Pacific Island Artists

Navigating the Global Art World

Edited by
Karen Stevenson

Pacific Island Artists: Navigating the Global Art World

Edited by Karen Stevenson

Published by:
Masalai Press
368 Capricorn Avenue
Oakland, CA 94611 USA

masalaipress@gmail.com

© 2011

All rights reserved. No part of this publication may be reproduced or transmitted in any form or by any means, electronic or mechanical, including photocopy, recording, or any information storage or retrieval system, without permission in writing from the publisher.

ISBN 0-9714127-7-4

The front cover illustration, *Melanesie,* is by Moses Jobo (Vanuatu). Photograph is courtesy of Ken Mayer. See Chapter 7 for more details.

The back cover illustration, *Turtles: Endangered Species,* is by Larry Santana. Photograph courtesy of Larry Santana. See Chapter 5 for more details.

Table of Contents

Acknowledgements

This volume represents the work of many people over many years. It is unique in that it not only attempts but also succeeds at providing a variety of voices concerned about the contemporary arts of the Pacific. For decades debates have raged amongst academics, which focused on the topics of authenticity, tradition, identity, and tourist arts and seemingly avoided discussion with their practitioners. This volume, bringing together artists (essays and interviewsstr), academics, museum curators, and gallery owners moves gallantly towards spanning this divide; opening up and maintaining a dialogue amongst the different stakeholders in the contemporary arts of the Pacific.

Pamela Rosi (Bridgewater State University) and Eric Kjellgren (The Metropolitan Museum of Art) introduced this concept as an informal session for the Association of Social Anthropologists of Oceania's (ASAO) annual conference in Vancouver (2003). Both have contributed to this volume and worked tirelessly to see the ASAO process to completion. They felt that the 'scope and nature of Pacific art itself has in recent years become contested terrain,' and therefore created an opportunity to discuss 'issues of artistic agency, construction of personal and group identity, gender, authorship, copyright, gate-keeping, and the unequal power relations between indigenous artists and the global art system.' With the goal of facilitating creative dialogue between artists and academics, they succeeded in integrating their voices.

The ASAO process needs to be addressed, as it is unique within the academic conference format. It spans a period of 3 years; chairs introduce the idea, and in an 'informal session' gather people together to discuss ideas about the topic and to narrow the scope for continued sessions. This is then followed by a 'working session' where interested participants have written and circulated papers prior to attending the conference. Frequently 'discussants' join the group and ideas and conversations build. A final 'symposium' is convened in the third year where papers (rewritten to incorporate the discussion of the previous years) are presented. Frequently plans are discussed for possible publication — for an ASAO volume, another press, or a special journal volume. Because this process is a lengthy one (and frequently a financial burden), there is often a high attrition rate as other commitments take precedence. Participants may be quite vocal at one session, never to return. As such, many voices were a part of these sessions and many people were influenced by the exhibitions and performances created. I would very much like to thank all of those individuals whose voices enhanced this volume. [1]

It is unusual for the ASAO to hold exhibitions in association with their conferences. However, when the focus is the arts attempts to create exhibition venues are essential. A special thank you to Pamela Rosi and Rosanna Raymond for their efforts to find, assure, and create exhibition spaces and possibilities. Vince Reyes and Judy Flores were invaluable as fundraisers to enable the Inetnon Gef Pa'go dance troupe to both attend and perform at the symposium in Kauai. I must also thank the Pacific Island Scholarship Fund committee of the ASAO who contributed significantly over the 3 years to this session. Through their travel and minigrant programs funds were provided for numerous artists and academics [2] to attend and participate in this project.

At the working session Rob Welsch (Franklin Pierce University) acted as discussant, and at the symposium both Robert Welsch and Vilsoni Hereniko (University of the South Pacific) offered direction for the discussion and suggestions for publication. They critiqued papers and suggested possibilities to 'open-up' conversation among artists, academics, and institutions. In so doing a variety of voices were brought together to address myriad agendas associated with contemporary arts in the Pacific. I would like to thank all of these participants for their time and passion for Pacific arts.

Prior to my taking on the stewardship of this volume, both Rob Welsch and Vilsoni Hereniko spent their time and efforts as discussants. I would like to thank them for their input into the format of the sessions and content of the essays. Rob was the project's first editor before other commitments took precedence. I thank him for his time and work on the structure of this volume. With my involvement in this project I have asked for the authors to revisit their essays and as such thank them for their patience and perseverance. I would also like to thank and acknowledge the contribution of those who are not represented here, but played a role in these discussions. Finally I must thank Pamela and Eric for creating and convening these sessions. A special thank you to Pamela for her work over the 3-year period, especially for attaining funding and exhibition space for their participants; and more importantly her persistence to see this volume to publication. Without her resolve, this volume would not have come to fruition. Her passion toward the arts of the Pacific as well as her compassion for the artists was the driving forces behind this project. The need to bridge the gap between artist, academic and institution, to dissolve the role of gatekeeper, and to promote the contemporary arts of the Pacific is a global arena is the heart and soul of this volume. For this I thank all of the participants whose voices have both influenced and inspired this volume. A final thank you to Tom Slone and Masalai Press for supporting this venture.

Karen Stevenson

Notes

1 The 'academic' participants over this 3-year period were: Anne D'Alleva, Judy Flores, Vilsoni Hereniko, Anna-Karina Hermkens, Carol Ivory, Eric Kjellgren, Mary N. MacDonald, Carol E. Mayer, Elaine Monds, Eva Raabe, Pamela Rosi, Eric Silverman, Teri Sowell, Marion Struck-Garbe, and Robert L. Welsch. The artists attending were: Konousi Aisake, Tusiata Avia, Wharetuturu Edward Vere Heke, Santi Hitorangi, Shigeyuki Kihara, Ake Lianga, Julie Mota, George Nuku, Rosanna Raymond, Vince Reyes and 'his' dance troupe Inetnon Gef Pa'go, and Michelle M. Kamakanoenoe Tupou.

2 Funding came from various sources, which demonstrates the commitment that artists and academics have to the contemporary arts of the Pacific. The ASAO Pacific Island Scholarship Fund provided travel grants to: Vilsoni Hereniko, Rosanna Raymond, Vince Reyes, Ake Lianga, Tusiata Avia, and Shigeyuki Kihara. Mini-grants were awarded to: Wharetuturu Edward Vere Heke, George Nuku and Santi Hitorangi, Rosanna Raymond and Konousi Aisake.

List of Illustrations

Chapter 5

Chapter 6

Chapter 7

Chapter 8

Chapter 9

Chapter 10

Chapter 11

Chapter 12

Chapter 13

Chapter 14

Introduction

Karen Stevenson

Misconception, misrepresentation, and misplaced intentions have shrouded the Pacific since Cook sailed into its waters more than 200 years ago. Ever since, fact has blended with fantasy to create the myth of the Pacific — a paradise with sun-drenched beaches, blue lagoons, and coconut palms. Images of Pacific beauties and noble savages [1] living in harmony with nature and far from the taint of civilization complete the picture. Today, Pacific nations market this myth to enhance their tourist industry. This has created a sense that Pacific peoples and their lives remain in the 18th century — that missionization, colonization, and independence have not occurred. Albeit, Pacific peoples have taken these changes in stride (when possible) integrating introduced goods and ideologies into their culture. Even so, a glimmer of a distant lifestyle remains, and is vigorously promoted. The desire to sample and enjoy this fantastical paradise brings millions of tourists into the Pacific each year... the myth continues. These visions, however, are difficult to balance with the realities facing the Pacific: global warming, poverty, political corruption, and nuclear waste are all very real and the subject of much artistic endeavour.

Pacific peoples today live in towns, they educate their children, and they play a role in the global economy. They have also become their own culture's critics. Artists, in particular, have taken on this role and in so doing often create artwork that addresses issues of social, economic and political unease. This too is hard to balance against the perception of art from the Pacific. For many in the west it is primitive. It is most often carving/sculpture. Created in association with a non-Christian belief system; it is Other.

These clichés are constant in the lives of Pacific peoples and are the basis of the issues addressed in this volume. Here, artists, academics, museum curators and art dealers come together to discuss the creation and promotion of Pacific arts in the global art world. These different voices also represent a long-standing complex of misconceptions. There are myriad issues that coincide with myriad perspectives, which both allow for generalisation and beg for specificity. In our post-modern world different voices and different identities are asserted (which at times makes one yearn for the simple days when things were black and white); even the term Pacific is not unanimously accepted.

If we begin with the Cook era, Europe's introduction to the Pacific equates to Tahiti. Wallis, Cook and Bougainville all visited Tahiti — but it was tales of the old trade [2], an endless supply of food, and what appeared to be an idyllic lifestyle (not far from Rousseau's notion of paradise) that held Europe's attention. Tahiti became a watering hole for explorers and relationships developed, which did not occur with other island groups. When reading the journals [3], Tahiti became the island of comparison — Tahiti became the Pacific. In contrast, the inhabitants of those island groups that did not welcome explorers (especially those in Melanesia) were frequently deemed savages. Tales of headhunters and cannibals inflamed the west's imagination. [4] These two stereotypes created the dichotomy between the noble and ignoble savage.

This type of generalisation has endured and has created misconceptions about the Pacific and its peoples. Even with the geographical divisions (set up by the west) of Polynesia, Micronesia, and Melanesia (which offer some distinctions), the gloss endures. Polynesia (many islands), Micronesia (small islands) and Melanesia (black islands) provide geographical (large/small), cultural (typically Polynesian social structures are chiefly systems, Melanesian societies are Big Man systems) and racial distinctions. However, they, clearly, do not offer the kind of specificity necessary to understand a culture.

Those who attempt to understand the belief systems (religions) and the artwork associated with the gods have also created skewed perceptions about art in the Pacific. As belief systems are, for the most part, under the aegis of men the artwork created for and utilised in rituals was recognised as this regions art. This meant that art was limited in scope and created by men. As a result, the west frequently ignored the arts of women, and at best designated them as craft.

This gloss perpetuates misconceptions and enables the myth to continue. Misconception are: first that art was only produced for ritual purposes, and therefore any other material production was deemed craft; and, two, that these artists perpetuated objects needed for these purposes, and therefore, there was little individual creativity involved — which meant there were no artists.

These perceptions created a dichotomy in the 20th century that pitted the original/traditional Masterpieces of Primitive Arts against the contemporary crafts/tourist arts. Following this argument, the only authentic art from the Pacific region was not only that that was produced for ritual/traditional purposes, it was art that was created prior to contact with/not contaminated by the west. [5] There was a recognition that the peoples of the Pacific continued to live their idyllic lifestyle, but that this life had changed. The west did not give the art this recognition. As Albert Wendt commented (1983: 198):

> My objection to this literature is that it gives the impression that our ancestors' art is still the Oceanic Art of today; or that if it isn't, it ought to be; or that we have not produced any worthwhile art since the papalagi came: or that if we are producing some art it is not 'authentic' Oceanic Art and therefore not worthy of serious discussion. This kind of one-eyed judgement does not happen only in books — it spills over into real life. And for practicing Pacific Island artists it has been a bitter source of anger and humiliation.

Here Wendt addresses the gulf between artists and academics — an issue at the heart of this volume. The authors who contributed here have witnessed many changes in attitude about the arts of the Pacific within the last 30 years. [6] These essays hope to change these attitudes. Here we speak of the value of contemporary Pacific art while coming to terms with such issues and terms as; art/craft, authenticity, and primitive/*avant garde*. To further complicate contemporary Pacific art, much of it is ensconced in traditional ideologies. It frequently incorporates motifs drawn from a historical past — used to both honour and assert a genealogical association with one's heritage. It becomes, therefore, political and tied to post-colonial economic realities as well as assertions of indigenous identities. To understand contemporary works one must understand the issues and the complexities they raise both in their homelands and abroad where they are exhibited and marketed to an often-prejudicial audience.

These prejudices are not new. In the 18th century, the artificial curiosities [7] brought back to Britain by Cook and his men were seen as artefacts. These eventually became part of ethnographic museum collections. Collecting the world as part of the explorer/colonial process enabled the appreciation of these works, but little understanding. Some, acknowledged for their manufacture however, were gathered together and exhibited as curiosities — not Art. [8] It is on the rare occasion that art museums exhibit these creations.

As museum culture has changed (Raabe, Mayer), shifts have taken place. Many institutions with traditional collections are updating, with the desire to demonstrate a continuum of cultural production over the centuries. However, in the past 30 years, artists have begun to create art using western media and techniques, combining technology with traditional motifs. Museums have begun to collect these works as well; however, they have struggled to find their place in the west's art market, and to be appreciated as contemporary art.

Many essays in this volume grapple with all of the above, and as such are unique in the scope of their investigation. There have been few volumes with their focus on Pacific art, and those that do exist are both surveys and regional in scope. Cochrane and Stevenson's *Luk Luk Gen* focuses on the beginnings of contemporary art in Papua New Guinea, Cochrane's *Beretara, Contemporary Pacific Art* highlights the collections of the Jean-Marie Tjibaou Cultural Centre and Stevenson's *The Frangipani is Dead, Contemporary Pacific Art in New Zealand 1985-2000* focuses it's attention on New Zealand. As these volumes address a specific area, they provide the reader with a snapshot of that region and the issues that those particular artists address in their works. In contrast, this volume not only looks at art production from various places within the Pacific region (Australia, Papua, Papua New Guinea, the Solomon Islands, Vanuatu, Fiji, Rotuma, Samoa, Tonga, New Zealand, Guam, Hawaii, and the Northwest Coast of Canada), it also discusses how these arts are exhibited and marketed in the United States, Canada, England, and Germany. This creates the opportunity for a global dialogue, which clearly demonstrates that different groups in different locations perceive contemporary indigenous arts differently. The inspiration for these arts is as diverse as the people who collect, exhibit, and discuss them. As such, we explore the diversity and complexities of contemporary Pacific art and reveal the issues surrounding their acceptance in the global art world.

In so doing, these authors address a variety of issues associated with the production and marketing of contemporary Pacific art. These essays stem from meetings of the Association of Social Anthropologists of Oceania (ASAO). [9] Key to this volume and to the discussions that originally took place with the ASAO sessions was the importance of moving beyond boundaries set by academia and to involve artists and dealers in discussions about the globalizing art world;

therefore this volume provides a different voice. It enables the reader an opportunity for insight into the creative process, but also into the dialogue between artists, academics, museum personnel, and dealers. It offers insight into the creative process with essays by artists (Reyes, Raymond, Lianga, and Castro); speaking for themselves about their art, their cultural heritage, and their identity as artists. We also hear the artist voice through interviews (Kihara, Konousi); a strategy specifically utilized here to enhance the dialogue amongst the conference participants (and ideally our readers). Other essays offer insight into the complexities that museum personnel and academics struggle with in their attempts to move Pacific art into the western world. Considerable time is spent offering a context for contemporary Pacific art and as such, education is a key issue in these discussions. The importance of context, of providing information to enhance the viewers experience is addressed from the gallery/dealer perspective. This volume recognizes the dynamic complexities of processes of interaction between the local and the global as contemporary Pacific art moves from the Pacific into the global art world.

The Issues

Authenticity became an important concept when discussing indigenous arts in the 1970s and 1980s. [10] Anthropologists and art historians were attempting to make distinctions between arts produced for internal consumption (traditional arts that may have undergone some changes over the last 200 years) or for tourism (that produced strictly to sell to outsiders). At the same time, issues of identity and the desire to speak for oneself came to the fore, which enhanced the debate. [11] This created a dichotomy between academics and artists, indigenous and other (this time the other being the westerner), and created the opportunity for Pacific people to make assertions about how they positioned their art. 30 years on, this debate continues to simmer just below the surface as it, too, glosses and generalizes the Pacific.

Eric Kjellgren discusses issues of ownership and obligation amongst Kimberley painters of Australia. Cultural beliefs about the production of images associated with country both assert and contradict the notion of a contemporary Aboriginal art movement. The artists from the Kimberley region find the label of artist placed upon them as 'welcoming but somewhat mysterious.' To these artists, being an artist is a job — it is a source of income. However, in this process they assert their tradition — the laws and obligations associated with ownership. They do not create for the sake of creation — their abstract artworks are not abstract, but representations of landscape, of country. These works become opportunities to visualize histories and assert ownership over lands. Creativity and artistic ability take a back seat to issues of ownership and guardianship. These artists paint to tell stories passed through the generations. Executing these in acrylic, is a contemporary manifestation, one that brings them money and recognition. Kjellgren also points out that they too have changed. The politics and economics of art have reinforced the Dreamings power to make changes, assert ideologies, and reconfigure Aboriginal law.

Clearly this essay demonstrates that there is a relationship between the past and present in the Pacific, that contemporary is a current manifestation of a traditional mode of representation; as Elaine Monds asserts, contemporary art can be both traditional and new. In her essay, Monds tells of Sepik River carvers creating imagery drawing upon myths and parables, which demonstrate the importance of traditional wisdom. More importantly, the money they earn is used to refurbish their traditional men's houses and as such, the role of contemporary artists is enhanced as they reinforce, comment on, and maintain tradition. The role of tradition in contemporary art is also addressed in the artist statement by Lianga and the interview of Aisake. These chapters relate traditional upbringings to a contemporary art practice — a practice that asserts traditional ideologies but also offers individual and cultural identity.

The uneasy relationship between tradition-contemporary/primitive-modern is exacerbated by the west's perception of both Papua New Guinea and its artists. Eva Raabe reiterates this issue as she relays her struggle to create exhibition environments that will both enhance a viewers experience and their understanding of Papua New Guinea cultures and traditions. Her essay describes the work of Trobriand Island artist Samuel Luguna and the process she undertook to display his work at the Museum of World Cultures, in Frankfurt am Main. She has found that exhibition design as well as working collaboratively with the artists and the design team, are the essential components to creating an educational experience that will change some attitudes toward Pacific art. Breaking through the stereotypes as well as the expectations of the German public has not been easy as they bring their perception of what art from PNG should be — something exotic and unfamiliar.

Carol Mayer speaking from an institutional position, details the obstacles that an enlightened viewing public bring to the University of British Colombia Museum of Anthropology. Her audience has become acquainted with the necessity to understand cultural protocols in the process of exhibition display. Offering a history of the museum's collections and display policies, Mayer addresses the changes in both attitudes and laws governing indigenous art and artists in Canada. Their experiences with First Nations People have broadened their perceptions of indigenous arts. However, misconceptions present themselves when these notions are placed on all indigenous peoples. Detailing an interesting case from Vanuatu, Mayer questions the various manifestations different cultures and their protocols bring to legal issues and exhibition processes.

Pamela Rosi addresses not only the dichotomy between the traditional and contemporary, but pushes the argument further to investigate issues of national support and perception. In places such as Papua New Guinea, where tradition remains strong, contemporary imagery that does not rely on customary knowledge or motifs is not as accepted in the global art market. As Raabe also notes, images that draw upon the stereotype of the primitive are more frequently accepted, than those with social criticism at their core. Rosi details some of the many obstacles that Larry Santana has incurred, including a lack of creative support and freedom, the lack of venues to exhibit his work, as well as the social, economic and political realities of a developing nation. It is interesting, though, that his works, based on social and economic critique — typical in contemporary western art practice, have difficulty finding a market as they do not reflect the west's preconceived notions about what art from Papua New Guinea should be.

Again, both the complexities and contradictions in contemporary art circles come to the fore. With an artist such as Santana, whose work stems from his personal experiences (which unfortunately are often bleak), his practice should meld easily into the contemporary genre.

Even though the west thrives on the clichés of the starving and the moody genius artist, these are not applicable to the artists of the Pacific. The west believes that if you are an indigenous artist you create indigenous art — not contemporary art with indigenous motifs or subject matter. Governments reinforce and exploit these perceptions; marketing their country as a tourist destination — a paradise where time has stood still. In contrast to tourist brochures, both Rosi and Raabe reveal the constant struggle for recognition within a very fragile country such as Papua New Guinea. Here, the traditional and contemporary are in contention with one another as the country itself endeavors to balance the past with visions of the future.

Another topic of importance within the Pacific is the issue surrounding gender and inequality. These are brought to the fore by Anna-Karina Hermkens as she explores the dynamic between tradition and Art in her essay. Drawing upon the Lake Sentani/Humboldt Bay area of Papua and the Collingwood Bay region of Oro Province of Papua New Guinea, Hermkens provides us with the history of barkcloth production in the area. Barkcloth collected in the early 20th century was one of the few female art forms given the Masterpiece label. However, over time and with cultural interventions, men now paint barkcloth. Men utilizing the patriarchal system of the west (reinforced by the traditional social system) have taken women's wealth [12] and asserted that their cloth is Art and that they are artists. Women, however, are relegated to produce cloth to wear and for the tourist market — this work is craft. Here, the complexities brought about by change coupled with the strength of traditional social and economic parameters provide an interesting case study of these interwoven issues. Hermkens questions governmental/patriarchal authority which has enabled men to position themselves as artists, whereas women, creating the same product, are just part of the traditional economy. Gender, and in particular, the lack of recognition for the Pacific's female artists, remains unresolved.

This issue is also the focus of Marion Struck-Garbe's essay, which addresses social and political issues surrounding the precarious situation of women artists in PNG. Similar to the case above where the men in essence, stole a woman's art tradition, here the women struggle for recognition in a male dominated world. Struck-Garbe details the differing gender relationships that exist in Papua New Guinea and how these become important issues/motifs in the work of these female artists. In particular, she alludes to the relationship (or lack thereof) between the Highlands and Coastal Provinces. These inherent differences create unease as peoples from all over the country live side by side in Port Moresby. The complexity of these social situations hinders the development of women artists — even when opportunities of travel and exhibitions in Europe are provided. [13] As Struck-Garbe points out, the struggles that Papua New Guinea women encounter could be alleviated with an artist alliance; yet social networks seem to counter this. Without this support, their position as artists' wanes, particularly as the perception of Pacific art is a male art form. Again, an understanding of these obstacles and of the Papua New Guinea that these women live in is necessary to fully value their art.

In contrast, the contemporary artists of Vanuatu have created an arts alliance. Nawita enables its members a voice, a venue, and the opportunity to discuss issues of importance to them. Identity, as opposed to gender (though these are often interrelated), provides the platform for Haidy Geismar to focus upon Vanuatu and the very distinct division between kastom (tradition) and contemporary art. She states; "through the rendering of ideas and identities in acrylic, wool, and wood contemporary artists in Vanuatu are able to synthesize global and local styles, classifications and values." This strong sense of identity allows the artists to work and create within their own terms and boundaries. Ni-Vanuatu artists have the ability to be either kastom or contemporary — both genres are accepted as culturally significant. Geismar suggests that it is the long history of cross-cultural political and economic exchange that has created these perceptions, both from within and without.

Notwithstanding, the question remains does the global art market truly understand the linkages between the traditional/contemporary offered by indigenous artists? On the other hand, as is discussed by Raabe, is the western viewer compelled to devalue this work according to their perception of Pacific art? Elaine Monds and Carol Mayer offer interesting perspectives on this issue in reference to exhibiting contemporary Pacific art. Monds explains the strategies that she uses to situate contemporary Pacific art in a gallery setting — one acknowledged to house Art within the west. Exhibitions are displayed in a professional manner, information is generated about the artist/s, and openings often provide the gallery patron with the opportunity to meet the artist. These strategies reinforce the educational, but also diminish the stereotype of the primitive/ exotic other.

The position as a contemporary artist, as opposed to an exotic other, is frequently countered by inviting artists to exhibition openings where they can meet potential patrons (or to participate in conference proceedings such as this). Galleries in conjunction with institutions have also utilized residency programs to enable artists, not only the time and materials to create, but also to enable a connection with the local community and resources, both of which support the artist as they enable the continuation of the creative process as well as networking. Jewel Castro discusses the importance of residencies as well as projects that are co-curated with artists. Institutional support becomes key, otherwise finding exhibition space/venues become obstacles in the promotion of Pacific art. An issue addressed by many in this volume, finding a gallery space, somewhere that exhibits Art, is essential for the promotion of contemporary Pacific art as contemporary art. Without a legitimate venue, artists feel that they are just objects/subjects of investigation. The lack of exhibition space not only demeans the art, it allows for the perpetuation of stereotypes and hinders these artists from crossing the boundaries into the global art world.

These varying attitudes also come to the fore in essays by the artists. Some artists believe that academics continue to exoticize the Pacific other. Raymond comments:

> To read about yourself labeled as hybrid and having your authenticity questioned by people outside of your community left me feeling disempowered.

Castro, on the other hand, finds the balance between artist and other a compelling tightrope. The ability to attend conferences, to speak for oneself, to network without boundaries is countered by the frustration of a debate no longer relevant to many contemporary artists. On the other hand, academics and galleries have provided opportunities (exchanges/collaborative projects) for Pacific artists.

Perceptions and labels are the hurdles that both the artist and dealer must overcome. However, in a postmodern world where people may assert different identities, the issue of self-promotion versus academic writing or critique escalates. Artists abhor the stereotype, but they also play into it. This issue, in particular, comes to the fore in the interview with Shigeyuki Kihara. When artists are able to decide which traditions they will draw upon, which stereotypes they will embrace, it becomes a component of their artistic practice. However, sensitivity surfaces if these same stereotypes are placed upon them. The west frequently uses the term 'hybrid' for contemporary Pacific art, but this label brings with it a sense of scientific classification. It becomes an issue of semantics, but one where misunderstandings and misconceptions can create obstacles in the process of contemporary Pacific art's integration into the art world.

Raymond speaks to the importance of Museums as resources, as guardians of living treasures from the Pacific's past. In her relationships, especially with the Pitt-Rivers and British Museum, opportunities to reclaim one's heritage and assert a Pacific identity allow her practice to flourish. She notes that her practice is a celebration of her cultural heritage — it makes her culture relevant to her. In turn, museums have also become quite interested in developing relationships with artists and have opened their storehouses to them. This relationship has enabled the creation of new works inspired by the past. [14] These opportunities enable artists to become acquainted with the objects their ancestors created, which shifts the power balance (if ever so slightly) of the colonial past. It also provides the artists an opportunity to reclaim and assert a cultural identity.

Reclaiming a cultural identity and creating artwork of cultural significance is just one of the many social, political, and economic factors associated with Pacific arts. Vince Reyes and Judy Flores both look at contemporary Chamorro art, one as a practitioner the other tracing recent developments. The Chamorro of Guam are another interesting case study, one where issues of authenticity often arise. Reyes' essay describes his passion for Chamorro dance and the important role it plays in sustaining a Chamorro identity in Guam today. Flores, however, puts critics at ease as she traces the development of contemporary art in Guam and its relationship to a Chamorro identity. For those artists drawing from the past, however vague the inspiration may be, enables them to assert their identity and create artwork that is culturally significant to them. The issue of authenticity is side-stepped as the Guamanian government has supported these efforts and acknowledges these practitioners as both artists and cultural ambassadors who promote both Guam and the Chamorro people.

Embedded in many of these discussions are issues that simmer below the surface, but issues nonetheless that are key to the artists' creative process. Social and economic policies create different realities across the Pacific. This becomes quite apparent in Struck-Garbe's discussion concerning the plight/lack of support for PNG women artists. The lack of equality becomes a monumental obstacle to overcome. Gender, the lack of equality, and the lack of possibility, are important issues that are raised in many of the essays in this volume. These issues go hand in hand with the reality of different social structures with the Pacific region. A communal work ethic is seen in Australia, whereas in New Zealand community remains important but as a support structure for an individual artist. In Papua New Guinea and Papua the patriarchal structure limits female artists greatly.

In contrast to the women of PNG, Rosanna Raymond, Shigeyuki Kihara and Jewel Castro are able to move seamlessly within the global art world — their work fully acknowledged as Art – Kihara is the first contemporary Pacific artist to be collected by the Metropolitan Museum in New York. Yet these artists continue to grapple with labels — being exotic or hybrid — both of which are drawn upon, but neither of which are embraced. Interestingly, it appears that either the artist or the artwork must fit the exotic mold for acceptance. As Raabe explains most German viewers do not have the anthropological background to comprehend either the motifs or inclusion of traditional and cultural values in the artwork. What they do understand is that the work, to them, does not appear exotic; nor is it *avant-garde*. This in turn, brings up, once again, issues of authenticity and identity. The academic and artistic shift that has taken place is discussed here. The public, through the efforts of curators and writers have begun to embrace both change and other cultures in a more holistic manner. These shifts, particularly in alignment with governmental and creative community support will enable contemporary Pacific artists to, not only negotiate, but also embrace the global art market.

Developments

Since the discussions of the ASAO meetings and the writing of these essays, Pacific artists have made inroads into the global art market. Kihara's work is held by the Metropolitan Museum, Michel Tuffery is now in the collection of the British Museum; and Ake Lianga is completing a commission for the Solomon Islands Embassy in Canberra, Australia. This has been accomplished in many ways, most of which are the result of determined work at realigning the west's perceptions about the Pacific. Many of these essays reflect these changes and how they have come to be. Monds addresses the importance of publications, the Internet and websites in the promotion of Pacific Arts. Rosi speaks of the need for governmental support, and Castro and Struck-Garbe for the importance of venues. In the past decade, Creative New Zealand has supported important exhibitions in the United States and Europe [15]. Other foundations, trusts, and endowments have supported the continued drive by Pacific artists in their quest for acknowledgement by the global art market. [16] Writers and curators have also published a number of essays and books that have added to the general knowledge about Pacific art. [17] Perhaps most important to the current success of contemporary Pacific artists is the interconnected web between governmental agencies, institutions, curators, dealers, academics and artists. Networking and the opportunities that brings have advanced the position of Pacific art in the global art market. Unfortunately, a crash in the world's economy has not aided the attempts to promote contemporary Pacific art, but those involved persevere. The issues remain, but they also create the diversity and complexities found in these artists work.

The importance of identity, for instance, may ease as the artist becomes more self-assured; yet, at the same time identity remains essential as artists interact within the global art market. Difference sells, but exoticism irks. All artists want their work to be acknowledged, not for the stereotype a viewer places upon it, but for its ability to convey meaning, to touch the viewer in some way. As Michael Somare (1979: xiii) stated, 35 years ago:

> The time is long overdue for the people of Oceania to tell the world, in our own way, what rich variety we have in the fine arts, which capture the inner depths of man.

In the same address Somare (1979: xv) also stated:

> Our art and our cultures must be appreciated and judged, if that is necessary, on our own merit, and not by arbitrary comparisons with those of the East and West.

Hence, contemporary Pacific artists are seeking a global marketplace free from the stereotypes of the Pacific, free from the gatekeepers who hinder their reception as artists or their work as art, and free from the tendency to exoticize both their work and themselves.

Artists who convey stories (be they traditional or new) combine the past and the future. This enables their culture (it's stories, ideals, and problems) a voice in the global art market. Valuing this work, providing access to this marketplace, adjusting preconceived notions, provides the possibility for artists to create. These essays not only address the complexities and dynamics of Pacific issues, they also focus their attention on the art world — on the academics, the gallery owners, the curators, the institutions, as well as the viewing public — all of whom are interrelated in this global art market.

The essays in this volume make reference to various exhibitions, festivals, and residencies [18] that have supported Pacific art and artists. These, however, are not a complete list of the opportunities that contemporary Pacific artists have had in the past decade. Clearly these artists and artistic practices are making waves and becoming recognized within the global art market. This encouragement, coupled with new technologies (the internet, websites, YouTube, artists blogs) provides an optimistic future as these Pacific Island artists negotiate the global art world.

Indigenous Acrylic: Art and Identity in Vanuatu

Haidy Geismar

Introduction

> Art is colonial. Art works can take you outside of yourself, impose their values on you, make you see the world in a different way, get you on side and make you over afresh... Art gives us an opportunity to think again, and again, and again. (Anon. 1992: 13).

This essay aims to dissect some of the tightly meshed connections between art objects and concepts of the indigenous, drawing on fieldwork within the marketplace for the growing contemporary arts movement in Vanuatu. At a time when the term 'indigenous' is increasingly fraught with political contestation in the global arena, a positive connection between art and indigeneity in the Pacific is only growing stronger [1]. Through the rendering of ideas and identities in acrylic, wool, and wood, contemporary artists in Vanuatu are able to synthesize global and local styles, classification and values, providing some alternative resolutions to more analytic quandaries about the cultural authenticity of their economic and political interests. Rather than promoting authenticity as an absolute and external value judgment assessing the legitimacy of identity and economic and political entitlement, the dialogue and exchange engendered by the production and transaction of artworks demonstrates how authenticity is also a strategy used to establish important and efficacious ideas about local identity in cross-cultural contexts.

In a controversial article, Adam Kuper (2002) mounted a broad critique of the category 'indigenous' (and implicitly of those who use the term, whether they be native, activist or academic, or all three) that, if accepted entirely, has serious ramifications for the present utility of the term. Drawing on his readings of the work of various indigenous people's movements concerned primarily with land restitution in Southern Africa, and North and South America, Kuper outlined and challenged the key notions he identifies as salient to the construction of indigenous identities — a latent primitivism and celebration of 'nature' as opposed to culture, a reliance on blood rights, and the elevation of an idealized (pre-colonial) mythic past into the political present. He noted that such forgings of identity are also "popular with extreme right-wing parties in Europe", citing the attempts of South African Boers to participate at a meeting of the United Nations Forum of Indigenous Peoples in 1996 (2002: 390). Kuper (2002: 395) also suggests that these indigenous rights movements generically utilize understandings of race, culture and biology that anthropologists, and others, are intensely uncomfortable with in other circumstances:

> The conventional lines of argument currently used to justify "indigenous" land claims rely on obsolete anthropological notions [of primitivism, race, and an opposition between culture and nature] and false ethnographic vision. Fostering essentialist ideologies of culture and identity, they may have dangerous political consequences.

The (ongoing) response to Kuper's piece has varied from measured to vehement critique (see Kenrick and Lewis 2004). Nearly all commentators have highlighted the importance of acknowledging how 'dangerous politics' have long and adversely affected indigenous peoples, and the very real necessity for restitution and empowerment for dispossessed and politically marginalized first peoples. As Suzman comments, "San people are frustrated not because they cannot pursue their "traditional culture" but because they are impoverished, marginalized, and exploited by the dominant population" (2002: 400). It also remains a fact that many groups of people share an understanding of what it means to be 'native', 'first nation', 'fourth world', 'tribal' or 'indigenous' with many other collectives from very different places around the world (see Smith 1999), sharing a broad experience of cultural and political encounter and co-option. Divisions between colonized/colonizer, native/settler, black-brown-red/white, to name but a few problematic but profound distinctions that feed into the criteria of who may be defined as indigenous, are thus very real. What to make then of Kuper's challenge to their authenticity?

Anthropologists working in the Pacific, especially those working with art and other kinds of cultural production, are particularly well suited to respond to Kuper's polemic. Kuper's critique of primitivism and identification of the political strategy surrounding many indigenous land claims intersects with a well-worn discussion that, whilst by no means unique to

Oceanic anthropology, has played a defining role within our discipline: the 'invention of tradition' (see Hobsbawm and Ranger 1983, Hanson 1989, Keesing and Tonkinson eds. 1981, Jolly and Thomas 1992, Linnekin 1990). In the context of the growing battle for empowerment and self-determination by native peoples living in lands later settled by others and, equally, by post-colonial nations struggling for recognition on a world stage, Kuper exposes indigenous identities to be politically contingent, and infinitely malleable even as they are promoted as timeless, natural kinds. He deconstructs the concept of indigenous much as anthropologists once did that of tradition or kastom, and by extension nationalism. As with much of the early invention of tradition debates, Kuper himself reifies terms such as invention, tradition and identity, assuming that there may be some pristine (authentic) meaning of each which is being corrupted by those with explicit political agendas. In doing so he crucially ignores local determinations and experiences of what it might mean to be native (Gegeo 2001: 492, Smith 1999, Trask 1991 [2]).

Kuper is right to an extent: indigenous identities, like all identities, are political, contested and fraught with controversy and dissent (both from within and from without) and there are provocative slippages between indigenous and national identities. What is interesting to me is how ideas and discussions about art in the Pacific may be seen to circumvent critiques such as Kuper, and how the anthropology of art has developed a parallel form of communicating about indigeneity and nationhood, one which acknowledges shared territories as well as political inequalities; which shows us that categories like 'primitive' and 'modern' or 'nature' and 'culture' are permeable and contingent. Perhaps most importantly, this perspective also incorporates diverse voices, and media, into the analytic framework, exemplified by the participants in this volume. As Ngahiraka Mason, curator Maori at the Auckland Art Gallery has written: Indigenous artists contribute and bring vitality to contemporary art and, inasmuch as they provide sweeping panoramic views of a rapidly changing world, they also offer departure points from which to discuss new directions... (Mason 2000: 24). The "post-postcolonial" imaginaries developed by many artists working in the Pacific offer "a counter-discursive Aboriginal imaginary that is crucial to their contemporary self-production" (Ginsberg and Myers 2006: 29).

Historically, the anthropology of art has been deeply interested in the cross-cultural applicability of categories (such as aesthetics, art and tradition); with the ways in which values (such as that of authenticity) are produced and reproduced in social and historical context; and with the symbolic and/or representational meaning of images in relation to identity politics (Morphy and Perkins, 2006). Increasingly, artists, and their work, have entered into these academic discussions, not only as illustrations, but also as active participants (Mithlo 2006). Over the past few years, there has been growing collaborative engagement with practicing artists, exemplified by the symposium from which this very volume emerges (Schneider and Wright 2005). Despite growing academic and political dispute over the linkages between concepts of indigenous and land or law (Brown 1998, 2003), the connections between 'indigenous' and 'art' have been powerfully reinforced, celebrated and consumed in recent years. The intellectual sophistication and political activism of many native artists, coupled with the very real powers of art to reproduce, not just represent, knowledge about the world increasingly informs our critical analyses. It is this ability to merge diverse opinion and discourse with culturally specific aesthetic forms that makes contemporary art in the Pacific a powerful tool for discussions about cultural, local and national identities.

Working closely in dialogue with artists and their work forces us to consider alternative forms of cultural expression to our own, and to open our analyses to fresh perspectives and ways of understanding, and indeed visualizing or experiencing, identity politics. As Fred Myers comments, referring to Aboriginal Australian acrylic painting, "its real power and lasting value is that it appears to be *of* "tradition" while violating it. This ambiguity constitutes its unsettlement" (2004: 263) and by extension the potential to unsettle mainstream political debates. The creative synthesis of, and intellectual engagement with, diverse art worlds demonstrates how art practices are extremely fertile ground for the expression, and even resolution, of provocative issues and more discursive divides.

Kuper's polemic emerges from the problematic of discursively policing the borders of cultural identity with tools that change shape and more often than not slip out of ones hands. In this essay, I want to exploit the fluid tools of the anthropology of art and draw on my own research in Vanuatu to emphasize how ni-Vanuatu artists may empower and connect differing definitions of authenticity and the indigenous, to more constructive and analytic, rather than dangerous political effect. It is here, I suggest, that the anthropology of art might become central, rather than marginal, to some of the fundamental concerns of anthropology (regarding identity, ethnicity, and globalization). Indeed, in Australia, New Zealand, and other settler-societies, indigenous art is frequently intrinsically linked to land rights and claims making it far from marginal to these issues (Ginsberg and Myers 2006, Myers 2002, 2004, Morphy 1991, Morphy and Smith Boles 1999).

Art in Vanuatu

The canonization of contemporary art in Vanuatu is a relatively recent phenomenon yet, despite the overt associations of the category with social and political concepts that have arrived from afar, contemporary art objects are used as much in the presentation and development of ideas about indigenous culture and tradition as they are in the development of local participation in an international art world. In this way, categories considered by many commentators to be non-local (such as art) are, in places like Vanuatu, prime grounds for the production and manifestation of local identity.

This essay draws upon research with people interested in art in Vanuatu — makers, dealers and collectors — to discuss how ideas about authenticity and indigenous identity are mediated in this cross-cultural context. The negotiations about value and identity that have emerged in the Vanuatu art world present an alternative view of identity politics to Kuper, where categories and values are conceived as intrinsically opposed to one another rather than as mutually constituted, dynamic and imbued with creativity. As Sero Kuautonga, a leading ni-Vanuatu painter, commented on this synthesis in describing one of his paintings: "Since independence, our kastom, church and independence have all come together. Vanuatu as a nation must be referred to in my painting. My painting is my culture." [3]

Authenticity in the Art Market

The Vanuatu art world is therefore a place where complex relations between local, national and international contexts converge in paint, wood and wool. In this, it is primarily an urban phenomenon -- the exhibition hall of the French embassy on the main high street in the capital, Port Vila, is one of the few places ni-Vanuatu, resident expatriates and tourists meet and mingle comfortably, providing a space for cross-cultural conversation and more often than not, provocative discussion (Geismar 2004). This kind of art market is a good place to start in examining how ideas about authenticity and identity are both entangled and negotiated. For instance, in most marketplaces concerned with artifacts categorized as art, buyers may think that they are simply buying objects of pure aesthetic value, but in reality they are often purchasing a relationship between the object and its producer (e.g. it is not only the image created by Picasso that a collector buys, but that fact that Picasso himself made it). This perspective exposes that authenticity is relational, and socially and politically constructed rather than inherent to any particular object.

In turn, it is often the case that objects made for sale are valued as somewhat less authentic than those that are perceived to be more embedded in local practice and society. The notion that economic gain has become the guiding motivation for many cultural productions and presentations in the Pacific is salient within much anthropological analysis (Stanley 1998). Ton Otto's paper entitled *Empty Tins for Lost Traditions* (1993) exemplifies this attitude. He comments "in the tourism and artifact business expatriate entrepreneurs and local agents share a complicit interest in sustaining dreams of primitivism and exoticism" (1993: 13), and laments the loss of authentic local culture. Chris Tilley on the other hand, interprets the performance of grade-taking ceremonies for tourists on Wala island, North-East Malakula, as a way in which islanders may creatively negotiate between modernity and traditionalism: "By virtue of the practice of objectifying culture in the show people are beginning to learn that they have to *negotiate and transform it*." (1999 [1997]: 259). In this analysis he raises an important critique of entrenched concepts of authenticity that view hybrid interactions between islanders and tourists (or indeed any other foreigner) as somehow spurious.

There is an implicit economic morality that places the market at the opposite end of the spectrum of authenticity to tradition. Dean MacCannell concludes melancholically, that tourism and globalisation are the creators of 'empty meeting grounds' (1992), unequally separating the world into consumers (tourists, and perhaps even anthropologists) and commodities ("ex-primitives" selling themselves as cultural productions). In this view, values such as traditional and modern are created by a hierarchical market forces, dominated by a cannibalistic white culture, which is "an enormous totalization" (Ibid: 129, see also Stanley 1998).

In the case of the art market in Port Vila, discourses of collectors and dealers may be seen to converge with those of artists, complicating some of these more pessimistic discussions. Whilst it cannot be denied that making money through the circulation of art is the primary agenda, art production also entails an ongoing public conversation about what it means to be ni-Vanuatu. Unlike mainstream artists in Europe, Australasia or North America, whose work tends to be evaluated primarily in terms of their art education, their originality, or their individual creativity, artists in the Pacific tend to be judged in the art market more by their place in a broader community, their connection to their ancestral and customary heritage, and the formal continuities of their work and practice between past and present. In this context, contemporary art straddles many discursive divides, being both traditional and modern, made for the market, and embodying traditional practices and identities.

Many collectors of Pacific art follow the archetypal collector, Nelson Rockefeller, in linking so-called non-western arts to forces of nature, to spirituality and to some kind of collective unconscious:

> There are inner forces in one's life that sometimes seem to be unrelated to conscious thought. This can be true of appreciation as well as creation of art. Much of so-called primitive art was created as direct response to strong feelings. [4]

However, many artists also share this attitude across the Pacific, who do not see this as incompatible with their lives as professional artists. For instance Michael Busai, from Futuna in Vanuatu, works full time for National Bank of Vanuatu as well as being internationally renowned for his pen and ink drawings. He describes the customary basis for his work:

> My work is based on traditional art, the art of the island environment that I come from. But it is in a new style, that I have invented.... The thing that really inspires me is the environment of my childhood days. There are many things that really inspired me in early childhood, which are unique to the village environment. [In my art] you can see the birds that I shot as a child when I was in the bush, the fish and seafood... it reflects the natural scenery of the natural environment of the village and also our cultural background, our legends and myths, because the area I am from is one that I really want to research. I think it is very interesting how all the myths and legends are related to our real environment... So in other words, you have a link to the supernatural, through our myths, from the physical world.... This is a secret behind my own painting. My painting has the same foundation that is behind our myths and legends — it has a strong spiritual force that really motivates me. [5]

As well as forging commercial value in the marketplace, art in Vanuatu is an important way to reinforce identities bound up in connections to ancestral power as well as in connection to development projects, churches, and tourist ventures. There is little doubt that the artworks produced in this context inculcate a shared discourse — as convergences, or materializations, of both self-definition and outsider interest, in the context of multiple investments made within a complex field of cross-cultural engagement.

Dealers and Artists Making Value Together

The marketplace becomes a place where a variety of different kinds of authenticity are produced, and where local identities are consolidated within broader spheres of exchange. Ni-Vanuatu often enter dealer stores in Port Vila, the capital of Vanuatu, commenting on the pieces on display. Such pieces must therefore be legitimated in front of a local audience as well as for visiting tourists. The market may be seen as a border zone, a public space that foregrounds "the unresolvable oscillations, the restless toing-and-froing, and the cultural, commercial, and political crossings" that develop value (Spyer 1998: 1). Ni-Vanuatu want to make and sell artifacts that represent them properly to others and that are perceived to be locally unique. They also want and need to earn money to survive in the growing urban settlements of Vanuatu. Market sales become grounds of political negotiation and cultural navigation by local people, who use concepts of the indigenous and of authenticity as their tools. Authenticity, which in this context hinges on a series of proscriptions about what it means to be indigenous, is a notion utilized on both sides of a transaction in order to strategically maximize political and economic relations in a variety of different contexts. Here, it is a category made in wood or paint, out of the relations between ni-Vanuatu and others.

In Port Vila, values of authenticity, and the promotion, through artwork, of ni-Vanuatu identities, are therefore made jointly between art producers and traders. Hanging around the newly opened store of a French dealer, gave me some good examples of this. Madame X came to Vanuatu after many years in Senegal, and has lived in Port Vila since 1988. She is married to a prominent Vietnamese businessman, who has close family ties with a nearby peri-urban village. Her husband was a vital resource in helping her consolidate her trade links with ni-Vanuatu. Madame X's priority was to sell kastom, which she initially defined as focusing purely on objects, valuing age, ritual use, and island production rather than the urban context of settlements in Port Vila. When she first opened, Madame X often visited the Vanuatu National Museum using the objects on display there as a marker for defining authentic kastom artifacts. On occasion, before she had established her own trade connections, she even bought things from the museum store and resold them downtown at a higher price. Around these objects, she placed photocopied pages from the exhibition catalogue, Arts of Vanuatu, in order to give scholarly validation and authenticity to her selections, and she also gave photocopied pages to local producers and asked them to make the objects illustrated: for example, she had a variety of hair

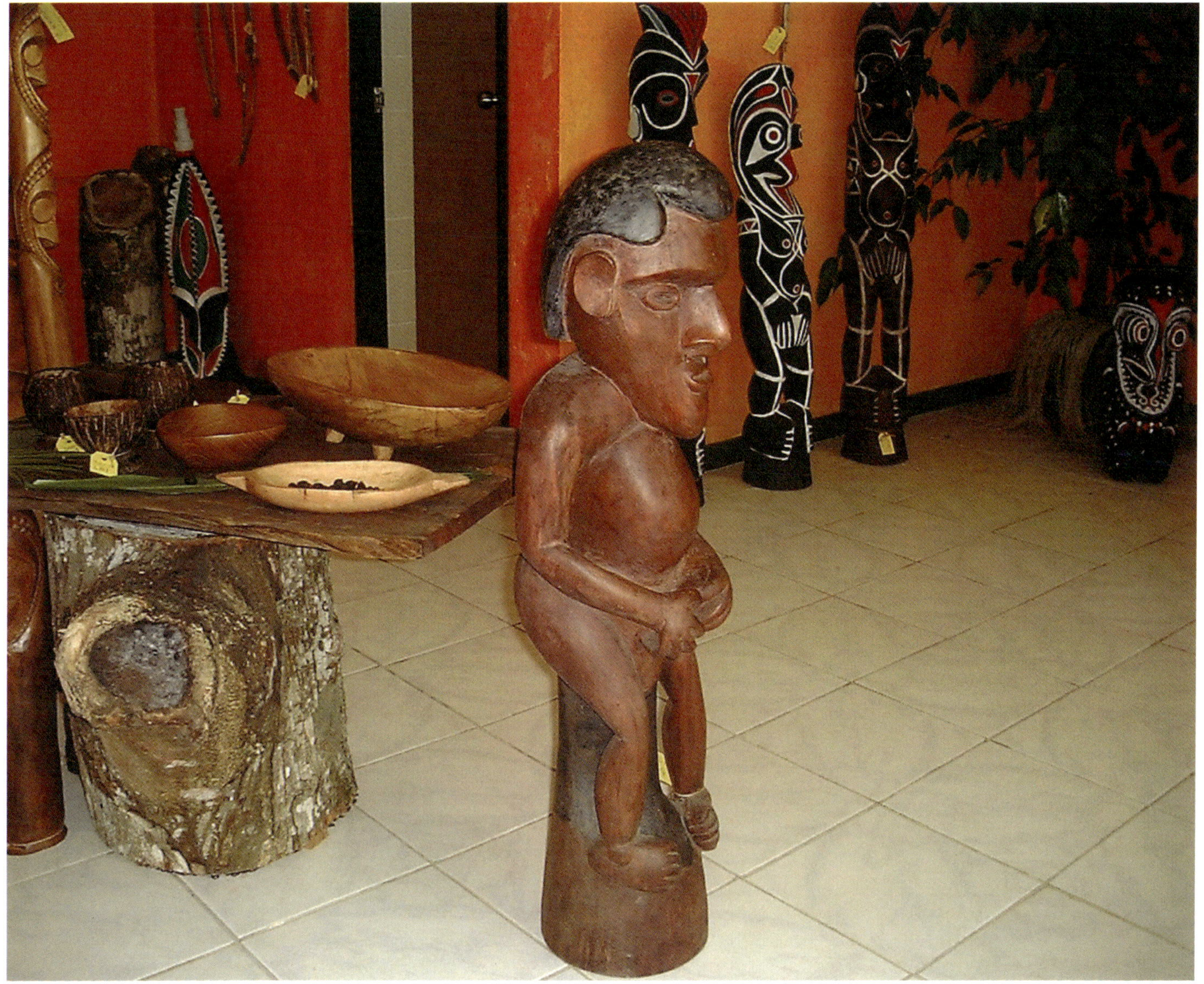

Figure 1.1 Falibak carving from Ambrym on display in Madame X's store and the story that was given to her by its maker to put by it in the store. Photograph by Haidy Geismar.

combs from Pentecost island collected in this manner (Bonnemaison et al. 1996: 141)

After she had established her own trade connections, Madame X moved away from this museological definition of kastom, to one that emerged more out of interaction with the people she was working with. One day when I was in the store, a woman from Tongoa island who had entered to look at some carved wooden storyboards from her island, commented loudly: "You should have the stories up around the objects, they'll sell better." Madame X had realised early on that real kastom was a complex social phenomenon, and that kastom objects needed to be socially embedded to be valuable. She began to request vendors to write down information about the artefacts [fig. 1.1], not just any information but kastom storian (kastom stories).

Story from Falibak: How Man was Formed

Once upon a time, a little child was borne of a liana vine. This vine was in the shape of a serpent, and hung from the branches of a big Banyan tree. After the child was born, he lived in the Banyan tree where he grew up into a big man. He saw a man from Wakon who had a pig. This pig was walking by the ocean carrying its babies on its shoulders, and came up to the roots of the Banyan tree. The man from Wakon was searching for his pig and found him asleep with its babies under the Banyan tree. He looked up into the branches and saw the child sitting in the tree. He asked, "What is your name". The child replied, "My name is Mel". Then Mel asked him "Who are you? What are you doing?" The man replied in his own language, meaning that he was walking around trying to find his pig. Mel gave the man a name: Bangbangon. Bangbangon tried to get his pig to go down to the village, but the pig could not move because Mel had tied him to a root of the tree. The man from Wakon wanted to go to work on his house in the village, but because he couldn't move his pig, he stayed there under the tree with Mel.

They stayed there together and Bangbangon saw that Mel was feeding the pig with his long hair to make the pig big and fat. The pigs grew and grew and gave birth to many more pigs. As he watched, Mel taking out his hair and feeding it to the pig, Bangbangon said: "Now your name is no longer Mel, it is Melfel because now you have a bald head!"

He stayed a long time with the ageing Melfel. He said to Bangbangon, "If I die, you will not bury me. You must put me in the Banyan tree where I can sit and look over everything." Bangbang did as Melfel told him to do, he put him up in the branches of the Banyan tree, and over time, he became like a stone.

All the people from Falibak used this stone (in the language of Falibak, called Muyuepu) to nourish their pigs, and they say that they make the pigs grow big and reproduce making all men rich in pigs.

And these stones of Bangbangon were used by Rengrengaim after Bangbangon died. When Rengrengaim died then Meleun Batken used them, when he died, they were used by Lokbaro Tungon, when he died they were passed to Bangdomal. Bangdomal used them until 1913, the year of the big volcano eruption at Deep Point. Now the volcano has buried the stones in the village of Falibak in West Ambrym at Deep Point.

So this figure represents this power, and belongs to me, Joseph Tungon from Falibak. I carved the figure again and no one else is allowed to carve him. [6]

The story above was given to Madame X by a carver from Ambrym Island along with a wooden figure to sell in her store. The narrative links the wooden carving to a mythic ancestor figure and explains how the carver knows how to carve this particular image. In presenting the complex genealogies and connections to place that this ancestor embodies, the carver not only represents crucial parts of his heritage to the consumer, but he also consolidates his local knowledge and identity to a more local audience — stating for example that he alone is entitled to carve (and sell) this particular image because of his genealogy.

Such complex criteria of authenticity are balanced around the principles of self-definition as well as external interest, and rather than evaluating their legitimacy we need to accept the political contingency and dynamism of this principle and process. Ultimately in this context, expatriate dealers may suffer because they themselves do not fulfill the particular criteria of authenticity that is most salient to definitions of indigenous identity: that of personhood, made incontrovertible by deep connections to local place, This form of authenticity serves ni-Vanuatu well in the marketplace, drawing upon an oppositional identity politics that privileges indigenous knowledge and market participation, to the detriment of expatriates who will always be 'outsiders' in these terms. Even as Madame X was building up her store, other more established dealers stores were closing shop, disaffected with their lack of success in navigating the customary regulations surrounding the production of kastom artifacts and with the complex identity politics which did not legitimate them (Geismar 2005).

Dealer stores in Port Vila are thus spaces within which ni-Vanuatu can subvert some of the inequalities between themselves and generally more affluent expatriates, and, increasingly assert economic and political self-determination. In this way, the production and circulation of artworks is a way in which dynamic local and national politics are worked out in practice, more often as not as a way of articulating shared values and mutual engagements.

Art Making the Indigenous

The negotiations around indigeneity and authenticity in dealer' stores and the growth of the marketplace has also given rise to the production of new kinds of objects, made specifically for this context. The growing contemporary arts movement in Vanuatu has provided an avenue for debates around the relationship between tradition and modernity to be made more explicit to a wide audience. For ni-Vanuatu engaged as artists, contemporary art (in contrast to kastom material culture) is a way in which social and political concerns may be articulated, a method for capitalising on culture as a resource to profit from the sale of artworks, a way in which they can present and discuss ideas about indigeneity and nationhood to each other and to strangers, and a material marker and maker of these classifications and distinctions. As Ralph Regenvanu, the director of the Vanuatu Cultural Centre, and a practicing artist, has noted:

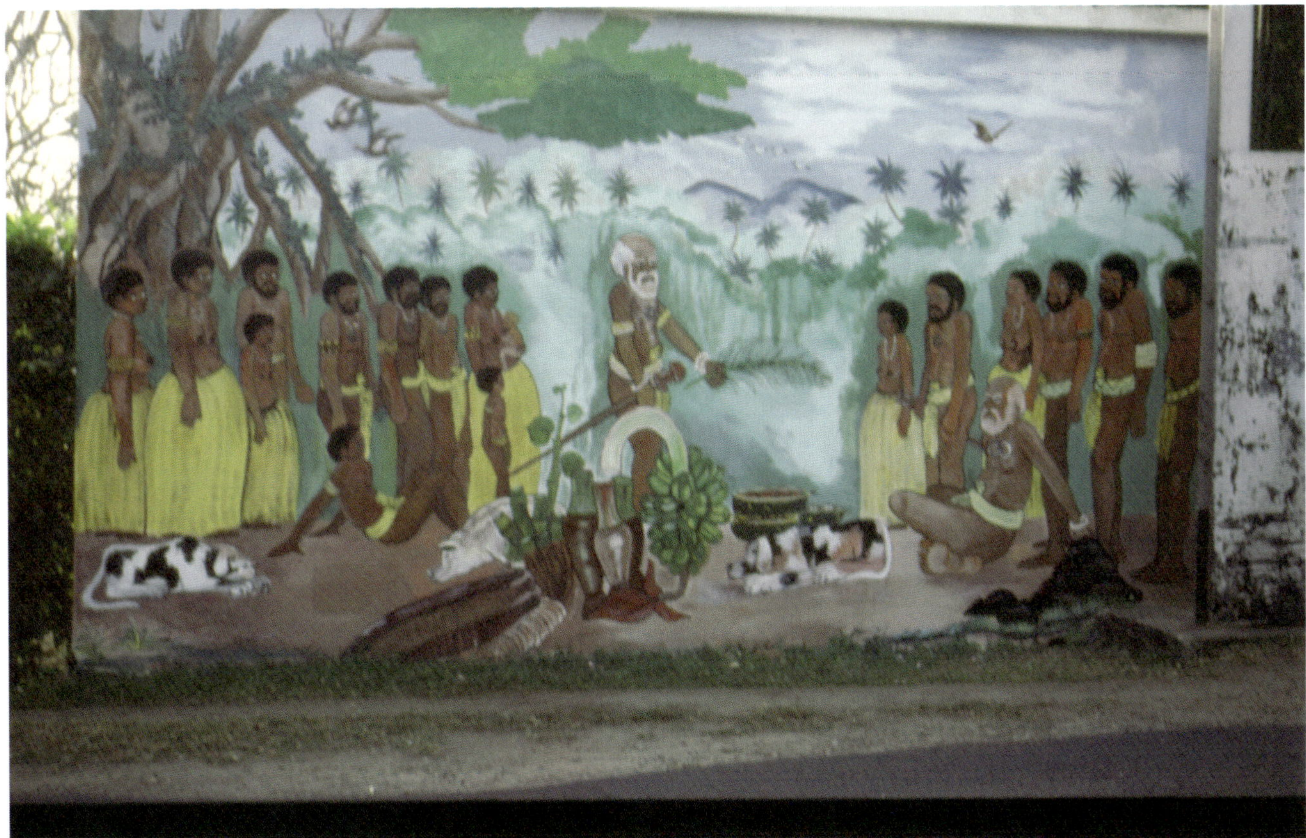

Figure 1.2 Moses Jobo, synthesizes the local and the national in his decorations of a UNELCO electricity shed, Port Vila, Vanuatu, 2001. This scene is about tribal reconciliation in Erromango. Photograph by Haidy Geismar.

> What is called "art" in Vanuatu today is based on many of the same principles as the traditional creative forms that preceded it. Contemporary art is perhaps distinguishable from its forebears only in terms of the wider range of media used and the sources of inspiration and motivation for creative expression...Although the tradition of contemporary art in Vanuatu has its origins in the drawing and paintings of the colonial settlers and European visitors to these islands, the contemporary art scene in Vanuatu today features a prominent ni-Vanuatu as well as European presence, with the primary Western form being increasingly transformed by creations inspired by indigenous conceptions. As an expression of the individual and collective experience, contemporary art in Vanuatu is perhaps uniquely placed to provide an ongoing representation of life in a country in which the latest Western technology coexists with a living and vital Melanesian spirituality. (Regenvanu 1997: 5)

Image production has been an important ground for thinking about the specificities of being ni-Vanuatu — a particular kind of indigenous identity defined in relation to national citizenship. In 1990, to commemorate ten years of independence, the Government of Vanuatu published a book celebrating the newly forged national culture of Vanuatu (Vanuatu 1990). In a section entitled National Symbols, the anonymous writer claims that the basis of independent identity is to be found in the natural resources of Vanuatu (of which culture is a constituent part), and goes on to describe a corpus of national symbols, all of which are stylised motifs connecting culture and nature [figs. 1.2, 1.3, and 1.4]. Thus, the national coat of arms, the symbol of *Long God yumi stanap* [In God we stand] incorporates culture into the natural resources of the country. [7]

The symbol is explained:

> The man is a ni-Vanuatu, a Melanesian and a chief. The spear he holds represents his role as defender and protector of his people. His armbands (shell money) denote his role as the dealer in economic exchanges and distributor of services, goods and resources. His headdress and loincloth represent the various modes of attire found throughout the country. The man

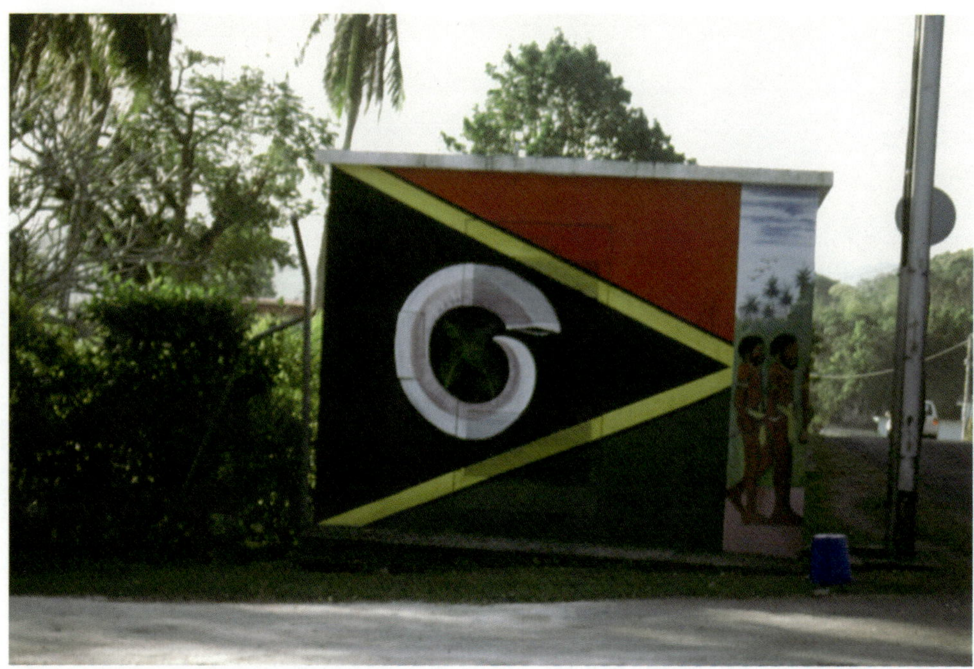

Figure 1.3 Moses Jobo, synthesizes the local and the national in his decorations of a UNELCO electricity shed, Port Vila, Vanuatu, 2001. Pigs tusk flanks the national flag of Vanuatu. Photograph by Haidy Geismar.

> stands with his feet firmly on the ground, in the soil of his land, Vanuatu. The crossed cycad leaves in the background signify the peace derived from chiefly authority and jurisprudence. The circular pig tusk symbolises unity, wealth, and prosperity, an outgrowth of human interaction, authority and peace. The mat in front of the man recalls the importance of agriculture in our traditional economy. Mats are the product of women's labour, and women are the producers and managers of our agricultural economy. Our motto, 'Long god yumi stanap', reminds us to give back to God our Creator, in sacrifice, all that He has abundantly bestowed upon us. (Ibid: 28-29)

Here is the contemporary nation-state drawn large. The conflation of nature with culture as indigenous resources that can be stylised and circulated as a series of images (consolidating the local and the national) has had great affect on the production of artefacts categorised explicitly as contemporary art.

Contemporary art mediates kastom

The production of contemporary art in Vanuatu entails a constant negotiation between continuity and change. Images made from tapestry, paint on canvas, or watercolour on paper, are seen as explicitly contemporary in ways that images created by technologies and materials that have been institutionalised within kastom are not. However, they are made indigenous by virtue of the symbols drawn upon and the identity of the people that produce them.

Newly found national material such as contemporary art not only mediates between the locality and the nation, but between national and international domains. The first organisation of ni-Vanuatu contemporary artists emerged in this context, out of a series of interactions between urban ni-Vanuatu and expatriate artists. In 1987, artists Emmanual Watt, Sero Kuautonga, Fidel Yoringmal, Juliette Pita and French expatriate Patrice Cujo, met at *L'Atelier*, the French gallery owned by dealer Suzanne Bastien, in Port Vila to discuss the establishment of an organisation of contemporary art. The meeting was also attended by ni-Vanuatu who had been trained in art at INTV (the technical training college in Port Vila) during the four years that the course was available, including Juliette Pita, John Joseph, Michael Busai, and Sylvester Bulesa. Prior to this, contemporary art in Vanuatu had only been produced by foreigners; exemplified by the work of French artists Nicholai Michoutouchkine and Robert Tatin (Regenvanu 1996, Geismar 2004). Following a suggestion of Pita's, they decided that the organisation be named Nawita, the Bislama term for octopus. Each tentacle of the octopus represents a different artistic medium or material form of expression, highlighting the diverse talents of the group, united in a single association.

In terms of expatriate relations, the association is still predominantly Francophile — the constitution was initially written in French — affirming a free member-

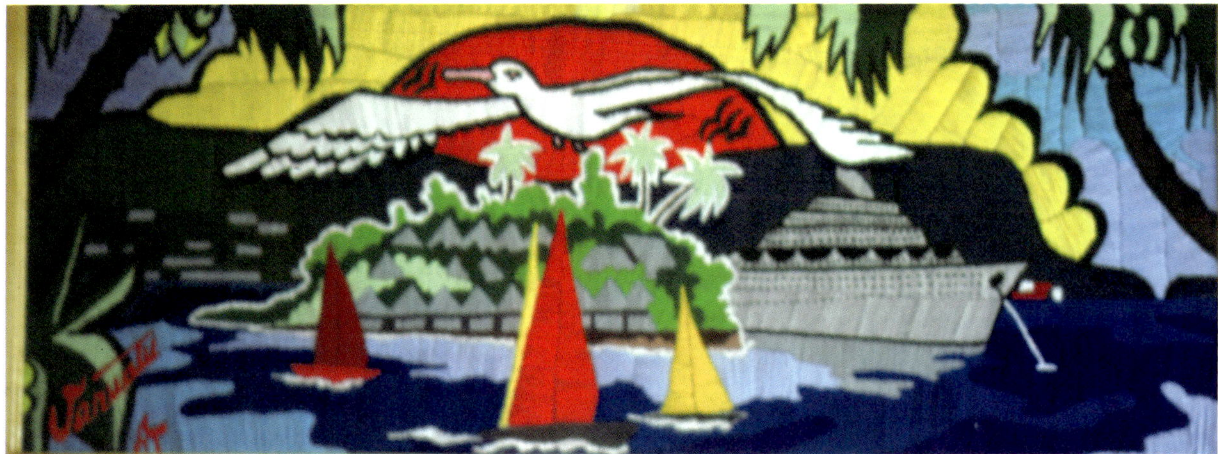

Figure 1.4 Andrew Tovovur. Tapestry depicting the arrival of the Pacific Sky cruise ship in Vila harbor. Photograph by Haidy Geismar.

ship open to expatriates and ni-Vanuatu alike. Despite these connections, Nawita presents itself as an indigenous organisation [8]. Expatriate artists act as teachers and facilitators, but maintain a lower public profile, keeping up the indigenous appearance of the association. Now with nearly a hundred members, Nawita continues to hold yearly exhibitions, in the gallery of the French Embassy, and remains the most prolific and high profile artists association in Vanuatu

Out of this framework, the primary criteria of the association's membership define the contemporary as explicitly *against* the concept of kastom. This is primarily a material distinction: artists or artisans using traditional media and traditional principles are excluded (Regenvanu 1996: 312). The use of tradition-as-image, transforms kastom. Whilst contemporary art objects are not regarded to have ritual efficacy, or be emplaced in local tradition, their reliance on customary imagery defines them as indigenous. For example, an expatriate accountant who crafted a miniature replica of the Pentecost Land Dive out of matchsticks and won first prize at an art competition in 1995, was deposed of his prize once his nationality was fully realized by the kastom chiefs acting as judges [9] — he was working with new materials, but was, as a foreigner not allowed to use the land dive as a representational resource. Such criteria of authentic personhood are not yet extended to ni-Vanuatu and it is still legitimate for artists such as Juliette Pita, from Erromango Island, to create versions of the Pentecost land dive out of tapestry.

Nawita members conscientiously follow the same rules of indigenous entitlement in place for material classified as kastom: they perceive kastom objects to be the entitlements of authentic persons (determined by natal affiliations with particular islands) expressed using authentic materials, usually those with a basis in the locality, or in nature. Ralph Regenvanu, describes how his work [fig. 1.5] negotiates this relationship:

> I always use symbols when I work; I think maybe a lot of artists here do. Basically the symbols are to do with the distinction between kastom and non-kastom. Kastom is taken to mean anything that has aspects of, or any aspect that represents the pre-European past, like the indigenous cultures of Vanuatu. Kastom is obviously made to be a distinct thing from anything that is not kastom, which has aspects of the post-European contact history of Vanuatu. For example, money or cash, or even the church, Christianity or things like their clothes and so on are not kastom.
>
> In all the work I do I try to create images of Vanuatu, pictures that I'm interested in. All my work is based around Vanuatu themes. I don't do anything that isn't. Always I want to represent the fact that this conflict exists in everything. Everything that happens in Vanuatu has the kastom and non-kastom side. So you have to find symbols for them and how they interact. That's a lot of my art, and all the other artists' work here in Vanuatu. All the contemporary artists have aspects of both in their drawings and their art.
>
> For me, I use a motif of a face from a drum, a slit-gong and also Black Palm figures that they carve on my island. I'm very conscious about using things that I have a right to use. I don't use symbols from other islands that belong to other groups of people. But you'll find that many of the contemporary artists in Vanuatu today, and most of them have contributed to this exhibition, do use symbols from other islands, which aren't really theirs. But they use them in the terms of a national idea of kastom. When they

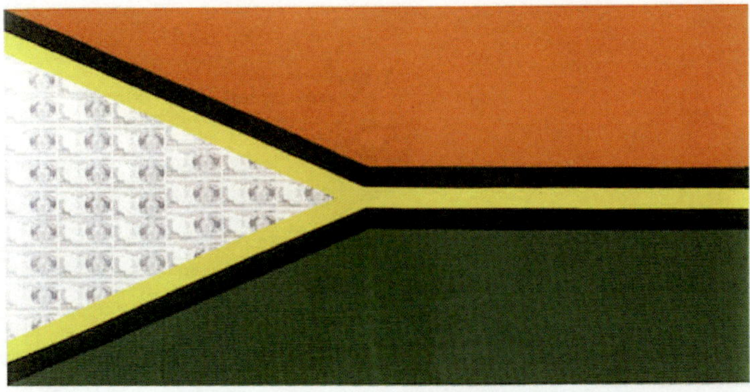

Figure 1.5 Ralph Regenvanu. *Development After Independence* (Vanuatu 1998). Mixed media on custom board. Photograph by Haidy Geismar.

> use it, for example, they use an image of a face from another island where they're not from, to represent kastom in a national context. Artists have got into trouble for doing that, and it's something they have got to be careful about. I totally avoid it at all costs.
>
> I just try not to use anything at all, any traditional design that doesn't come from my area. So I stick to a certain range of options that I can use to represent kastom when I do any designs. At the same time there's a different range of options that I can use from the non-kastom side. Obviously a wider range because there aren't really these issues of copyright that I have to be sensitive about. [10]

New Traditions

Given that the criteria for authentic personal identity is extended into the production of contemporary arts, it soon becomes apparent that the material form of contemporary art pieces are grounds upon which crucial definition and distinctions are formed and synthesised. An example of such synthesis can be drawn out of an exhibition entitled *New Traditions: Contemporary Art from Vanuatu*, which was held at the VCC in 1999-2000 (VCC 2000) and subsequently toured Australia and New Zealand [11]. In the exhibition, connections were made between contemporary art made by individual artists (all ni-Vanuatu citizens) [12], and contemporary objects (traditional, but newly made) that were associated with general island styles more than specific individuals. The new traditions of the title of the exhibition accentuated the strong relationships between traditional and contemporary arts in the forging of ni-Vanuatu identities.

Ten contemporary artists from the Nawita association were asked to interpret ten periods from the history of Vanuatu [13]. These pieces were then placed alongside examples of recently made traditional artifacts in order to demonstrate "both the similarities and contrasts between modern and traditional art" (Ibid). In his comment above, Regenvanu emphasizes that he views kastom as a parallel way of being to that of the ways of the west (epitomized by clothes, money, and Christianity). In his painting *Development After Independence*, the ultimate national symbol includes not only the national flag, but is made partly from images of vatu banknotes. Regevanu's comment that "Everything that happens in Vanuatu has the kastom and non-kastom side" emphasizes the synthetic capability of contemporary arts in Vanuatu to forge some kind of material resolution between the often-problematic opposition of tradition and modernity in a national indigenous identity.

Equally, painter Sero Kuautonga reflected upon his own piece, *The Future* [fig. 1.6] in the *New Traditions* exhibition:

> My idea behind this picture is our future. To me our future is based on the past, and our past is based on our culture. So based on our cultural heritage and our cultural knowledge, we can enter the future. In this picture I have expressed an aspect of our cultural heritage that is copyright. We cannot create or copy those designs but we can get inspiration from those images and create new ones. I have stylized all the traditional designs. You can see the face of a slit-drum. You can also see a pig's tusk, a rock design and a footprint. The footprint symbolizes standing in your own culture so that you can enter the future, which is the bright space. The namele leaf is the bridge so that we can speak to each other. It symbolizes staying in the past so that you can enter the future. That is how we can communicate. There is also a show print. The show print steps on the footprint as it steps into the future. So knowing our cultural heritage and our cultural knowledge we can enter

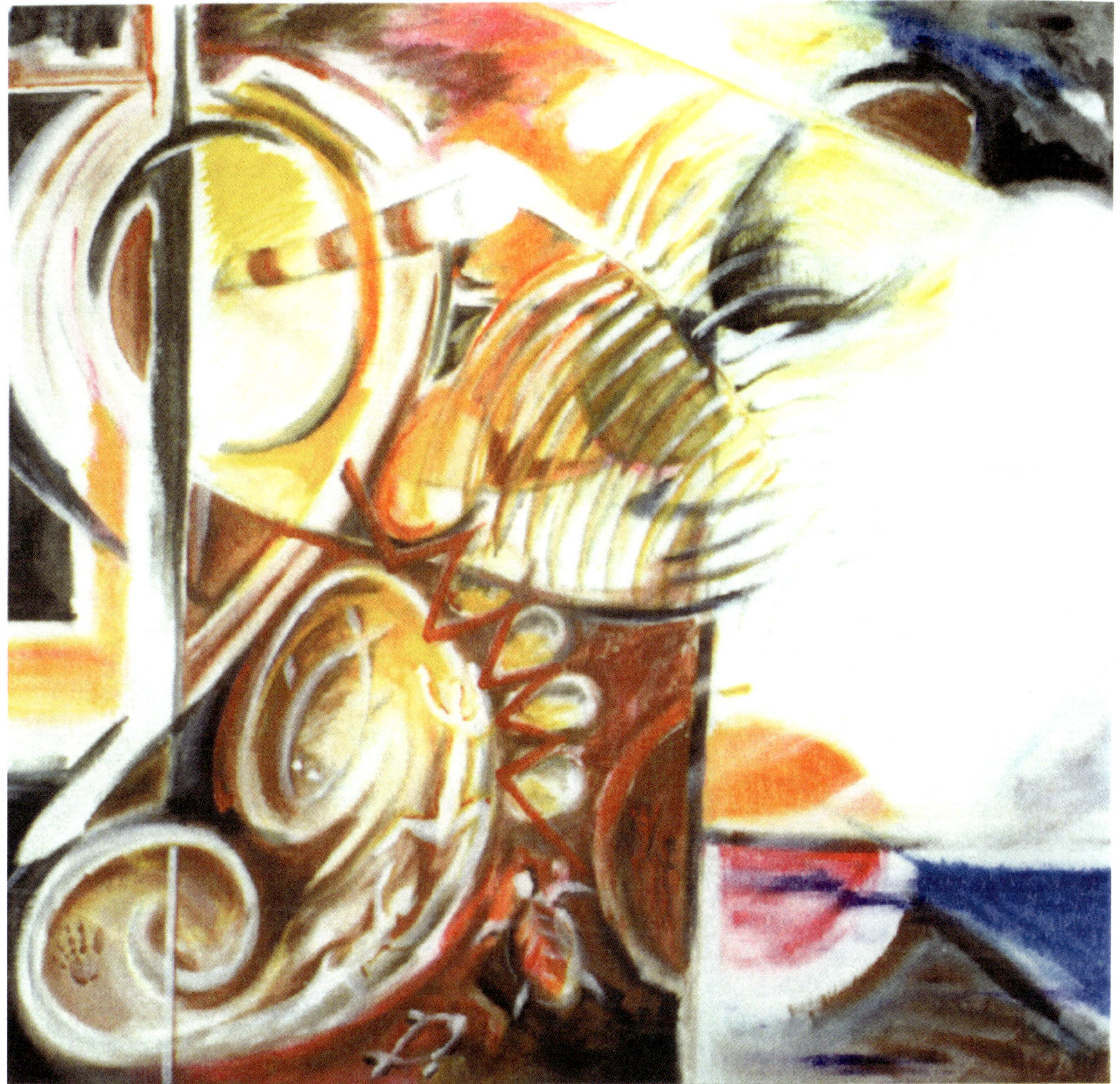

Figure 1.6 Sero Kuautonga, *The future*, Oil on Canvas. 1998. Photograph by Haidy Geismar.

> the new world, which is the modern world… In Vanuatu we have an association of modern contemporary artists. For me, the association is symbolic of a keyhole that we can use to open a new door, which is contemporary art.

Since the *New Traditions* show, contemporary artists in Vanuatu have increasingly reflected upon what makes their work unique as ni-Vanuatu artists, as they participate in international workshops, art festivals and biennials. The *Nawita* association has expanded its membership, and other artists associations have been founded. For instance, a young carver from Tongoa Island, Kake Buko, participated in an exhibition of Tongoan carvings at the French Embassy in Port Vila in 2001. He described to me how he defined his unique style and subject matter. His training in traditional carving in his island home was supplemented by his work with the US Peace Corps office in Port Vila and by carving workshops in Australia and the Solomon

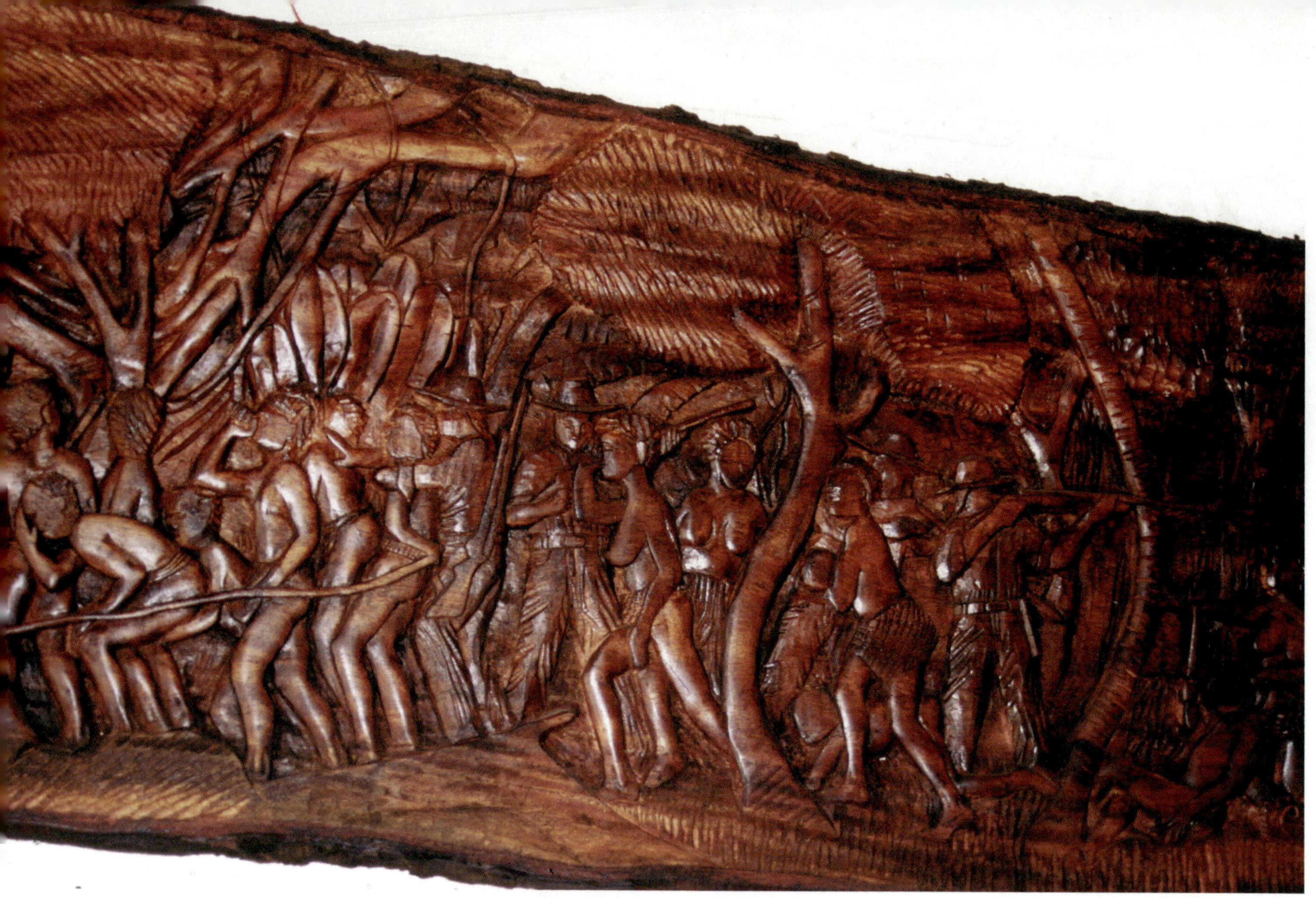

Figure 1.7 Kake Buko, *Blackbirding*. Storyboard. 2001. Detail. Photograph by Haidy Geismar.

Islands. He draws on the traditional carving techniques of his island, storyboards [figs. 1.7 and 1.8], to depict periods of Vanuatu's colonial history and his experiences of Pacific multiculturalism:

> I want to address in my work some styles of Vanuatu that everyone here knows about. Since I was in Australia, I have been researching the story of the experiences of the workers from Vanuatu who went to Australia one hundred years ago to work on the sugar plantations. I have carved their story onto a traditional Tongoan storyboard. My work reflects both my own experiences and wider Pacific art. [14]

Buko also incorporates techniques learned in the Solomon Islands such as pearl-shell inlay to his relief carving. The material consolidation of ni-Vanuatu experience and identity is thus forged in the wider context of the exchange of ideas, styles, and of overlapping histories, and Buko's work is also part of a growing pan-Pacific visual style, one which highlights shared connections of experience between the indigenous peoples of Oceania.

Looking at the work and comments of contemporary artists in Vanuatu demonstrates that the Port Vila art world is a place where ideas about indigenous authenticity are re-made *over* the tension lines of tradition/modernity. As in the marketplace, the key to the authentic production of contemporary art objects is the same as for other artifacts: they must be made by indigenous, entitled producers, who in turn set the boundaries and definitions of their own indigeneity. During one conversation I had with Sero Kuautonga and Richard Abong, a chief from Southern Malakula, who is responsible for producing the ritual material culture used by his family in important ceremonial rites of status acquisition, they began to talk about what made objects real, or authentic:

> **Richard Abong:** Yes, our art must have its time. The things that we are making now, come from our desire to revive the masks which were used before... we have to go inside our kastom of the past, and make these masks part of our activities today... When we make them we follow the 'originality' of the masks that were made before. All of the new masks that we make; we

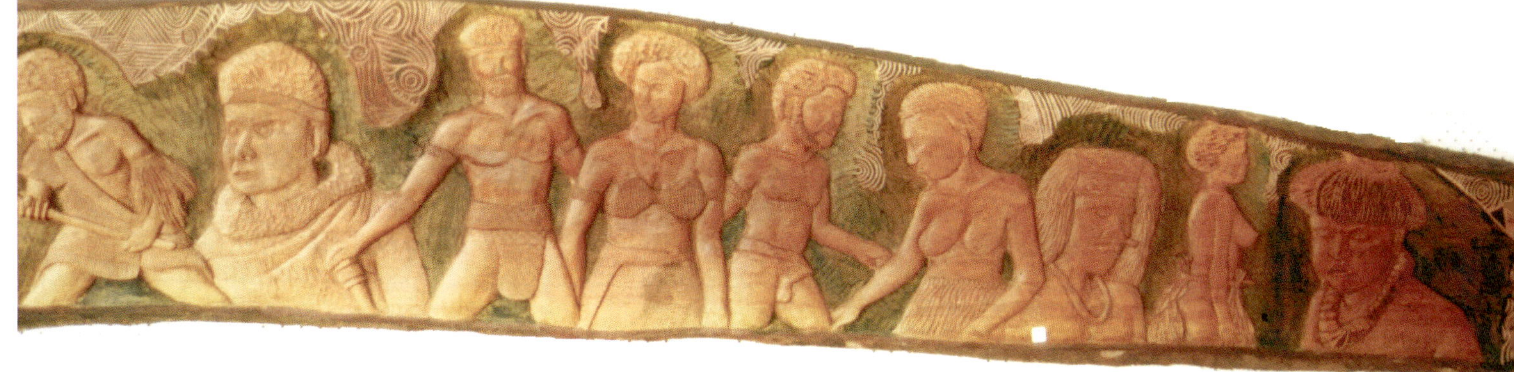

Figure 1.8 Kake Buko: *Kastom dress*, Storyboard. Photograph by Haidy Geismar.

> try our best to make them follow the originality of the old masks.
>
> **Sero**: Yes, for example, in making a mask, it isn't just the creation of art or artefact. It must be made with how you behave around the time of preparation, to collect the right material, then to slowly build up the mask, then at the end there must be a ceremony with a dance, so everything is part of this bigger thing. The object or artefact that you look at, it isn't just an artefact, it is a full process. Otherwise there is no meaning to the mask, you are just making it to sell. You must make it with a purpose. The purpose is the mask, the activity that goes with it, kastom dance, or whatever it is. But if you just 'make it', and you leave it as it is, the thinking of old tells us that you will be affected by this, it will go against you. [15]

For Sero, a contemporary artist, and Richard, a ritual practitioner, the ancestral past is the ultimate source of authenticity and of indigenous identity. Ancestors are the link between living people, local places and their productions. As such contemporary art practice takes mythic history and kastom and makes it into indigenous national cultural heritage.

Conclusions

Contemporary indigenous art can be used as a window to view how some seemingly opposite ways of being are united materially in everyday life for many ni-Vanuatu. Localized notions of the indigenous and of authenticity are drawn through increasingly international relations: the internationalist environment of the market and the internationally recognized language of contemporary arts. Both categories emerge from a web of connections, which might incorporate foreigners in Vanuatu and in other countries, as well as neighboring islanders from throughout the archipelago, but never forgets to foreground difference as much as relationality. In this way, objects (especially contemporary art objects) become sites upon which oppositional tensions between tradition and modernity, continuity and change can coexist. To make an authentic artwork in Vanuatu, one that is legitimately viable in cultural and economic terms, one must be an authentic (indigenous) person. To be an authentic person means claiming indisputable rights in particular places. Both authentic places and persons are ascribed and described by objects. It is important to realize that there is space for dispute, controversy, and dissent within this process. Making and presenting contemporary art can help us to develop an academic language that can incorporate diversity, fluidity and dynamic change in our understandings of how people talk about their sense of identity and their understandings of authenticity.

This discussion of the machinations of the art market in Vanuatu has highlighted that rather than analytically sweeping the value of authenticity under the carpet, we should recognize it as a powerful mechanism by which the category of the indigenous is made by local agents in tandem with diverse external interest groups. In addition, by focusing on some ways in which the contemporary artists of Vanuatu *construct their own* concepts of the indigenous that acknowledge both mythic pasts and contemporary historical and political realities, this essay has emphasized how criteria of the indigenous are currently played out in the production of art. Contemporary art objects may be understood as cross-cultural meeting grounds, which may facilitate the reconciliation between sharply contrasting domains of political and cultural experience and the classifications and values that are attendant to them (Thomas 1991).

In summary, looking closely at contemporary indigenous art can show how authenticity and indigeneity are made or materialized out of a long history of *cross-cultural* political and economic exchange and interaction. Kuper's discussion, in ignoring local exegesis of these categories, is curiously limited. Focusing on the ways in which dealers, collectors and artists in the Pacific, describe authenticity shows that there is a very real efficacy to the category, as it is negotiated between these different interest groups, and consolidated in the very form of artworks themselves. It is still vital for many native artists to integrate their cultural identity into their work; tourists and collectors still ask whether pieces they buy are truly authentic; dealers discuss authenticity amongst themselves as well as with the people that they buy or sell to (albeit in somewhat different terms). Asking what it means for a person or an object to be real or really indigenous is asking a question about authenticity: a judgment that determines the worth of something in terms of the strength of its identity claims. As Regenvanu and Kuautonga both acknowledge in their artist's statements, being indigenous is also a value of entitlement. In this way, the relationship between classifications and values pertaining to authenticity and indigenous identity are extremely powerful and it is for this reason that they continue to be used and to resonate as important categories of thought.

In Unknown Country: East Kimberley Artists and the Art World

Eric Kjellgren

As the work of Aboriginal artists from the East Kimberley region of Western Australia has achieved greater prominence in the art world over the last two decades, both the paintings and their creators have been increasingly drawn, both fiscally and physically, into the global art market. This interaction represents a new type of encounter with Europeans and their settler descendants, who East Kimberley Aboriginals refer to as kartiya. [1] That kartiya, who, within living memory, sought to eradicate Aboriginals and their culture, now frequently idealize Aboriginal art, artists, and culture, elicits mixed reactions from painters in the East Kimberley. [2]

As their works have attained growing recognition on the national and international art scene, many East Kimberley painters have traveled extensively to exhibitions of their work in Australia and abroad and had the opportunity to ponder the ways in which their works are recontextualized by their kartiya consumers. Pleased with the respect for Aboriginal culture and income that their art brings, many also voice concerns over who primarily profits from the art market and the appropriate display of their paintings by museums and galleries (see Kjellgren 2000). Their efforts to understand and critique the art world in terms of Aboriginal cultural conventions and priorities represent an important and often neglected voice in the cross-cultural dialogue between Aboriginals and kartiya.

As East Kimberley painters, in turn, have become aware of art world responses to their works, they have reacted to them in ways, which address not art world agendas or concerns but their own cultural and political priorities. Unconcerned with the majority of the aesthetic and political agendas of the art world, at those points where its discourses intersect with issues East Kimberley painters regard as important, such as land rights, they respond accordingly, becoming active agents in ongoing cross cultural dialogues on the meaning and nature of Aboriginal art. Many artists, in their initial encounters with the art world, were at first reticent to express certain concerns or address certain themes, such as the devastating massacres of Aboriginal people that occurred during the colonial period in the East Kimberley. However, their growing familiarity with, and newfound acceptance within, the art world has given both painters and performers the resolve, courage and venue to address the violent events of the colonial period. In doing so they seek not simply to document the tragic events of the past but also to reach out to kartiya audiences as an important step in the ongoing process of Aboriginal-kartiya reconciliation.

This essay examines East Kimberley Aboriginal artists' perspectives on and encounters with the art world between the mid 1990s and 2003. It is based primarily on the author's interviews with many of the original founders of the contemporary East Kimberley painting movement including Queenie McKenzie, Jack Britten, Hector Jandulu (also called Hector Jandany), Rover Thomas, and Freddie Timms as well as members of the second generation of artists who followed them such as Shirley Purdie and Peggy Patrick. These artists were generally the first members of their communities to have any significant interaction with the art world and many of the comments recorded here constitute their initial reactions to what was at that time a completely novel cultural milieu. However, as these and subsequent generations of East Kimberley painters continue to interact and become increasingly familiar with the art world, their perspectives are constantly evolving. Since the interviews described here were conducted, nearly all of the founding artists of the East Kimberley movement have passed away and many of the members of the second (and now third) generation of artists, if interviewed today, might express significantly different views on the same issues. Aboriginal culture in the East Kimberley remains a living and highly dynamic phenomenon. Thus, the present study seeks not to present an ahistorical description of East Kimberley artists' perspectives on the art world as if they were unchanging. Instead it examines those perspectives during a specific and highly significant period in the history of the contemporary painting movement, which encompassed many of the earliest encounters between East Kimberley artists and the art world.

Contemporary East Kimberley Painting

The East Kimberley forms a distinctive area within the larger Kimberley region situated in the northeast corner of the state of Western Australia. Culturally, the East Kimberley includes the peoples of the eastern portion of the Kimberley and adjacent sections of the Northern Territory. At its core lie the homelands of the Gija and Miriwoong peoples but a diversity of local Aboriginal groups, including the Gajirrawoong, Ngaliwurru, Jaminjung, and Jaru, as well as individuals from the desert peoples of the interior, also live and paint in the region.

Contemporary East Kimberley Aboriginal painting represents a distinctive regional tradition within contemporary Aboriginal art. Centered in and around the Aboriginal communities at Warmun (also called Turkey Creek) and Kununurra the contemporary painting movement began in the mid 1970s and remains vigorous. The best-known East Kimberley painter was Rover Thomas who lived and painted at Warmun. Other prominent Warmun painters include Jack Britten, Queenie McKenzie, Freddie Timms, Hector Jandulu, Lena Nyadbi, Shirley Purdie, Paddy Bedford, Peggy Patrick, and Henry Wambiny. Notable painters from the Kununurra area include Paddy Carlton, Alan and Peggy Griffiths, and Billy Thomas.

East Kimberley painting constitutes a unique and largely self-contained school within contemporary Aboriginal painting. Distinct from the brightly colored acrylic (or "dot") paintings of the deserts to the south and the bark painting traditions of Arnhem Land to the east, East Kimberley painting overall is characterized by compositions in which large areas of monochrome ochre are set apart from each other by borders consisting of a single line of dots [fig. 2.1]. Within this broad set of stylistic conventions, however, each painter in the region has developed his or her own unique individual style.

The imagery of East Kimberley paintings frequently appears abstract to non-Aboriginal observers. However, virtually all contemporary East Kimberley paintings are, in one form or another, representations of landscape. Each depicts aspects of the inseparable phenomena of country and dreamings — the landscape and its sacred oral history, which lie at the center of indigenous religious practices, land tenure, and conceptions of self in the East Kimberley.

The peoples of the East Kimberley were originally hunter-gatherers living in small, semi-nomadic bands of related individuals who moved from place to place within a well defined home territory known in Kriol (Aboriginal English) as their country. Although Aboriginals in the region today live in permanent settlements, country still remains central to Aboriginal identity, politics, and religion. At birth each member of Aboriginal society inherits ownership rights to, and ceremonial responsibility for, particular portions of the land owned by his or her language and/or kin group. Each country, in turn, is associated with one or more dreamings, the ancestral beings and events that created its physical features during the dreaming [3] or creation period and whose creative (and destructive) power still remains at specific places in the landscape.

A country's history, however, does not end with its dreamings. The often tragic events of the colonial era are linked to the land in Aboriginal oral traditions in the same way as dreaming events. Aboriginal narratives of massacres and other encounters with kartiya settlers have also become an integral part of the landscape in which they occurred. Like the mountains or waterholes created by dreaming beings, a rock charred during the burning of massacre victims or a massive tree standing at a massacre site now form indelible features of country. Although Aboriginals distinguish between dreaming stories and the oral histories of the colonial era, each type of narrative is inextricably linked to landscape. Country is the embodiment of history, a history that includes the dreaming, the events of the colonial encounter, as well as incidents from more recent times.

Although some paintings are produced for local ceremonial use, the vast majority of contemporary East Kimberley paintings are produced for sale to kartiya. This fact is openly acknowledged by the artists who generally view painting as a type of job, similar to being a stockworker or government employee. This pragmatic attitude on the part of East Kimberley painters toward the act of painting or being an artist (activities which have attained almost mystical significance in kartiya culture) contrasts with the underlying cultural importance of the subject matter of the paintings themselves (country and dreamings).

When asked to comment on the importance of, and aesthetic criteria for evaluating, their own works and those of others, Aboriginal painters in the East Kimberley above all cite the knowledge and ownership of the country, dreamings, and other narratives their paintings portray as the source of their significance and value. In contrast to the visually based aesthetics of the art world, it is the cultural content rather than the physical or visual qualities of the work itself, which is the source of a painting's value among East Kimberley Aboriginals. To many senior artists, the money they receive for their canvases is perceived as payment for sharing this knowledge rather than for the image itself. While the kartiya think they are buying the image, the artist often believes he or she is selling the knowledge of the country and dreamings from which the image derives.

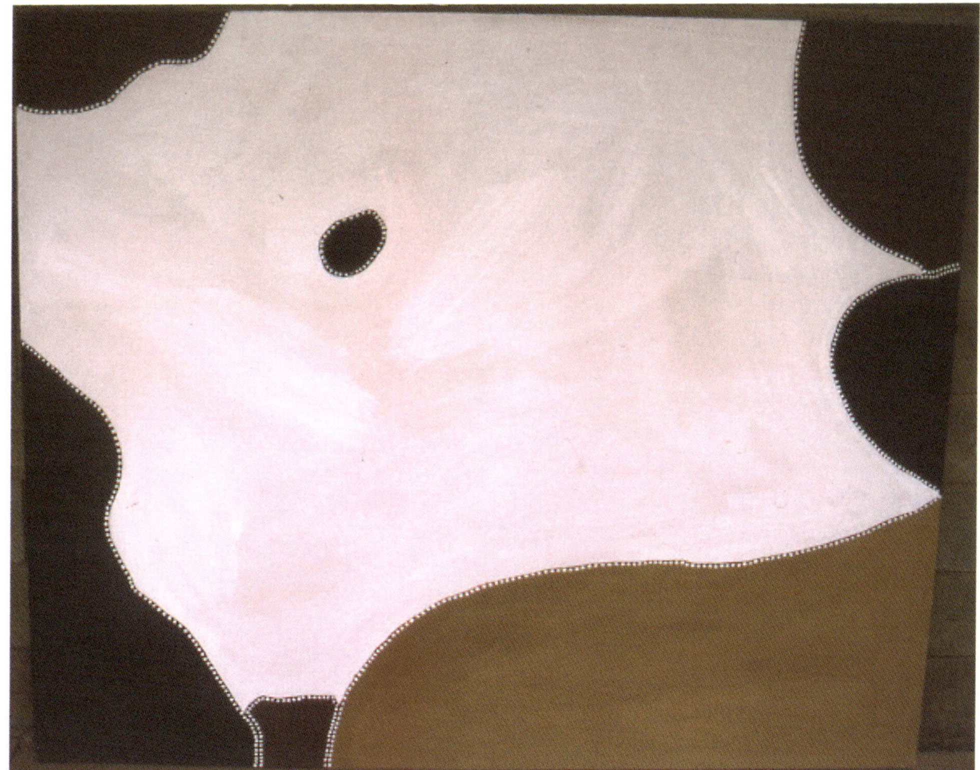

Figure. 2.1. Freddie Timms, *Lake Argyle Country*, ca. 1995, ocher on canvas. Featuring large areas of monochrome ochre set off by dotted borders, this work exemplifies the distinctive stylistic conventions of Warmun painting. © Freddie Timms, used with permission.

Both the attitude toward painting as a job undertaken to meet the demands of kartiya buyers and of the sale of paintings as primarily a transaction in cultural knowledge rather than objects are reflected in painters' perspectives on their dealings with the art world. The late Gija painter Jack Britten, for example, emphasized the central importance of cultural content in paintings as the source of their importance and value in his dealings with kartiya art buyers:

> We don't want to give our culture away. The kartiya said "This is your culture... We will pay you for that [i.e. making paintings]." Well, they pay you for drawing the country. [...] That's the way we do it. And the kartiya love that. [4]

Thus, although art world consumers concentrate on the imagery when purchasing Aboriginal paintings, from the perspective of many East Kimberley artists, especially members of the older generation, these transactions with the art market are interpreted in wholly Aboriginal terms. Just as young people in Aboriginal societies must pay in food, money, or work for the knowledge of dreaming and country they receive from elders, kartiya too must pay for the dreamings imparted to them through Aboriginal paintings.

In addition to selling their work to local art cooperatives and art dealers, a transaction that often takes place in the East Kimberley itself, many East Kimberley painters have traveled extensively to exhibitions at galleries and museums in major Australian cities. A number have also been overseas, as all international destinations are referred to in Kriol, to places as distant as Tokyo, Paris, Venice and Miami. For the artists, most of whom had not previously had the opportunity to travel outside the East Kimberley and whose primary experience of kartiya was based on encounters with pastoralists, government workers, missionaries (and the occasional anthropologist), exposure to the subcultures of the metropolitan art world and the huge cities in which it operates, was, at first, a novel and often surprising experience.

Based on the author's interviews, East Kimberley painters seem pleased with their encounters with the art world and their experiences at exhibitions. Indeed, many take advantage of every opportunity they have for further travel. However, they also express amusement (or bewilderment) with such unfamiliar activities as posing for photographers, answering questions from journalists and the public, or navigating through the crowded streets of cities whose vast size and enormous populations have no parallels in their home countries. [5] Freddie Timms, for example, describes walking the streets of Tokyo:

> I went to Tokyo. But the [kartiya] never bought any paintings. I was there for a week and we had all the paintings hanging up [in the gallery]... I walked around there. I walked all over the city looking around. [It impressed me] to meet that many people. To see *that many* people... And they haven't got much room. They have houses everywhere. [...] It's very jammed up. The people are jammed up together. [6]

Commenting on the same trip, Rover Thomas' sole observation was that Tokyo had "Huge numbers of kartiya, and huge numbers of Japanese." [7]

Miriwoong artist Peggy Patrick, who accompanied a group of Warmun painters, musicians, and dancers to an exhibition in Paris in 1997 describes the kartiya fascination with Aboriginal culture. She also attempts to explain why she believes the French audiences were so enthusiastic about Gija paintings and dances:

> [In Paris the French people] wanted to see how Aboriginals make paintings. We had a grindstone there with pieces of charcoal and white and yellow ochre. And we showed them how to grind them up to make paint... I don't think they had ever seen a grindstone in France... Another time we danced. It was good. And the French people wanted to find out how Aboriginal people live... There were huge numbers of people living in Paris, people living everywhere. [...] Every day we taught them. Every morning we went to the museum. We were singing and the men played the didgeridu. [The French] wanted to find out what music means to Aboriginal people. "Well, that's our law" [8] we told them, "we don't just dance for the sake of dancing." We make paintings. And our paintings are related to our songs and dances. They are songs and dances. They make people feel happy inside. [...] And the French went mad for those things now. For painting and singing... I think they had never seen a painting before and never seen people dancing. [9]

The late Gija painter Hector Jandulu, who traveled extensively throughout Australia both as a representative to conferences on Aboriginal issues and, later, in connection with his paintings, mentioned his concern with the need to be cautious when in the unfamiliar country where such events take place:

> I'm going all over for work with my paintings. To Queensland, Melbourne, Canberra, Sydney, Perth. [...] It's not so bad. As long as you look after yourself you will be alright... I look after myself when I go to a big city. I have been to cities many times... All around to big cities. To Perth... even Melbourne. We [artists] have to travel to far away places. I look around to see what is good there. [10]

Another equally well-traveled artist, the late Gija painter Queenie McKenzie, recounted being tired out by photographers repeatedly asking her to pose for photographs at an exhibition in Melbourne. Seemingly both amused and puzzled by the experience, she announced her intentions to record the incident in a painting:

> All the pictures that [the photographers] took. It exhausted me completely. [...] Someday I'll put it in a painting... I'll show what they did to me... I have to make a painting of that. [Of the photographers telling me] to sit in a chair, get up from the chair, walk that way and walk back. [...] I have to put all that in a painting. [11]

Unfortunately, McKenzie never carried out her plans to paint this encounter, a work or works that would have presented a uniquely Aboriginal vision, and wry criticism of the ways of the art world. For, as McKenzie's experience reveals, at exhibition openings it is often as much the artist as the art that is on display (a problem not unique to, although perhaps more acute for, Aboriginal painters).

What emerges from the comments of McKenzie and the other painters about their initial encounters with the art world are visions of galleries and the cities as generally welcoming but somewhat mysterious places where vast numbers of kartiya go about engaging in unfamiliar, often inexplicable activities. From the perspectives of painters in the East Kimberley, exhibitions and the cities are wholly a kartiya phenomena — amusing but of little lasting relevance to their lives or culture.

"The Kartiya Own Them Now": Paintings, Museums, and Display

While most East Kimberley artists characterize attending exhibitions as an amusing diversion, the collection and display of Aboriginal paintings by museums and collectors raises a more serious set of cultural issues. A number of artists who have had the opportunity to visit museums and private collections of their work voice concerns on a range of topics, some of which clash directly with the conventions and practices of the art world.

Painters frequently lament losing control of their works as they are purchased and displayed by unfamiliar buyers. The movement of paintings from the Aboriginal to the kartiya world is perceived as (and largely is) a process over which the painters have little or no control. Once painted, virtually all East Kimberley canvases eventually pass into kartiya hands. Though artists appreciate the income and recognition they receive for their work and are aware it must ultimately leave the community, at the same time they also express regret over the loss of control they experience after the paintings are sold. Asked how he felt about seeing his paintings on display at a gallery in Canberra, for example, Hector Jandulu replied:

> I don't know!... It's all up to the kartiya. The kartiya buy the paintings. And we have already been paid for them. The kartiya own them now. And they might sell them somewhere, maybe to a foreign country. On and on and all the way [to distant places] the paintings go... [12]

He later added:

> When we make a painting somebody buys it from us in this country and takes it to the city. Then maybe a kartiya comes from overseas and buys it again and takes it away. Say you bought a painting from me. You might take it overseas to America. Well, that's the kind of thing the kartiya do. You can't stop it... If I bought something from America... you couldn't stop me. I'd bring it right back here [to Warmun]. [13]

Other artists, however, express pleasure at seeing their paintings in museums, often many years after they originally created them. Queenie McKenzie, for example, proudly described viewing several of her early works in the storeroom at the National Gallery of Victoria in Melbourne. On a subsequent trip to Sydney, McKenzie recalled seeing her works in a museum but was more profoundly moved by another artist's work, which showed Aboriginal people in prison. This painting, for her, brought back sad memories of the imprisonment of Aboriginals by early kartiya settlers in the Kimberley:

> I went to Sydney and saw the museum. I went in and my paintings were there. That's what I went in for. [But] I saw a painting there of Aboriginals in prison too... In the old days they [kartiya] put all the Aboriginals in jail... It made me sad... to see that picture in the museum. [14]

Descriptions and critiques of the art world by East Kimberley painters generally have little bearing on mainstream art world discourses but rather reflect wholly Aboriginal priorities. Some painters, for example, express regret that representations of important dreamings now reside far from their home country. Asked how she felt about East Kimberley paintings leaving their home country and being spread all over the world, Gija painter Shirley Purdie responded:

> I think it's alright. But sometimes when Aboriginal people come down [to see the paintings in exhibitions] we feel sorry. We say "Oh, we painted that country and it will being going to another place now." [15]

An equally important issue for some East Kimberley painters concerns the appropriateness (or lack thereof) of displaying paintings by deceased individuals. Art world discourses typically emphasize a painter's legacy in which his or her works serve as a lasting monument to his or her artistic achievement and form a permanent part of museum displays and collections. However, such Western notions of artistic immortality stand in direct contradiction to the conventions of respect for the dead in many Aboriginal societies. Aboriginal law in the East Kimberley customarily calls for the destruction of all images of (and items belonging to) a deceased person and forbids the living to utter his or her name. However, the situation, at least in regards to photographs, paintings and other possessions, is gradually changing. In 1996, for example, Shirley Purdie, although explicitly noting that Aboriginal law requires that the belongings of the dead be destroyed, described telling her children that it was permissible to keep photographs of her, as well as her paintings, after her death:

> I tell all my kids now. If anything happens to me... they can keep my photographs. They can keep my paintings... [In the past] people used to burn them. You couldn't keep anything. But now it's different because kids are growing up more or less like kartiya now... and they like to keep things so they can remember me. [16]

During the same 1996 interview, however, Purdie expressed concerns about the (in)appropriateness of displaying paintings by deceased artists in museums and galleries. Asked her thoughts on seeing a group of paintings on exhibit at the National Gallery of Victoria in Melbourne, she specifically mentioned being "worried" about the inclusion of works by Warmun painter Paddy Jaminji, who at the time was only recently deceased (note that she does not mention him by name):

> That old man that we lost [i.e. Jaminji]... We saw one of his paintings there [in the museum]. We were a bit worried about that. But you can't help it. When you do a painting that painting will still be there [in the museum after you die]. You can't help it really. [17]

To judge from my 1996 interview with Purdie, the practice of displaying works by deceased artists in museums and art galleries was at best unsettling and, at worst, offensive to those Aboriginals who continue to practice the customary proscriptions associated with the dead.

Over the ensuing four years, however, Purdie's opinion on the issue underwent a noticeable change. When I interviewed her about the same topic in 2000, she began by expressing the notion that having paintings by deceased artists in museums was appropriate since it preserves the memory of the dead for their descendants. Significantly, however, she prefaced the statement by noting that this was her own opinion:

> Well, it's my idea, but I think it's alright [to display paintings by deceased artists in museums]. As long as they are there when people want to see them... Like with the old people now. When they are gone... if their paintings are still there we can still see them. The ones they keep in the museum. It's the same with us living artists. If we die, well, maybe our children or... some other family members will want to see our paintings. They can now. As long as the paintings are there [in the museum] all the time. [18]

More interestingly, she subsequently went on to give a significantly different account of the customary Aboriginal prohibitions regarding the works of the dead than she had in 1996 — one that can accommodate both art world conventions and Aboriginal law. According to her 2000 description of Aboriginal law, works by deceased individuals, rather than being permanently withdrawn (and, ideally, destroyed) can be displayed following an appropriate period of mourning, as seen in this excerpt from the 2000 interview:

> Some families don't worry [about having paintings by deceased family members on view in museums]. As long as they think they evoke good memories about the person. [...] In the past it was different. They always put the deceased person's possessions away... until maybe two years had passed and them put them out again... They say that when the rainy season [19] comes it washes away all the restrictions associated with the people who have passed on. The next year it will be alright. That's what the old people used to say. After the rainy season it will be alright... They believed that the rain would wash away everything. Like it washes away a [human or animal] track... [20]

The significant differences not only in Purdie's personal perspective on the subject but also in her account of relevant Aboriginal law again highlight the ongoing development of the relationship between East Kimberley painters and the art world. Although its fundamental principles are stated by Aboriginals in the East Kimberley to be permanent and unchanging, Aboriginal law exhibits considerable flexibility, allowing it to accommodate, on Aboriginal cultural terms, the growing interaction between local Aboriginal peoples and the wider art world.

Though East Kimberley painters have both an understanding of and definite opinions on how their works are kept and displayed by museums and collectors, the question of *why* the kartiya are interested in Aboriginal paintings at all remains largely a mystery to their creators. That kartiya, who are known to have no dreaming of their own, should be willing to pay hundreds or thousands of dollars for images (or knowledge) of dreamings and country that they do not own and, in the vast majority of instances, have never seen often seems inexplicable to Aboriginal painters in the East Kimberley. While painters are willing to fulfill the growing kartiya desire for Aboriginal paintings, the origins of that desire, like many other aspects of kartiya culture and behavior, remain obscure.

When asked why they think kartiya want Aboriginal paintings or what they do with the paintings after they purchase them, East Kimberley painters almost invariably responded "I don't know" and offered little further explanation. Hector Jandulu, however, suggested that the motivation might be at least partially economic, describing art transactions as a straightforward exchange in which Aboriginals obtain what they want (money) while kartiya obtain what they want (paintings), stating "Kartiya love paintings from Aboriginal people. And I love the paper money from the kartiya." [21] Jandulu, however, ultimately ascribed an emotional basis to kartiya desire. Asked why kartiya wanted Aboriginal paintings in another interview he replied: "I don't know. Maybe kartiya simply take a fancy to Aboriginal paintings." [22]

Despite his unfamiliarity with art historical and other critical discourses, Jandulu's insight into the source of kartiya desire coincides closely with that of those art historians who cite emotional and aesthetic motivations for the collection and appreciation of art.

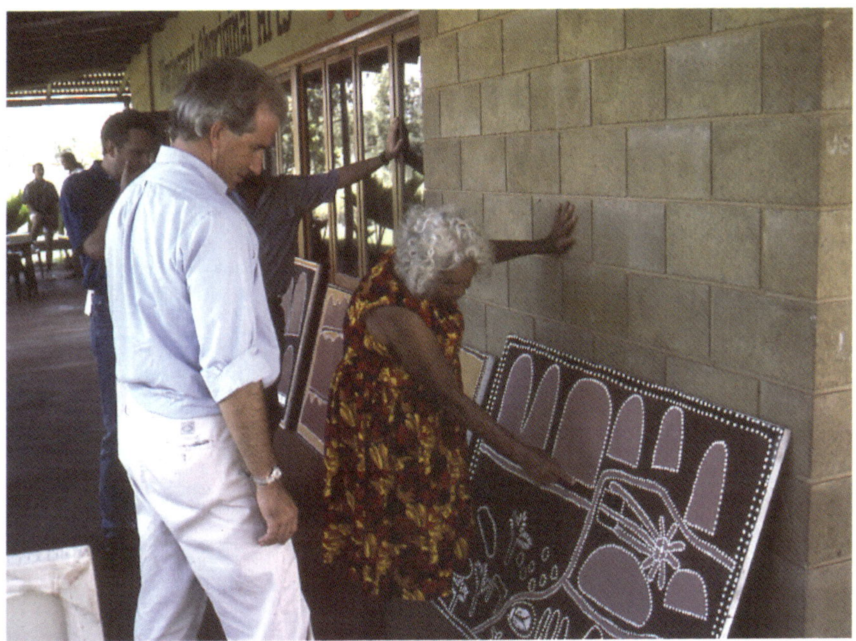

Figure. 2.2. Queenie McKenzie describing areas of Gija country portrayed in her paintings to a judge reviewing a mining rights case involving traditional Gija lands at Waringarri Arts in Kununurra, 1996.

Perhaps expressing some insight into the name-driven nature of the art market, the most renowned Warmun painter, Rover Thomas, ascribed the kartiya desire for his paintings to his own persona. Asked why kartiya wanted to buy his paintings he replied, "I don't know. They really like *me*" (emphasis original). [23]

On the issue of what kartiya do with Aboriginal paintings after they have purchased them, some East Kimberley painters offered more concrete theories. Asked what kartiya do with Aboriginal paintings the Gija painter Lorna Thomas replied:

> I don't know what kartiya do with the paintings afterwards. We just sell them here for a little bit of money and I don't know what they do with the paintings. They keep them in the gallery and maybe another kartiya comes and buys it from there. [24]

Others, more familiar with kartiya displays of Aboriginal art from their experiences at exhibitions, described the context of Aboriginal paintings in kartiya society. Shirley Purdie noted:

> I don't know what kartiya do with the paintings after they buy them here. Maybe they hang them up on the wall but I really don't know what they do. [25]

Miriwoong painter Juju Wilson observed that, after they have bought Aboriginal paintings, "Kartiya just hang them on the walls in their houses." [26] While these two artists and other East Kimberley painters are aware of what kartiya ultimately do with their works, the motivations behind this aspect of kartiya culture remain obscure.

Although the origins of the kartiya desire for Aboriginal paintings, like many other art world phenomena and practices, remain enigmatic to painters in the East Kimberley, the painters are quick to observe, and make positive use of, those aspects of the art world which help to further their own cultural and political priorities. This is particularly true in the case of the emerging relationship between Aboriginal paintings and land rights.

The current prominence in Australian politics of the issues of Aboriginal sovereignty and land tenure, especially since the landmark Mabo decision in 1993, which gave legal recognition to the existence of indigenous systems of land ownership prior to European colonization, has resulted in Aboriginal art and artists becoming increasingly active agents in the politics of Aboriginal land rights. In recent decades works by Western Desert and Arnhem Land painters have been perceived and represented by activists, art writers, and, increasingly, by the painters themselves, as assertions of ownership of, or even indigenous deeds to, the lands they portray. Bark paintings or canvases depicting an individual's or group's country have been used as evidence in support of Aboriginal land claims in government hearings and court cases (Jones 1988:

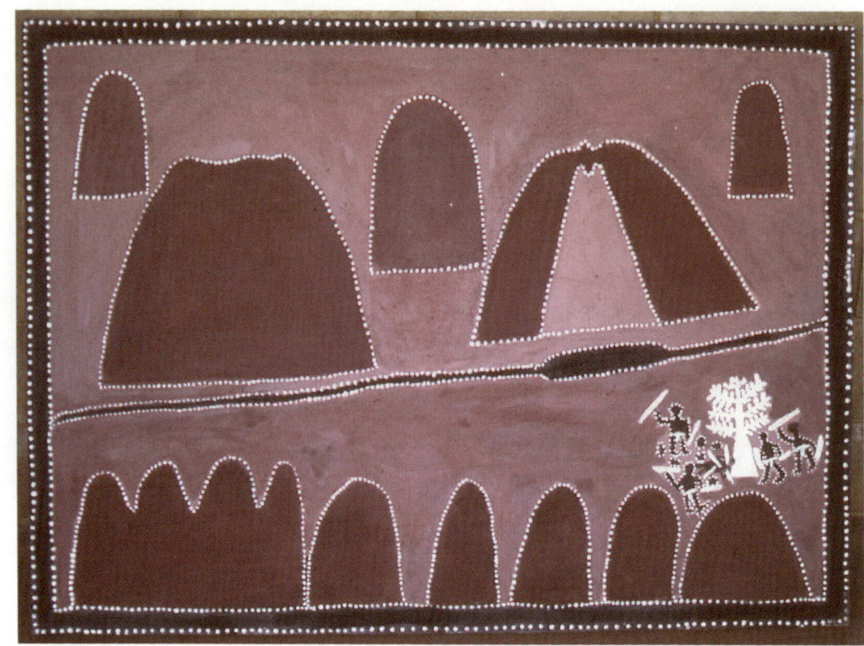

Figure. 2.3. Queenie McKenzie, *Stockman Spearing Story — Wirdim Country*, 1996, ochre on canvas. © The Estate of Queenie McKenzie.

177-8, Anderson and Dussart 1988: 139, Megaw and Megaw 1993: 165). As representations of Aboriginal country, paintings have become a significant voice in the debate over Aboriginal land rights.

Concerned primarily with local rather than national land politics, East Kimberley painters, nonetheless, take an active interest in the potential role that their works can play in achieving legal recognition of their land rights. In East Kimberley communities, the act of painting country is always, at least implicitly, an assertion of ownership. Producing visual representations of country is one of many ways in which individuals proclaim their rights to it — the income received from the sale of paintings being one of the benefits of such ownership. Creating a painting is simultaneously a religious and a political act — a celebration of country and dreamings and an assertion of control over them.

Such assertions are still generally made, understood, and contested within the context of local Aboriginal communities. But many East Kimberley painters have become increasingly aware of the broader political relationships between Aboriginal art and land rights and the fact that paintings have been used by other Aboriginal groups to support their land claims. As a result, painters in the East Kimberley are alert to the potential (in some instances, actual) role that their works can play in bolstering their claims to ownership of traditional lands, many of which remain alienated through pastoral leases and continue to be inaccessible to them.

One of the most politically savvy painters in relation to this issue was Queenie McKenzie. In 1996, when she learned that a judge involved in deciding whether she and other Gija elders had the right to be consulted as traditional land owners in a mining rights case, she asked the local art cooperative to bring out a series of canvases she had recently completed. With the canvases set up along the veranda of the cooperative, she led the judge to each in turn, explaining the sites and dreamings it depicted and their significance to herself and her people [fig. 2.2]. She later went on to relate the landforms in her paintings to features on the Western maps of the same country the judge had with him. In this and other ways, Aboriginal painters in the East Kimberley have begun to use their growing prominence within the art world as an important means to bolster their claims on traditional lands.

Revealing the Killing Times: Art, Dance, and Massacres

The early colonial period in the East Kimberley region was frequently marked by violent encounters between kartiya settlers and local Aboriginal peoples. Using incidences of cattle spearing or similar pretexts, kartiya stockmen (ranchers) often massacred entire encampments of Aboriginal people in reprisal. The people were shot, the bodies burned, and the matter hushed up and forgotten. But not by everyone. Long omitted from mainstream histories, the stories of these massacres survive in Aboriginal oral tradition. Aboriginals, however, were not simply passive victims of the colonial encounter. Some, often described as "outlaws" or "bush rangers" by kartiya historians, actively took up arms against the invading settlers (Shaw 1983). Others sought revenge through isolated killings of lone travelers. Lasting from the 1880s until the early decades of the twentieth century, this era of massacre and resistance is often referred to among the local Aboriginal population as the "killing times." Largely unwritten, the stories of the killing times constitute part of what anthropologist Deborah Bird Rose calls the "hidden history" of Aboriginal Australia (Rose 1991) — a history that is today being revealed to kartiya audiences through contemporary East Kimberley painting and dance.

The earliest painters to create works that focus on the killing times were Rover Thomas and Queenie McKenzie. Each approached the subject from a unique personal history and formal artistic perspective. Like his other works, Thomas' massacre paintings were stark portrayals of landscape, relying on narrative to reveal their underlying histories. During his career Thomas created images of a number of different massacres including killings at Ruby Plains, Beford Downs and at Lajibany (known to kartiya as Horseshoe Creek). Thomas, however, typically chose to depict only the physical features (hills, creeks, roads) of the sites at which the massacres occurred (see Thomas et al. 1994: 40-56, 60-61). [27] Queenie McKenzie, however, frequently represented the actual events through the use of enigmatic human figures who go about their sinister business amidst the sacred country and dreaming sites of the East Kimberley. McKenzie's paintings of the killing times are unique in their multifaceted vision of the colonial encounter, depicting both the victimization and resistance of Aboriginal people. Although her massacre scenes show the wholesale slaughter of Aboriginal people, works such as *Stockman Spearing Story — Wirdim Country* [fig. 2.3] also show instances where Aboriginals took up arms against the invading kartiya.

While Thomas created images of a number of different massacres, McKenzie focused almost exclusively on a single massacre event — the killings at Lajibany. The events at Lajibany began when a group of Aboriginals killed a bullock for food. The dead bullock was discovered by a group of kartiya stockmen from Texas Downs station, who attempted to shoot the entire encampment of Aboriginals in reprisal. The killings were witnessed by a man who crawled under the bullock carcass to avoid discovery and later followed the stockmen as they led the Aboriginals to the site where the killings took place.

Near the end of the massacre, the stockmen ran out of ammunition. At this point one of the Aboriginal

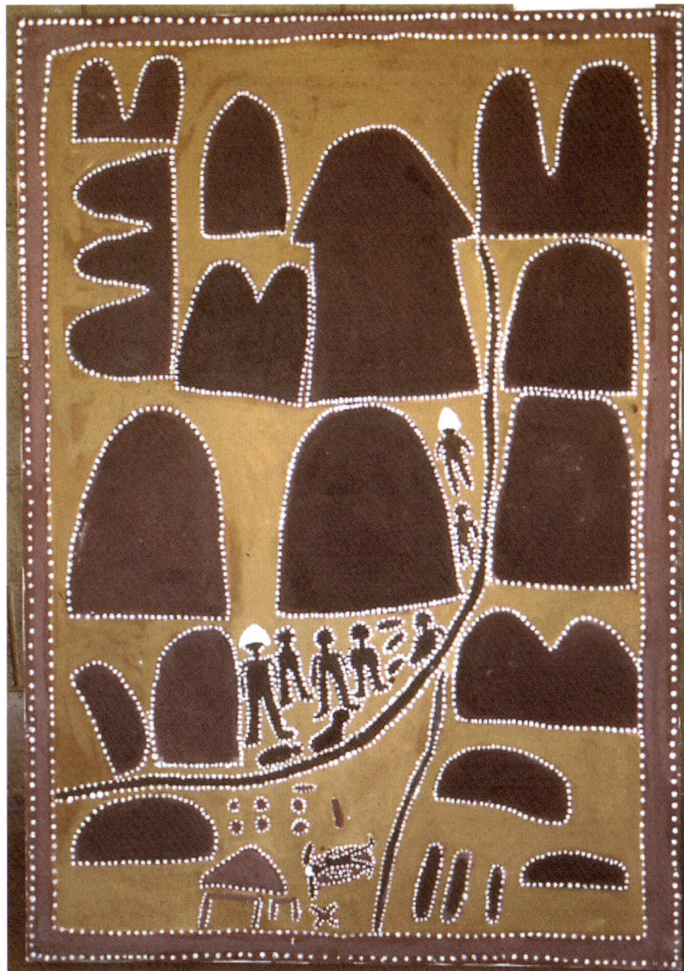

Figure. 2.4. Queenie McKenzie, *Massacre and Rover Thomas Story — Texas Downs Country*, 1996, ochre on canvas. © The Estate of Queenie McKenzie.

women offered them a bullet that she had been saving in her bag — and was shot with it. After shooting all the Aboriginals they could find, the stockmen burned the bodies and rode off. The man who had been hiding searched the area for survivors and found a baby, which had been hidden by its mother who had also managed to survive.

McKenzie painted a version of the Lajibany massacre in late 1995 entitled *Massacre and Rover Thomas Story — Texas Downs Country* [fig. 2.4]. Compressing time as well as space, the work actually shows two historic incidents that took place in McKenzie's country. As in Thomas' work, the hills and rivers of the country dominate the composition. However, unlike Thomas, McKenzie places human figures within the landscape, forming a series of tableaux that show the complex history of her country. At the upper center is the Lajibany massacre. Here the stockmen, ironically wearing white hats, descend upon the hatless Aboriginals in their camp just prior to the slaughter.

The scene at the lower left illustrates an incident from McKenzie's own life in which, as a young woman, she saved Rover Thomas' life by sewing a portion of his scalp back on after he had been kicked in the head by a horse (Kjellgren 2001: 14-15).

In relating the stories of the killing times Thomas and McKenzie followed separate visions, approaching the material from distinct formal and individual perspectives. While McKenzie chose to show massacre events explicitly, through depiction of the actual incidents, Thomas depicted the country in which the events occurred, relating the massacre events orally. What united these two pioneering painters was the need to tell the tale, to record and relate the stories of the killing times for a new generation of Aboriginals and kartiya.

The need to record and recount the events of the killing times has since been taken up by a new group of artists and performers who, together, brought the stories to an even wider audience. The late 1990s witnessed the revival of a traditional East Kimberley Joonba corroboree (song and dance performance), which recounted the events of the Bedford Downs massacre, on Bedford Downs Station west of the present day Aboriginal community at Warmun. Here the station manager and other kartiya stockmen had their Aboriginal workers gather a large amount of wood before feeding them a meal laced with strychnine. As the Aboriginals lay struggling from the effects of the poison, they were shot and then burned with the wood they had gathered. One man, who, suspecting something was wrong, had not eaten the poisoned food and managed to get to his feet and escape by taking refuge on a high hill where the stockmen could not get to him. This sole survivor later recounted the story of the massacre, which survives in Gija oral tradition (Thomas et al.1994:51-3, Ian Potter Museum of Art, 2002: 18-21).

In 2000 the late painter Timmy Timms, together with Peggy Patrick and other Gija elders made the decision to stage the corroboree recounting the events of the massacre for kartiya audiences using performers from the newly formed Neminuwarlin Performance Group, an ensemble of Gija dancers, singers, and musicians, which Patrick had founded several years earlier (Kofod 2002: 18). At first Patrick and others, fearful of what the response might be, were apprehensive about performing the corroboree in front of kartiya. In former times the corroboree, while free for any Aboriginal to witness, had been kept hidden from local kartiya in fear that they might take revenge as Patrick explained (in Oliver 2002: 10):

> It [the corroboree] was a very important thing which was kept hidden from white people. People who were still working on the stations were scared they might all be shot themselves if white people saw the Joonba or realised what it was about. The white people who killed Aboriginal people throughout the country never told anyone outside what they had done.

Finally, however, the artists and performers of Warmun decided that the story must be told, as both a record of the past and as a way of reaching out and continuing the process of reconciliation with the kartiya community. As Patrick put it "We want you [kartiya] to know what white people did to black people in the past... We hope there can be real peace and friendship between black and white." (Oliver 2002: 10) Neminuwarlin presented a fully staged production of the Bedford Downs Massacre corroboree, entitled *Fire, Fire Burning Bright (Marnem, Marnem Dililib Benuwarrenji)*, a reference to the burning of the Aboriginal victims after the massacre, at the Perth International Festival of the Arts. The following year, the performers brought the production to Melbourne where it was performed as part of the Melbourne Festival (Oliver 2002: 11). The corroboree, featuring an all East Kimberley Aboriginal cast, including several individuals made up in white face portraying the murderous kartiya stockmen, received an enthusiastic reception at both venues.

Inspired, in part, by the success of *Fire, Fire Burning Bright* a group of Gija painters, coordinated by Jirrawun Aboriginal Arts, a local art cooperative, decided to put together a group show of paintings depicting the killing times. This exhibition, entitled *Blood on the Spinifex* was presented at the Ian Potter Museum of Art at the University of Melbourne in 2003 (Ian Potter Museum of Art, 2002). Featuring works by ten different painters portraying a number of different massacres, the exhibition enjoyed considerable critical success. In a period of less than a decade, from the first massacre paintings by Thomas and McKenzie, through Fire, *Fire Burning Bright* and *Blood on the Spinifex*, the once secret histories of the killing times in the East Kimberley have now become widely known, using painting and performance as twin voices which, together, have helped to rewrite and correct the mainstream kartiya histories of the region.

Conclusion

In light of the comments of painters on their increasingly complex encounters with the kartiya art world it is evident that East Kimberley Aboriginals attempt to understand and explain the art world exactly as the art world seeks to understand and explain them — in terms of the conventions and idioms of their own culture. Just as kartiya observers attempt to comprehend and adapt Aboriginal art and culture to the dominant conventions and agendas of the contemporary art world, Aboriginal artists, in turn, perceive and challenge art world practices in terms of their own cultural values. This ongoing process of mutual (in)comprehension can result in (often unintentional) conflicts between Aboriginal and kartiya cultural values. To an art world audience, for example, displays of works by dead painters serve as a lasting memorial to their artistic achievement while, to some Aboriginals, the same displays are disrespectful. To kartiya, the image in a painting is the source of all (or most) of its aesthetic value, a reason in itself to collect the unfamiliar images produced by Aboriginal painters as art. To Aboriginals the content of the painting is paramount and the desire of kartiya to purchase paintings whose content is irrelevant to their lives seems inexplicable.

Although Aboriginal paintings and their creators can be physically transported to the art world with relative ease, both remain deeply embedded within Aboriginal culture. An Aboriginal painter may have become an artist in the kartiya world, and his or her paintings art, but to Aboriginals artist remains a job and paintings simply one expression of the country and its dreamings.

As expressions of country, Aboriginal paintings themselves have become active agents in the ongoing politics of Aboriginal land tenure. Originally created simply as images of country, the paintings now have increasingly become a means of asserting claim to it as well, entering into the complex political arena of land rights in Australia. Responding to their favorable reception by the art world, East Kimberley artists have also begun, in recent years, to use both the visual and performing arts as dynamic ways of retelling the long hidden histories of the killing times in East Kimberley country. Overall, although East Kimberley artists were initially somewhat wary of and unfamiliar with the art world, through their continuing engagement with it they have now become active agents in shaping how the art world perceives both themselves and their work. Rather than being an alien institution into which Aboriginal paintings are passively absorbed, the art world has become an active arena for the exposure (and debate) of issues that are of vital importance to Aboriginal people in the East Kimberley. Through their art, East Kimberley painters express those things that are central to their identity, their country, and their dreaming. And their art, in turn, proclaims them in the unknown countries of the wider world.

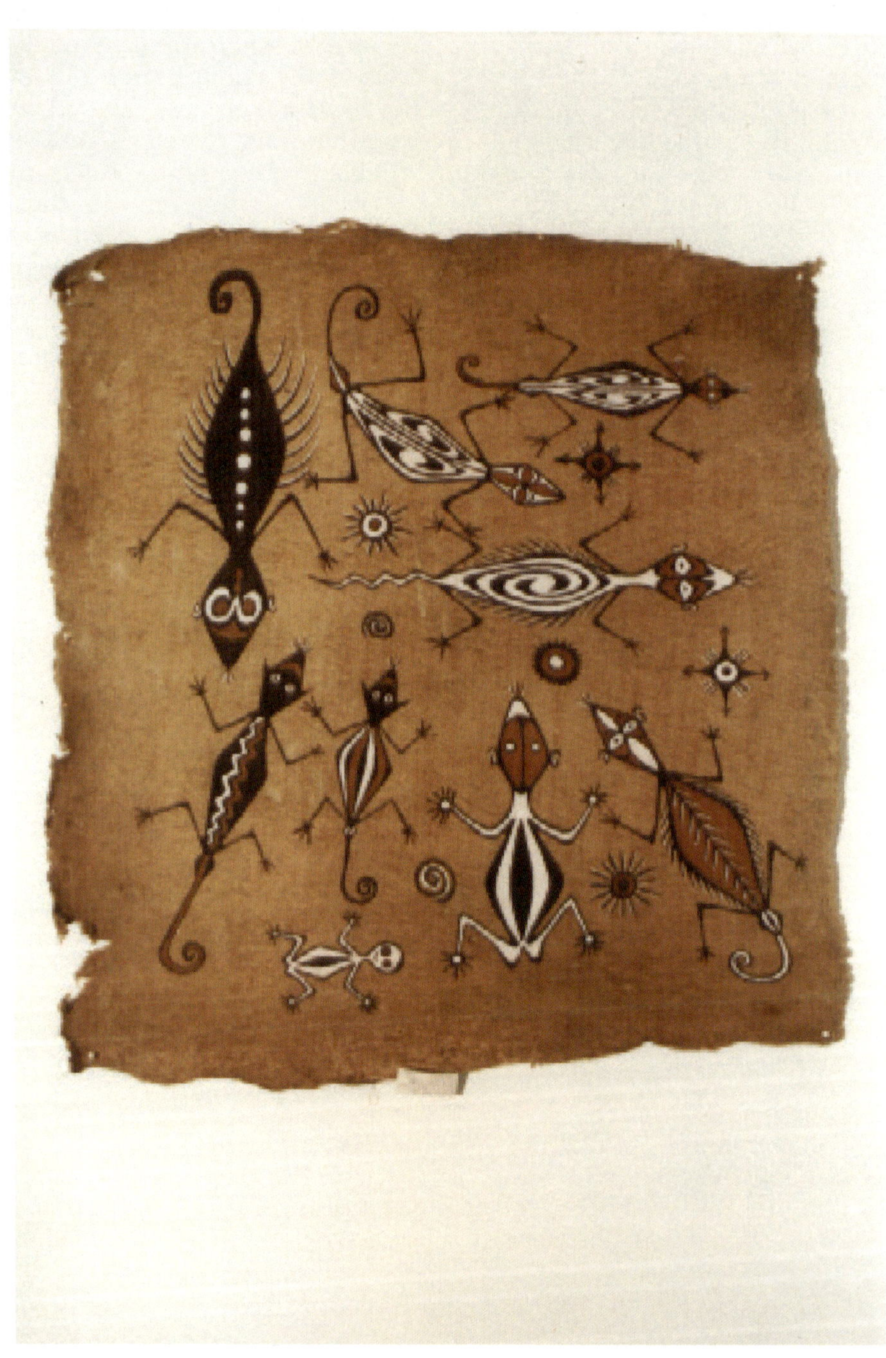

Figure. 3.1. Painted barkcloth from Lake Sentani, made by Agus Ongge in 1996. Photograph by Anna-Karina Hermkens.

Gendered (Hi-)stories of Cloth: Female Artists and Dynamics in the Art of Barkcloth Painting

Anna-Karina Hermkens

This chapter focuses on women and their artwork. The work of women artists may be constrained by various forces, limiting their mobility and also their ability to give voice to their work. In Melanesian societies that have traditionally been dominated by male decision-making and male representations, women have often been prohibited from speaking on behalf of themselves, their families, and the larger community or representing these concerns in art. As I will show, these restraints affect their ability to participate in national and international art settings. In addition, women's art was less accessible to early collectors (Hermkens 2007a: 9-12,18), and was often classified as non-art by collectors, anthropologists and the global art market. As a result, women's work has become to a large extent invisible.

Scholars interested in Melanesian material culture have tended to focus on the more visual and dominant male 'arts,' such as sculptures, and artifacts used in male dominated rituals and performances, such as ornaments and masks (for example, Malinowski 1922, Smidt 1995, Fajans 1997, Küchler 2002, Campbell 2002). Many of these objects were easily incorporated in the Western "primitive art" market and subsequently modern art galleries, as also seen in the contributions of Ake Lianga (this volume), Elaine Monds (this volume), and Eric Venbrux (2006).

In contrast, the role of women's objects in New Guinean and Melanesian societies has received little scholarly attention. In fact, Annette Weiner's analysis of Trobriand Island women's skirts and banana leaf bundles (1980, 1989), Maureen MacKenzie's analysis of Telefol string bags (1991), and Lissant Bolton's study of plaited mats made by Vanuatu women (1993, 1996, 2001, 2003) are the most significant studies that have been conducted so far. It seems that women's creations, such as cloth and mats, have typically been classified as crafts and, consequently, have received little scholarly attention. Moreover, they were of little interest to early collectors and, subsequently, the tribal art market (Thomas 1995:132). According to Thomas (ibid), the exception is barkcloth, which has long aroused the interest of Europeans. [1]

Here, I address the effects of the commercialization of painted barkcloth, or tapa as it is often called in the Pacific. The analysis compares two areas in New Guinea — Lake Sentani in Papua, Indonesia, and Collingwood Bay in the Oro Province of Papua New Guinea. [2] In both areas, women were traditionally the main producers of barkcloth [figs. 3.1 and 3.2], which was predominantly made into loincloths. In both areas, barkcloth is no longer used as a dress in daily life, and seems to be reduced to the status of production for tourists.

But barkcloth has not lost all its significance and has even gained new meanings. Depending on its context and the designs applied, these decorated loincloths are categorized locally either as inalienable clan properties or as alienable artifacts and commodities that can be sold to tourists. Simultaneously, alienable, commercial cloths are also markers of traditional, ethnic identity, and presented to foreigners as Papuan and Papua New Guinean art respectively. Locally, both men and women regard the production of barkcloth by women as part of women's responsibilities and work. Yet it is men who have responded to the emergence of art markets by making their own decorated barkcloth. And these men tend to define themselves — not women — as artists.

By comparing the production of barkcloth in these two regions, we can see both similar and divergent trajectories of the gendered production and commercialization of barkcloth. This comparison shows the tensions between traditional and commercial values of painted barkcloth. It also illustrates the implications for gender relations, particularly the agency and position of women, who used to be responsible for manufacturing these cloths. This comparison also elucidates the ways both dominant art markets as well as gender relations mute women's voices and, to a certain extent, even alienate their products.

Designing Barkcloth in Lake Sentani and Humboldt Bay

In the Indonesian provinces of West Papua and Papua (former Irian Jaya), the best-known area for barkcloth is the North Coast, especially the Lake Sentani and

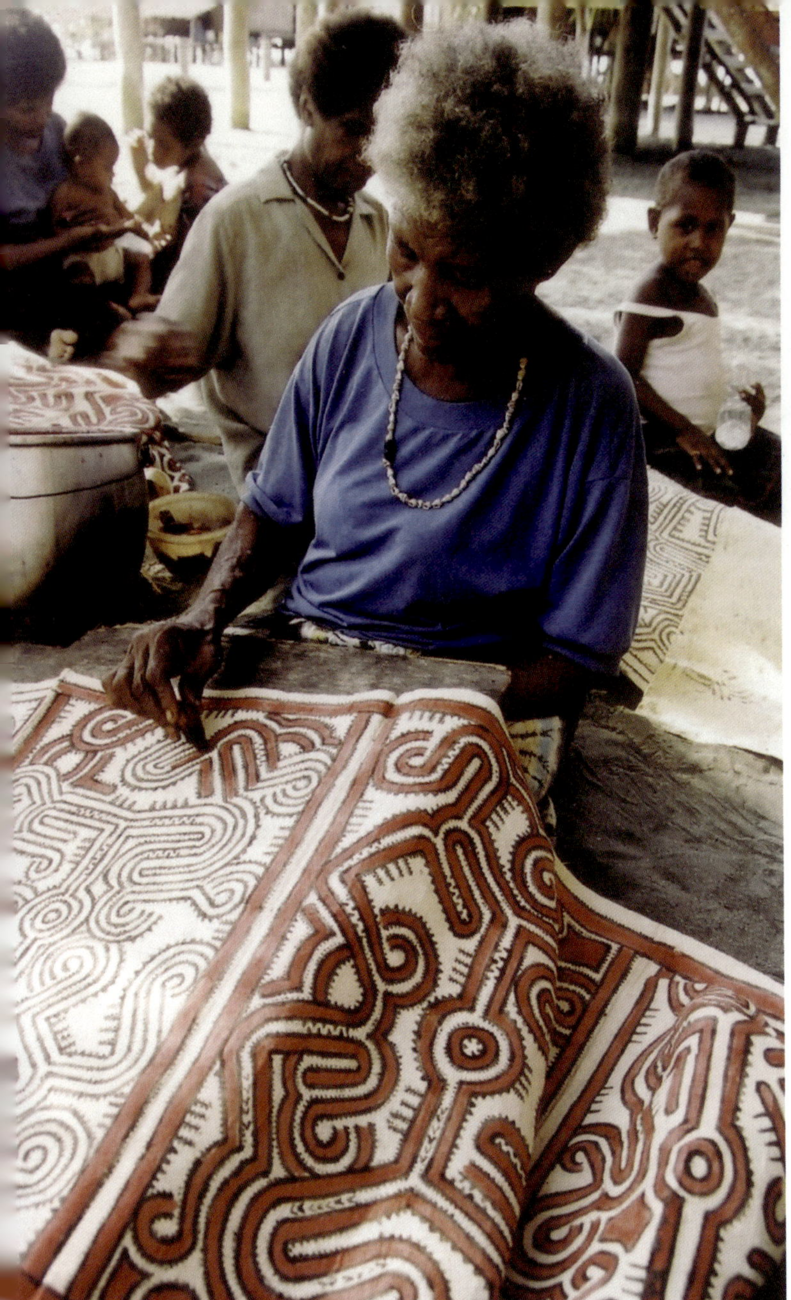

Figure 3.2. Women painting barkcloth, Airara Village, Collingwood Bay, 2001. Photograph by Anna-Karina Hermkens.

Humboldt Bay (now known as Teluk Yos Sudarso), located in the northeastern corner of Papua province. The pieces of barkcloth that caught the eyes of "primitive art" collectors were designed with black geometrical and figurative images, colored with red, white and occasionally other colors such as yellow and blue. Plain cloths were obviously less attractive for the early collectors and subsequent tribal art market, which, as argued by Thomas (1995: 132), "by no means indicated a lower status in indigenous terms." Among the Sentani and Humboldt Bay people, both plain and decorated barkcloth was strongly intertwined with women's life-cycle stages, their bodies and their status.

Until the beginning of the twentieth century, maro — as the barkcloth loincloth is called locally — was worn only by initiated and married women. In Humboldt Bay, girls had to wear a maro as soon as they were initiated (Galis 1955: 25). Their initiation into adulthood commenced upon instigation of the Ondofolo (the village chief) and usually took place when the girls were about 12 years of age. The loincloth they received consisted of a plain rectangular piece of barkcloth that was wound around the waist with a rope, covering the body from the hips to the thighs (Van der Goes 1862: 172, De Clercq 1893: 1010). Several scholars have reported that sometimes a decorated piece of barkcloth was worn over undecorated pieces (De Clercq and Schmeltz 1893: 47, Galis 1955: 92-93). The decorations consisted of shells (De Clercq 1893: 1010, Lorentz 1905: 2, Galis 1955: 93), or regularly drawn black figures (Van der Goes 1862: 172). At Lake Sentani, girls received their first loincloth, a long maro that hanged down below their knees, when they got married (Van der Goes 1862: 172, Bink 1896: 50, Van der Sande 1907: 38, 234). The maro was put on after the girl's parents had verified the bride price, and before the bride was handed over to the bridegroom (Van der Sande 1907: 38). Smaller pieces of painted barkcloth, which covered the thighs only, were worn during festivities (Bijkerk 1924: 42), while large decorated maro were put on women's graves (Wirz 1928: 297).

It is not clear whether all initiated or married women could wear decorated pieces of maro, or that these were restricted to women from a particular lineage. Each clan had its own designs and particular designs were reserved for Ondofolo lineages, which were only to be made by artisans from that particular lineage. So it could be that wearing a decorated piece of maro signalled a woman's status as being the chief's wife (Roper 1995: 96) and her identity as belonging to a particular lineage or clan.

Early reports describing maro attribute the manufacturing (Bijkerk 1924: 42, Wirz 1928: 291) and designing of barkcloth to women. Jacques Viot, a French collector of 'primitive art', stated in the 1920s that only a few old Humboldt Bay women still made and designed the painted barkcloth, which were being used by initiated girls (Peltier 1992: 170). Viot collected a maro from an old woman who had applied the traditional spiral design. Others, like government officer Halie and the collectors De Rautenfeld and Groenevelt, also noted that they obtained cloths from women, which suggests that women had been responsible for their manufacture. More recent scholars, such as Howard (1996, 1998) and Hoogerbrugge (1995) have attributed the painting of maro to men. These reports are informed by more recent gendered productions, as today it is mostly men

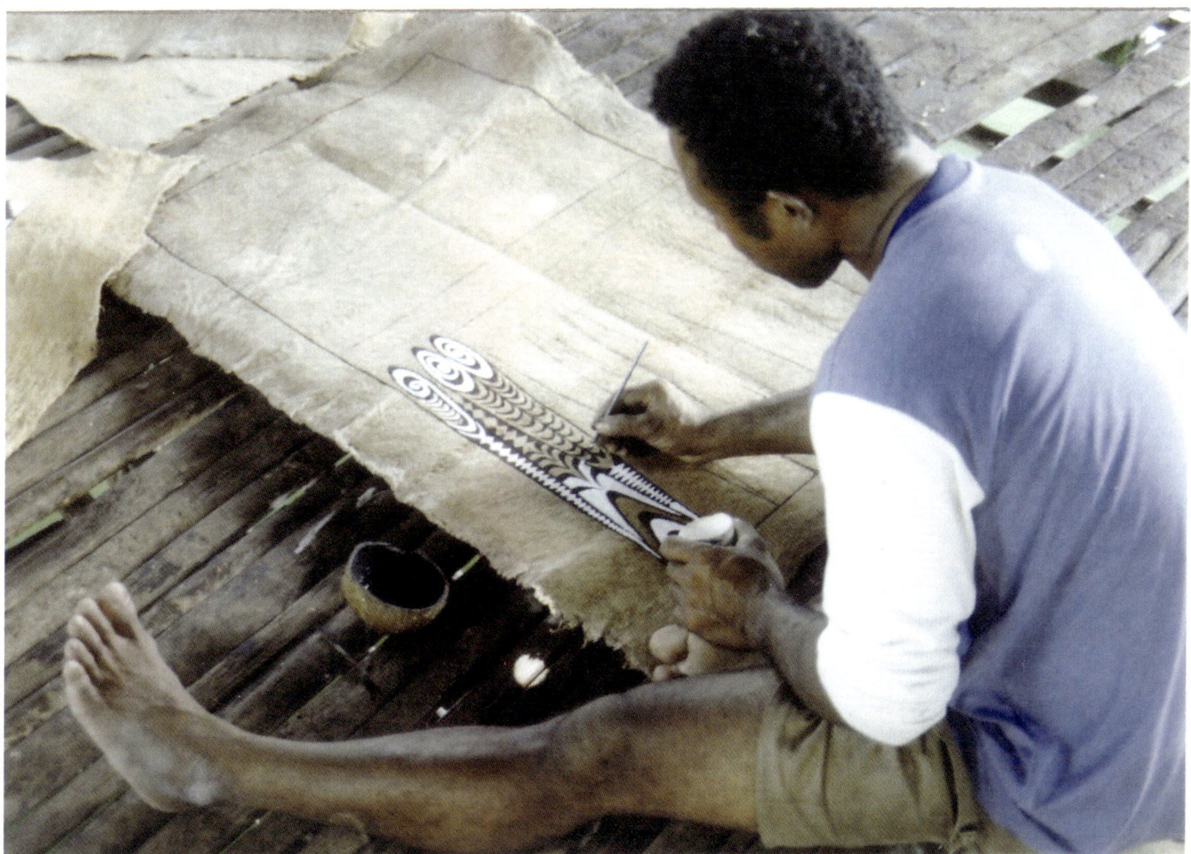

Figure. 3.3. Agus Ongge from the village Asei (Lake Sentani) drawing a barkcloth design. Photograph by Anna-Karina Hermkens, Asei 1996.

who are engaged in the artistic production of barkcloth (Roper 1995; Hermkens and Widjojo 2011), while women largely produce items that are not classified by outside markets and galleries as "art" but as "petty commodities."

In 1996, while doing fieldwork in the Lake Sentani village Asei Besar, a little island and village situated in the eastern end of this Lake, I encountered Agus Ongge [fig. 3.3]. This male artist claimed to be the best barkcloth designer and painter in the Lake Sentani area. He commenced painting in the early 1980s, asking his parents about the meaning and depictions of particular designs. Inspired by photographs of old maro in catalogues and art books, which he often copies, Ongge creates new pieces of barkcloth/art. To Ongge, these designs no longer refer to women's lifecycle stages, their bodies and status, but represent symbols of knowledge and identity, which he tries to control and commodify.

According to Ongge's statements, women cannot draw designs on barkcloth because this task is the prerogative of men, who possess the necessary skills and creativity to do so. However, when discussing the past with a group of women and Ongge, the women enthusiastically confirmed that in the past making barkcloth was women's work. This response brought an uneasy tension to the setting because of the awkward situation in which Ongge was placed. How could he as a man be engaged in a female activity? Trying to legitimize his involvement with barkcloth he fiercely uttered, "women can and may beat the cloth, but they are not capable of drawing it!" [3], whereupon the women sitting with us fell silent.

In practice, women do make drawings on barkcloth. Women as well as children often make smaller pieces of decorated barkcloth using stencil techniques. They may also help fill in the barkcloth design drawn by their husbands, fathers, or other relatives, like Agus's wife Maria and his daughter [fig. 3.4]. Some women also draw freehand style designs. During my stay on Asei Island in 1996, I obtained a piece of barkcloth from Maria Pepuho, an Asei woman who had applied and painted her own design. The male artists, however, did not acknowledge Pepuho's or any other women's works on cloth. When one takes into account the fact that in former times barkcloth was exclusively made by women and also decorated by them, this becomes all the more significant.

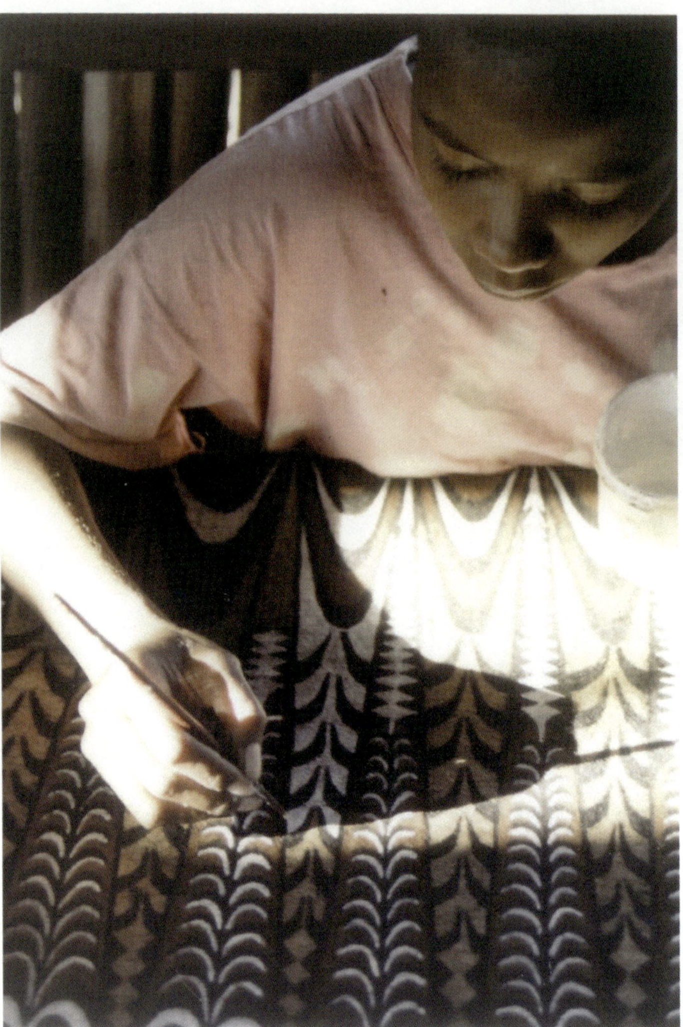

Figure. 3.4. Rodi Ongge (here 12 years), helping her father Agus applying white pigment made from a mixture of burned shells and water. Photograph by Anna-Karina Hermkens, Asei 1996.

On Asei, the sound of outboard-engines alerts the arrival of tourists. Upon hearing these sounds women and children stop their other work and run into their homes to fetch decorated pieces of barkcloth and other artifacts. These are carefully displayed on the gravel beach so the tourists may see their work and make their choices [fig. 3.5]. Just as women mainly do the selling of these objects, the production of this 'tourist-art' is equally in the hands of women, even young girls. The relatively small pieces of barkcloth are predominantly created using stencils that facilitate an easy and quick production. The few men engaged in designing barkcloth use larger pieces of barkcloth, sometimes applying free-hand designs.

In contrast to women's production, these larger pieces of barkcloth are generally not sold to tourists visiting Asei, but are brought to more profitable markets. For example, like other people living on Asei, Agus Ongge initially produced pieces of barkcloth for tourists visiting the island. He also sold them to Church organizations. As he gradually became more renowned for his skills, he produced fewer for these local markets and started to focus on other more lucrative buyers. Like other male craftsmen in the area, Ongge was able to specialize in art, which enabled him to travel abroad and identity himself as an artist. In contrast, Ongge's female relatives, who help him produce these objects, as well as other Asei women engaged in making barkcloth, in general do not have the time to specialize themselves, as their main responsibility lies in the care of their families.

However, during the last thirteen years, inspiration drawn from barkcloth painters such as Ongge and the need to get access to cash eventually also encouraged women to specialize themselves in the art of barkcloth painting. In 2009, Martha Ohee, a 39-year-old, strong and joyful Asei woman who is married to a local official with whom she has a 9-year-old child, has managed to become a renowned Sentani artist [fig. 3.6]. Inspired and partly trained by Ongge while in secondary school, she has developed a line of completely new barkcloth products, such as hats, purses, and bags, which she sells at local fairs and markets with great success. As expressed by Martha [4]:

> Up until recently, there were no women who made these paintings. In our customary law, there is no prohibition for women to do this work. However barkcloth painting has been basically a male job, with hardly any women doing this kind of work. So female artists are a new phenomenon here and when people found out about my paintings, they were pretty startled. In fact, I was the first woman to make these paintings, and now other female artists start to emerge as well.

However, most women find it difficult to follow Martha's example. Martha [5]:

> I have taught some local women here to make barkcloth handbags, which was a great success. The handbags were sold quickly. But unfortunately, these women did not continue their work, as they felt it was too difficult.

According to Martha, in 2009 only two other local women were making barkcloth paintings, following the more traditional style of Ongge and other male artists. Like her male colleagues, Martha thereby overlooks the fact that most of the male barkcloth painters depend on help of their female relatives. As in 1996, when I first encountered Sentani barkcloth painters,

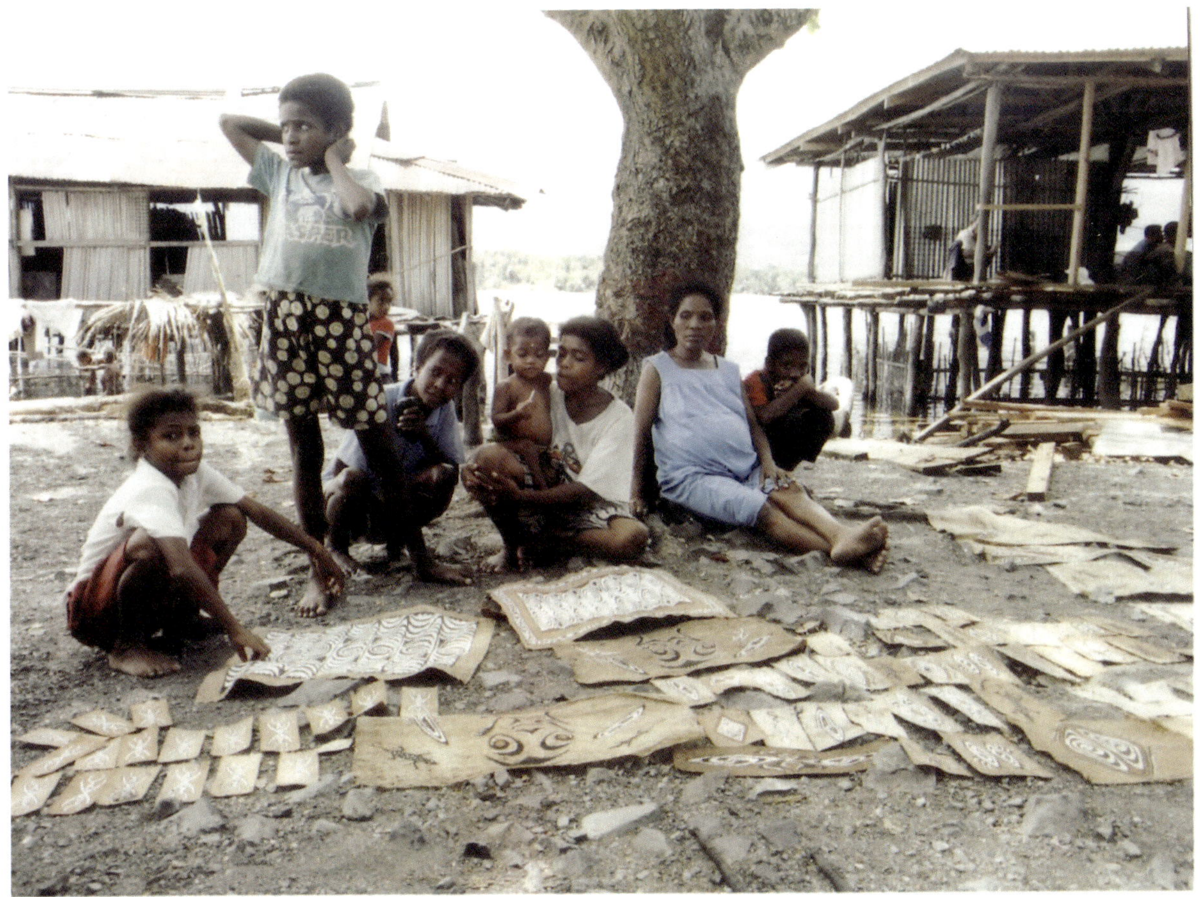

Figure. 3.5. Women and children placing their pieces of decorated barkcloth on the beach, waiting for the tourists, who just arrived on the small island of Asei, to come and see their work. Photograph by Anna-Karina Hermkens, Asei 1996.

this female labor is still not recognized as a significant contribution to the art of barkcloth painting.

Designing Barkcloth in Maisin

Roughly 1500 kilometer southeast of Lake Sentani in the Oro Province of Papua New Guinea, live the Maisin people. The members of this linguistic group live scattered in ten major villages along the coast of Collingwood Bay. Just as in the Lake Sentani area, these people have a long history of making and wearing barkcloth (locally in English referred to as tapa). Among the Maisin, women were traditionally responsible for manufacturing barkcloth, designing the decorative motifs, and its painting. The importance of barkcloth for Maisin people is reflected in the statement one often hears in the area "Maisin is tapa." In 2001, men in Airara village told me that because of its importance for Maisin, "all women, even those coming from the outside, have to learn how to make and design it." [6]

The production of barkcloth requires skill, strength, and creativity. It is intertwined with women's bodies, their knowledge, status, and their identity (Hermkens 2005a, 2005b, 2007b). This relationship between barkcloth and the female body is fourfold. It is physical, mental, social, and symbolic. Through the production of barkcloth, the female body is physically intertwined with the material, both in women's appropriation of skills and techniques, as well as in handling the material, which affects their bodies. Women learn to beat and design barkcloth from a young age onward. While beating barkcloth, women are required to sit in particular ways and exercise physical power (as beating barkcloth is an arduous and straining process), technical skill as well as patience and endurance. Since designs evolve out of women's imagination and creativity, women's minds are also linked to the making of barkcloth. The relationship between women and barkcloth becomes even more apparent when one considers how both men and women stress the responsibility Maisin women have in making barkcloth, both in cultural and in economic terms. Finally, due to women's symbolic relationship with the production and application of red paint, women are ritually connected with barkcloth.

Although each woman has her own design style, Maisin barkcloth is always clearly identifiable, as women remain within the boundaries of what is regarded as a

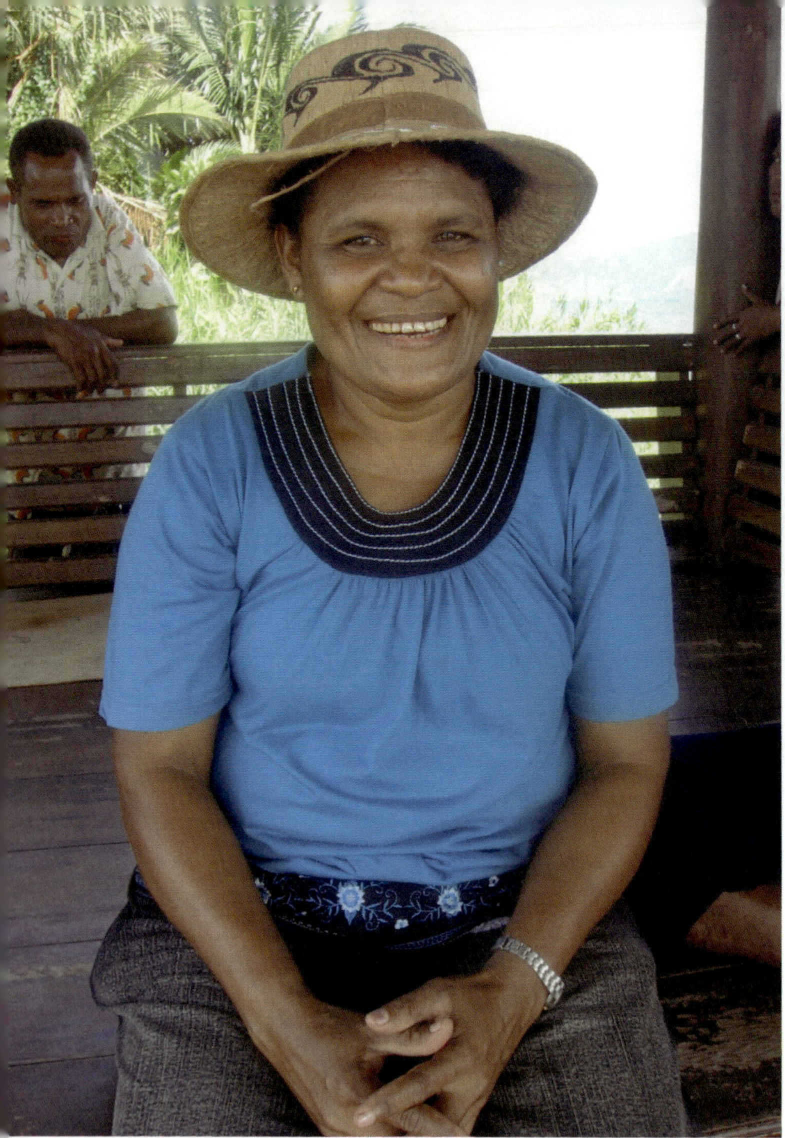

Figure. 3.6. Martha Ohee showing one of her products, a hat made from barkcloth. Photograph by Muridan Widjojo, Asei 2009.

good Maisin design [fig. 3.7]. Aesthetic concepts of what makes a good barkcloth and a good design are confined to the texture of the barkcloth, the structure of the design — it must consist of at least four lines — and women take great care not to spill red paint outside the black lines. Individual preferences for the work of particular women exist, but Maisin people will always stress that all Maisin women are capable barkcloth makers, both in drawing designs and as painters.

Whereas in Humboldt Bay and Lake Sentani only initiated and married women would wear loincloths, among the Maisin both men and women have a tradition of wearing barkcloth loincloths. The female garment embobi, is rectangular in shape and wrapped around the hips with a girdle, covering the thighs and the knees. Koefi, the male garment, is a long and narrow piece of barkcloth worn between the legs and wrapped around the hips, one end covering the genitals and the other pendant over the buttocks. Among the Maisin, these two types of loincloths are often decorated with designs outlined by black lines and filled with red pigment, producing a vivid display of meandering and curving red lines on the light barkcloth.

In contrast to many other societies in New Guinea, like Sentani and Humboldt Bay villages where people stopped wearing their traditional dress in the 1920s, the Maisin kept wearing their embobi and koefi for a relatively long time. Unlike many other congregations (Eves 1996, Colchester 2003), the Anglican Church based in the Maisin area unintentionally contributed to the continuation of their traditional clothing. Anglicans had no policy of converting Papuans by dressing them up in western clothes. As a result Collingwood Bay people generally, but especially the Maisin adhered to their koefi and embobi. While Papuans in the Sentani area were encouraged to replace their traditional clothing with western dress as soon as European missionaries, colonist, traders and collectors (Hermkens 2007a: 12-14) made their appearance around 1900, Anglican "missionaries who clothed Papuans were the exception rather than the rule." In fact, the missionaries "more frequently lamented the desire of Papuans for European clothes than complained about immodest dress" (Wetherell 1977: 202). This attitude provided a social and cultural context in which barkcloth was used as the principal Maisin garment until a few years after World War II.

In the past, barkcloth was not only used as clothing but also as blankets, and people used to wrap sago in barkcloth when they carried it from the gardens to the village. In some cases, loincloths were used in a secondary context as well — expressing a person's gender and identity, simply by displaying his or her barkcloth. Just as it was custom in Lake Sentani to decorate a woman's grave with a large decorated maro, Collingwood Bay people display a person's loincloth on his or her grave. In Wanigela, a village neighboring Maisin villages, people cover a women's grave with an embobi and a men's grave with a koefi. Among the Maisin, the garment of the deceased is hung underneath the house together with the deceased's yati (small string bag) with his or her personal belongings. The deceased's body was first wrapped in mats and subsequently covered with a piece of barkcloth. Today pieces of cotton cloth are also used for this purpose. In addition, barkcloth is used as an item to exchange for clay pots or canoes. People give barkcloth during life cycle rituals and bride-price payments, and people still use barkcloth as clothing during various festivities.

Maisin distinguish among evovi (patrilineal clan designs), imaginary designs and Anglican Church related designs. The individually named clan designs are often figurative, visualizing mountains, animals, or specific artifacts. These designs are rather static, being transmitted within each clan from one female generation to another. In contrast, imaginary designs evolve from individual women's imagination and creativity and, as such, are hardly ever the same. Church designs often display the Mother Union's logo (MU) [fig. 3.8], or Christian symbols, such as the crucifix or biblical scenes.

Wearing particular embobi and koefi provides an arena in which various identities and messages may be visualized and transmitted (Hermkens 2007c) [fig. 3.9]. For example, wearing one's clan design expresses one's clan identity; in much the same way other objects mark the clan. In addition to the clan designs drawn on barkcloth, clans claim necklaces and armlets with particular shapes, as well as particular shells and (colored) feathers, such as cockatoo feathers and black or white chicken feathers. Each clan has its own clan designs that are not allowed to be worn by members of other clans. In cases where people wear clan designs they are not entitled to wear, disputes and even violent outbursts could occur. As several Maisin men stressed, wearing someone else's clan design may result in being killed.

In the past, women predominantly drew clan designs. From my study of museum collections in the Australian Museum in Sydney and at the National Museum and Art Gallery of Papua New Guinea in Port Moresby, it appears that since the 1950s, there has been an increase in the production of imaginary designs. This shift coincides with initiatives to commercialize barkcloth. Whereas imaginary designs have been sold all over the world, clan designs are less easily turned into commodities. Maisin people who are concerned with their culture and identity have advocated against selling clan designs. Due to this prohibition and the commodification of imaginary designs, less clan barkcloth is being produced. At the same time, some clan designs are almost forgotten because they were not passed down to the next generation from senior women.

As the emphasis has shifted to imaginary designs that are alienable and may be freely sold to outsiders, women's monopoly on the creation of barkcloth is dissolving as men gradually enter its sphere of production (Hermkens 2007b). Attracted to the revenues, a few men have started to design pieces of barkcloth themselves, thereby crossing the boundaries of this previously gendered production. Such a shift was made possible because of the fading symbolic meaning of the red pigment, called dun or tambuta (red blood). The taboos that formerly surrounded the painting of barkcloth were abandoned, thereby making it possible for men to witness and sometimes participate in its production. Such an act was not possible a century ago, when it was strictly forbidden for men (and children) to witness the manufacture of red paint or its application to the barkcloth. The number of men actually designing barkcloth is still very limited. Moreover, none of them draws and creates clan designs, which are still a woman's responsibility.

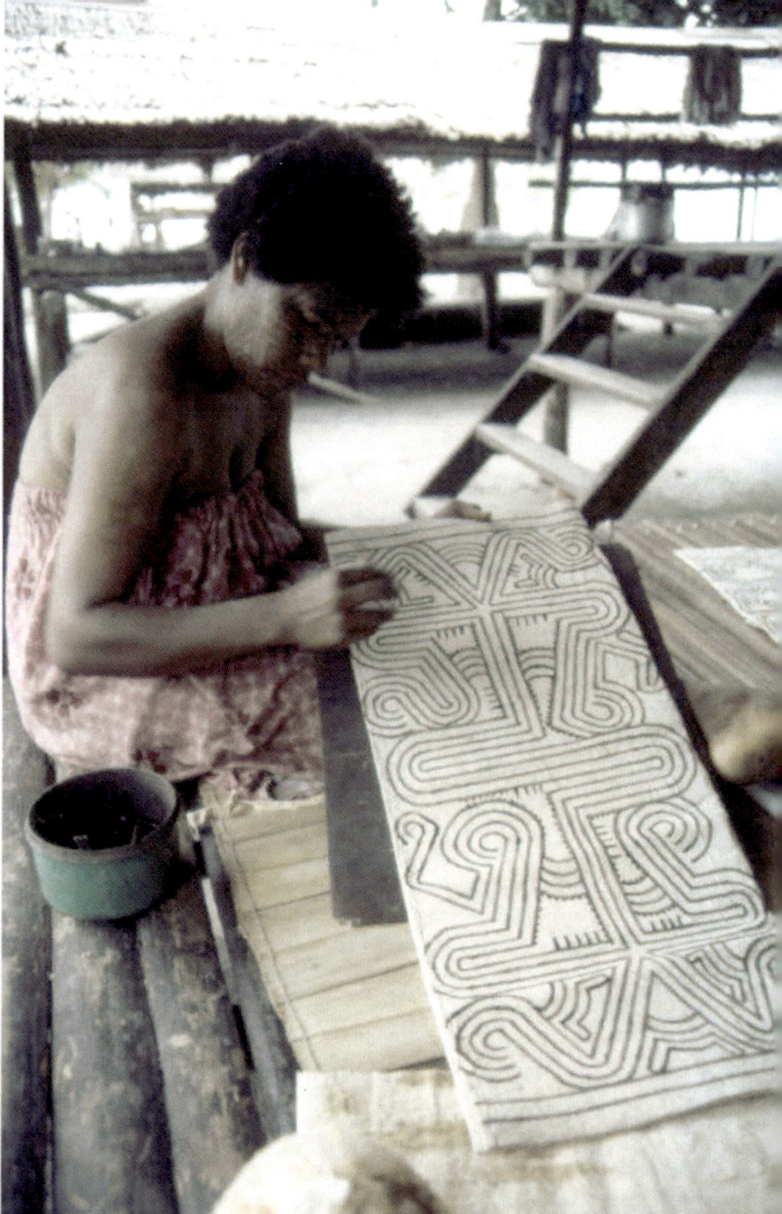

Figure. 3.7. Monica Taniova, one of the acknowledged excellent barkcloth artists among the Maisin. She designs a piece of barkcloth in her individual though typical Maisin style. Photograph by Anna-Karina Hermkens, Airara 2001.

Due to the commercialization of barkcloth and men's growing involvement in both its manufacturing and marketing, property rights over barkcloth are also changing. While string bags, pottery, and pandanus mats still belong to the women who made them, and

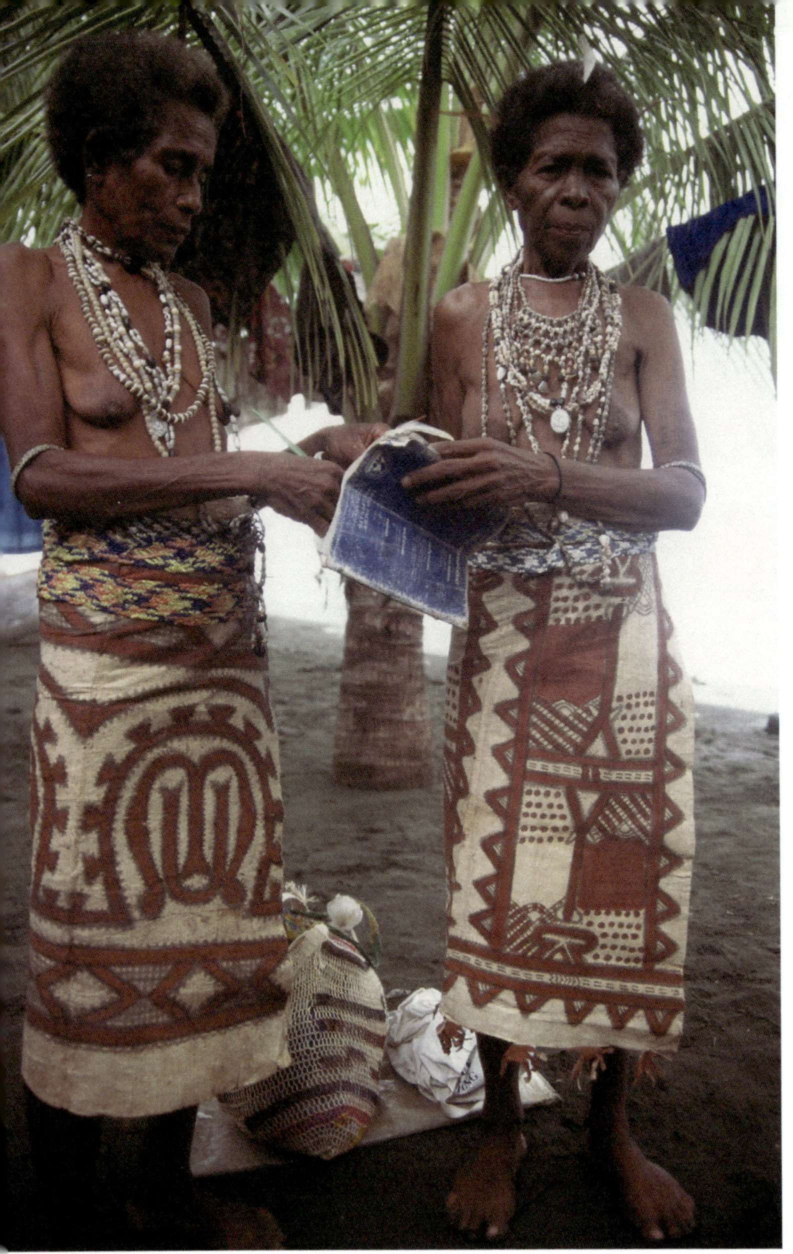

Figure. 3.8. Two Maisin women, one wearing a clan design (right) and the other a barkcloth featuring the Mother's Union (MU) logo. Photograph by Anna-Karina Hermkens, Airara 2001.

it is up to them to decide whether to give it away in exchange or sell it, men are trying to gain control over barkcloth and its revenues. In contrast to previously mentioned products of women's labor, many women cannot give or sell barkcloth as they please, since they need their husband's consent to do so. Young and middle-aged couples (between 30-45 years old) that I interviewed on this topic stressed the commercial value of the alienable barkcloth and its importance for the entire family. They argued that ideally both husband and wife should consult each other before giving barkcloth away or selling it. Monica's husband Clifford, however, argued that: "Monica cannot sell tapa without letting me know, but if I want to sell a finished tapa, I can do it without letting her know! Once, when I was not at home, she gave someone three pieces who promised to sell them in town. But he didn't give her the money he received for the tapa and I am still angry with that." Clifford is, like other husbands, less concerned with regard to the more traditional purpose of barkcloth as a gift or item for barter. "If she wants to give tapa to contribute to ceremonies, such as a ro-babassi [end of mourning ceremony] or to a sauki jobi [bride-price payment], that's okay. But if I am at home, we should first talk about it." [7]

Thus, while women can decide for themselves either to give, exchange, or sell string bags, clay pots, and mats, commercial barkcloth is no longer considered to be woman's property. As such, women's production of barkcloth, and especially commercial barkcloth seems to have become alienated from them. Whether, and to what extent, she can control her own products depends upon a woman's age and status, and in particular on her residence. If adult women live within their father's clan, they can produce for their own support, whereas women who live with their husband's clan are subjected to the wishes of their husbands and his extended family, and other claims from their in-laws. Also, elderly and widowed women stated that they could decide for themselves, since the barkcloth belongs to them. As Lina, a 65-year old widow, put it, "I own the wuwusi [barkcloth tree], my brother gave me the seeds, but I took care of them so I own the tapa." When Lina's husband was still alive, "he could not decide on giving or selling tapa, I did!" [8] For much younger women, however, this is not the case and they have to accept their husbands' control over barkcloth and its destinations, as well as its revenues.

This does not imply that women silently accept their husbands' control over barkcloth revenues, or, more generally, the monopoly of men in the barkcloth business. Almost all women in Airara village have produced several pieces of barkcloth that were sold either by or to male relatives, but the women have never seen the money paid for the barkcloth. This mismanagement of women's products and its revenues gives rise to critique and caution among women, as well as among men. As various couples involved in selling barkcloth stressed, the money obtained from the sale of barkcloth is meant for the family and not just for the husband. Ironically, many men admitted that they do not trust themselves with money and as a result, their wives often keep the barkcloth revenues forcing the men to ask for money, simultaneously allowing women to keep track of expenditures. Despite these precautions, barkcloth money still "disappears" from men's pockets through their gambling or other non-lucrative business activities.

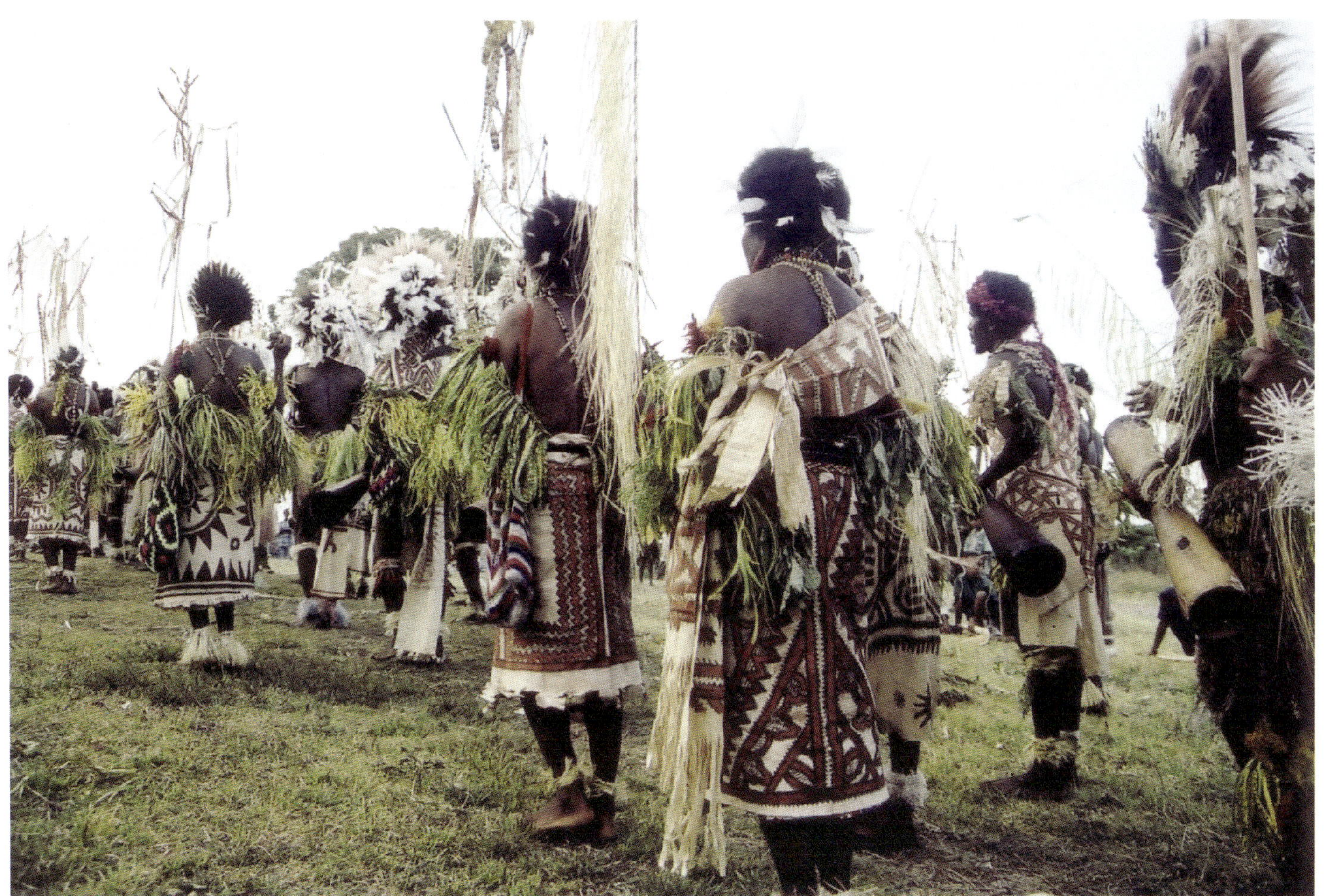

Figure. 3.9. Maisin men and women dressed up in their traditional regalia, performing a dance during a church festival in Sefoa, Cape Nelson. Photograph by Anna-Karina Hermkens, Airara 2001.

Barkcloth: From Female Cloth to Male Art

We have seen that among both the Sentani and Maisin people the production and design of barkcloth was traditionally the product of women's labor and creativity. In both areas, the commercialization of barkcloth has led to the incongruous role of male artists. Although Maisin women still dominate the domestic production of barkcloth, just as Sentani women dominate the local commodity production, male Maisin and Sentani artists dominate the global exposure of barkcloth as art. This section will question how this transformation of creativity and the (restricted) ability to act as agents in the global art world has came about among Sentani and Maisin men and women.

In order to understand how Sentani and Humboldt Bay maro transformed from a women's garment into a commodity, we need to consider the Dutch colonial past in which the collecting and display of maro was a thoroughly gendered and racial enterprise. As I argue elsewhere, colonial collecting and, in particular, local colonial relations affected the way we have represented both maro and Papuans in the past and today (Hermkens 2007a).

The earliest descriptions and documentation of painted barkcloth date from 1858 by members of the Etna expedition. Van der Goes (1862: 172) described them as featuring regularly drawn, black figures. The artist C. B. H. von Rosenberg made a drawing of a Humboldt Bay couple, the woman wearing a decorated piece of maro with patterns similar to those depicted on the barkcloth) collected by his colleague, F. G. Beckman in 1858 in Humboldt Bay [fig. 3.10].

Large military expeditions visited the North Coast of Dutch New Guinea in 1887 and 1903, but these collectors only acquired a few undecorated pieces. It would take almost twenty years before collectors collected more painted barkcloth. In 1921 and 1926, Wirz managed to collect two decorated maro in Lake Sentani, followed by De Rautenfeld (in 1929) and Halie (1929-1931) who each brought home one piece of decorated barkcloth. In contrast, the collecting of maro in

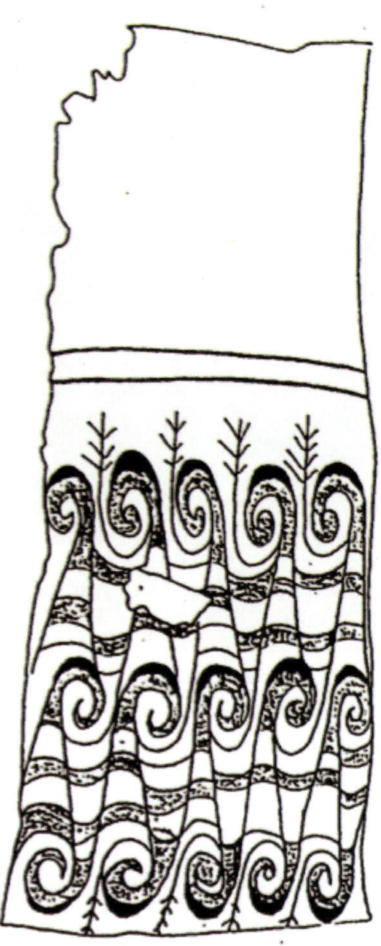

Figure. 3.10. Drawing of the decorated maro collected by F. G. Beckman in 1858 (Collection RMV).

Humboldt Bay rose to previous unknown heights from 1929 onwards.

One wonders why there was such a noticeable increase of barkcloth collecting — and probably production — in Humboldt Bay. According to Hoogerbrugge (1995: 175), the reasons for this rise in creative activity in especially Tobati village could be The Arts and Crafts Exhibition organized in May 1929 to mark the occasion of the Fourth Pacific Science Congress. The exhibition was held at the museum of the Koninklijk Bataviaasch Genootschap van Kunsten en Wetenschappen (Royal Batavian Society for the Arts and Sciences) — now the National Museum in Jakarta. A group of 35 men and women from the North coast of West Papua went to the exhibition. The women all wore plain barkcloth, but painted pieces were sold at their stand and were described as "naive drawings in bright colors" (Hoogerbrugge 1995: 178). Soon after they returned, the art collector Jacques Viot travelled to Humboldt Bay, followed in 1931 by an American couple named Fleischmann. This foreign interest in the painted maro must have stimulated local production as Viot and the Fleischmann's managed to collect in total some 90 pieces of decorated barkcloth! Importantly, due to this growing interest amongst French and American collectors, barkcloth was placed on the international agenda. In fact, the maro from the Humboldt Bay and Lake Sentani area became important examples of "primitive art" (Peltier 1992).

When comparing the maro from the early 1930s with the old maro from 1858 and those collected by Wirz between 1921 and 1926, the general shape and layout of the maro and paintings are seen to have changed. Instead of an elongated shape, which was needed if the barkcloth was to be around the hips, most of the cloths collected in the late 1920s and 1930s are nearly square. The overall orientation of the decorations is centered, rather than at one end (the shorter sides of the earlier elongated form). These changes are due to the changing function of the maro. Starting out as loincloths whose undecorated part would be wound underneath the decorated part, the maro soon became a piece of decoration and primitive art. Unfortunately, World War II brought both the collecting and production of maro to a halt.

After the war, few collectors visited the region. In the 1950s, Galis (1955: 116) recorded that items made from barkcloth were rare in the Humboldt area. A similar situation was found in lake Sentani. C.M.A. Groenevelt was able to collect only one painted barkcloth for the museums in Amsterdam and Rotterdam during his first year (1951-1952) of residence in Hollandia, present-day Jayapura. Since Groenevelt collected many artifacts in Lake Sentani, the presence of only one piece of maro in his collection is as disappointing as it is surprising. As Groenevelt mentions in a letter he wrote in 1952, older maro paintings were no longer to be found around Lake Sentani and few new ones were being produced (Van Duuren 1992: 210). Groenevelt was so keen on acquiring (old style) maro paintings that he asked a Sentani chief to make some new pieces. He was, however, very disappointed with the results (Hollander 2007: 75).

In the 1960s, the Dutch ex-colonial officer, and collector Jacq Hoogerbrugge came to a similar conclusion. He had shown photographs of eight barkcloth paintings from Simon Kooijman's book The Art of Lake Sentani (1959) to several Sentani villagers, asking them to find him "a man capable of making a maro" (Hoogerbrugge 1995: 167: emphasis mine). Although Hoogerbrugge had promised attractive rewards, responses were slow and the common explanation was that "the preparation of the cloth was a woman's affair." When he returned in the early 1970's, Hoogerbrugge visited the village of Nafri in Humboldt Bay. After asking around again, two old men claimed to be capable barkcloth painters in the "old-style," one of which, after lengthy discussions with his female relatives who would have to make the cloth, produced four painted maro (Hoogerbrugge 1992: 131; 1995: 168). It appears that by Hoogerbrugge's search for maro artists, men were encouraged to make these paintings and earn some money. This may have triggered a revival in barkcloth paintings, but executed by men. By the end of the decade the two artists had died and Hoogerbrugge (1992: 139; 1995: 169) feared that barkcloth painting had disappeared forever. Twenty years later he returned to notice that this 'art' was more alive then ever.

This revival is linked to the emergence of two new phenomena: the growing tourist industry and government-sponsored arts and crafts festivals (Howard 1996). According to Howard (1996, 1998), the revival of barkcloth paintings has specifically been encouraged by the staff of the Anthropology Museum (Museum Loka Budaya) at the Cenderawasih University (UNCEN), which is situated between Humboldt Bay and Lake Sentani. In 1992 this interest led to an exhibition of barkcloth paintings, which were predominantly made by Seru Ongge living at Asei village (Howard 1996). A year later, Seru's nephew Agus Ongge was able to show his barkcloth paintings at an exhibition of Sentani art in Jakarta. This exhibition was sponsored by the Jakarta Post and arranged with help of one of the organisers of the UNCEN exhibition, who also happens to own an art-shop in which maro are sold.

This short overview of the history of maro shows that with the advent of ethnographic and primitive art collectors in the late 1920s and early 1930s, Sentani and Humboldt Bay barkcloth started to cross international borders. The tradition of making and painting maro was almost lost after the Second World War, but slowly regained new impetus with outside encouragement from the 1970s, and especially from the 1990s onwards. These dynamics in the production and circulation of maro express some of the changes in the colonial relationships, just as they express changes in the production, meaning, and designs of the object itself. It foremost demonstrates how the global art market turned female garments produced by women into pieces of art made by men.

Transformations in Barkcloth and Gender Among the Maisin

In Collingwood Bay, the commodification of barkcloth was not so much a response to primitive art collectors, but rather was inspired by the Anglican Church. From the moment Anglican missionaries based themselves in Collingwood Bay (1898), they collected barkcloth, selling it as well as other artifacts to museums. They also sold barkcloth to people interested in ethnographic artifacts (Hermkens 2005).

Sister Helen Roberts (1920-1992) continued these early attempts to commercialize barkcloth, but also incorporated it in the Christian way of life and worship (Barker 1985), amongst others by supporting the use of painted barkcloth in Church decorations and as dress during Church celebrations. In addition, she arranged that the Archbishop of Canterbury be dressed in a barkcloth cape and mitre on the occasion of the Anglican Church's centenary celebration in 1991. Roberts had come to Wanigela Mission Station as a young woman a few years after World War II. In the early 1970s, she started to sell pieces of barkcloth to visiting friends and other foreigners in order to assist in costs related to the education of local youth. [9]

Maisin people have been able to promote themselves via the display and exhibition of barkcloth partly as a result of the travels of one Maisin man, Franklin Seri. In the 1980s several international Art Festivals were held, which included a Maisin representative illustrating barkcloth. At these festivals barkcloth was designed and sold to an international audience. In Edinburgh, Seri demonstrated the art of barkcloth making, and even had the opportunity to give two pieces of barkcloth to Prince Charles and Princess Diana, thereby placing Maisin barkcloth in the Royal collection at Westminster Abbey. And in 2004, Seri once more represented Maisin and Papua New Guinea's artistic culture by attending the Pacific Arts Festival on Palau, bringing several pieces of barkcloth, as well as barkcloth hats and other artifacts made from designed barkcloth. It is striking that of all international festivals where Maisin barkcloth was displayed and sold, only during one occasion a Maisin woman demonstrated the art of barkcloth-making (this was during a festival held in Japan where a small group of Maisin men and women performed their dances and showed their barkcloth loincloths). On all other occasions, a male representative displayed the art of making barkcloth. This male, as well as foreign, domination over the commercialization of barkcloth is still present.

In the mid-1990s, the Maisin came to the attention of environmental activists when villagers launched a public campaign to prevent the national government from permitting commercial logging on their ancestral lands. In their struggle, the Maisin received support from Greenpeace, which actively used Maisin barkcloth to promote their cause and the fight against logging. "Painting a sustainable future: Maisin art and rainforest conservation," was the slogan for an international campaign. It presented the Maisin as a tribal people whose ancestral barkcloth art could save the rainforest and bring development in their lives at the same time. Environmentalists were, as John Barker (2008: 188) formulates, effectively "kayapoing" the Maisin, making them a famous tribe. In this process, the Maisin were encouraged to run an "integrated conservation and development" (ICAD) organization, in order to prevent extensive logging in their area. The idea was to set up national and international tapa markets to sustain the organization, but people began to depend more and more on MICAD (Maisin Integrated Conservation and Development) to provide alternative ways of development, especially other possibilities for selling barkcloth.

The Anglican Church provided another market for barkcloth, and especially the former priest stationed in Uiaku. He tried to create new markets to sell barkcloth. During my stay among the Maisin, two Maisin women and a man working in the tapa business were given the opportunity to travel to South Korea to promote and sell barkcloth. The women in this delegation were members of the Mothers Union, which had been established among the Maisin about 50 years ago. This organization provides a structure through which the Anglican Church encourages local female members to produce barkcloth for Anglican markets. These sales would support the church's expenses as well as generate income for the women and their families. But unlike many of the other MU activities, this Anglican commercialization of barkcloth attracted the involvement of various local men who were either invited to give advice to the MU about the selling of barkcloth, or they volunteered. As such, even within a MU context, which is largely dominated by women's activities and decision-making, men became involved in the Anglican barkcloth business. Until now, many projects have failed; the barkcloth was sold, but the priest and the women have yet to see their money as, in particular, local middlemen kept or spend the revenues.

The economic importance of barkcloth becomes clear when one considers the few alternatives for generating an income; especially after the copra market collapsed several years ago. In addition to markets where women sell their garden produce, prepared dishes, and pandanus mats, and the small trade-stores where men sell goods like kerosene, rice, sugar, and salt, the barkcloth selling provides one of the few ways of getting money. Since women are the main producers of barkcloth, households depend on their wives and mothers to manufacture this special kind of cash crop. The increase in barkcloth production thus leads to an increase in women's labor. Groups of Airara women can regularly be seen painting large amounts of barkcloth because one of their husbands suddenly decided to make a selling trip to the nearest city. In such cases, female friends and relatives help the wife to design or paint barkcloth. In these contexts, when the pressure to produce many pieces of commercial barkcloth is high, the still somewhat incongruity of men designing barkcloth is not considered problematic. As Lina, an elderly Maisin woman expressed: "It's not good for men to remain lazy. It is good they started to design tapa for themselves." [10]

The symbolic and economic changes in barkcloth have clearly had an impact on local gender relations as well. First, women are held responsible for the production of commercial barkcloth. As one Maisin man argued, "Maisin is tapa. It is our living! If a woman does not make tapa, her family's life is very poor." [11] But while women's workloads and responsibilities as providers of cash for their families have increased, their control over the destination and revenues of barkcloth is diminishing. Moreover, because of the foreign interest in barkcloth, which stresses the importance of women's involvement as the main producers, gender relations have become strained. This tension resulted due to the establishment of Maisin Integrated Conservation and Development (MICAD), which allowed women to attend meetings and speak up, which had previously been prohibited. In addition, much to the disapproval of many Maisin men, women were invited to demonstrate their barkcloth skills abroad, and to participate in exchange programs.

For example, in the late 1990s, the Fabric Workshop in Philadelphia invited three Papuan leaders and two female artists to visit Philadelphia and experiment with new ways of interpreting barkcloth. During a follow-up visit, three women, including Monica Taniova [fig. 3.6], travelled to Philadelphia. Their barkcloth designs were printed on various kinds of fabric (on rugs, synthetics and cotton) and exhibited in the museum of the Fabric Workshop in Philadelphia in 1998 (Rice 1998). In June 2001, a delegation of seven Maisin — five men and two women — travelled to Canada to spend two weeks with people from the Sto:lo tribe (First Nation people), who had previously visited Maisin. The trip was presented as an effort to set up exchange relationships, facilitating mutual understanding with regard to environmental and cultural heritage. The result was a film. The initial request of the organizers was to have a Maisin delegation of three men and three women. But Maisin men protested against this request. After long and angry debates in which it was expressed that only men should represent Maisin people and that it was morally dangerous to have women travel with men who were not relatives, it was decided two, instead of three Maisin women were allowed to travel abroad. By allowing only two women to participate, Maisin men protested against the foreign pressure for gender equality. Most women I spoke to did not agree with this decision, but did not publicly challenge it either.

Ironically, these processes of integrating women in local decision making policies and foreign exchanges eventually backfired. According to John Barker, in the 1990s women regularly attended MICAD meetings to express their opinions. Upon his return in 2000, he noticed, as I did in 2001, that this female participation had ceased. The women were sitting outside the meeting platform, as before. Below on the grass, they were not able to participate in the discussions and decisions being made by the men present. As such, the commodification of barkcloth predominantly reinforced conservative gender and power relations whereby men attempt to dominate the markets and revenues of this traditionally female produced object.

From Gender Identity to Ethnic Identity

The previous descriptions of Sentani and Maisin barkcloth showed how the commercialisation of barkcloth has led, or is leading, to a shift in gender and production relations, in which women are no longer the sole producers of the barkcloth they— and in the Maisin case their husbands—used to wear. But this shift suggests another transition as well. Whereas in the past the production of this type of cloth was symbolically intertwined with women's bodies and their sexuality, barkcloth no longer denotes specific gender or even clan identity, but increasingly it marks ethnic or even national identity.

Typical Lake Sentani designs drawn on barkcloth also occur on Indonesian national monuments and are printed on cotton cloth, which is referred to as Batik Irian. When Papuan leader Theys Hiyo Eluay was arrested for conspiracy against the Indonesian state on 29 November 2000, he wore this novel kind of maro, a cotton lap-lap with Sentani batik designs. Eluay was not only one of the major Papua leaders, struggling for independence from Indonesia; he was also the Ondofolo of all the Lake Sentani villages. Wearing a lap-lap with Sentani designs therefore marked his identity as a Sentani chief. In combination with a T-shirt featuring his own portrait set against the flag of West Papua, his identity as a Papua leader and Sentani man was both enhanced and expressed. Just a few weeks before his arrest Theys had participated in an exhibition, Art forms of Papua Culture at the Hotel Borobudur in Jakarta (20-26 October 2000). Among the artists present was Agus Ongge who exhibited many decorated maro and demonstrated his painting during the exhibition. Theys Eluay's presence at the exhibition made explicit the new status of maro as a representation of Sentani and, more generally, Papuan identity. In this context, the maro became a (silent) political protest against the Indonesian authorities, and the urge for independence.

Thus, loincloths used by initiated or married women were transformed into political images, made and used by men. In so doing, Sentani as well as Papuan identity is being expressed. Wearing pieces of barkcloth with Sentani designs at the Kamoro Art festival in Mimika in 2001 similarly reflected this feature of contemporary maro as a marker of Papuan identity (Roper 2001).

In Maisin, a similar tendency may be discerned. The manufacturing and display of Maisin barkcloth in the Papua New Guinea stands at the Pacific Art Festivals, visualizes traditional Papua New Guinea culture. In fact, since neighboring and adjacent cultural groups have stopped manufacturing barkcloth, Maisin barkcloth decorated with imaginary designs has also become a traditional garment used by other linguistic groups, even by people who have no tradition of wearing barkcloth, including for example, the Biniguni people, who live in the mountains behind the South-eastern Maisin villages. Besides borrowing coastal dances and songs, Biniguni men have incorporated Maisin koefi in their traditional outfit, while their women still wear grass-skirts. In the same way, through the intermediary of the Anglican Church, cultural groups in New Britain have recently bought a large number of koefi and embobi to wear during festivities. Thus, also in a more local setting, Maisin barkcloth no longer refers just to gender and clan identity, but is increasingly a symbol of traditional identity. Maisin barkcloth is therefore crossing its boundaries and acquiring new value as a neo-traditional symbol of cultural identity.

Conclusion

Whether stimulated by foreign collectors or by missionaries, the production of painted barkcloth for commercial markets in both Sentani and Maisin has brought a change in gender roles (either of men or women) in the production of barkcloth as well as changes in the designs depicted on the cloth. In both regions tourism demanded fast production techniques and created the opportunity for male artists to specialize in activities heretofore associated with women. These processes of change were not merely the result of the external factors discussed above, but also reflect changes in life at a local level.

Commercialization of barkcloth in both Lake Sentani and Maisin areas could have resulted in increased status and global mobility for women, however this did not happen. Local men dominate the international and global markets of barkcloth art, while women were confined to domestic production for local markets. In the 1920s Humboldt Bay women travelled all the way to Jakarta to show and sell their barkcloth designs. Today this mobility is the prerogative of a few Humboldt Bay and Lake Sentani men, like Agus Ongge. In a similar way, the international representation of Maisin and Maisin barkcloth has largely become a male affair. Among Maisin, Franklin Seri is the one who has turned himself in a professional barkcloth artist, travelling the world over demonstrating his skills and selling barkcloth. Unlike Maisin women making barkcloth, he has registered himself as an artist at the Culture and Tourism bureau in Port Moresby, thereby being officially recognized as a Papua New Guinea artist.

Why do Sentani and Maisin women not actively present or register themselves as artists, thereby gaining local, national, and international recognition? The answer to this question lies first of all in the relationship that exists between women and the object of art they produce, and secondly women's domestic roles as mothers and wives that is believed to be in conflict with a career as an artist. The relationship between women and barkcloth and the possibilities women have to own or claim their product, touches upon notions of property. According to Carrier (1998:86-88), Melanesians have an "inclusive" notion of property, in which objects reflect and are embedded in relationships between people, while Western societies tend to have a more "exclusive" form of property in which objects are controlled and associated with the person who owns it. Sentani and Maisin people live in both of these worlds and deploy both forms of property as they negotiate their daily experiences into the capitalistic economy. Within this setting, people have both inalienable "inclusive" forms of property, as well as alienable and "exclusive" forms of property (Carrier 1998:101). But who can exercise control over what form of property?

In Maisin, we have seen that the commercialization of barkcloth alienates women from their product in the sense that they can no longer control it, as they must consult with their husbands or other male relatives over its use. In contrast, women can still exercise control over inalienable barkcloth and barkcloth given in the gift economy or in barter exchange. Thus, it depends upon the involvement of money, whether women can exercise control or not. According to Whitehead (1984:180), women's ability to act "as fully operative individuals in relation to property is always less than that of men." In her view, "it is the kinship or family-system which constructs women in such a way." In Lake Sentani and Maisin villages, the kinship or family-system emphasizes the roles of women as mothers, wives and sisters, leaving little space for alternative roles and identities, such as being an artist. Also, their responsibility for providing for their families prevents them from spending too much time creating barkcloth. As Monica Taniova [fig. 3.6], a 35-year-old barkcloth maker, but most of all mother of five children living with her parents-in-law and husband, expressed: "I really like designing and painting and I would like to paint whole day. In fact, I used to do that, but now I have plenty work to do for my parents in-law, husband, and children." [12]

Both Sentani and Maisin women have to plan when to spend time on making or designing barkcloth since this takes them away from going to the gardens and harvesting food. They must make sure enough food is in the house for the entire family to be able to stay at home. On average, Maisin women go to the gardens four times per week, leaving one day for communal activities, such as clearing the school grounds or Mothers Union activities and, of course, Sunday, which to most of the Maisin people was acknowledged as resting day. Some women took the opportunity to work on their barkcloth on Sunday, either beating or painting it. Like their Maisin sisters, Sentani women take care of their families and spend most of their time fishing and processing sago, which is a women's job in the Lake Sentani area. In addition, childrearing demands women's time, leaving little time for mothers to spend on artistic activities.

This aspect of time and domestic chores interfering with women's creativity becomes especially salient when considering that husbands, brothers, and sons, are often not around to lessen women's burdens. Among the Maisin, many young men find employment elsewhere. Even married men regularly travelled outside the village for business. On Asei, many adult and young men migrated from the village in order to find paid jobs, as there is no work for money available on Asei. The young men who stayed, like Agus Ongge, have considerable time to spend making barkcloth and specializing themselves in this particular art. Because of this male mobility — and often the absence of husbands and brothers — women find themselves contributing greatly to the subsistence economy. While those

Sentani and Maisin men who remain in the village have much more time to spend on the creative arts.

In short, it seems that in particular rural women must overcome prevailing gender norms and a gendered division of care-taking and labor before they can claim and give voice to their work, and enter the world as local and globally acknowledged artists. As the Sentani and Maisin cases show, this can only work with the cooperation of local men who have to both allow and support their daughters and wives in being and becoming artists. Until then, women's artistic work will remain silent; anonymous art that cannot be claimed by women themselves, but, instead, is appropriated by local men who are eager to get acknowledged by the global art-market.

Acknowledgements

With thanks to Dr. Muridan Widjojo for conducting interviews in Lake Sentani in 2009 on my behalf and for sharing his photographs. Some parts of this article have been published previously in the *Journal of Pacific History* and in the *Journal of Pacific Arts*.

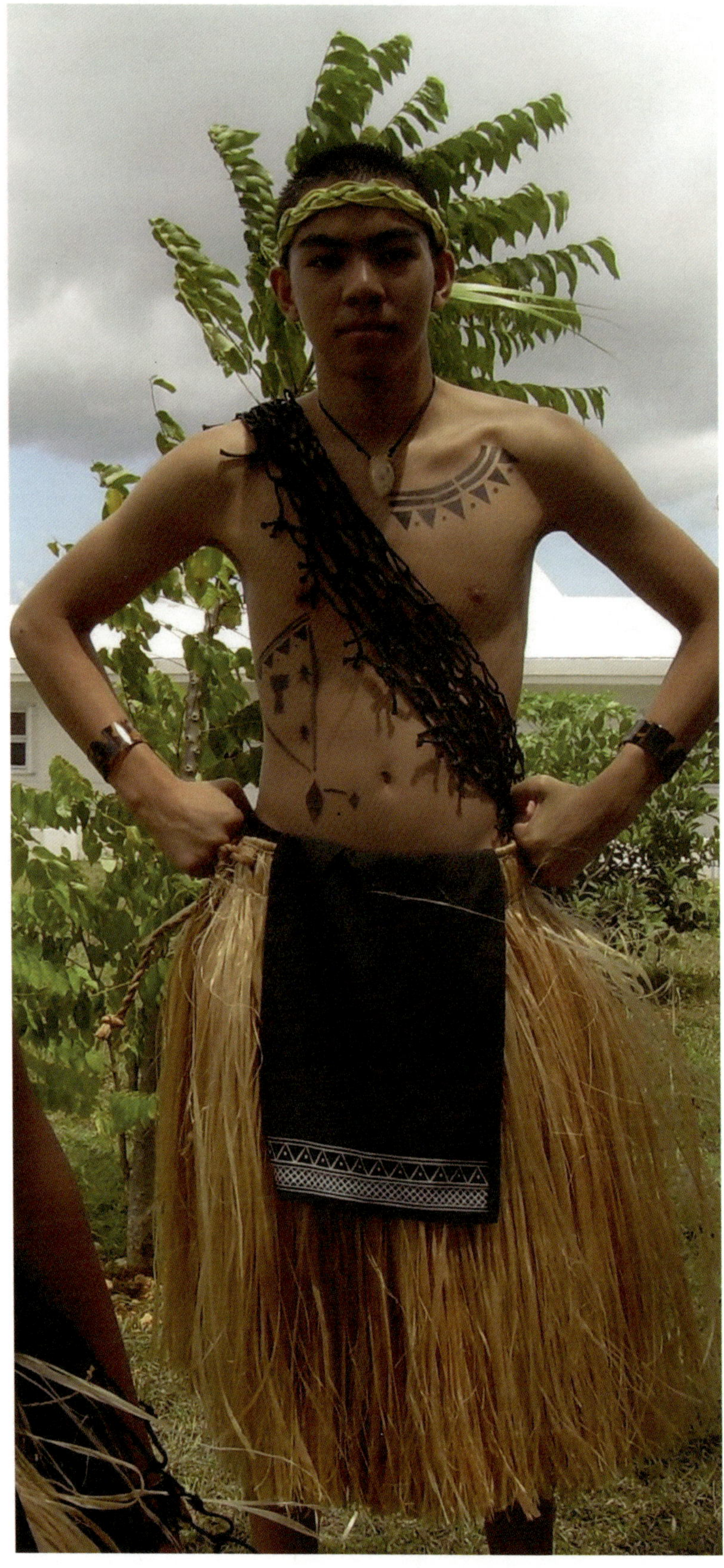

Figure 4.1. Painted Tattoo worn by a Dance Group member of Inetnon Gef Pa'go. Photograph by Judy Flores, 2009.

Navigating Chamorro Art and Identity

Judy Flores

The painted tattoo of bold black geometric shapes began at his neckline and spread across his torso in a scattering of design. A repeat row of geometric shapes edged his loincloth. [fig. 4.1]. The designs accentuated his graceful moves in unison with the dance group. The group of teenage boys and girls moved with confidence through a series of choreographed movements using long decorated sticks to strike cadence. Their leader gave commands in the Chamorro language, to which the group responded melodically, in unison. At the end of their performance they received enthusiastic applause from the audience seated around the elegantly decorated ballroom.

Inetnon Gef Pa'go dance group is among a growing number of community-based Chamorro dance groups that have been active from the mid-1990s, performing for schools, family and community celebrations, official ceremonial functions and festivals. Vince Reyes, the dance leader for the group, learned to dance from a former student of Master Frank Rabon, who started the Chamorro dance movement in 1984. Frank Rabon has been awarded the title, Traditional Master of Chamorro Dance, by the governor, for his pioneering efforts to re-create ancient Chamorro dance and to revitalize dance traditions.

Twenty years ago, the hotel ballrooms in Guam were more likely to have Big Band and Cha Cha music. Dance entertainment groups were imported from Polynesia, and the few local groups were dancing hula. In the twenty-first century, Chamorro dance groups are replacing Polynesian entertainment groups in hotels. A Chamorro chant is an accepted, almost required, opening ritual at government functions. The Guam Visitors Bureau holds auditions each year to select the best dancers to represent Guam in cultural promotions in Japan, Korea, Hong Kong and other Asian visitor markets. A generation of school children has grown up with the opportunity to learn Chamorro dance within their school programs or in community dance groups.

Chamorro crafts and visual arts forms have exhibited a similar renaissance over the same period. Indigenous art is often given as official gifts to visiting dignitaries. The Guam delegation to the Festival of Pacific Arts in Palau in 2004 included a large contingent of contemporary Chamorro artists who created carvings and body adornment from wood, bone and seashell. Paintings and drawings by contemporary artists were displayed in the new Palau National Museum. The 2008 Festival in American Samoa was again comprised of a strong group of visual and performing artists who used their art to proclaim their identity with Chamorro heritage.

Dance groups tend to use adornment influenced by the work of contemporary artists. The most popular items for purchase by the general Guam public as well as by dance groups have been items that replicate ancient objects. The development of ancient replicas and reconstructed ancient dance seems to have taken place simultaneously over the past twenty-five years. What has fueled this renaissance? How do artists interact with their community and environment to create these symbols? How has the community accepted or rejected this movement?

This paper will examine the dynamics of artists and their use of symbols to create an identity that emphasizes and affirms their connection to their ancient heritage. I will describe this movement as it relates to the native Chamorro people of Guam, the artists who create the symbols, and the particular influences that guide their creation of Chamorro identity markers. These identity markers draw on the cultural past but acquire new meaning and become emotionally weighty in the present (Linnekin 1990:159).

Initially, the renaissance of a Chamorro cultural consciousness can be traced to historical experiences of a global nature — the rising activism of minorities to establish their rights and secure a recognized place in the world order. In the 1960s and 1970s ethnicity became a focus of activism in American universities. This quickly spread to the Pacific and raised ethnic consciousness among Hawaiian Americans, Australian Aborigines, New Zealand Maori (Howard 1990: 270) and the Mariana Island Chamorros. Discourse on this ethnic (cultural) consciousness makes connections with consequent artistic manifestations termed variously as reconstruction (Thomas 1991), transformation (Kaeppler 1992: 314 [quoting Howard]), cultural rearticulations, ethnic symbolism (Perez, M., 1997), summarizing symbols (Ortner 1973), artistic inventions (Peterson 1992, Keesing 1989), and reinventions (Flores 1996). Sidney Mead points out that "Pacific cultures everywhere are actively pursuing and promoting their indigenous art forms... the more the arts are developed, the greater the indication that the people are taking charge of their heritage and their destiny" (1993: 229). Cultural self-consciousness is emerging among Pacific peoples as they "struggle for the first time with who they are — their cultural identity — in an increasingly complex social world" (Howard 1990: 259). These quotations, from authors familiar with late twentieth-century issues in Pacific cultures, point out the linkages between art and identity.

Art and identity are manifested in symbolism. Certain artifacts became pervasive symbols employed by artists in this national identity movement. Artists seem to be particularly sensitive to the power of the symbol to represent a broader, emotionally charged idea. As Chamorros reaffirm their identity as a people, artists act as the receptors and filters for ideas that they are then able to give tangible form. These symbols serve as rallying points that sustain and re-energize the movement. The artist and the community interact in the processing of ideas and energy to create, accept, reject or re-configure symbols of the identity formation, nation-building movement. The success or failure of their innovations depends on how their work is construed, rewarded or criticized in the community (Layton 1991: 239).

Contemporary Chamorros who seek to re-establish more visible links to their pre-contact past are faced with two main problems: There are only sparse descriptions of pre-contact cultural art forms; and the long historical period of outside influences largely obliterated the oral traditions and cultural practices associated with the continuity of traditional Chamorro art forms. Therefore the creation of neo-Chamorro art that identifies present-day Chamorros with their ancient ancestors is perceived by some as being built upon a myth; of not being grounded in visible, tangible manifestations of a continuous peoplehood. How does the contemporary Chamorro artist create these links to the past and how does the community respond and authenticate these creations? How does contemporary artistic production reflect or influence Chamorro identity and the nation building movement? Furthermore, how are Chamorro artists participating in local and global markets?

Cecelia (Lee) Perez uses her creative writing skills to document the politics of cultural identity and historical memory in a process which she calls "decolonization of the Chamoru mind." She feels that art forms play an important role [1]:

> I bear witness to a growing Grass Roots-based, village-based political movement toward decolonization through intellectual and sensory awareness and stimulation. Sensory and intellectual engagement invoke memories of a Chamoru past that are best expressed through sensory and intellectual actions. Dancers, choirs, musicians, painters, weavers, carvers, writers, chefs, photographers, chanters, and even athletes have become the major proponents of a Chamoru presence of Guam.

The 'decolonization of the Chamoru mind' is a fitting term to apply to the processional steps involving identity crises, cultural resistance and subsequent cultural rearticulation; the last being concerned with artistic production. In an attempt to analyze the role of art in the decolonization movement I will first look at what others have written about the effects of colonialism on artistic production with regard to the processional steps suggested above.

Richard Anderson (1990: 234) in *Calliope's Sisters: A Comparative Study of Philosophies of Art*, proposes that traditional cultures possess philosophies of art that convey "significant cultural meaning," which decline or disappear under colonization and are replaced by values which emphasize the artist's technical skill, economic value, and "considerations of ethnic identity or subcultural pride" (*ibid.*: 235). He offers what he considers a cross-culturally applicable definition of art: "Art is culturally significant meaning, skillfully encoded in an affecting, sensuous medium" (*ibid.*: 238). In other words, the art being produced is related in some way to the social cultural matrix from which it comes. According to his definition, art usually contains the power to elicit feelings or emotion from those who experience it; and its production is executed with exceptional skill (*ibid.*: 262). As contemporary Chamorros produce art which has 'significant cultural meaning' in today's society, they may choose to perpetuate old forms or to create new forms based on their own perceptions of what has significance in modern Chamorro society. Daniel Miller argues that the authenticity of art forms derives "from their active participation in a process of social self-creation in which they are directly constitutive of our understanding of ourselves and others" (1987: 215). His perspective places less emphasis on colonial agency in determining the quality of artistic production and places it on local perspectives. Using weaving as an example, Chamorros considered this form of artistic expression important to their society and continue to employ it into the twenty-first century. Significant cultural meaning can be used to describe its continued practice. Contemporary Chamorro artists are creating a variety of unprecedented art forms that seem to have significant cultural meaning in the ways they reflect

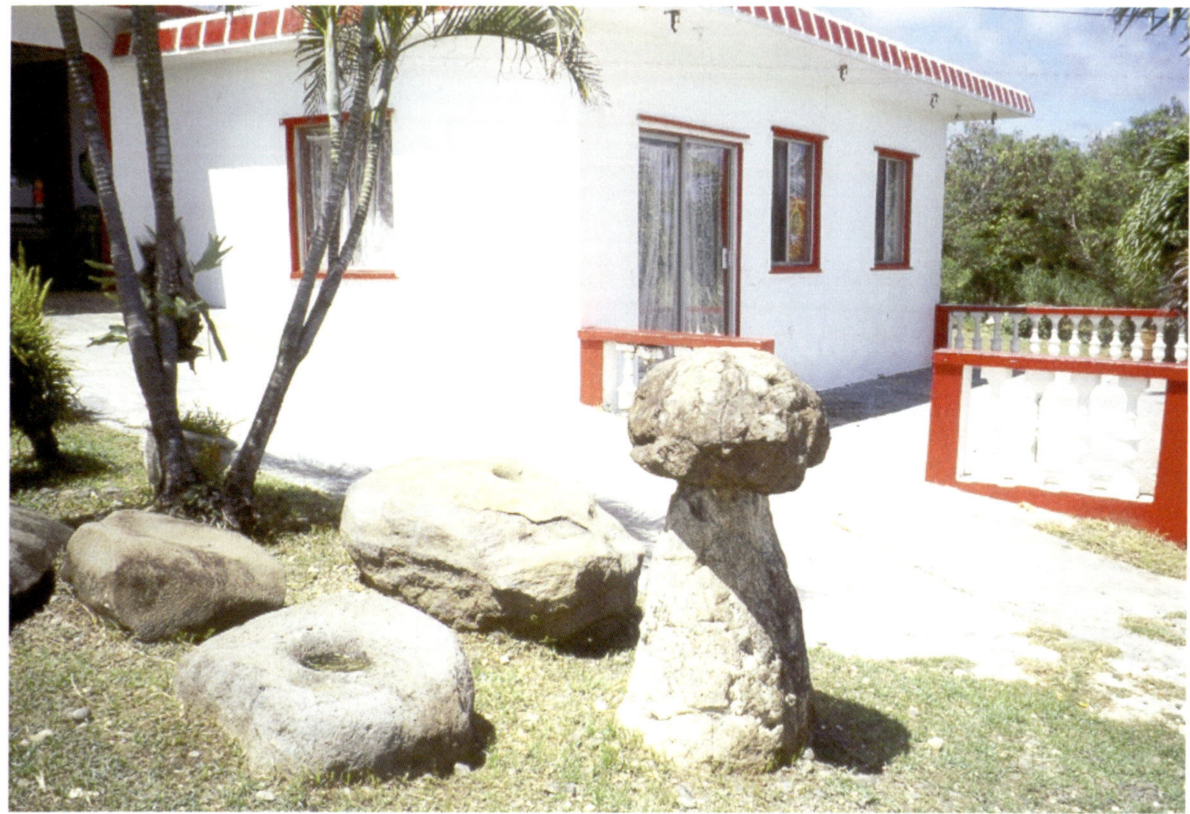

Figure 4.2. Lusong, ancient grinding stones, and Latte, ancient stone house posts. Photograph by Judy Flores, courtesy of the Francisco Crisostomo family, 1998.

cultural resistance movements embodied in decolonization and political activism.

Michael Perez (1997) proposes that Chamorros have collectively experienced two main episodes of identity crises, each occurring during a time of rapid cultural change in a colonial situation. The first occurred during the Spanish missionization and colonization period, when disease and near genocide threatened the existence of the Chamorro people. Cultural resistance at that time took the form of adaptation to new ideas and materials while maintaining a value system that found ways to work through the imposed changes. A second identity crisis was experienced by many Chamorros during the rapid social changes of the 1970s, when a developing cultural consciousness led many Chamorros to re-discover their indigenous past. Cultural rearticulation then took the form of a reconstruction of that past based on contemporary perspectives. Alan Howard suggests that in Oceania, "continual reconstruction — process rather than structure — appears to be the norm" (1990: 267).

Jocelyn Linnekin proposes that cultural identity is a potent basis for political mobilization among peoples disenfranchised under colonial rule (1990: 150). She argues that the past is often used to validate the present, particularly to justify contemporary political relations, and this rearticulation of the past 'a sense of predisposed continuity.' Manifestations of ways contemporary Chamorros are validating their connections with the past can be seen in the community at large. Many Chamorro homes use ancient artifacts to decorate their lawns. Lusong (grinding stones) and latte (ancient stone house posts) have become part of garden decoration [fig. 4.2]. Replicas of latte are seen as decorative fences. Bus shelters as well as many public buildings have the latte shape incorporated into their construction. This community manifestation of links to an ancient past becomes fodder for activists and government officials to validate their claims to indigenous rights. In keeping with this community movement towards establishing links to the past, John Davis argues that time — the past, history, myth, precedent, and biography — is absolutely central for identity (1992: 21). To create a collective identity one would "...create customs, traditions — a history, all tending to show that the collectivity is old and encrusted with the signs of antiquity and hence has a claim to recognition by significant others, in this case, usually governments of nation-states" (Davis 1992: 21).

Since the first Spanish Catholic school was established in Guam in 1669, western education has influenced the perception of art as that of western culture, to the extent that Chamorro art forms were relegated to crafts and folkways, and, as such, considered inferior. Throughout their colonial history, Chamorros have embraced western art forms to become fine visual artists, goldsmiths, musicians and singers. The renaissance of the 1970s included a renewed interest in indigenous arts, such as carving, palm leaf weaving, traditional singing and dancing. This blend of global and local artistic expressions have value in terms of how they reflect contemporary Chamorro society. The particular focus of this study is on artists of Chamorro lineage who are using their creativity to express a connection with their indigenous roots. In the process, they respond to community perceptions of Chamorro identity that are being influenced by a growing sense of Pacific brotherhood in an ever-increasing global environment.

The artists featured here represent a cross-section of artistic forms in performance, body adornment and visual-material creation. They were selected according to their recognition in two spheres: They have been officially chosen to represent the Chamorro culture through their art at public functions or have been given public awards for their work; or their work has been accepted by their peers through buying, wearing or emulating their artistic creations. The stories related here are primarily from specific, open-structured interviews I conducted with each artist in which they told me what they thought was important in their upbringing, education, religious experiences and other relationships which influenced their art. Their stories tell how they are reaching back in time in a variety of ways, in an attempt to re-affirm their connection to their ancestral roots and to re-establish tangible links between the present and the past. I propose that their efforts significantly contribute to the national identity-building movement as Guam struggles with issues of decolonization from the United States.

The experiences of these artists exemplify steps held in common by indigenous groups as they reconstruct their racial and ethnic identity through political and cultural resistance (Perez, M. 1997: 3-4). First, one discovers a consciousness, or self-realization, of an identity apart from their colonizer. Then a search for ways to express that indigenous identity is explored in terms of cultural rearticulation. Artists employ various sources of inspiration in this rearticultion process. Political contestation informed by identity reconstruction is then explained by codification of this identity into symbols or icons that are shared by the group. Artists enter into local and global markets in varying degrees throughout the process.

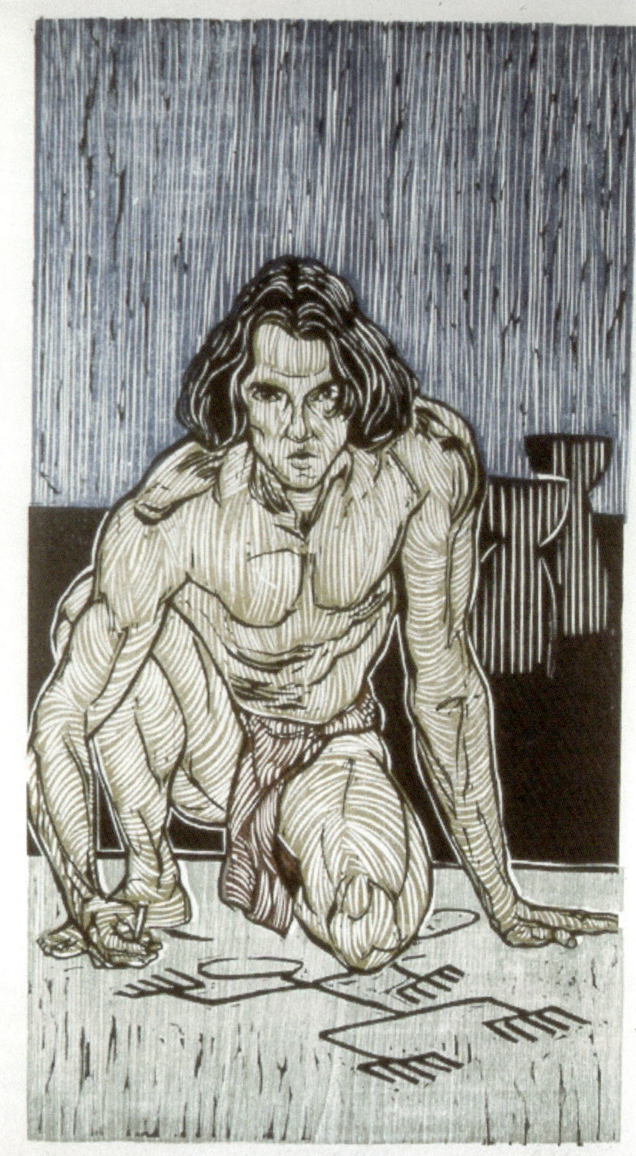

Figure 4.3. Ric Castro, *Chamorro Warrior*, woodblock print, 1994. Depicts an ancient warrior drawing the Gadao Cave figures, also known as taotao tano' figures, meaning "people of the land". Photograph courtesy of Ric Castro.

Identity-building through Artistic Expression

As modernization and neo-colonialism continue to erode cultural practices, indigenous artists use cultural rearticulation to establish tangible evidence of their connections to the past (Perez, M. 1997: 212). One of their reasons for producing and supporting indigenous art is to promote their ethnic identity. It is a strategy to transcend the dominant reference group (such as American ideals) by relocating their frames of reference and empowering themselves. They strive to perpetuate (and in some cases, return to) an indigenous worldview as opposed to the constructed world created by popular culture. "In other words, colonized groups have the potential of symbolically locating their source of strength within their ancestral identity" (Perez, M. 1997: 75). A term coined for this strategy is *symbolic ethnicity.* "Symbolic ethnicity not only facilitates cultural renewal, rearticulation, and continuity, but also provides a powerful emotive force of consciousness crucial to political contestation, organization, and mobilization that ultimately propels indigenous resistance and an identity movement" (*ibid.*: 73). Symbolic ethnicity links the ancestral past to the present. I propose that these processional steps of identity formation are embodied in the following stories told by a selection of contemporary Chamorro artists.

Ric Castro is a native of Guam, who grew up in a military family, living on U.S. bases all over the world. His family returned to live in Guam when he was a young man. Ric worked in commercial art in Guam before returning to art school and graduating from the Pennsylvania Academy of the Fine Arts in Philadelphia in 1998. He subsequently entered a career as a professor of Fine Arts at the University of Guam. Ric uses his remote family ranch in northern Guam as a touchstone to his ancient heritage. His paintings, over a period of several years, show an evolution from realistic depictions of familiar symbols of Chamorro heritage to more abstract symbolism in recent works [fig. 4.3]. His work in woodblock prints as well as oil paintings incorporated Chamorro iconographic symbols such as the Gadao cave drawings and tropical marine life. These symbols were especially evident during a period of realistic executions in oils employing ancient warrior figures along with cave drawing symbols. He explained that the use of these symbols of his Chamorro identity was important to him and gave his work a distinguishing feature among his colleagues at the art academy [fig. 4.4]. At the same time, rather than working from a narrative, in which interpretation was often needed for the viewer, the direction of his later work has become more non-representational and derived the core of its influence, not only from the visible, but also the invisible spiritual world of his Chamorro heritage. His art became loose and flowing, yet evidence of the symbols remained recognizable to anyone familiar with them. His abstract work was now more primal and emotional in its approach, which also allowed the audience to become a participant. The general public could appreciate it for its artistic qualities. Yet his Chamorro identity within the work remains there for those who know the symbols [fig. 4.5].

Joe Babauta, born and raised in Guam, became a practicing artist in the 1970s and subsequently earned an MFA degree in California. Serving as professor, then head of the Fine Arts Division at the University of Guam since the early 1990s, Joe stated that he has been and still is searching for ways to express his identity through his art. He is working toward imagery that fits his aesthetic sensibility through his oil paintings and watercolors. He does not believe that it is political or cultural identity so much as it is a search for personal identity. The images he paints are more regional than strictly Guam or Chamorro, he feels. In a 1997 exhibit at the University of Guam Isla Center for the Arts he pointed to his paintings in watercolor. The images, of brightly colored tropical plants, are those which are familiar to him, but he has treated them in terms of "isms" he learned in art school: Cubism, Expressionism, Impressionism, all flat and combined. He asks, "who am I painting for? Me? Or what I perceive an artist to be." He went on to talk about his background, being from the Chamorro culture that does not have a category for art in the Western sense of the word. He questions whether many of his cousins would appreciate or even notice art hanging on the wall. Their contemporary imagery is more focused on the prevalent symbols of Nike, Toyota, Budweiser and the like. He points to his paintings in the exhibit as being the end of a phase in his search to express his identity. Whereas his images have been nature-oriented, he now feels that this landscape is being replaced by a more commercial landscape that dominates the Guam scene today. He has begun to move into contemporary imagery — the images he sees in the particular group he interacts with — the laid-back barbecue-and-Budweiser, boom-box, earthy, pick-up truck contemporary young Chamorros [fig. 4.6]. This new imagery will speak to his questions of "what are these changes doing to me? Pacificism or McDonaldism?" Although his subject matter and points of view have changed, his search for identity through his art continues. His art now explores the symbolic ethnicity manifested in cultural connections to the land through commercial materialism evident in the lives of today's islanders.

Joe Babauta's imagery of contemporary Guam reveals the two worlds in which today's Chamorros live. The native Chamorros of Guam now comprise 43% of the 160,000 population of the island. [2] Their subsistence economy of farming and fishing changed rapidly after the U.S. military reclaimed the island from three years of Japanese occupation during World War II. Farmlands were destroyed or taken by the U.S. military, who brought in foreign skilled labor from the Philippines to reconstruct and modernize the island. Many Filipinos became residents and brought their families to live; they now comprise 28% of the population. Tourism and land investments brought a new generation of Japanese back as visitors and businessmen in the 1970s. Many Chamorros sold their land and happily joined the burgeoning economy, sending their children to U.S. universities. Many families relocated to California — the "mainstream American life" taught to

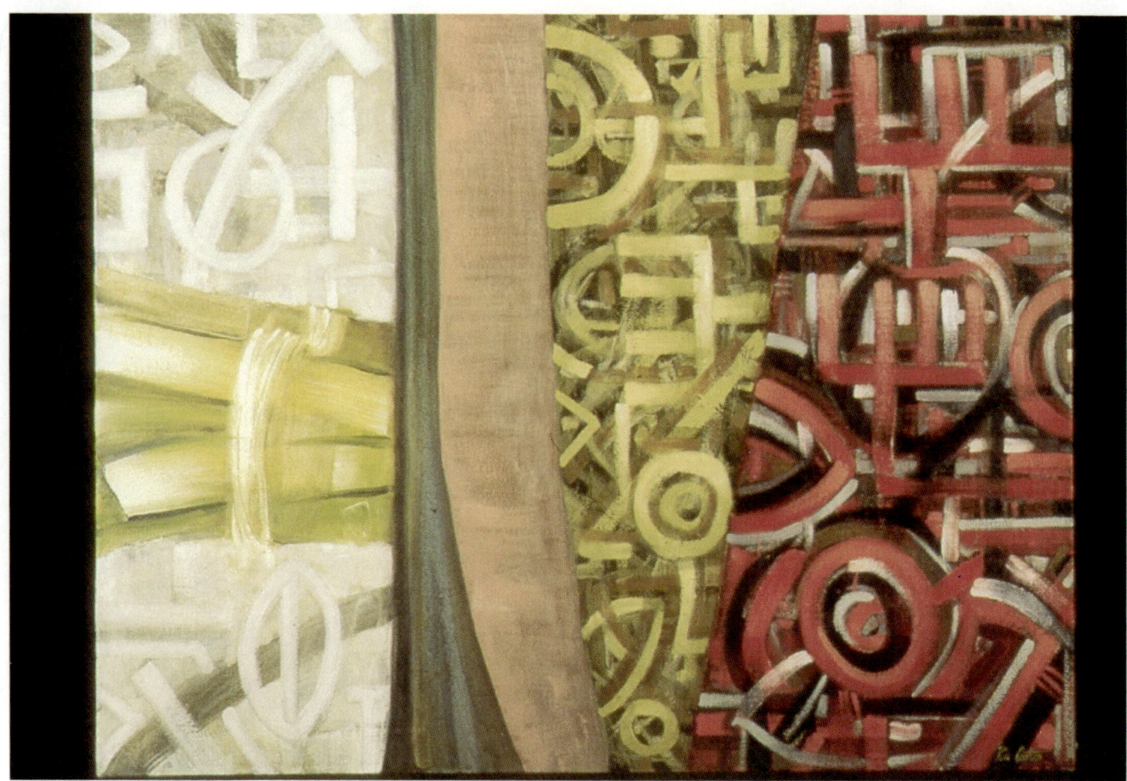

Figure 4.4. Ric Castro, Untitled, oil painting, 1997. Although the in abstract style, Gadao Cave figures are evident in the form of forked hands and feet. The circle draws from the figure but also suggests a reef fish eye. Photographs courtesy of Ric Castro.

them in school and advertised on cable TV complete with commercials from Los Angeles.

The rapid social changes over a period of just three generations have created different perspectives and tensions between age groups. While grandparents tenaciously cling to colonial neo-Chamorro traditions which shaped their lives, their adult children are torn between values and ideals they have been taught and the realities of Westernisation which they see facing their own children. This is especially problematic for the youth, who are attracted by the materialism and individualism presented by modern media, and because of the ambiguity in which they have been raised, are forced to create their own meaningful paths between tradition and modernity. "[I]f formerly culture was something the older people handed down to the younger ones in their society, now for the first time culture means that which can be sold or consumed" (Wassman 1998: 7).

The 'barbecue and Budweiser' generation described above seem to construct their identity around a matrix of global and local influences. The global concept of California street culture and consumerism, with lowriders, high riders and other popular modes of status and transportation, has become entangled with a love of vehicles that indicate connections with the land — hunting, farming and roaming the jungle (not on foot but in powerful vehicles!). They like the global status symbols such as Nike and Budweiser, and are proud to be called "CHamoru" [3] within this context. This lifestyle contrasts with the lives of those who are traditionalist in their search to reclaim connections to an indigenous past.

A product of the middle, transitional generation, Vince Reyes grew up in a family whose parents chose to prepare their children for the modern world by speaking only English in their household and embracing an American lifestyle. In speaking about his own upbringing, Vince talks about being among the generation in-between traditionalism and modernity. While in high school, he became interested in his Chamorro identity during an intergenerational oral history, storytelling project where he had the opportunity to listen to stories from his elders and to interact with them. [4] He made a concerted effort as a young adult to reconnect to the generation of his grandparents, to re-immerse himself in his native language and to rediscover his heritage through Chamorro dance. He spent several years as a member of a Chamorro dance group while continuing his education to become a schoolteacher. He began to teach Chamorro dance as a way to help his students understand their heritage. He was instrumental in developing the Cultural Arts program for his

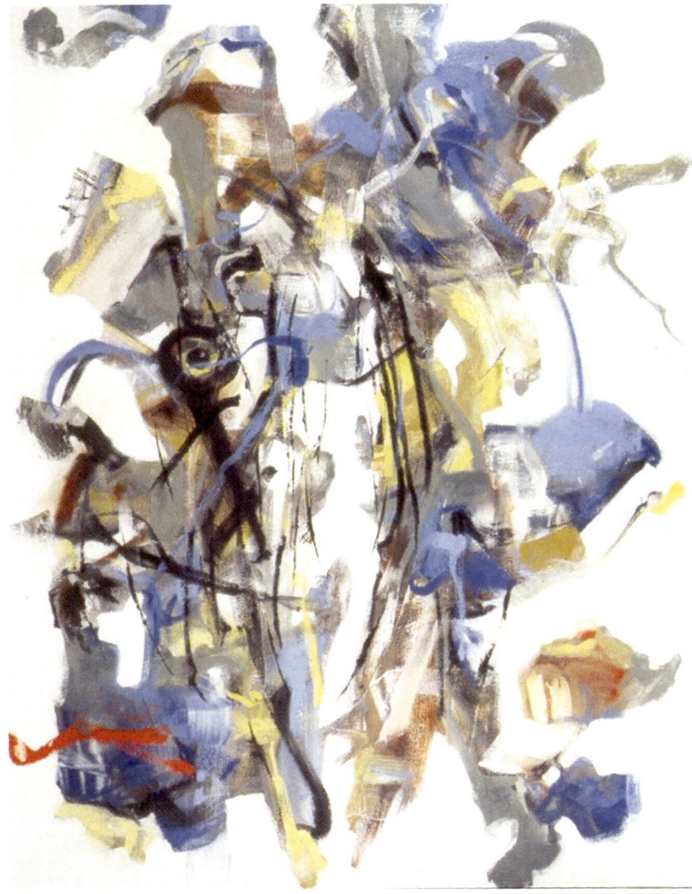

Figure 4.5. Ric Castro, Untitled, oil painting), 1998. This shows a more abstracted rendering, with a suggestion of the Gadao Cave figures in black. The circular head carries on with the fish eye form, further reinforced by a suggestion of a yellow, black and gray reef fish above the eye. Photographs courtesy of Ric Castro.

Inarajan middle school, where his eighth-grade students learn the basics of Chamorro dance. He formed a partnership with the nearby Gef Pa'go Chamorro Cultural Village whereby every semester his students go to the center to learn other cultural folkways from the elders. He now runs an after-school program for the cultural village, where his students have the opportunity to continue their cultural activities beyond their eighth-grade class. His dance group, Inetnon Gef Pa'go, has garnered local and international awards and they have represented Guam for the Guam Visitors Bureau in off-island visitor markets. His personal challenge has been to help the next generation reconnect to their heritage through the activities of his dance group. Vince's use of modern marketing methods to entice students to participate is detailed elsewhere in this volume.

These and the following case studies show that ethnic symbolism is manifested through various artistic forms of expression that attempt to link Chamorro heritage to contemporary lifestyles. Each artist tells of experiencing a self-conscious awareness of their indigenous identity followed by artistic efforts to link their contemporary world to their heritage. Contemporary Chamorro artists are creating artistic connections to their indigenous identity in ways that respond to community issues and public awareness. Their sources of inspiration for these cultural rearticulations are revealed in the following stories.

Sources of Inspiration

Projects in archaeology, historical document research and Chamorro cultural programs in schools and other institutions have provided initial inspiration for artists. They have then sought further inspiration in more spiritual ways, such as observing nature and communing with the spirits in ancient jungle sites. Artifacts themselves in some cases became sources of inspiration as well as vessels of spiritual essence. Influences from other Pacific islands have become more prevalent with increased opportunities for cultural exchange. All of these influences have fueled the cultural rearticulation movement and inspired artistic development.

Public awareness of ancient Chamorro burials was created in the course of increased tourism development and large-scale construction projects that began in the 1970s in Guam. Archaeological monitoring and salvage operations during construction excavations highlighted the discovery of ancient burials and other artifacts, which publicly informed an ancient Chamorro past. [5] Some artists were influenced by artifacts made public from such excavations. Others were more directly involved in archaeological work, which inspired their artistic creations.

Alejandro (Al) Lizama came from a very traditional family, deeply connected to the land through ancestry, language and cultural practices. Al became interested in ancient Chamorro society when he studied anthropology with an emphasis in archaeology at the University of Guam. His fieldwork studies led him to work with archaeologist Fred Reinman, surveying Guam's major archaeological sites for inclusion in the Guam and National Register of Historic Places. [6] He subsequently worked for the Department of Parks and Recreation Historic Resources Division since the late 1970s when archaeological excavations of Ypao Beach Park were being conducted. His job was to monitor this and other archaeological projects. Being artistically inclined, he began to make pen and ink drawings based on artifacts unearthed in various projects. He used specific artifacts as inspiration on which to build his perception of ancient Chamorro society. He called on his artist friend, David Sablan, to make drawings at excavation sites as well, which inspired David to begin

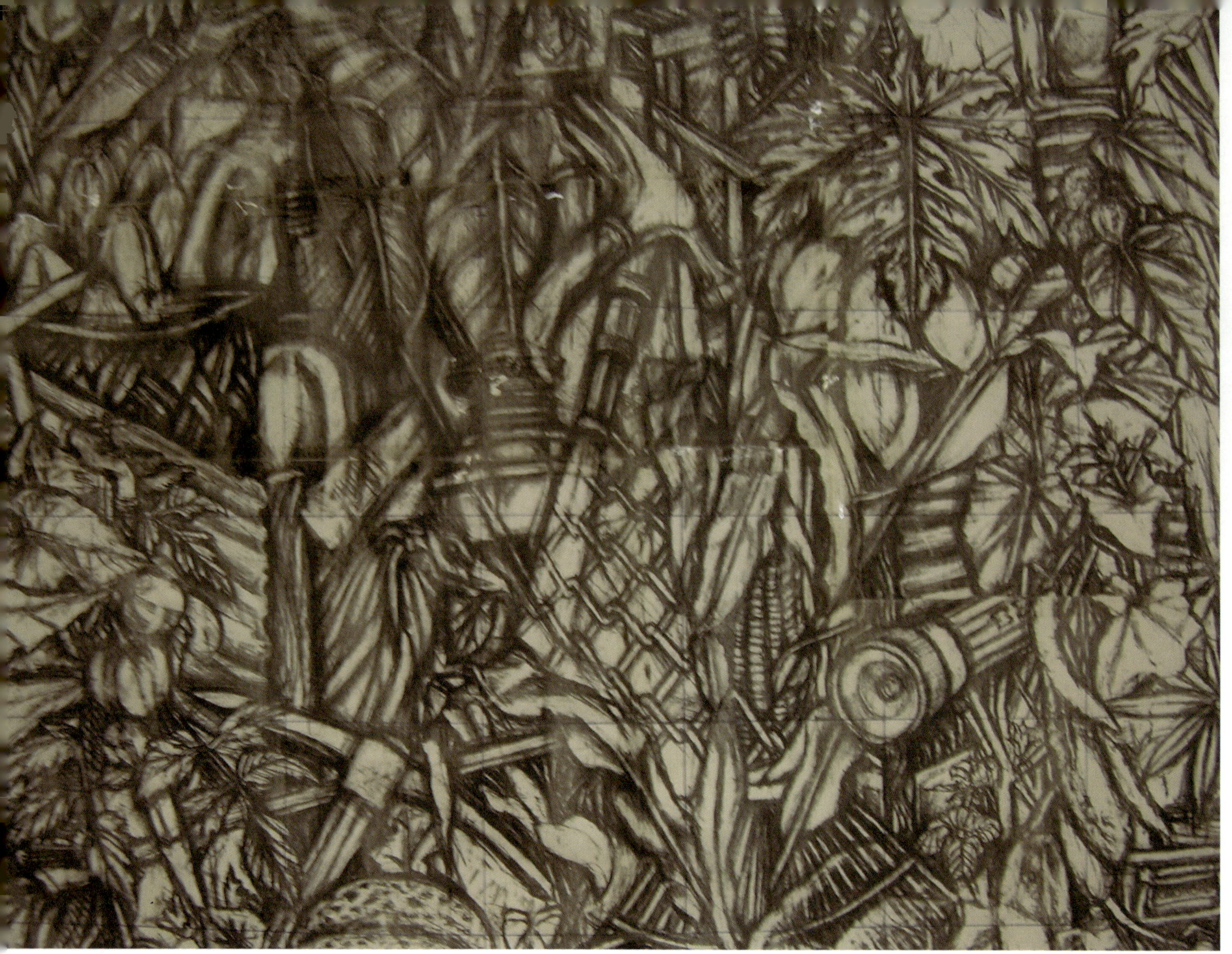

Figure 4.6. Jose Babauta, Detail of *Lancho* drawing, c. 2006. This work includes contemporary commercial icons prevalent in Guam society today together with symbols of connections to the land, through the family farm, called "lancho". Photograph by Judy Flores courtesy of Jose Babauta, 2009.

painting his concept of ancient Chamorro society. [7] Both of these artists' works show detailed interpretations of their ancient heritage. Their depictions of ancient latte houses, ways of preparing food, and flora and fauna of the ancient period have influenced successive artists.

Other artists began by researching historical documents and then turned to practical application of that knowledge to re-create their art forms. Canoe Carver Rob Limtiaco began his study of ancient Chamorro canoes by researching early accounts and drawings. He soon became frustrated with inadequate historical descriptions and turned to more practical methods of reconstructing the Chamorro canoe. He sought help from the Guam Council on the Arts & Humanities Agency who provided assistance for him to apprentice under Segundo Blas, a Chamorro woodcarver who had learned to build canoes in Saipan and Palau in his youth. That apprenticeship produced a fifteen-foot outrigger sailing canoe that was put on display in the Guam Museum. Wanting to learn more, Rob turned to the Caroline island of Polowat for answers. This remote atoll, 400-miles south of Guam, still retains its ancient canoe and navigation traditions. Rob and fellow apprentice Gary Guerrero spent more than a year on Polowat, learning to build an ocean-going canoe from master canoe builder and navigator Tawa Tilimwar [fig. 4.7]. They returned to Guam and shared their knowledge through school presentations and further canoe-building projects (Celes 1995: 38-45). [8]

Leonard Iriarte was inspired by other Pacific indigenous artists he encountered at the South Pacific Arts Festival in 1976. [9] Raised in the United States, his Chamorro parents spoke only English to him and only

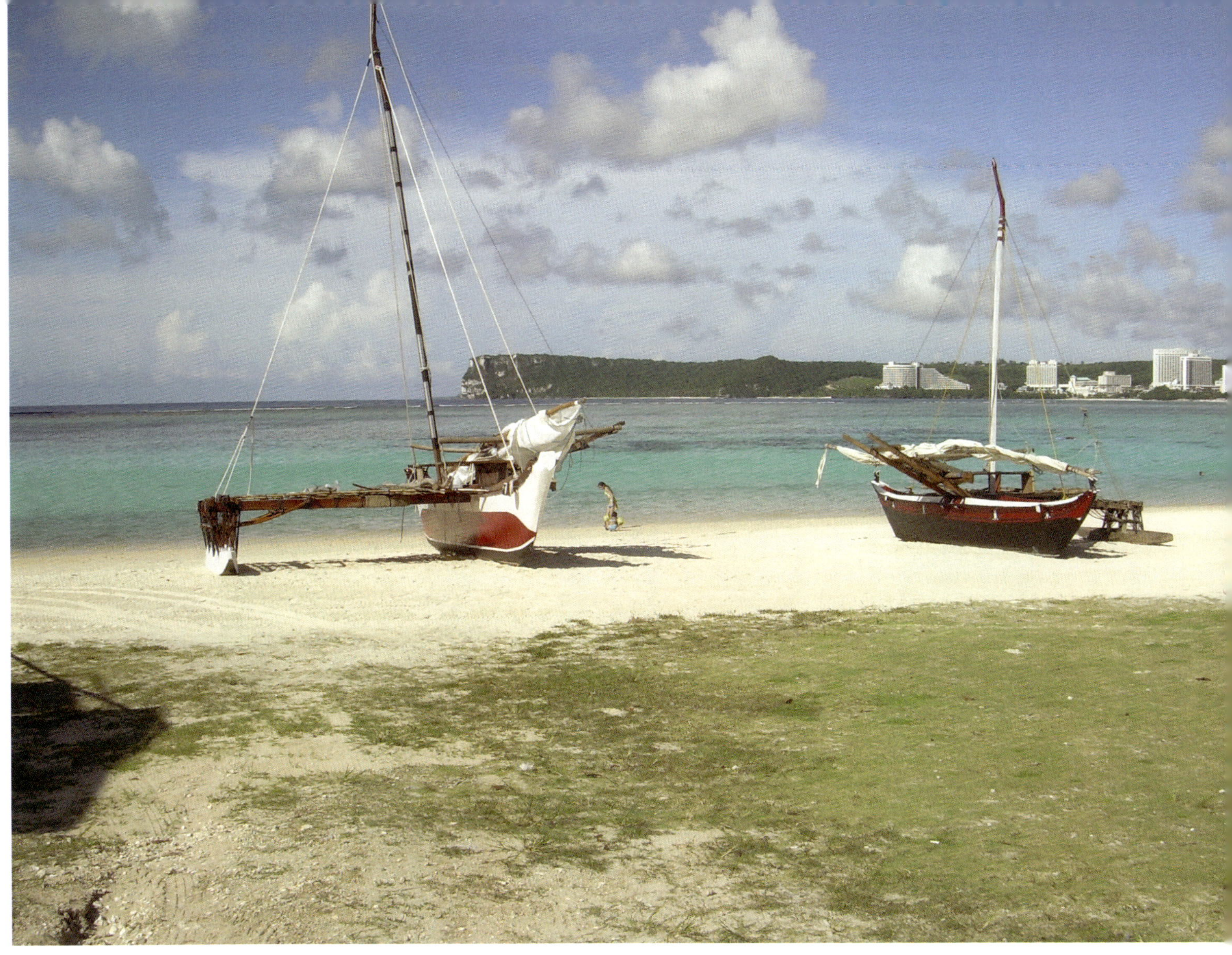

Figure 4.7. Canoes "Quest" and "Saina" carved by members of the TASI organization in the style Rob Limtiaco learned from Polowat master canoe builder Tawa Tilimwar. Photograph by Judy Flores at the Guam Micronesia Island Fair, 2008.

spoke their native tongue to each other. Leonard said he felt left out, and longed to speak his language. He returned to Guam as a teenager and in 1976 traveled with his family band and a contemporary Guam dance group to represent Guam at the South Pacific Arts Festival in New Zealand. He sensed immediately that the Guam group did not fit with the other Pacific islanders who presented indigenous art forms. He vowed that he must learn about his indigenous heritage so that he and fellow Chamorro artists could proudly present indigenous art. Through research and oral history interviews he began to learn about his ancient past. He created replicas of indigenous artifacts and pen-and-ink drawings of ancient lifestyles. He later began to retrieve ancient words that were being lost from the language and incorporated pre-Spanish words into chants. His chant group, Fanlalaihan, has a research team who study the entomology of pre-Spanish words to make ancient connections, which the chant group uses to compose chants. [10]

The natural and spiritual environment served as inspiration for other artists. In the 1990s Joe Guerrero began exploring the properties of natural materials such as wood, stone, shell, bone, and afok (quicklime) to create symbols of Chamorro culture. The lime-impressed designs he created combined techniques similar to those used in ancient lime-impressed pottery. He said that he didn't know about the ancient pottery when he incised designs in ifil (*Intsia bajuga*, an indigenous wood) and filled in the incisions with quicklime. He was looking more at the aesthetic qualities of white lime against dark wood. Others who saw his creations told him of the 'lime-impressed' term used to describe the ancient pottery, so he began to use the term to describe his pieces. He continued to refine his

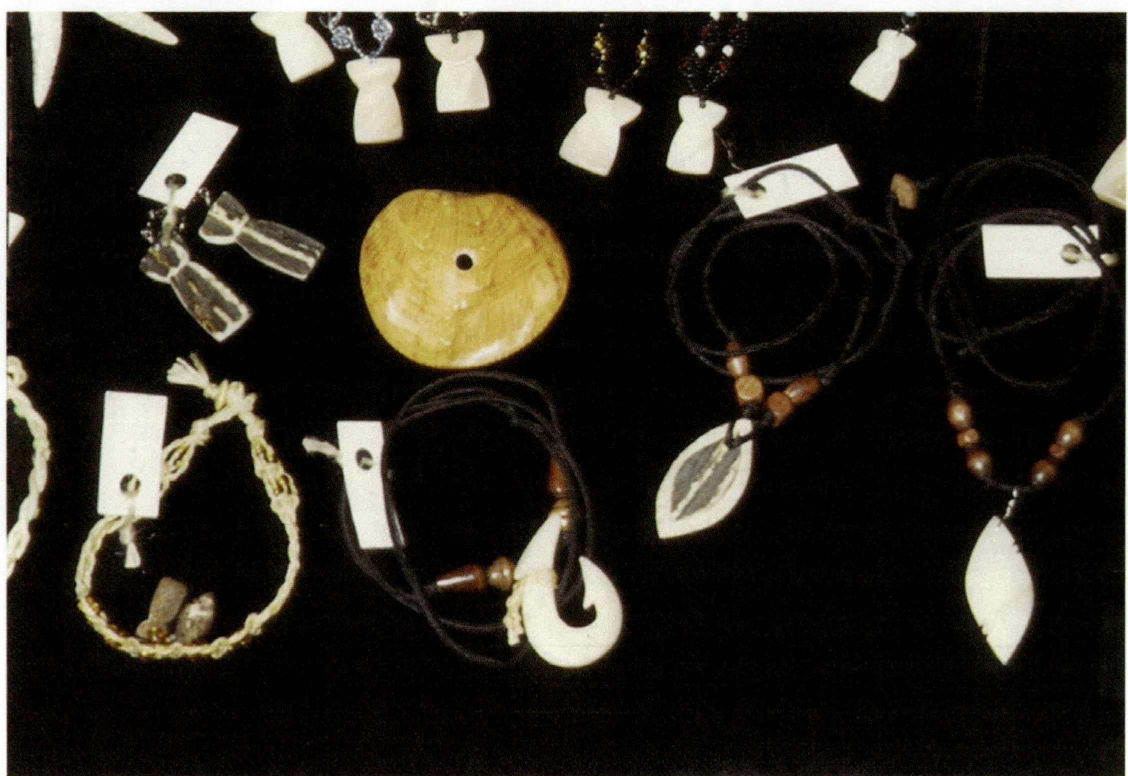

Figure 4.8. Examples of *Spondylus* shell and contemporary jewelry based on ancient artifacts, by Jill Benavente. Photograph by Judy Flores, 1998.

methods of working in natural materials to create symbols based on the latte, fishhooks, cave drawings and other Chamorro artifacts that he made into jewelry and other ornamental pieces. In some instances he wrote poems and chants that ascribed special ancient associations to specific pieces, which he framed and displayed next to his art pieces.

Jewelry maker and carver Frank "Ko" San Nicolas came from a traditional family who held strong beliefs in the ancestral spirits, called taotaomo'na (the first people). Ko's first artwork was tattoo on his own body, which he started when he was nine years old. His schoolmates encouraged these first crude tattoos. By the time he was thirteen, he was making more sophisticated, elaborate tattoos. He describes his tattooed body as a story of his life experiences, from the crude tattoos of a young boy to traditional icons of his Chamorro heritage. One example is the galaide (canoe) design he wears. "This canoe can take me where I want to go in life, and also it reminds me that I must keep paddling to get anywhere." [11]

Shapes created by the ancestors and the materials they used have influenced and inspired many artists. Chamorro jewelry makers have incorporated the use of *Spondylus* shell into their items of adornment [fig. 4.8]. As rare today as it was in ancient times [12], contemporary artists value this orange spiny oyster shell both for its color and for its association with a noble past. The crescent-shaped, highly polished giant clamshell neckpiece called senahi (crescent moon) has also become a culturally-significant symbol of Chamorro identity. Based on rare pieces found in caves and ancient burials, the replicas have become expensive, fine art pieces that testify to the skill of the maker.

Cultural exchanges with other Pacific islands have influenced many of Guam's indigenous artists. Ko San Nicolas and Joe Guerrero are among many artists who have participated in the Festival of Pacific Arts since 1992, proudly representing Guam with their artistic creations of stone, bone, shell and wood; etched, carved, and inlaid with culturally significant symbols of Chamorro identity. Artists who have attended these and other cultural exchanges return home with a renewed awareness of indigenous identity as well as creative ideas that they apply to their own work.

Symbols of Chamorro identity appear in contemporary tattoo designs worn particularly as dance adornment by some groups and increasingly as permanent body art among the general island population. Maria Yatar McDonald studied tattoo art internationally in the 1970s and 1980s and is highly respected in international circles for her knowledge. She returned home in the late 1980s and began creating designs based on Chamorro ancient icons. Her documentation of tattoo art on the bodies of elder Micronesians led her to believe that Chamorros, as geographically situated in Micronesia, must have practiced tattoo at some point in their history. The fact that there is no known historical documentation of Chamorro tattoo practice has not discouraged her or others from creating and using tattoo in their contemporary art.

Polynesian movements, sounds and instrumentation have been prevalent in the reconstruction of Chamorro dance, due to influences from Hawaiians (and their families) who came to work for the United States Naval civil service after World War II. The romanticization of Hawaiian hula by Hollywood (movies) was further impressed on the Chamorro community when Guam hotels brought in and employed Polynesian dance groups in the 1970s. Almost all current Chamorro dance leaders received their first formal cultural dance training in Polynesian dance. The type and amount of appropriation of hula elements is a matter of continuing debate among dance leaders, Chamorro arts advocates, practitioners, and government officials who support and promote cultural activities. Vince Reyes, elsewhere in this book, analyzes the philosophies of key players in this movement and positions himself among the new generation of searchers for particular Chamorro sounds and movements.

In some cases, the imitation of Polynesian styles has been indirect and on a subconscious level. I observed Ko San Nicolas working on a woodcarving during the Festival of Pacific Arts in Samoa (1996). The swirling designs with anthropomorphic figures looked very much to me like a Maori design. I asked Ko where he got his inspiration for the piece, commenting on its similarity to Maori art. He launched into a detailed explanation of the meaning of the various designs, which he related to the Chamorro legend of Chief Gadao. He also added that he had drawn the design for the carving before he came to the Festival. When asked about his experiences at the Festival, Ko said, "It purified me, and made me want to do more to advance the Chamorro culture. I feel like the spirits helped me get there, and they also answered me there. I felt like I was home." [13]

We can see how cultural exchanges such as the Festival of Pacific Arts have influenced Chamorro artists in a variety of ways. Such cultural interaction has created a sense of cultural consciousness whereby Chamorros began to perceive themselves as being Pacific islanders. This in itself is a big step from American colonial perceptions of Guam as an extension of the United States. A significant minority has accepted that Chamorros are geographically Micronesian and are beginning to look towards their Carolinian neighbors to explore artistic expression. This is very evident in the dress and movements of Leonard's chant group. But it seems that most are using their cultural exchange inspirations to develop a Chamorro identity based on a more pan-Pacific model.

Spiritual Beliefs and Influences

Many artists have turned to the ancient spirits for inspiration. Chamorro dance master Frank Rabon often takes group members to jungle latte sites to create chants. Some artists have had a life-long association with the ancient spirits, while for others it has been a recent experience. Chamorro ancient spirits are usually referred to as the taotaomo'na. The jungle is their domain, especially ancient latte sites and the Nunu (Banyan) tree. If their sites are disrespected or disturbed, the violator is often afflicted with an illness (Onedera 1994: 7-13). Sometimes an insulted taotaomo'na will follow the trespasser home to inflict emmok (damage in kind).

Ko told a story of his association with the taotaomo'na since he was a child, wherein his family home became haunted by three young taotaomo'na and required the intervention of a traditional suruhana (healer) to make them leave. [14] "Not all taotaomo'na are bad. Some are good, and they have helped me many times," Ko stated. His favorite pastime is to wear his sadi' (loincloth) and walk in the jungle, communing with the spirits. He has seen the taotaomo'na many times. [15] When he is in the jungle, he is often "in a spiritual world," where, in the presence of a spirit, the climate will become very cold."[16] He stated that he has often taken people who are afflicted with a malady — either spiritual or physical — into the jungle overnight, called out for the spirits' help, and cured their affliction.

For his work in helping such afflicted people, the good taotaomo'na will often reward Ko with artifacts. They may tell him where to look nearby, or he may open his hand and find an item there. Ko says he has always been gifted with the ability to see and commune with the taotaomo'na, and also gifted in that he can sense if a slingstone, a fishhook, or other artifact is nearby in the jungle. More often, the spirits help him with successful fishing expeditions or abundant crab hunting. He collects artifacts in disturbed sites, where land has been cleared or trees uprooted. When he finds such an artifact, he will begin a prayer, or chant, with "Saina, kao sina...," or "Elder one, can I . . . keep this piece safely for you so that I may use it to teach others..." Several other artists and interviewees have spoken of their chanting or asking the spirits to help them find artifacts, and that they have received such help. In other words, the ancestors retained a close association with the artifacts they made, and in some cases the object embodied or attracted that spirit.

Belief in taotaomo'na continues to be very strong, as can be seen in the stories told by these artists. Other artists and community members show varying degrees of respect for the taotaomo'na, ranging from seeking guidance to begging forgiveness for a transgression, to merely acknowledging and respecting possible spiritual locations. In my opinion, the artists reflect the varying attitudes of the general Chamorro community regarding spiritual intercession in human activity.

Contemporary Chamorro artists are continuously reconstituting fragments from the past in their efforts to create identity symbols, which have meaning in the present. For what audience or consumer is this art being produced? I have shown examples of what I believe are attempts by indigenous Chamorro artists to create a distinct space for themselves (and their fellow Chamorros) within an increasingly global, homogenized world. This implies that they are creating art for their own community consumption — "inwardly directed arts — that are made for, appreciated, and used by peoples within their own part-society..."[T]hese arts have important functions in maintaining ethnic identity and social structure, and in didactically instilling the important values in group members" (Graburn 1976: 4-5). These artists sell their work in various, limited ways such as in crafts fairs, in small shops or galleries and cultural festivals. Their primary audience seems to be members of their own island community. At the same time, they are presenting their art forms to the external, dominant world as symbols of their internal and external boundaries.

The life stories told by this sampling of contemporary Chamorro artists point to processional steps in the identity-formation process proposed by Michael Perez (Perez, M 1997: 304). First, one discovers a consciousness, or self-realization, of an identity apart from their colonizer. Then, a search for ways to express that indigenous identity is explored in terms of cultural rearticulation. Various sources of inspiration are employed by artists in this rearticulation process.

Perez goes on to describe the subsequent step of political contestation informed by identity reconstruction, which is then explained by codification of this identity into symbols or icons that are shared by the group. In my observations, political contestation is manifested in varied degrees and broad terms, ranging from individual use of culturally significant symbols to declare an indigenous heritage separate from the colonizer, to group organization of nation building, decolonization activities. In any case, indigenous artists have played an important role in the development of culturally significant symbols that become accepted and used by the general public or nation-building groups to help them navigate indigenous agendas in the modern world.

According to Perez, artists enter into local and global markets in varying degrees throughout the process. This was noted briefly in the above life stories of Chamorro artists. As their artistic expression gained local support, both dancers and visual artists began to seek external audiences for their artistic productions. Travel has always been a valuable commodity, especially for remote islands such as Guam, where the price of airfare is a significant investment. The government began to support cultural exchange travel for Guam's artists with the 1976 South Pacific Arts Festival held in New Zealand. Since that time, the Government of Guam has sent delegations of up to 100 artists to participate in the Festival of Pacific Arts. In order to qualify as a member of the delegation, individual artists, dance and music groups were required to be consistently active in community arts events at home. Auditions, combined with informal evaluations of artists' presentations at local festivals determined their selection as a delegate. [17] Through this process, Guam's best and most active artists traveled and were exposed to other cultures across the Pacific. In the late 1980s and early 1990s, the government assisted the Chamorro communities in California to organize festivals, to which Guam groups were sent as participants. Several artists began to raise funds and seek sponsors for their own tours. Traditional Dance Master Frank Rabon and members of Pa'a Taotao Tano linked up with international festival tours in Europe and traveled the European festival tour for five weeks in 2001. Paraisu Dance Group led by Tom Concepcion has represented Guam at Austronesian Youth festivals in Taiwan for several years. Vince Reyes uses travel as one of the enticements for his dancers to join his middle school dance class and then to strive to reach the level of skill required to join the traveling group, Inetnon Gef Pa'go. The Guam Visitor's Bureau selects dancers and musicians through an annual audition whereby those selected travel to visitor markets in Asia, primarily in Japan, to provide cultural presentations to entice audiences to visit Guam. These travel opportunities allowed them to present their symbolic icons to a more commercial audience.

Among visual artists, Ben Del Rosario has become known as one of the most skilled creators of the senahi

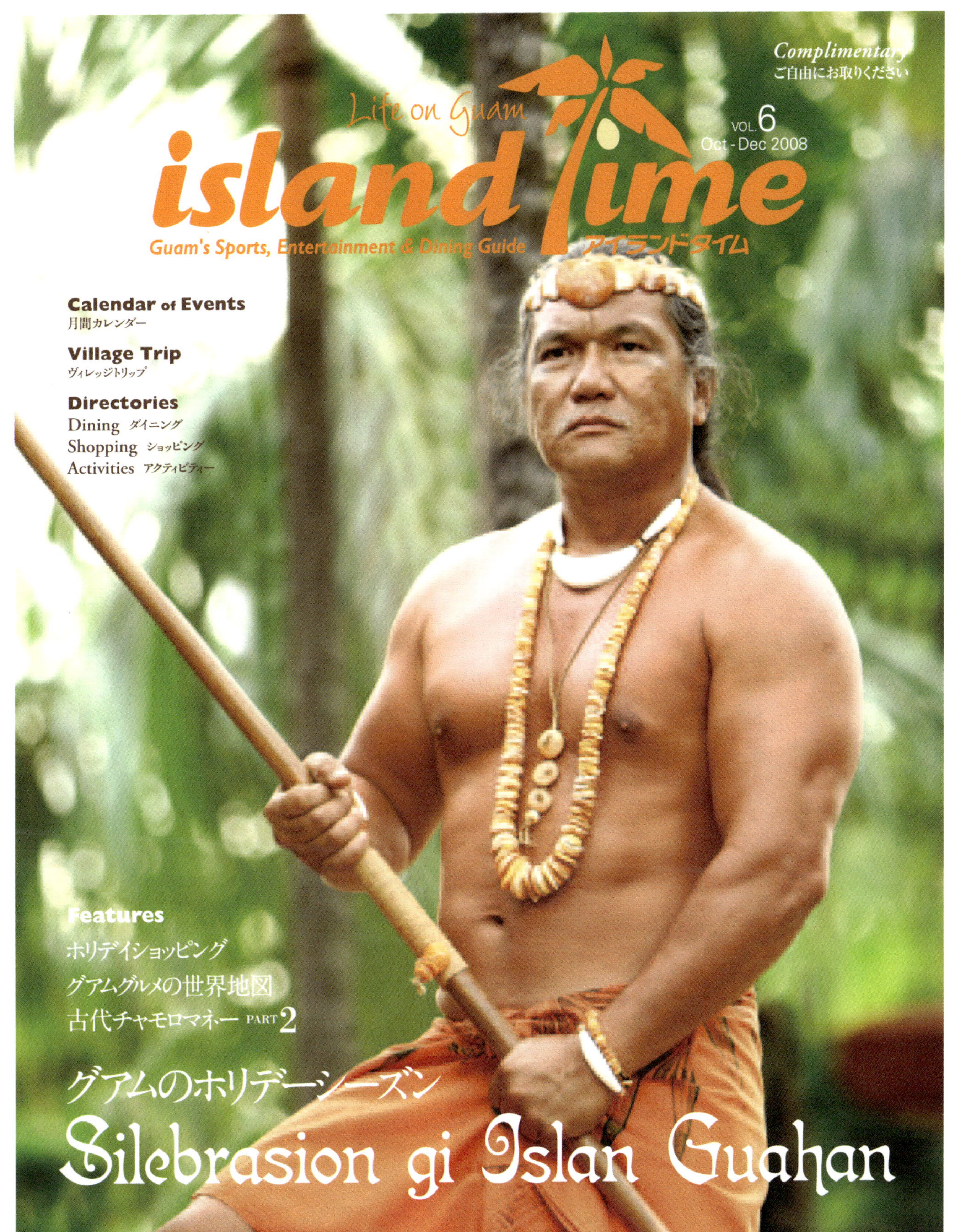

Figure 4.9. Ben Del Rosario (Senahi) wearing his senahi carvings from giant clam shell and Spondylus jewelry. Photograph courtesy of Island Time magazine, Front Cover Vol. 6 (Oct-Dec 2008), Guam.

[fig. 4.9], a replica of an ancient artifact made of giant clam shell noted earlier. He has consistently exhibited exceptional skill in shaping, polishing, and then drilling through each end of this dense, brittle material without breaking or chipping it in the process. His work commands hundreds of dollars in today's market. Senahi have become a symbol of Chamorro identity, worn by local government officials as well as Chamorros and others who have come to appreciate the heritage embodied in the piece and the skill of the maker. Jill Benavente is another indigenous artist who skillfully creates senahi and other culturally significant jewelry at her gift shop in Guam. The Rosario family helped their sons develop several culturally-significant designs to market as stickers and decals as a start of their Che'lu business in the early 1990s. Their shop at the Hagatna Chamorro Village is well-known as a source of Chamorro art and icons.

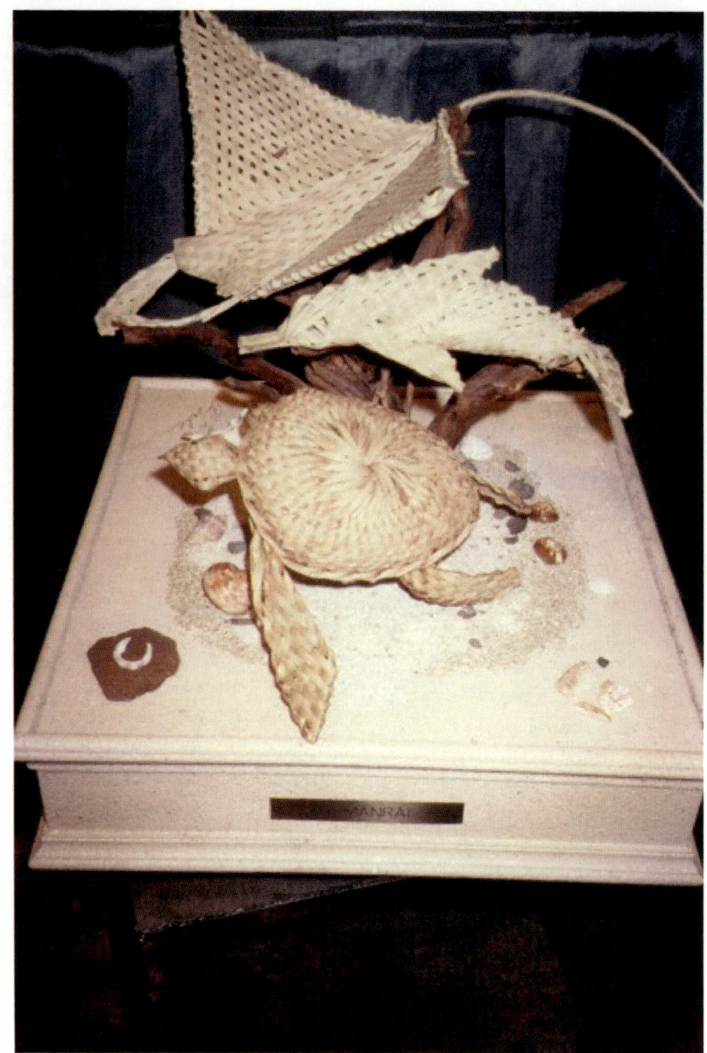

Figure 4.10. Philip Sablan, *Galaide, Tuninos yan Haggan* (Canoe, Marlin and Turtle), woven coconut leaf sculpture. Photograph by Judy Flores, 1999.

Philip Sablan was among a small group of artists who demonstrated their artistic skills at a space in DFS, Inc., in the heart of the Tumon tourist district. Philip learned coconut leaf weaving from master weaver Lucia Torres. He then elaborated upon these skills and wove three-dimensional sculptural forms in coconut leaf. Delicately woven coconut crabs, fruit bats, turtles and other endemic animal forms are displayed in acrylic exhibit cases [fig. 4.10]; or larger pieces are hung from the ceiling. Philip calls himself the "Monster Weaver." He also began to work in local stone, along with artist Rick Guerrero, who has perfected his carving skills in stone, coral and sometimes wood. These artists are seeking recognition in the global market by exhibiting their work in Hawaii, the mainland United States and in other, larger Pacific markets. They were among the more than twenty Guam artists who demonstrated and exhibited in the Guam booth at the Festival of Pacific Arts in Palau (2004). The quality of their work compared well with that of other Pacific island artists, and they received a lot of interest at this event, demonstrated by numerous sales.

The above examples indicate that a significant number of artists are attempting to pursue both local and global markets as a means to sustain themselves. There are many others who have been influenced by these pioneers and are now beginning to exhibit at local art festivals. The increasing number of indigenous artists attests to the growing movement of cultural rearticulation among contemporary Chamorro artists. Most are currently creating their art for a sense of personal recognition, group identity and as an opportunity to promote their culture through travel. I propose that an increasing number of indigenous artists will continue building on symbols that resonate with the community as being culturally significant.

The Power of Symbolism

"The essence of symbolism lies in the recognition of one thing as standing for (re-presenting) another, the relation between them normally being that of concrete to abstract, particular to general" (Firth, R. 1973: 15). The symbols noted above represent different levels of meaning to various segments of the Chamorro community. They are also used in different ways to convey specific meanings in particular situations. In other words, it is not their particular nature but their relationships that account for their selection as symbols. [18] Activists have attributed special status to the senahi neckpiece, equating it with the warrior or Chamorri class from ancient times. The latte has been appropriated as a symbol of Chamorro identity on many levels. Government agencies have used this symbol to signify ties to ancient roots. For example, a replica of a giant latte was erected on the grounds of the Crafts Village at the 1996 Festival of Pacific Arts in Samoa. The Guam international airport (both the old and new buildings) has latte-support motifs incorporated into their architecture. Latte designs and taotaotano' figures incorporated into T-shirt logos can be read on various levels. Dance group members take pride in wearing their T-shirts, which proclaim their membership in a particular group. Tourists might buy a similar T-shirt as a souvenir of their visit to Guam.

Emerging symbols of Chamorro identity are used by various segments of the community to fit multiple agendas. For some people it may be a nostalgic reaction to globalization or perhaps a strategy that provides symbolic benefits without jeopardizing an urban or modern condition (Cruces and Rada 1992: 77). Such may be the case with Chamorro youth who wear ancient symbols and dance ancient dances. This may also apply on another level to the Nike and Budweiser generation who are proud to be called Chamoru on their own terms, as long as they do not have to give up their boom boxes and pick-up trucks. Middle-class professionals who identify with their colonial heritage subscribe to symbols of Chamorro identity on a different level. To them, Spanish-era Chamorro gold jewelry is just as much a part of their heritage as is the latte and the taotaotano' cave figures. The two worlds — global and traditional — occupied by contemporary Chamorros have produced multiple identities whose members respond to symbols of ancient roots on various levels. Artists and activists, however, seem to be the driving force behind the creation of a cultural consciousness that acknowledges these symbols of Chamorro identity.

In some cases, contemporary Chamorro artists are selectively ignoring their colonial heritage in their attempts to strengthen links to their ancient past. Spanish-era dances and songs are being minimized while ancient period dance interpretations continue to proliferate. Chants are formulated with an attempt to use only pre-contact Chamorro words. This seems to be prevalent in decolonization movements, most likely as an act of cultural resistance against the colonizing power. By refusing to acknowledge the changes imposed by the colonizer, the links to a pre-colonial past can be reconstructed more thoroughly. However, while the colonized are engaged in actions of cultural resistance, they are at the same time reconstructing an ancient past in innovative ways that make that past meaningful in the present. Innovation and cultural change in the present continue while reconstructions of the past attempt to fix that era in unchanging timelessness.

Indigenous reconstruction of the past has been proclaimed by some observers as a myth, something made-up or not real. How then, can these historical reconstructions be authenticated, and by whom? I suggest that the authenticity of artistic reconstructions is based upon community acceptance, emulation and use of the art forms by the community, a concept proposed by Robert Layton (1991). Historical reconstructions are related to these concepts, but so far we have only seen the visual, tangible artistic symbols of that reconstruction. We need to examine culture as lived in contemporary daily life in order to see how the arts fit into the picture.

Official, ritualistic representations of Chamorro culture are exhibited in the promotion of Chamorro art forms at official government functions and in tourist promotions. Welcoming chants are heard in official Chamorro language greetings in speeches and formal events and in associated lavish food presentations. Activists and government officials employ symbolic ornamentation and phraseology in talks on decolonization with each other and with national governments, particularly in presentations to the United States Congress and the United Nations. Simultaneously, people's daily lives are regulated by kinship and other relationships, manifested in how many funerals one must attend over a weekend and in how many rosaries one is obligated to participate, or by who is getting married or baptising a child. All of these events involve various degrees of social obligations along with how much chenchule' (reciprocal money gift) is required at each event. Increasingly, Chamorro dance will take place, perhaps at a wedding or baptism, as a presentation by a dance group that is watched as entertainment by guests. Life crisis events are attended by Chamorros from all levels of society. Some will wear Chamorro stone, bone, or shell jewelry; others will wear gold bracelets, necklaces and earrings based on classic Spanish-era designs. Many will wear international name brand clothing and jewelry. Leisure time is spent in very Americanized ways. Most Chamorro teen-agers spend their spare time in beach barbecues, shopping, watching American videos, movies or television. In the daily westernized world of the modern Chamorro, has cultural identity become something that one puts on like a piece of culturally significant jewelry, then puts away until the next occasion where one's heritage is displayed? What is Chamorro identity as practiced today?

I believe that all of these cultural practices represent contemporary Chamorro society. There seems to be a dual existence in the official conventions and the daily life activities of the people. A contrast is made between "culture as a way of life as 'simply living' and culture as a reified symbol of a way of life, between tradition as inheritance from the ancestors and tradition as the manipulative rhetoric of contemporary politicians" (Jolly 1992: 49). Traditional dance master Frank Rabon voices his concern that culture should not be something put on and then laid aside at one's convenience. [19] Cultural Arts teacher Vince Reyes (see Reyes this volume) states that one of his goals for his dance group is that the members move from the concept of dancing as performance to the idea that cultural dance is an intrinsic part of life.

The official cultural symbols are not being practiced on a daily basis by the Chamorro community at large. They are not contradictory, however. The ritualistic and symbolic is performed on one official, ritualistic level and the pragmatic takes place on another, daily level. However, they co-exist and are equal aspects of the same Chamorro culture. When asked to give examples of their culture, most Chamorros would use examples from the official cultural model — the art forms, the food presentations and the language usage. They are using symbolic action to describe their culture. By their own admission, Chamorros generally accept official versions of their culture. To them it is no less real than their daily life practices. It is also recognized and readily acknowledged that today's official rituals were not practiced before the 1980s. Does this make reconstructed indigenous art less authentic? The reconstruction of ancient Chamorro chants and dances continue to be a subject of passionate discussion among practitioners

In an Intergenerational Conference on Chamoru Language and Culture panel discussion in 1999, a group of Chamorro singer/songwriters and dance masters voiced their thoughts about these rearticulations. Dance instructor Benjie Santiago said, "I told my Natibu Dance members that we are going to advance our culture by taking the old times and the new times and using them together. This is how we advance our culture." [20] Musician songwriter Joe Peredo added,

> We here must carry the culture forward. Those things we borrow and make our own we must 'distinguish' because we see what we like and take it and make it Chamorro. Let's keep what we want and make it Chamorro. I write original Chamorro songs. I want to pass those on to future generations. If you hear a little Spanish, Chamorros are singing it, so it is Chamorro. We must pick up pieces from our heritage. [21]

Church choir director and songwriter Bill Paulino provided a summarizing statement, "Everything that comes from within is yours and part of your culture." [22] Frank Rabon (2001: 18) explains his re-creation of ancient Chamorro dance as follows:

> This segment depicting the pre-contact period of our people exists only in the hearts of some of the Chamorro people. I am not trying to bring back thousands of years of lost traditions; I am only creating an awareness to show that we existed thousands of years before colonization occurred. There are people who choose not to acknowledge their ancient heritage. I choose to embrace it and teach younger generations to be proud of our ancestors, where we came from, and who we are now. I do not feel that we are authenticating lost traditions, but instead are re-creating traditions through researched concepts.

Margaret Jolly questions whether anyone, anywhere, anytime is simply living their culture without an awareness of cultural alternatives (1992: 58). She challenges the notion that cultural unselfconsciousness equates with authenticity and by implication, self-consciousness with inauthenticity. [23] Chamorros seem to generally accept both historical realities and artistic reconstructions of their culture. Both have significant cultural meaning for them in their contemporary lives. If Chamorros accept certain contemporary versions of their past as authentic, do others have a right to denigrate it as myth?

The artists who have spoken through these pages point to the importance of indigenous identity on many levels and in many genres. They have incorporated connections to their ancient roots and to their homeland that proclaim their place in the modern world. They are using symbols that hark back to an indigenous past that has been accepted by their own Chamorro community. Contemporary versions of their past are accepted despite their recent beginnings, because they have become culturally-significant.

Conclusion

Contemporary Chamorro artistic creations are based on a reality created by the socio/cultural matrix of Chamorro life today. No other ethnic group can legitimately lay claim to latte stones, taotaotano' rock art or senahi neckpieces, nor can these symbols evoke emotive responses from any other social group except Chamorros. These are symbols from an indigenous past that are finding significant cultural meaning in the present as a means of identity formation.

The processional steps experienced by contemporary Chamorro artists resonate with that of other indigenous people who have been marginalized by colonial powers; their beliefs, folkways and arts devalued or obliterated. A conscious awakening to an indigenous past inspired artists to create culturally significant art that has resonated with the community. Artists are engaging in cultural rearticulation to establish their indigenous identity with their Pacific brothers and sisters. They are using their art as a means of reflecting a social situation and mirroring how one wants to be seen by others, but also as a form of cultural resistance that fuels nation-building efforts.

The renaissance of Chamorro arts over the past twenty-five years has been fueled by a variety of factors. Cultural consciousness of the 1970s was brought on by a global cry for recognition of indigenous rights, and reinforced locally by public awareness of an indigenous heritage revealed in archaeological finds and research into historic documents. Political activism of the 1980s and 1990s relied on symbols from the past to establish legitimacy of a continuous peoplehood to drive the decolonization movement. Artists provided the visual, sensual and emotive symbols that fueled cultural rearticulation and influenced public opinion. Increased travel and cultural exchange with other Pacific islands helped Chamorros develop a sense of connection with their Pacific brothers, as artists explored similarities while promoting Guam's specific cultural differences through dances, chants and visual artistic creations. Specific artistic icons, movements and sounds are now accepted and emulated in the Guam community and recognized in the Pacific community.

But the voyage has only begun. McDonaldism, Nike and Budweiser are powerful forces for small indigenous groups to contend with. When the young Chamorro dancer washes off his painted tattoo, will he also discard his cultural values and put aside his cultural heritage until the next dance? Or will leaders like Vince Reyes continue to create dances and activities that have significant cultural meaning in their modern lives.

Pioneers of this renaissance have set the sail and will eventually hand the rudder to the next generation. In the course of conversations with the artists mentioned here, several expressed concern that they have not yet retrieved enough information from the past to sustain the next generation; or that the glitz and glamour of the modern world will overwhelm their efforts to instill cultural values.

I believe that cultural rearticulation will continue to evolve in the hands of future indigenous artists, in new and exciting ways that hopefully will take into account lessons from the past. As noted earlier, continuous reconstruction of indigenous identity is the norm for Chamorro Pacific Islanders as they navigate their way into the future. The resilient, adaptive nature of the Chamorro people has carried them through many crises for over 4000 years of their existence. I believe that the powerful synergy between artists, activists and nation builders will continue to produce culturally-significant symbols of a proud, enduring heritage. The voyage continues.

Painting My Country Papua New Guinea: The Creative (Contested) Vision of Larry Santana

Pamela Rosi

> Contemporary artists have a unique place in Papua New Guinea history… they express what lies deep in our hearts, a longing to be new, yet rooted in our rich and ancient past. [1]

In the mid-1960s, when Australia moved to expedite national sovereignty for its territory Papua and New Guinea, eighty years of colonialism had done little to create sentiments of "nationness" in local peoples divided by regional politics, tribal loyalties, and cultural diversity. Confronting the task of nation-making following Independence in 1975, the state government swiftly initiated policies to further national integration among new citizens. As discussions surrounding post-colonial Papua New Guinean nation making have noted (Foster 1995, 2002; Otto and Thomas 1997; Zimmer-Tamakoshi 1998), it takes more than constructing schools, bridges, and roads to unite people and create sentiments of national consciousness and identity. It requires symbols and narratives of national life as well as a collective memory to materialize what Benedict Anderson (1983) calls an "imagined community" — one that depends on emotional attachments affecting what it means to be Papua New Guinea or a Papua New Guinean.

Given the diversity of its traditional societies and the impact of colonialism and globalization, PNG culture is subject to critical debate and negotiation — a process that necessitates integrating old and new life ways and evaluating national goals (Lindstrom 1998). If imagination plays a role in nation making, whose images have contributed to constructs of nationness? Scholars have proposed the agency of various media, including reading national newspapers (Anderson 1983), consuming national advertisements (Foster 1995, 2002), or viewing national TV, as these engage national life and raise national consciousness.

Yet beyond the powers of modern media to report national events and concerns, PNG leaders have recognized the agency of contemporary artists to create images of national culture and ancestral heritage. To promote this idea, Sir Michael Somare, the country's first Prime Minister, sent a message to the first meeting of the Pacific Arts Association in 1974 urging recognition for the role of Papua New Guinea art in nation making and for respecting every artist's work in creating "a vision of the cosmos as he/she envisions it" (Somare 1979a, xv). In a similar way, constitutional lawyer and playwright Bernard Narokobi has called for supporting artistic vision because it expresses "the spirit" of Papua New Guinea and the search for "selfhood, nationalism, and identity" (Narokobi 1990, 17). As stated in his well-known book The Melanesian Way, artists should question: "What was Papua New Guinea? What is happening to Papua New Guinea? Where are we going?" [2]

To make these statements more than rhetoric, the national government acted before Independence to provide institutional support for the arts. Policies included introducing art education into the country's four national high schools; opening technical colleges to teach contemporary design; and the establishment in 1973 of a Creative Arts Center in Port Moresby, the national capital. Renamed the National Arts School in 1976, the institution had a broad mission: to train artists in new media and technology; to fund exhibitions to sell artwork professionally; and to maintain a production workshop to make new art visible in national life. [3]

Given the value that Michael Somare and other civic leaders have placed on the importance of individual artistic vision in creating representations of PNG culture and identity, this chapter focuses on the work of contemporary painter and designer — Larry Santana. My discussion has two goals: to consider how Santana depicts images of national culture and identity, including the tensions he perceives in contemporary national life; and to comment on how Papua New Guineans and other viewers in the global art world have perceived and responded to Santana's repertoire of work. Evaluating the responses of these audiences is instructive because, as Nelson Graburn (1976:24-26) has noted, national identity is a relational concept that engages internal collectivity while also displaying distinction to outsiders. In either case, national identity is contingent because it is a dynamic process that is subject to public debate.

To investigate these observations, I consider two aspects of Santana's art. First, in what ways can his repertoire of images be interpreted as a narrative of Papua New Guinean life that engages questions about national identity and personhood? Second, as an artist participating in global art worlds (Becker 1982; Rosi 1998a; Venbrux et al. 2006), how successful has he been in marketing his work both at home and overseas and, if not, why not? While Santana is proud to be an artist who has had the opportunity to represent his country abroad, his career as a professional artist has been a struggle to survive as he confronted economic hardships, difficult family obligations, and increasing government indifference to supporting the arts as an integral aspect of national development. Consequently, expressions of personal frustration and criticism about the difficult conditions of contemporary life surface in his art encouraged by modern values of self-awareness.

Although a few scholars have begun to document contemporary PNG art as cultural expressions of Papua New Guinea's modernizing culture, there has been little in-depth examination of individual artists leading this contemporary art movement. Drawing on long-term research, this chapter contributes a case study to an area of scholarship that invites further attention if key issues underlying the imagery and careers of contemporary PNG artists are to be better understood.

Larry Santana: A Career of Achievements, Constraints, and Struggle

The eldest of four children, Larry Santana was born in 1962 in his mother's village on the Ramu River. At three, he moved to Madang when his father found work as a mechanic. At ten, his father's sudden death made town life precarious and to supplement his mother's meager wages as a domestic and to pay for school fees he collected bottles from the streets. Keeping the family together was a struggle (Sisii 2004). Like other contemporary PNG artists growing up in the early 1960s, Santana's artistic development was influenced by late colonial policies of education which aimed at encouraging students to take pride in their own traditions while learning Western knowledge (G. Beier 1974, Rosi 1994). At Tusbab High School, he took art classes from a New Zealand art teacher who stimulated his creative skills and helped him gain admittance to Goroka Technical College. He studied graphics and painting and obtained his diploma in 1980. [4]

Santana's first job was for an advertising firm in Port Moresby where the Waigani Arts Center and the new National Arts School exposed him to an emerging art world. He began to paint professionally and, in 1983, held his first exhibition at the Waigani Arts Center. In 1986, one of his paintings was selected to represent Papua New Guinea at a conference in Brussels. Santana recalls this achievement with pride as his work was recognized as promoting his country's culture. Since then, when travelling abroad to attend exhibitions of PNG art, he regards himself as a "Cultural Ambassador" (Rosi 1989; 1992). At the 1998 opening of an exhibition of Contemporary PNG art in Boston attended by the Santana family and the PNG Ambassador, Larry's wife and daughter wore distinctive meri (women) blouses and long skirts made from fabric designed as the PNG flag (Rosi 2002).

Although Santana has gained national recognition as a painter, his artistic career has been sustained by income earned as a graphic designer. Port Moresby is, however, notorious for its exorbitant prices and employers often offer jobs that include housing. But this practice has a downside since losing a job can also result in being homeless. Santana has experienced this situation twice. In 1988, the advertising firm he worked for went bankrupt and he lived for several months on the city dump, scavenging to feed his family. In 1993, a fire destroyed his apartment and his possessions. Fortunately, he recovered his losses quickly. He was working at a TV station and his advertising sponsors permitted him to broadcast a public appeal for help. Response was swift: the family was offered new housing and friends gave money.

In the mid-1990's, as Santana gained increasing recognition as an artist, he began attracting growing numbers of private clients seeking his design services, including commissions from wantoks (relatives) working in the national Parliament. He therefore decided to open his own graphic design company Sai Arts, and his business from the mid to late 90' was strong. Commissions included painting murals in the capital, furnishing offices to give them a "PNG look," and designing Christmas cards and calendars that were distributed by national companies, including Air Niugini and Chevron Oil Niugini (Rosi 2002). These favorable circumstances then changed and business ceased.

In 2000, when I visited Santana in Port Moresby, his business had fallen off sharply due to government budget cuts caused by a deepening national recession. Since most of his projects — including his commission to design the Prime Minister's 2000 Christmas card — came through his wantoks working in the Parliament House, he was fearful that this patronage would also end if the next election brought in a new administration. When this happened in 2002, the loss of income, further devaluation of the kina, and eviction from his house for failure to pay rent convinced Santana and his wife that living in Port Moresby was no longer tenable. In 2002, he moved his family to Madang where he could draw support from his maternal relatives and, he believed, re-start his career.

After living in Madang for eight years, Santana's professional and personal life remains a struggle to maintain his exposure as a national artist and to support his family. When he first arrived and failed to find work as a graphic designer, he eked out a living selling screen-printed T-shirts at the market and drawings to tourists. To attend school his children moved in with relatives and he built a one-room house for his wife and himself in one of Madang's squatter settlements.

In 2003, Santana's national reputation secured him a job teaching visual arts at Tusbab High School, and he retained this position until 2007. The salary was small but it provided two benefits: a small house, and an outside studio where he could create large paintings to sell to corporate and expatriate clients securing funds for his children's tertiary education. [5] In 2008, when World Vision offered him a better salary and housing as a field officer, he resigned from Tusbab High School. While he has enjoyed working with craftsmen living in remote bush villages, the constant travel has left no time for painting. When his contract expires in 2010, he plans to return to Madang and work as an independent artist.

As discussed next, connections between art and life are evident in Santana's repertoire as his paintings image old and new life ways, which are familiar to Papua New Guineans but are also contentious. In this respect, his gaze brackets contemporary PNG culture as a melding of Melanesian ancestral heritage with collective aspirations for modernization — including its conflicts. In discourses about national development, a key metaphor for shared experience grounded in local traditions is "Unity in Diversity". Now widely promoted, this slogan encourages people, including artists like Santana, to draw inspiration from their own cultural traditions but also to recognize that respecting diversity does not preclude common denominators for making national culture, including framing a collective history and posing questions about the future (Iamo and Simet 1998; Mel 2002).

Narratives of the Nation and Ideas of Time

To some degree all nations re-imagine cultural traditions to assert pride in traditional heritage as the cultural foundation on which the nation should develop (Keesing and Tonkinson 1982, Lindstrom and White 1994, Foster 1995, Mathews 2000). Papua New Guinea is no exception. Indigenous traditions have often been devalued by Christian missionaries and their converts as belonging to an age of darkness, but the ideal of honoring ancestral ways (pasin bilong tambuna) is nevertheless enshrined in the national constitution. The same ideal is also emblazoned for all to see on the gabled façade of the national Parliament House, with its roof shaped as a traditional arrowhead flying into the future (Rosi 1991). At the same time, national leaders have also cautioned that hegemonic forces of western colonialism have threatened the country's ancestral heritage, leaving native people in the perilous condition of losing the sustaining force of their culture and the essence of their identity (Somare 1979b).

To halt this officially proclaimed legacy of loss, the PNG Government passed the Cultural Development Act in 1974. This established a National Cultural Council whose task was to oversee, preserve, and revitalize traditional customs by encouraging dynamic new forms of creativity. Papua New Guineans, including artists, have responded to this directive in two ways: by recording and rearticulating indigenous cultural traditions as vital resources for contemporary culture making (Narokobi 1983, Iamo and Simet 1998), and by linking ideas of national identity to notions of time, which people talk about as: taim bipo (the mythic past of sacred origins, customs and histories that existed before western contact); taim bilong masta (the colonial period with its destruction of traditional ways and instigation of modernity); taim nau (the present with its hybrid life styles, cultural tensions, and goals of national development); and taim behain (the future with its alternative possibilities). Boundaries of these time periods are nevertheless fluid; the past envelops the present and the present engages the future (Foster 1995, Powell 1987, Mel 2002).

Santana's artworks similarly mingle concepts of time, creating a narrative of national life that frames ideas of the past, present, and future. But unlike the West where movement ahead is equated with progress, Santana depicts the past as ahead of the present and future.

Taim Bipo — Pasin bilong Tambuna

When explaining his work, Santana underscores the point that traditional lifestyles and culture are the most important sources of his artistic inspiration. Like other national artists I have worked with (Rosi 1994), he explains this by saying that his art is a way of recording (hence preserving) traditional life and knowledge for future generations. He also expresses national pride in village traditions, with his art constructing collective memories to honor ideas of national heritage. Many of Santana's paintings and drawings reflect this sentiment by drawing on traditional myths and stories told to him by relatives who come from different regions of the country. For example, paintings from his first exhibition in 1985 — with titles: *Hunting the Magic Cassowary* or *Masalai bilong diwai (Spirits of the Forest)* — are inspired by legends that come from the Sepik River, the Ramu Valley, and Central Province. The multiple cultural sources of Santana's traditional imagery reflect a wide mixing and sharing of local cultural traditions now occurring in many other aspects

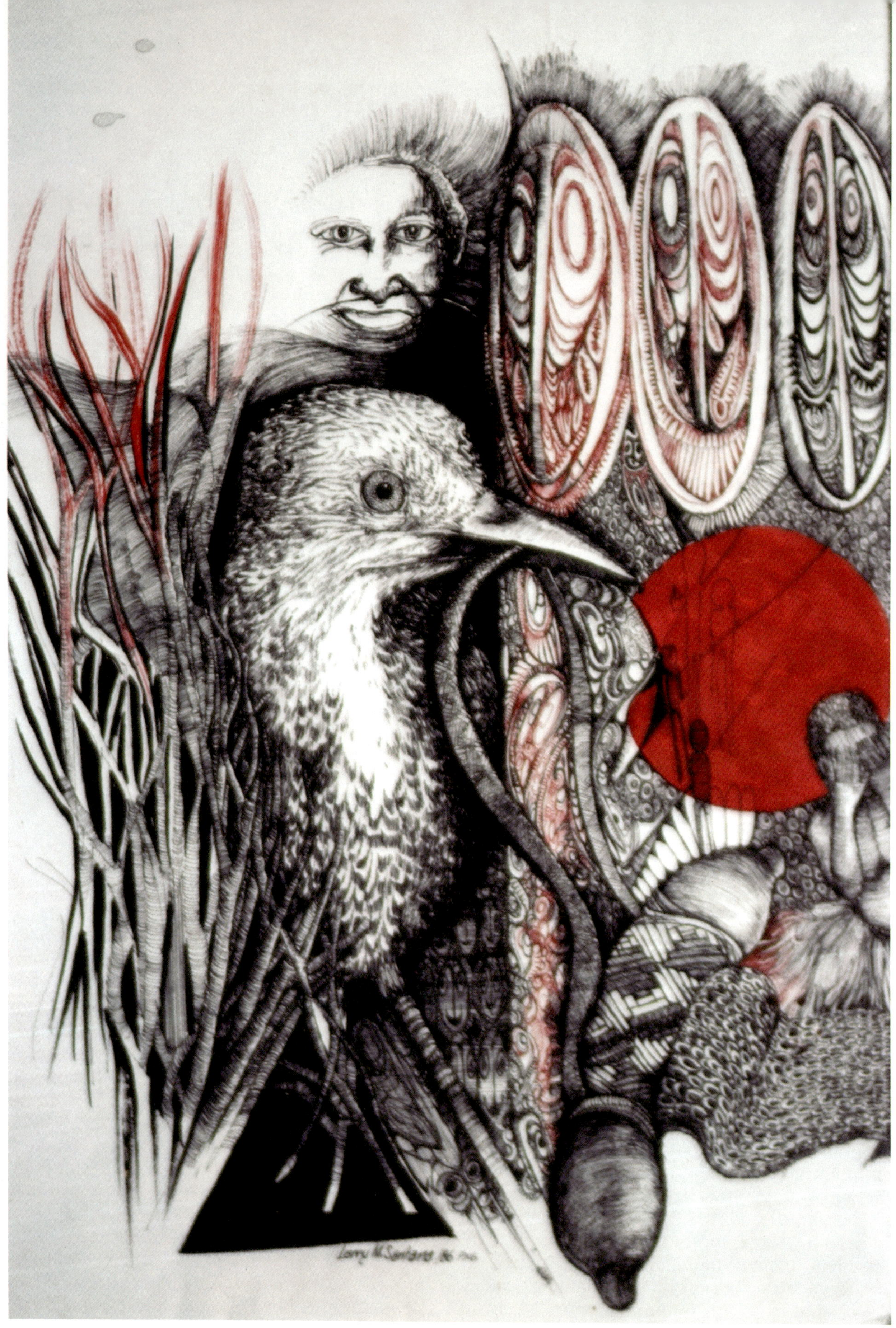

Figure 5.1. Larry Santana. *Immiwang the Bird of Warning.* Pen and ink and colored wash, 1986. Collection of Pamela Rosi.

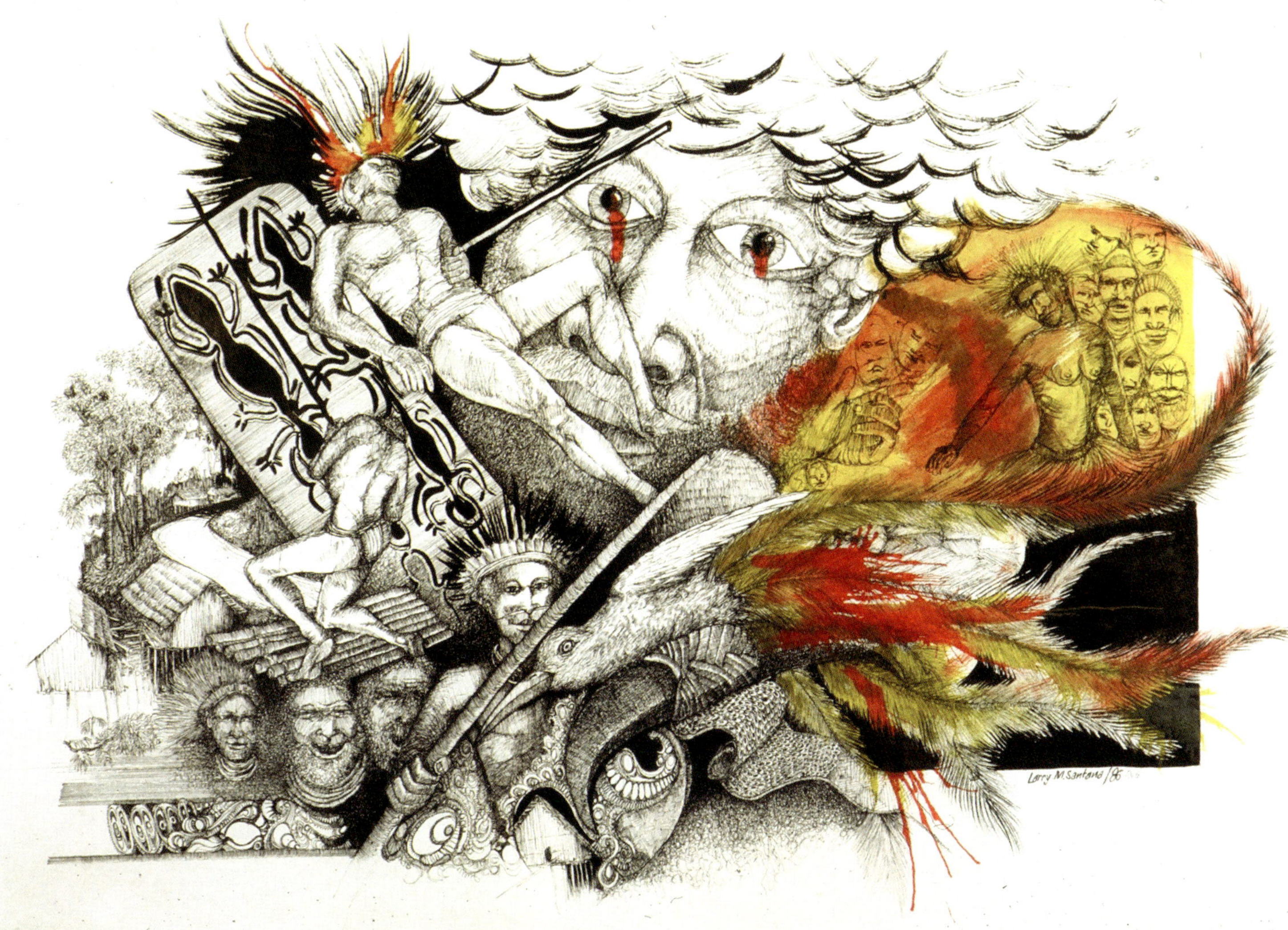

Figure 5.2. Larry Santana. *Kombong'abe: the River Spirit*, Pen and ink and colored wash, 1986. Collection of Pamela Rosi.

of national life and serving as a well of indigenous knowledge.

The mixing and sharing of local motifs raises issues of traditional copyright and, as discussed by Geismar in this volume, these are being raised in Vanuatu as well as in other Pacific states, including Papua New Guinea. Santana responds to this concern by saying he only paints popular stories he has heard from his own family or his wife's, which are known and shared by everybody. With regard to his use of traditional motifs, he informed me that he does not copy designs that are owned and restricted. Instead, he twists them so their use won't be challenged and he will not be asked for compensation for their use. Consequently, his designs, like those used in the Parliament house, are drawn from common motifs, which he blends in his own style. [6]

Santana's repertoire of imagery from taim bipo also includes images of spirits, heroes, and wildlife of symbolic importance — notably, the Bird of Paradise (the national symbol that appears on the flag and on money). When interpreting many of Santana's images of traditional life, it is important to recognize that they embody a moral message for modern society and that traditional values must continue to guide Papua New Guinean life. Santana wants to assert that traditional customs can be superior to Western values (see Flores this volume).

This point can be illustrated with two drawings: *Immiwang, the Bird of Warning* [fig. 5.1] and *Kombong'abe: The River Spirit* [fig. 5.2]. Each is done in a semi-realistic style that includes narrative elements, expressive color washes, and traditional motifs that symbolize a traditional connection with the past. According to the artist, *Immiwang, the Bird of Warning* is inspired by a traditional tale about greed and envy but also the kinship existing between humans and the natural world. Shown in the center of the image, *Immiwang* holds a traditional ornament in his beak. His friend — a young man who makes these decorations that others envy and kill him to possess — is seen above. *Immiwang* brings news of his friend's death to his wife, who is shown weeping with a red

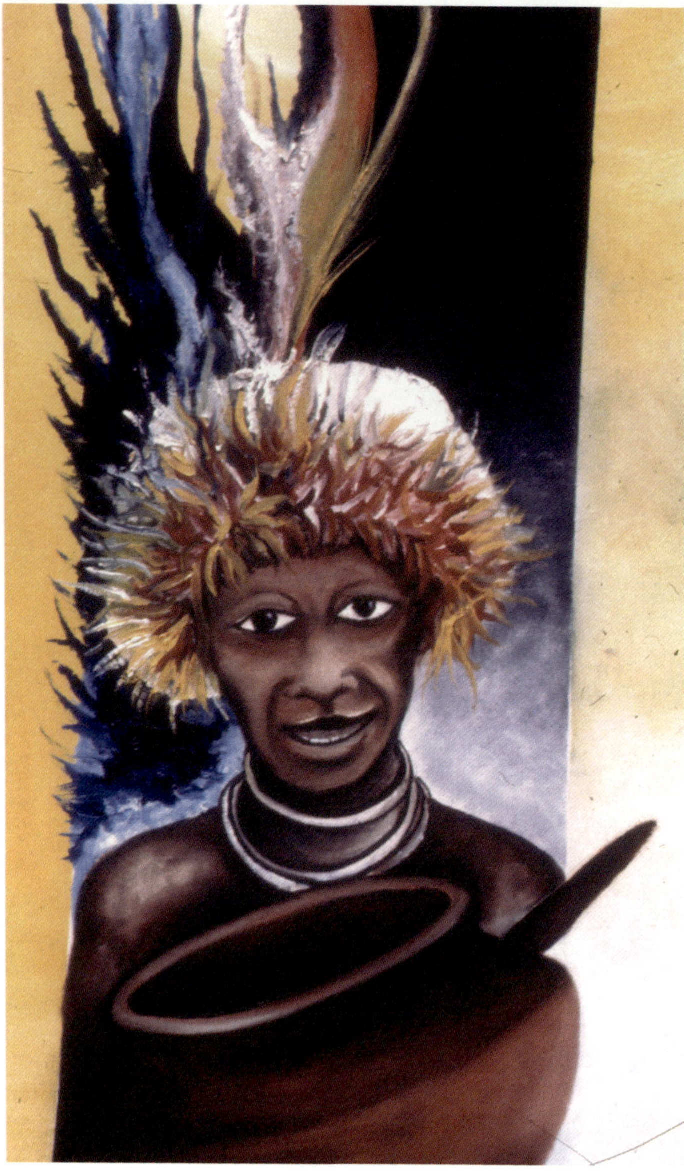

Figure 5.3. Larry Santana. *Maniki Maker of Pots,* Acrylic on Wood, 1985. Photograph courtesy of Larry Santana.

circle behind her head symbolizing death. This story may also be interpreted as a parable for contemporary life, which metaphorically warns Papua New Guineans to recognize forces now destroying the country's natural environment and its wild life (Rosi 1998b).

Kombong'abe: The River Spirit illustrates another traditional story with a moral meaning and a warning for contemporary society. It tells of traditional warfare between the Bandicoot and Parrot peoples of the Karam River. In Santana's drawing, the Parrot people have speared two Bandicoot warriors and, for peace to be achieved, the Parrots are shown compensating the Bandicoots for these deaths with objects of value. Also imaged is the customary exchange of women as wives. The face of Kombong'abe is, however, shown weeping. Santana comments (Rosi 1998b, 20):

> ...In our traditional warfare, damage was limited and enemies ended up marrying one another. We created new life from death and compensated losers. Tears spill from *Kombong'abe's* eyes because the old beliefs and customs he once sustained are breaking down. I use red to denote fire and pain, mixing it with yellow, a color that signifies tradition. Our old ways are being consumed by ideas of progress.

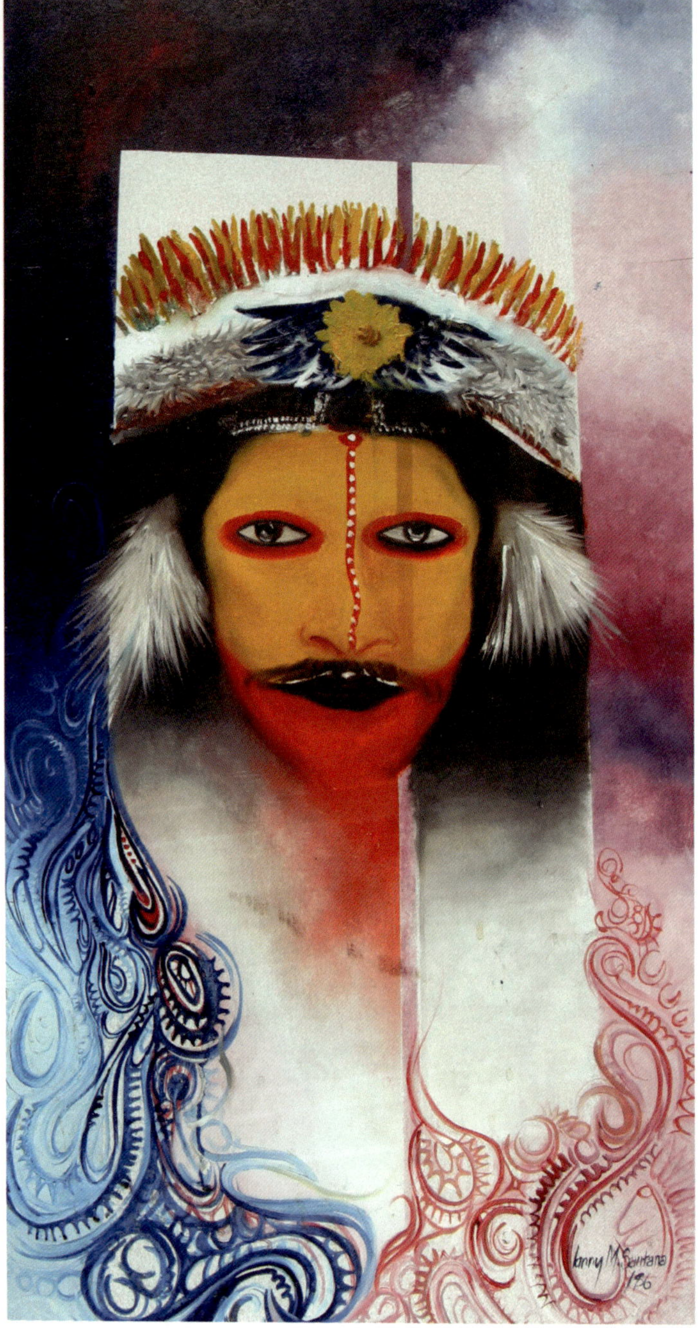

Figure 5.4. Larry Santana. *Traditional Huli Man,* Acrylic on wood, 1986. Collection of Pamela Rosi.

Taim bilong Masta — Western Colonialism

When the history of Papua New Guinea is taught to PNG school children today, colonialism is portrayed as having both positive and negative aspects. While suppressing many revered ancestral customs (*pasin bilong tambuna*), it also introduced modern tools of progress, including Christianity, which Papua New Guineans wish to embrace. Indeed, as preparations were made for Independence, many Papua New Guineans did not believe the country was sufficiently prepared for statehood and they wanted Australia to continue its administrative rule. On Independence Day, as recorded in Dennis O'Rourke's (1977) film *Yumi Yet*, some Papua New Guineans shed tears watching the Australians leave. Attitudes toward the colonial period are consequently mixed and this ambiguity is reflected in Santana's imagery. He references colonialism either by recording particular events or enterprises, or by making images that depict the loss of cultural practices resulting from colonial rule. Loss, destruction, and pain are conveyed by several symbols: sfumato to suggest fading; fire for destruction; cracking to connote erosion or breaking; and tears and the color red express pain. Three of Santana's works, in particular, illustrate these ideas.

Maniki: Maker of Pots [fig. 5.3] was inspired by a childhood story Santana heard about a young woman who was so skilled in pottery making that many village men wanted to marry her. But as people in her village began to desire things brought by white men, they wanted metal not clay pots. Symbolizing this material replacement and devaluation of PNG women as pot-makers, Santana depicts Maniki and her pots consumed by fire. He comments: [7]

> I wanted to show that powers of village women are being destroyed like the pots. Before white ways and things came to village life, a traditional woman was respected for making pots, beating sago, or weaving mats. What PNG women did in the village was more important than the work of a colonial woman. My painting shows respect for Maniki's work... Colonialism has made us forget our traditional skills.

Santana's painting of Maniki reflects a preoccupation held by many of the national elite and art educators that ancient skills and artifacts of village life have been destroyed or threatened by modernization and need to be creatively revitalized. Although few PNG women today make pots in traditional ways, the knowledge and practice of pot-making is not lost but redirected to fill a new market opened up by tourism and a growing interest in pottery as fine art and a medium for expressing personal, regional, and national identity (Cochrane 1997).

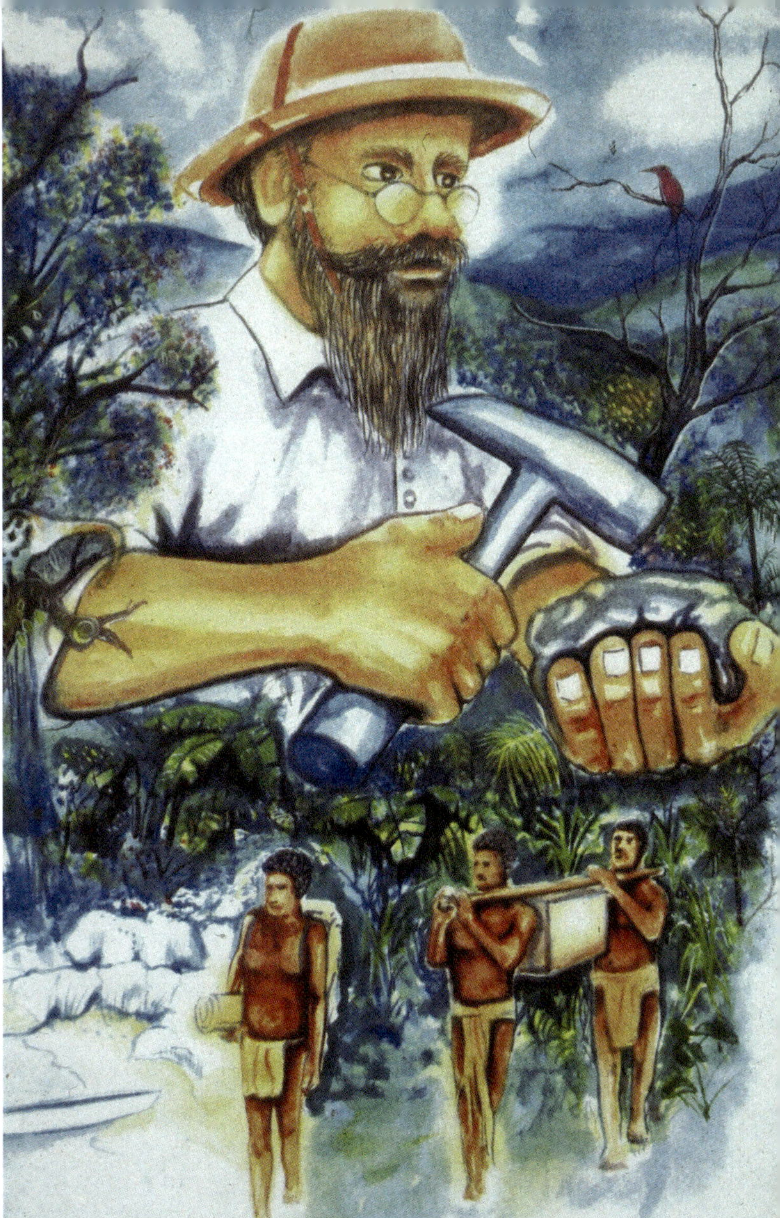

Figure 5.5. Larry Santana. *Explorers begin digging.* Chevron Oil Calendar, Watercolor and gouache, 1997. Collection of Pamela Rosi. Photograph courtesy of Larry Santana.

In *Traditional Huli Man* [fig. 5.4], Santana images an elaborately decorated Huli man from the Southern Highlands. Like Maniki, the painting is motivated by respect for ancient customs, but also concern that they are eroding. As the artist noted: [8]

> You may not notice the crack down the face, but it is something important. Before the Australians came, pigments for face painting were made of local clays and traded between villages. But now, after years of westernization, traditional customs are not like they used to be. Yes, people may decorate, but now they buy paints and pigments from the store...to get what they want right away.

While images mourning the loss of traditional customs as a result of colonialism are a regular theme

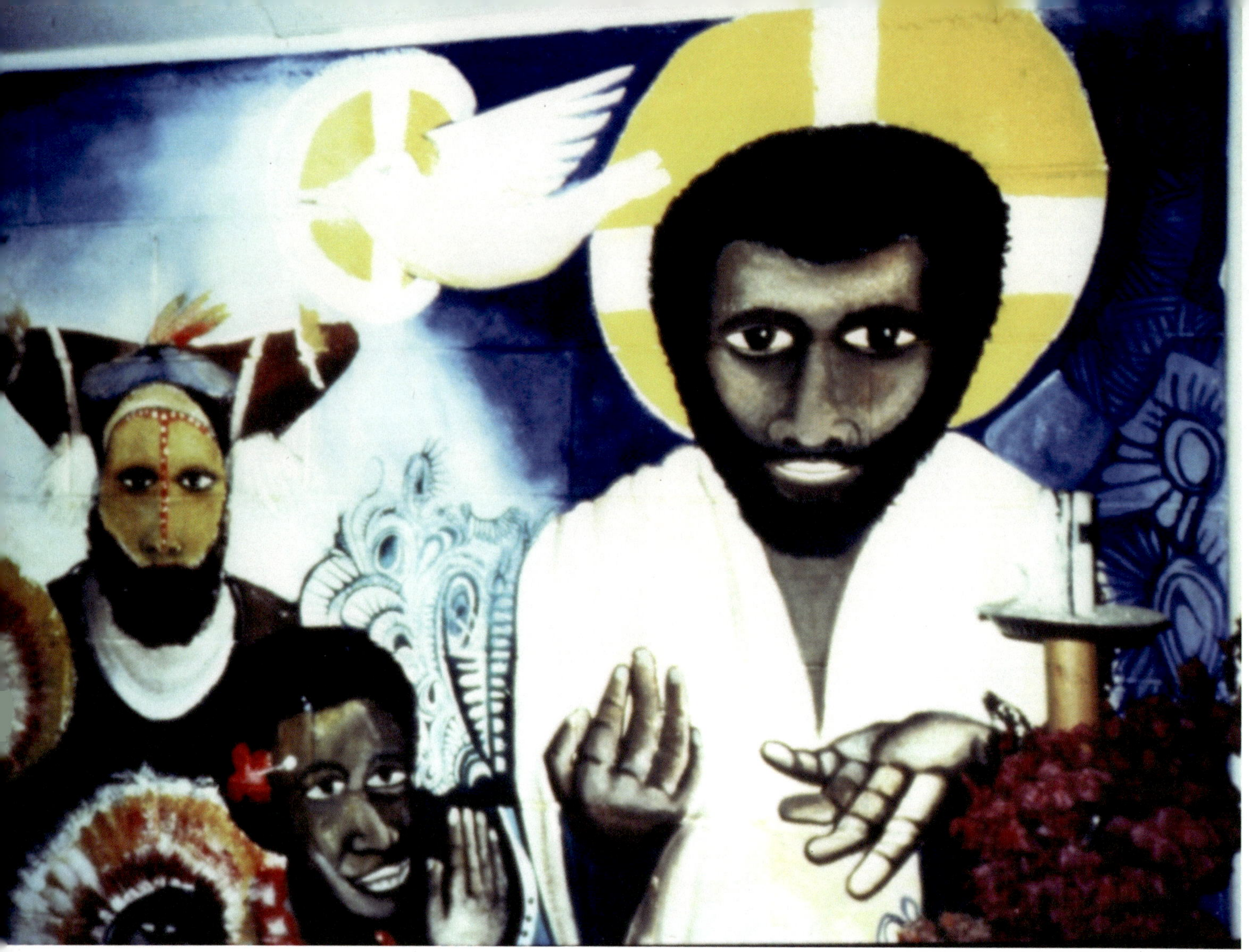

Figure 5.6. Larry Santana. Church Mural, 1986. Photograph by Pamela Rosi.

in Santana's art, specific events in colonial history also occur. In 1997, Santana designed a calendar for Chevron Oil Niugini, which offers a visual history of oil exploration and production at Lake Kutubu through twelve narrative images — one for each month. For example, March is titled *Early Exploration* and April [fig. 5.5] *Explorers begin digging.* [9]

Developing the country's natural resources is a key component of the state's commitment to modernization. As I describe next, changing lifestyles, values, and tensions associated with modernization are recurring subjects of Santana's art, visualizing the panorama of contemporary PNG life. When considered collectively, several themes draw his gaze. These include: reimaging Christianity to give it an indigenous identity, creating critical or humorous images of new life ways, and expressing a personal biography and personhood.

Taim Nau: Cultural Diversity, Mixed Identities, and Tensions in Contemporary PNG Life

In the arena of nation-states, Papua New Guinea identifies itself as a Christian nation. Santana is a Catholic and indigenizing Christianity is an important theme in his art. Unlike protestant evangelical traditions, his art is ecumenical but embraces references to local custom. A good example of his vision of Papua New Guinea as a Christian community is a church mural he executed in Port Moresby, in 1984. [fig. 5.6] Christ's skin is shown black and the congregation — adorned in traditional headdresses and face painting — is represented from all regions of the country. Santana has also created a series of Christmas cards which image baby Jesus in a bilum bag and represent the Holy family as Papua New Guinean. In doing this, he is giving Christianity a local national identity and face.

In addition to these religious images, Santana also uses Christmas card images to critique Papua New Guineans

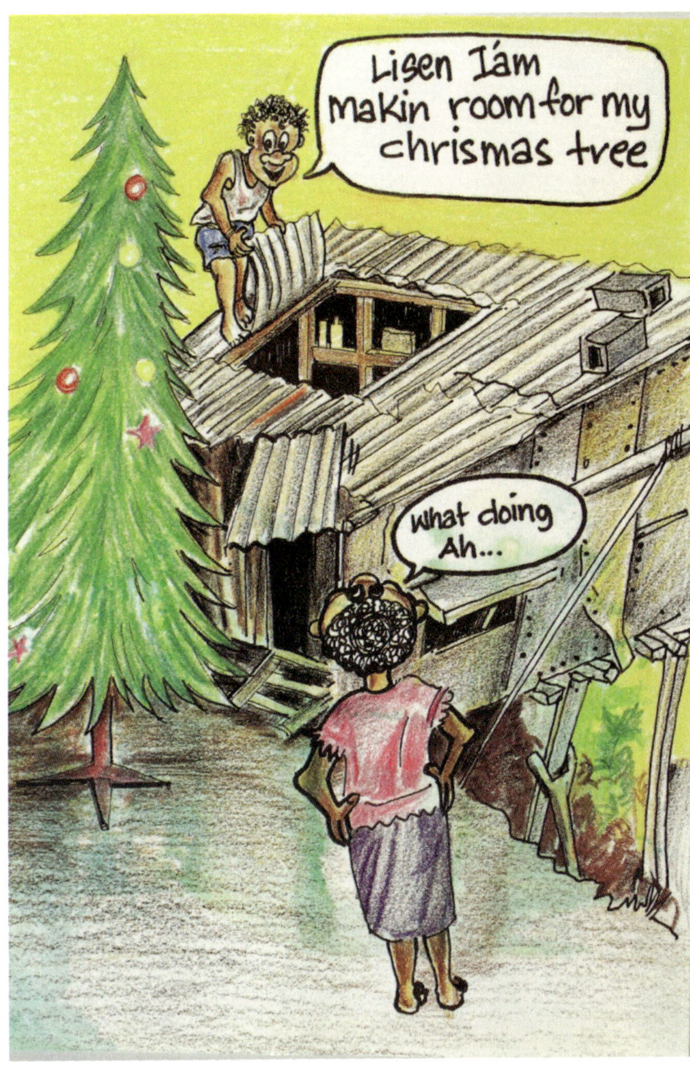

Figure 5.7. Larry Santana. Christmas card. Aktinruts Series, 1989. Photograph courtesy of Larry Santana.

who ape western Christmas traditions. One image pictures a village couple breaking a hole through their traditional bush house to accommodate a Christmas tree. [fig. 5.7] Others depict Christmas as a time to get drunk or steal desired consumer items, mocking the spirit of Christmas giving. The cartoon style of these cards, with the trade name *Aktinruts*, resonates to the popularity of the well-known *Post Courier* newspaper cartoon character Grass Roots. He is an urban rascal who gets into petty crime or other scrapes that readers recognize as all too familiar.

In contrast to humorous cartooning as a vehicle for social critique, Santana's serious social criticism is done in a realist style that is directed to behavior regarded as socially promiscuous or deeply shameful — particularly begging and prostitution. In the 1970s as urban poverty escalated in Port Moresby, beggars became the target of critical public discourse as well as artistic expression. The first example of this social genre appeared in 1977 in the work of Taba Silau because he was outraged that the crippled and the old were being placed on the streets by their relatives to solicit money (Rosi 1994:479). With similar sentiments, Santana has also included the lonely figure of the beggar in his images of urban life because, to him, they symbolize the depravity and misery created by so-called modern development and the power of money to corrupt traditional values of kinship obligations.

Prostitutes working in bars or discos are regarded as a source of AIDS, and therefore have become a symbol

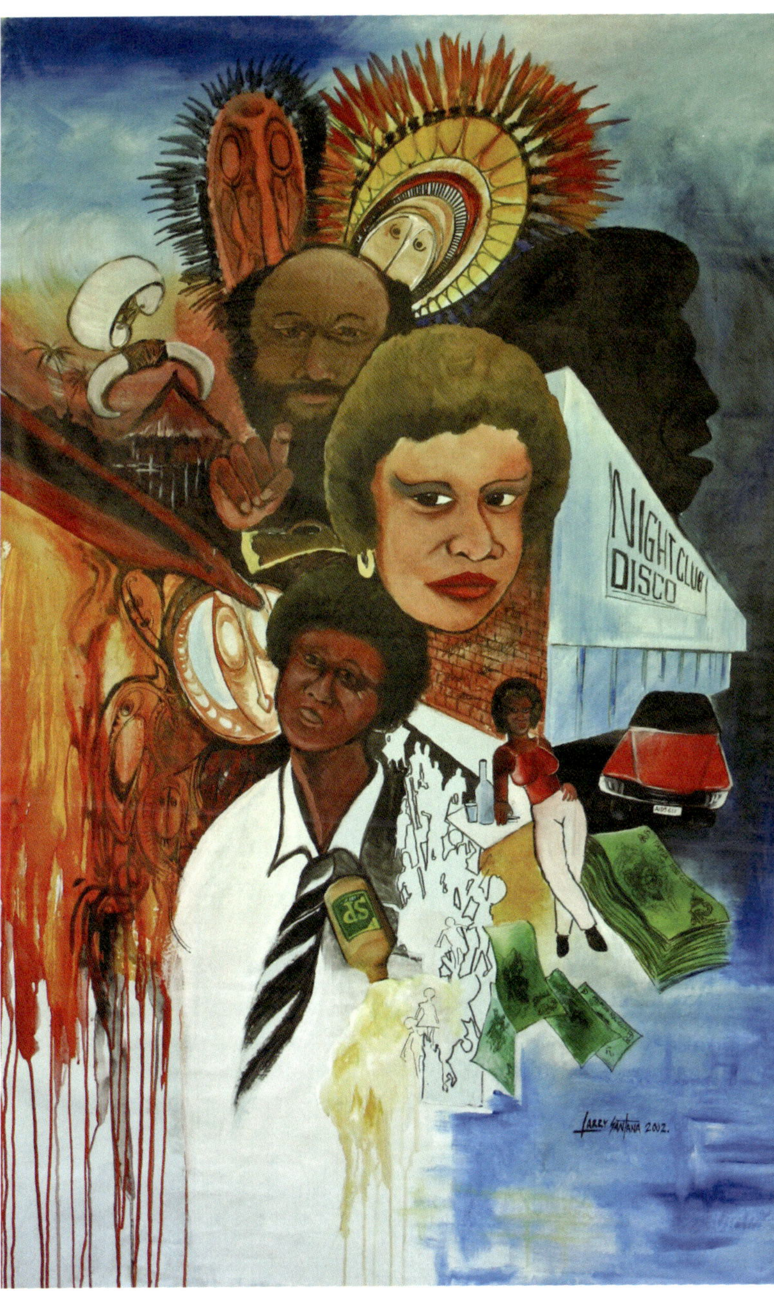

Figure 5.8. Larry Santana. *Modern Society*, acrylic painting, 2001 after original pen and ink drawing, 1986. Photograph courtesy of Larry Santana.

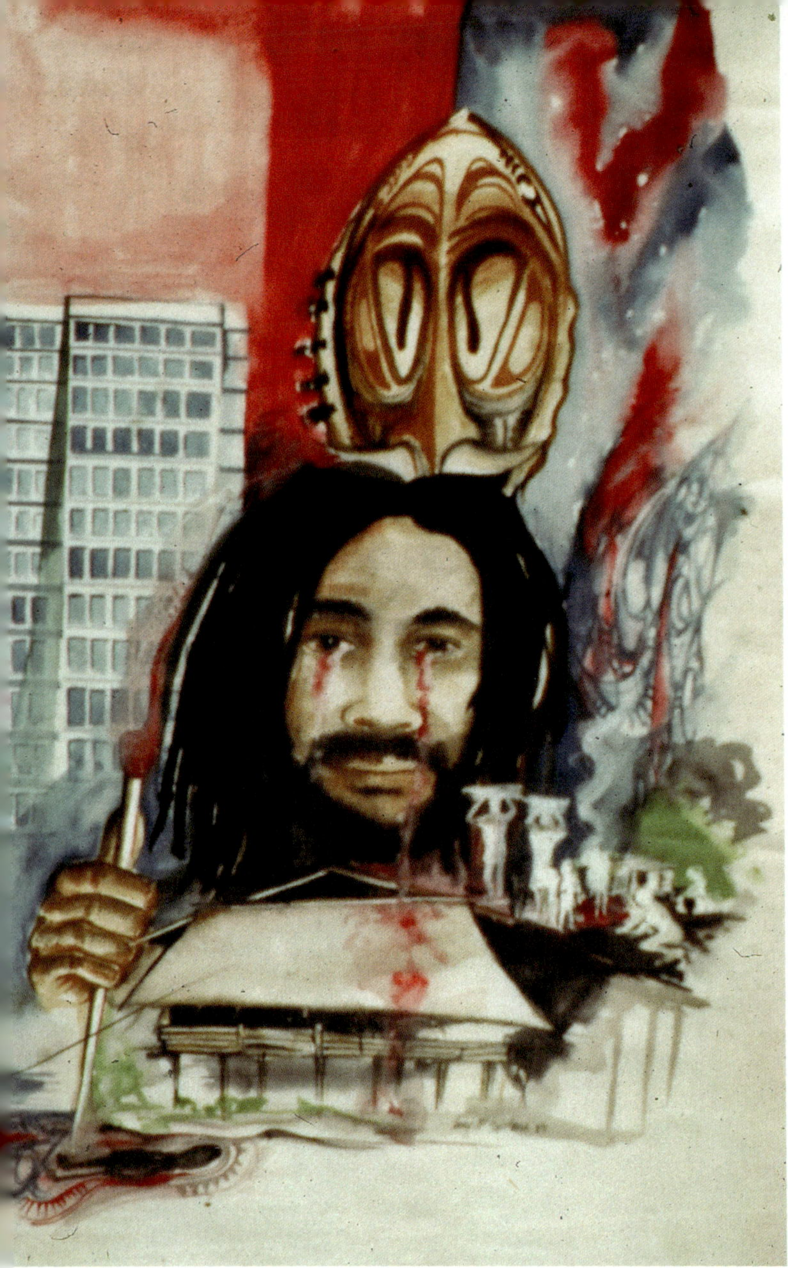

Figure 5.9. Larry Santana. *Pain and Sorrow at the Six-mile Dump*, Watercolor on paper, 1989. Collection of Pamela Rosi.

of the breakdown of traditional values. Santana and other PNG artists excoriate these women because their flamboyant dress and sexual soliciting are considered to break traditional rules of female modesty and sexual relations considered the prerogative of marriage contracted between groups. Santana therefore targets prostitutes as both the source of disease and as symbols of forces threatening traditional kinship and gender relations. Together with beggars, they represent what he calls the dark side of progress, an idea he first illustrated in a 1986 drawing *Modern Society* [fig. 5.8]. He commented:

> I show a nightclub… people are dancing in the back… a young prostitute looks for money outside… everybody wants to follow the bright lights. In the background an old traditional man points a finger and is telling them to come back... see the carvings, outriggers… and that handle. It is broken and there is no one to mend it. Only the old man has the skill but he will die soon and there is no one to pass his skill onto in the village. Everyone is coming to the city to enjoy ol *pasin masta* (Western ways). There is a dark side of progress — the prostitutes, the beggars—our dying crafts…

A darker side of the breakdown of kinship values has arisen from Papua New Guinea's civil war in Bougainville. To mark this decade of national upheaval, Santana created *A New Nation Going Through Struggle and Confusion Leading to Instability and War*. This painting was shown at the exhibition *Nation-Making and Cultural Tensions: Contemporary Art from Papua New Guinea* mounted in Boston, Massachusetts in 1998. Drawing on the symbol of fire, the image depicts the PNG flag held against a vast incendiary of flames and smoke that engulfs both villages and city offices in an inferno. Commenting on the bitter strife for the exhibition catalogue, Santana stated "the war has affected all Papua New Guineans since it caused deep dissent between the government and citizens, confusing people over issues of citizen loyalty and the instability war has caused." [10]

Beyond representing confusion and pain at the national level, Santana's images depict suffering connected to his life experiences where, as an aspect of modern individuality, his art expresses his own emotions and memories. His work has included the death of his father by sorcery, [11] the destruction of his home, and most heart-wrenchingly a period of homelessness with his family at Port Moresby's six-mile dump, where he scavenged for food discarded by Air Niugini. This dark period is reflected in the self-portrait *Struggle and Pain at the Six-mile Dump* (1989) [fig. 5.9]. He described the work (Rosi, 1998: 20):

> This is an image of myself and the little settlement house that I built is under me. Tears and blood are in my eyes. The silhouettes of the people in the back are my in-laws coming back from the dump where they have collected food scraps. The carving represents the traditional culture we have lost. The red wash is the pain of living in the city. The blue wash down below shows my little kids playing around the house. This is the struggle and pain I face when I have no job or money. Life is not worth living, but I have my family to care for. As an artist I work with my brush. But I can't paint. I see the kids

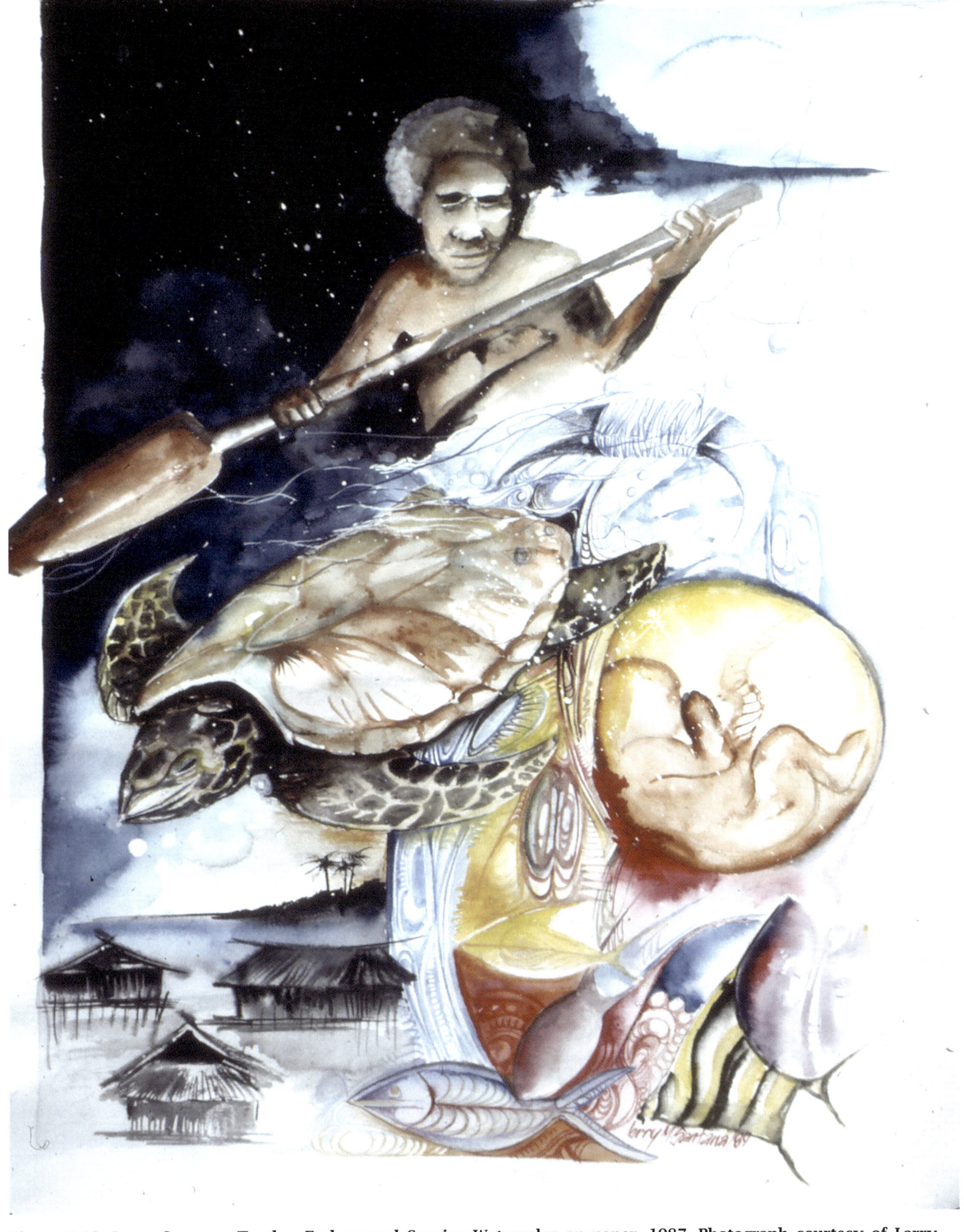

Figure 5.10. Larry Santana. *Turtles: Endangered Species*, Watercolor on paper, 1987. Photograph courtesy of Larry Santana.

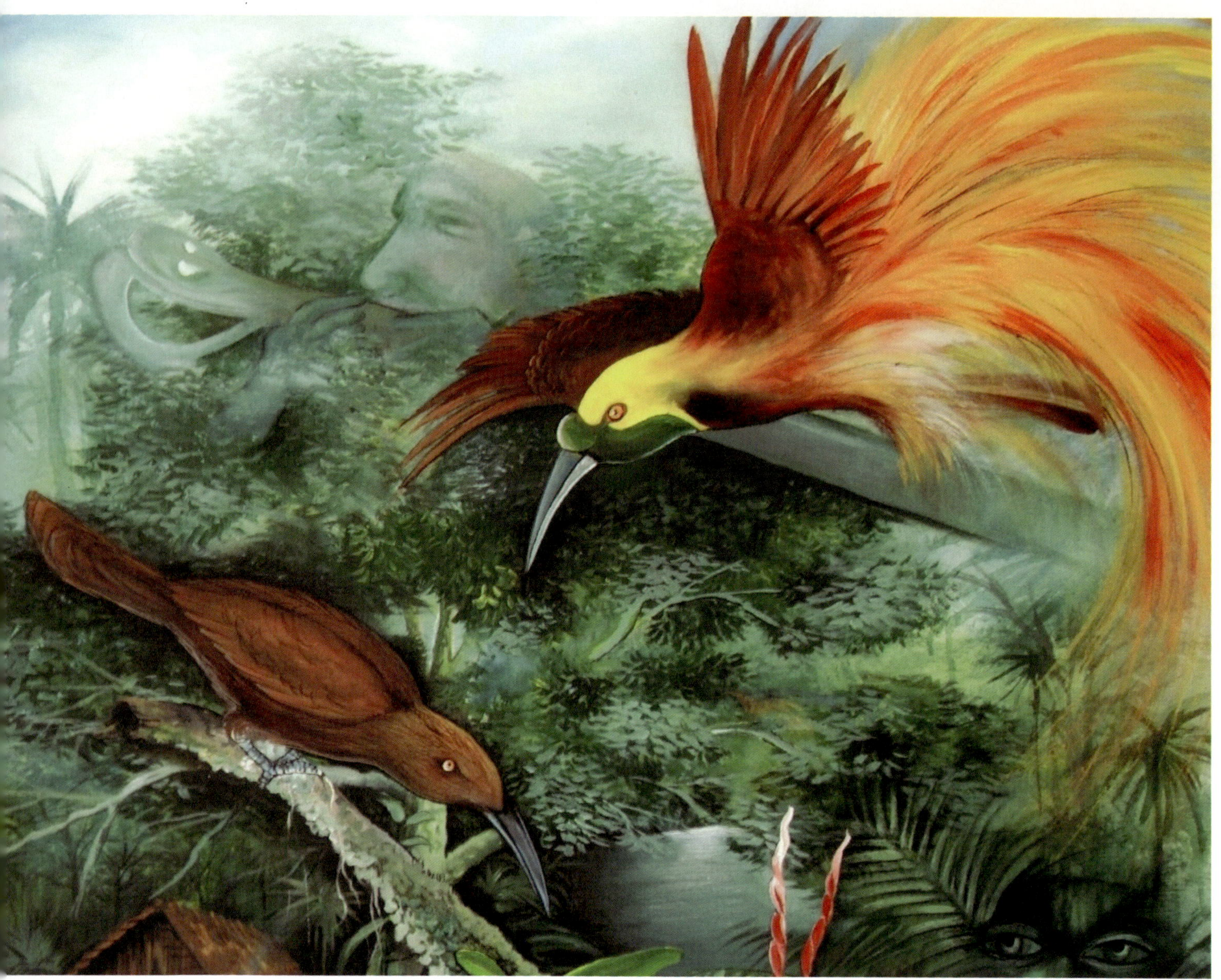

Figure 5.11. Larry Santana. *Bilas of the Forest,* acrylics on canvas, 2005. Photograph courtesy of Larry Santana.

> sick. It is such a struggle to keep us all together. Problems have grown worse, so I wanted to put them down on paper. As you can see the sketch is not neatly done. But it is a painting from my heart to let the world know what is happening to artists like myself as we struggle to survive on the garbage dump.

Although pain, struggle, and contested lifestyles are integral to Santana's representations of urban life and its dislocations, this is not the only vista he paints of his country. He is also drawn to rural village life. On visits to relatives in Madang Province or the mountains of the Central Province, he is inspired to create village landscapes, wild life, or portraits of village people — such as women making netted bags. When the rural images are seen together with the cityscapes, they create an imagined but also realistically grounded picture of the hybridizing complexity of Papua New Guinea life. These contrasting images illustrate the problematic relationship between tradition and development. For Santana, the past guides the future.

Taim Behain — Possible Futures

Santana's vision of the future is hopeful but cautionary, and focuses on four major concerns: conservation of the natural environment to prevent unregulated mining, logging, and fishing; the importance of universal education, women's demands for equal rights in national life [12], and breaking the cycle of economic dependency fostered by the world banking system.

Living in Madang, a beautiful seashore town, Santana's concerns for preserving local fauna and flora are strong. In Turtles: Endangered Species [fig.5.10] he includes a fetal image because, as he explained [13]:

> Turtles are an endangered species. If we want to preserve natural life for future generations of PNG children, we must save our rivers and wild life and not pollute or destroy them. But everyday we hear about politicians selling out to multinational companies to line their own pockets. It's the same old story of corruption.

A similar idea is imaged in his painting Bilas of the Forest (2005) [fig. 5.11], suggesting that the future of Papua New Guinea is linked to preservation of the Regiana Bird of Paradise, the national symbol.

> This is my vision of the forest that holds my identity, my traditions and my life. These beautiful birds are near extinction — they are the bilas (decorations) of my forest, the bilas of my culture. This painting is a call for people in authority to do something to help these birds from dying out—so our PNG culture will not die with them. [14]

In addition to managing Papua New Guinea's natural resources to provide for future generations, Santana sees education as a key to national development, which must include gender equality. Hoping that his daughter Maureen would complete her university degree Santana created *Educate a Woman and You Educate a Nation*, reflecting this aspiration. It pictures an unborn fetus representing the future, and a central figure of a young woman who wears an academic robe while holding a traditional pot in her left hand and a bible and diploma in her right. These objects signify that future generations of PNG women must be nurtured by traditional knowledge, Christian principles, and the skills of modern education to become strong leaders. In PNG's male dominated society, Santana is a strong advocate for women's rights and his painting *Bilum Hevi Tumas* [fig. 6.12] is an admonishment to men to share the heavy work and duties traditionally designated to women.

In engaging issues of economic development in his art, Santana's expressive realism reflects the hardships that grassroots people encounter in Papua New Guinea's capitalist economy. Providing food and education for their children while fulfilling kinship obligations that are the backbone of traditional Melanesian social structure is not easy. These predicaments and how they affect Papua New Guineans in managing their resources are relevant to the second part of this paper: namely, how successful has Santana been in marketing his contemporary art at home and abroad? As I will discuss next, the obstacles he encounters in promoting and selling his work are institutional and personal, but also engage the politics of representation which have economic repercussions because judgments made by art critics and collectors influence the art market (Venbrux et al. 2006).

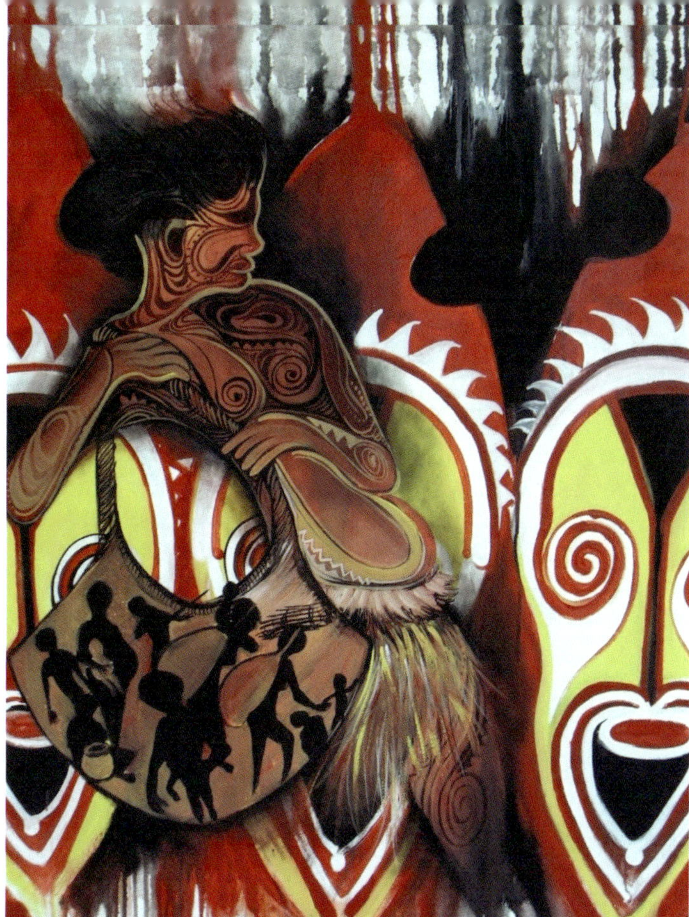

Figure 5.12. Larry Santana. *Bilum hevi tumas*, acrylics on Canvas, 2006. Collection of Pamela Rosi.

Local and Global Marketing of Contemporary PNG Art

To seek recognition and financial success in today's global art worlds, Santana and other PNG artists required institutional support and facilities, which have limited availability. With few art institutions and only one art gallery operating in Port Moresby, PNG artists have had to depend on the government, expatriates, or expatriate firms to provide venues for exhibiting their work. Several circumstances account for this lack of self-reliance: artists must fulfill family financial obligations; [15] they cannot afford to rent professional spaces for exhibitions; and many live in crowded high crime urban settlements where marketing art is potentially dangerous for customers (Rosi 2006).

Aware of these circumstances before Independence, the PNG government recognized that if contemporary artists were to contribute to creating a new national culture and pride in indigenous identity, the state needed to provide professional training and institutional facilities to help artists market their work. Expatriate organizations were also encouraged to support new art production by providing venues and patronage for the arts (Simons and Stevenson 1990, Rosi 1998b). Today, as in the 1970s and 1980s, most art production occurs in Port Moresby, though Artists also find limited outlets for their work in provincial cultural centers and tourist areas, including Madang and the Highlands.

Until 1990, government support for contemporary art in Port Moresby was channeled through the Creative Arts Center, which opened in 1972. Renamed the National Arts School in 1975, it operated a gallery and production workshop. With these two facilities, the school mounted a regular program of exhibitions and carried out commissioned work employing students and a team of carvers and welders (Rosi 1994). Throughout the 1970s and early 1980s, the well publicized National Arts School exhibition openings were attended by government officials and the expatriate community. As Marsha Berman (1990) has noted, urban migrants and villagers had little interest in contemporary art forms since these works had little value in local systems of meaning. In contrast, decorated T-shirts and tie-dyed clothing sold in local markets or on the street were popular in local communities.

The situation changed in the mid-1980s when Mathias Kauage, one of Papua New Guinea's best known Highlander village migrant artists living in Port Moresby, and his Simbu relatives began selling paintings at the Ela Beach arts and craft market and outside the Islander Hotel. Since then, many more artists now exhibit their work at the Ela Beach market (held once a month) out of financial necessity. However, some professionally trained artists consider this practice debases the value of contemporary PNG art. The willingness of village artists to haggle with tourists over price is also viewed as unseemly because it transforms artists into vendors and art into a commodity without spiritual value. Professionally trained artists also note that if PNG artists want their work recognized as fine art in the global art world, they must display it in galleries, museums, or high-end shops.

However, in commenting about the rich diversity visible in contemporary Papua New Guinea art forms, Bernard Narokobi is critical of people who make comparative judgments about their different stylistic forms. Doing this, he argues, misses an essential point. Regardless of whether these arts are t-shirts or murals adorning the Parliament House, each artistic expression speaks to the technological, political, and socio-cultural changes that have taken place in Papua New Guinea since Independence and embody these complex transformations no matter what they look like (Narokobi 1990). [16]

Daniel Waswas, a young PNG painter trained in New Zealand and recently appointed the Director of Melanesian Arts at the University of Papua New Guinea in Port Moresby, is a strong advocate of this position. With help from local sponsors he has given workshops to instruct street artists how to prepare their canvasses professionally and to use high quality acrylics and canvas (rather than house paint and calico). [17] He has also worked to find funds to support a permanent venue for art exhibitions. Because Papua New Guinea lacks exhibition venues, a new gallery in Port Moresby would be a welcome asset permitting artists to present their art professionally and seek gallery-scale prices from local collectors, business clients, and wealthy foreign tourists.

In the early 1980s, PNG had a large expatriate population still living in the country and, for several years after Independence, expatriate residents continued to patronize exhibitions at the National Art School and the Waigani Art Centre. In 1987, because of a deepening national fiscal crisis, the PNG government slashed all funding for public exhibitions at the National Art School. In addition, large numbers of expatriates left the country by the late 1980s prompted by two factors: post-independence government regulations which instigated national policies of self-reliance in the work place; and escalation of violent crime related to high urban unemployment, deep poverty, and criminal "raskol" gangs. The decline in attendance at Waigani Art Centre exhibitions exacerbated in the mid 1990s as urban violence escalated further and police curfews restricted travel after dark. Exhibitions became sporadic and the only institution that could have provided gallery space for contemporary art exhibitions was the National Museum. Unfortunately, staff and services were cut drastically. Therefore exhibitions of contemporary art at the Museum happen rarely and, when they do, are supported mainly by outside sponsors. With the demise of public art exhibitions at the National Art School and the Waigani Centre and with little funding available at the National Museum, Santana and other artists have had to look elsewhere for spaces to show and market their work.

Despite fewer opportunities to exhibit in Port Moresby, Santana was able to maintain his professional career from commissions he received as a graphic designer. But as I describe below, trying to manage the demands of his business, his ambitions as a painter, and his family became increasingly untenable from the mid-1980s. Santana worked to overcome a number of economic, social, and legal problems in the late 1990s until his business collapsed in 2000. Always resilient, Santana had high aspirations for restarting his professional career in Madang, where he planed to build a small thatched roof gallery near the airport. Because of contacts made during his art residency in Boston in 1998, he was also hopeful of exhibiting and selling paintings in the United States. But as the following discussion will point out, problems with his career management along with mixed reactions to the imagery of his paintings in the United Sates have limited the success of his art practice.

The Contending Worlds of Larry Santana: Problems in Career Management

When Santana arrived in Port Moresby in 1980, his aspirations for becoming a professional artist began well. He had a job in an advertising firm and was able to exhibit his paintings at the Waigani Art Centre as their open door policy supported all PNG artists. After art collector Hugh Stevenson favorably reviewed Santana's first exhibition in 1983, he regularly displayed his work at the Center's annual Independence Day show until this event was curtailed in the early 1990s. Up until the mid 1980s, he also participated in privately sponsored exhibitions and filled commissions for his paintings from local businesses and government agencies.

But in pursuing his ambitions as a painter, the production of his studio art competed with his job in advertising resulting in career management problems that stressed his health and his emotions. Such problems help to explain why many young Papua New Guineans with artistic talent decide to stop making art or are pressured by their families to move into jobs with better income. [18] In Santana's case, after long hours working at the office, he stayed up late at night to paint when his family was sleeping. The expenses required for purchasing imported paints and canvas also conflicted with his traditional obligations to support kinsmen. These demands were particularly hard in the first years of his marriage when his in-laws made threats to secure bride price, which he could not pay. [19] Because kinship obligations drew heavily on his finances and time, he was never able to mount a second solo exhibition at the Waigani Art Center. Yet, kinship obligations are based on reciprocity. After Santana lost his job and house in 1988, his in-laws aided his family while they squatted at the six-mile dump. In 1993, after his flat burned down, other wantoks helped him secure money to open his own graphic design business.

From 1993-2002, Santana's Sai Arts business provided facilities for his art practice. In the early 1990s when the Waigani Center eliminated exhibitions, he displayed his paintings in the restaurant of the Ela Beach Hotel, managed by an expatriate friend. At this popular nightspot patronized by an elite clientele, his paintings sold for about three thousand kina (US$1,000). His major source of income depended, however, on commissions for murals and graphic design projects he secured through his parliamentary wantoks. From the mid to late 1990s, these jobs were regular and lucrative enabling him to employ two young graphic designers to help with the workload.

But government work was not a panacea as party alliances in the national government shifted. Corrupt government practices also jeopardized payments for contracted jobs. Santana faced this situation in 1997 when, after a change of government, the new administration refused to make payment on a ten thousand kina contract made by their predecessors. Santana hired a lawyer to litigate but, after two years of court procedures, the judge rejected his case. The consequences of this loss in income, followed by the ouster of his wantoks (whom he depended on to secure government work) from the new government in 2002, had a severe impact on Santana's business. Despite selling his computers, trucks, and paintings, he could not cover his living expenses to stave off insolvency.

Santana's problems with time management; wantok obligations and government corruption are not singular to his career but are shared by many other contemporary artists having to accommodate old and new values, social systems, and economies. Even after moving to Madang in 2002, Santana faced familiar difficulties in managing his art practice. His duties teaching art at Tusbab High School left him little time to paint; his current job with World Vision is even more restricting as he is away in the bush for days at a time. Working in a bush house, the quality of some of his recent paintings has also declined, which knowledgeable patrons have noted. Aware that his current job situation is adversely affecting his reputation as a national artist, Santana has decided to return to Madang and build a studio where he can again produce paintings for exhibitions. [20]

Once back in town, Santana has plans to implement three possibilities to promote the sale of his work at home and abroad: first, to mount a solo exhibition of his paintings in a Madang resort hotel, which the owner has been waiting to sponsor for some time; second, network with his contacts in the United States to locate a gallery that would represent his work there; set up a Facebook page and network here. Given the limited market for contemporary arts in Papua New Guinea, the desire to tap lucrative sales in the growing traffic in art and culture (Marcus and Myers 1995) is one that Santana shares with many other PNG artists (Rosi 2002). His ambitious plans for these exhibitions must, however, deal realistically with two problems. He must still meet his kinship obligations to his family; and he needs to accumulate a sufficiently large body of work required for solo exhibitions.

Another question is whether or not his paintings will sell in the United States fine arts market. Based on evaluations I received after curating four exhibitions of contemporary PNG art in the United States, viewers reactions to the art works were mixed and engaged the cultural politics of representation which frame consumer interests and decisions about funding.

Critical Responses to Santana's Art: The Cultural Politics of Representation

A crucial problem that confronts exhibitions of contemporary PNG art in the United States is that the country is not well known outside the Asia-Pacific Rim. Even on the West coast, few people know anything about Papua New Guinea. Its economy has only regional importance, and it has no large populations of trans-global migrants living within the United States to make Americans aware of PNG people and their traditions. With the exception of veterans who fought in the Pacific during World War II, what most people know about Papua New Guinea is likely framed by images they have seen on the Discovery Channel or in National Geographic — namely plumed warriors living in a wild paradise of mountainous jungles and coasts fringed with white sandy beaches. [21] Because of these engrained stereotypes, American audiences typically respond to contemporary PNG art through their own cultural lenses of the exotic. To see the art in any other way, American viewers must have contextual information to help them interpret these images (see also Raabe and Struck-Garbe this volume). In the three exhibitions of PNG art I have curated at academic venues in the United States a catalogue, descriptive labels, and a video that showed artists speaking about their work aided viewers. Larry Santana attended two of these exhibitions and stayed for several weeks as an artist in residence. He discussed his art with students and visited local schools. For the 1998 exhibition in Boston, when he was accompanied by his family, public interest in the art was enhanced by television interviews, an article written by Christine Temin, the art critic of the Boston Globe, and attendance at the exhibition opening by the PNG Ambassador, who was interviewed for a student-made video to explain the significance of Papua New Guinea art in nation-making — the focus of the exhibition.

Yet, even with such efforts made to enhance understanding of the forms and meanings of contemporary PNG art, viewers' opinions varied about how the imagery should be evaluated. The art works that attracted people most were the decorative and imaginative representations of village artists, especially Kauage, Akis, and Jakupa. Exhibition visitors thought their work showed energy and saw their naïve (primitive) style as authentically Papua New Guinean. When school children visited the exhibition, parents said their children enjoyed the images of village artists because they resembled children's art and so, by implication, had spontaneous creative energy. Hugh Stevenson (1990) uses the term naïve artists to label this expressive quality. Ulli and Georgina Beier similarly value this spontaneity because it comes from the unconscious and most closely resembles uncolonized mentalities (Beier, U. 2005, Beier, G. 1974).

As Marianna Torgovnick (1990) and others have noted, tastes for the exotic reflect a long Western tradition of being attracted by the primitive — something that resonated with my informants in several ways. One Boston collector of traditional New Guinea art regarded the primitive style of Akis and Jakupa as evidence of their spiritual connections to village life. Because of this, he felt it appropriate to hang their art works alongside the traditional pieces in his collection. Like Hugh Stevenson, he saw the spontaneity and elaborate patterning of this "naïve" art as evidence of enduring village "mental landscapes" (Stevenson 1990: 47-56). A similar reaction to Akis' art has been noted by Elaine Monds (this volume) when Akis prints are displayed at the Alcheringa Gallery and on their webpage. Several artists viewing the Boston exhibition remarked that the multiple perspectives used by village artists called to mind old manuscript designs — something exotic that attracted their interest and admiration.

In contrast, reactions to the realistic imagery and use of three-dimensional space in the work of professionally trained PNG artists, including Santana, received less favorable responses. Some people criticized weak techniques, while others did not see anything aesthetically exciting in the work (see also Struck-Garbe this volume). For viewers accustomed to visiting galleries and museums, the imagery seemed westernized or slightly pallid.

Labeling contemporary PNG art as tourist art euphemistically calls into question whether it is art at all. The latter opinion is typical of critics who devalue the hybridity of the new art's styles and media, which are viewed as dispirited copies of Western art that lack cultural identity. This is one reason that Hugh Stevenson, even though he was an early collector of contemporary PNG art, criticized the westernized style of art education adopted at national Independence — describing it as "the last act of cultural colonialism imposed by a well-meaning white hierarchy" (Stevenson 1990:31). This view contrasts starkly with the view of Narokobi (1990) in the same exhibition catalog, who — speaking as a Papua New Guinean — argues that all contemporary PNG arts produced under this educational system be recognized as "national treasures" that embody the nation's changing lifestyles.

When asked to evaluate Santana's art, viewers consistently preferred his lyrical landscapes and representations of village people. Although, after speaking with him they were sympathetic to his images of urban life, they expressed no interest in buying them. Instead, when faculty at the two institutions where Santana was artist-in-residence purchased his art for their personal or college collections, they selected images of traditional myths. In Boston, *Nation-making and Cultural Tensions: Contemporary Art from Papua New Guinea* was very successful but the faculty at Pine Manor College did not purchase the image of civil war, which appeared on the exhibition cover, for the college collection. Instead, they chose *Amain — the Spirit of Good Fortune* because its theme of good will and sfumato coloring were aesthetically more appealing to them.

This preference for images of village life or indigenous flora and fauna was evident when an art historian at the college, who had professional and social connections in Boston's art world, offered to help Santana place his art at two venues: in a gallery in Florida, where she had a summer house, and a small regional gallery outside Boston. In discussing these possibilities with me, she tempered her offer with advice she thought would make Santana's work more marketable in the United States:

> Tell Larry that if he wants to sell his art over here, he must get rid of those pointing fingers and glowering faces of *Kombong'abe* and concentrate on making beautiful drawings of PNG flora and fauna or tropical landscapes that people will enjoy seeing on their walls. Prostitutes and beggars are not what people like to see; they are interested in cultural traditions and island life...the sun, birds, and beaches are what are appealing. And for the Florida market, he needs to improve the quality of his work... avoid signs of wear and tear...these are upscale buyers he is selling to. [22]

Such advice, while well intentioned, irritates Santana because he sees it as hypocritically censoring his work to remove its social commentary and confine him to romantic stereotyped images. As he remarked to me, westerners promote the modernization of Papua New Guinea but they critique new art forms that represent change. Western artists are expected to be innovative, but he is viewed negatively for experimenting with new styles and subject matter.

Unfortunately, the integrity of Santana's artistic vision does not translate into market success. As most Papua New Guineans have little interest in owning new paintings or sculptures, he and other contemporary artists compete to sell their fine art to a small clientele of expatriates and the new PNG elite who buy artworks as representations of national culture or class status. When access to this high-end market has been restricted, contemporary artists, including Santana, must diversify their art production and sell in local art and craft markets in order to earn an income. Today, the largest and important of these is at Ela Beach because most contemporary artists live and work in Port Moresby. [23]

In seeking access to global art markets, contemporary PNG artists also confront other problems that hamper marketing their work. The most important of these is the agency of western gatekeepers, who determine whether or not the public will see exhibitions of contemporary PNG art. Two instances from my own curatorial experience demonstrate how economics and cultural politics served to derail two exhibitions that I had hoped would be shown in the United Sates. The first was to be shown at a museum in the state of Washington. The curators were enthusiastic and planning went ahead for six months, after which the exhibition was suddenly cancelled. As I learned from the museum director, he had decided that without a large group of Papua New Guineans living in the area to draw an audience, the exhibition would be not profitable. Although, other Polynesian and Micronesian communities resided in the region, he did not believe they would attend without community leaders promoting bonds of specific ethnic affiliation and identity to attract an audience.

In the second case, a proposal submitted to a nonprofit arts organization to fund a traveling exhibition of contemporary Papua New Guinea art was rejected for similar reasons. The previous year the organization had supported an exhibition of Haitian art that was poorly attended even at venues with sizeable Caribbean communities. Following this financial loss, the selection committee decided it could not chance funding the art of an ethnic group that had no cultural visibility in the United States. The committee regretted this decision because they agreed that the PNG artwork was aesthetically striking. As Eva Raabe (this volume) has described, Western museums and curators play a mediating role in educating visitors to shift from using a Western gaze to look at contemporary Papua New Guinean art and to view it, instead, with an enhanced sensibility of indigenous perspectives. When successful, curatorial mediation can positively influence how the art is evaluated. However, this is not always possible as ethnocentrisms can be difficult to dislodge, as Struck-Garbe (this volume) suggests.

Given the dynamic power relations that regulate global art worlds, there are nevertheless indications that the contemporary arts of Pacific peoples are, incrementally, entering the mainstream consciousness of western art centers as assertions of cultural and political identity. In February 2004, the exhibition *Paradise Now: Contemporary Art from the Pacific* displayed forty-five pieces of work from leading artists from Aotearoa New Zealand and the Pacific Islands at the Asia Society in New York City. Described as "a striking expression of the fit between the practices of conceptual and performance art and the circumstances of postcolonial indigeneity and diaspora" (Myers 2005:273), the art reflected the high technology, numerous art facilities, and strong government support now available to Pacific Islander artists residing in New Zealand. In April 2006, *Pasifika Styles*, an exhibition of contemporary Maori and Pacific Islander art, opened at the Museum of Archaeology and Anthropology in Cambridge. Cocurated by Rosanna Raymond and Amiria Salmond, the show (which ran through May 2008), was promoted as exploring issues of migration, diaspora, race, and identity in Pacific cultures. The high caliber of the artworks, together with their creative technology and celebratory promotion, mark both shows as landmark exhibitions that bring contemporary Pacific art to major centers of the western art world (Petersen 2007; Rosi 2007a, b).

In October 2004, a new window of opportunity to increase public awareness of contemporary Papua New Guinea art also opened in the United States. The American art collector John Friede donated part of his extraordinary collection of traditional New Guinea art (the Jolika Collection) to the Fine Arts Museums of San Francisco de Young, whose new building opened in October 2005. At the same time, a new curatorial position was created to manage the collection. An artist-in residence program for Pacific artists was also established in the hope that artists would find artistic inspiration in these rare New Guinea pieces (many of ancient origin), and to provide the opportunity to show their work in San Francisco.

Daniel Waswas was the first recipient of this funding in 2006. The residency allowed him to lecture on his work at the de Young Museum; to present papers at the Association of Social Anthropologists in Oceania and College Art Association meetings; and to exhibit (and sell) a painting at *Turning Tides: Gender in Oceania* (Graduate Gallery, University of California, San Diego) curated by Samoan artist Jewel Castro. In 2007, this painting, as well as works by Larry Santana and Julie Mota was exhibited in *Island Affinities: Contemporary Art of Oceania.* [24] The de Young has since hosted other PNG contemporary artists, including Teddy Balangu, Michael Mel, Cathy Kata, and Martin Morubuna. [25]

Candidates for the Jolika artist-in-residence program are chosen in open competition and Larry Santana intends to apply. As described above, his credentials merit consideration as his art is regionally and nationally recognized. In 2006, his work was profiled in the *Contemporary Pacific* [26], directing Pan-Pacific attention to his art in raising consciousness about the need to preserve Papua New Guinea's natural environment and heritage (Rosi 2006a). Two years earlier, in 2004, his persistence as an artist struggling to survive received national recognition when he was selected as one of fourteen Papua New Guineans chosen by journalism students at Divine Word University for a publication *Inspirational People: Role Models for a Developing Nation* (Sisii 2004:34-35). National leaders Sir Michael Somare (PNG's first and current Prime Minister) and former Ambassador Meg Taylor headed the list. Larry Santana was selected because he created art "out of pain and hardship" and helped Papua New Guineans recognize their collective sense of peles (place). In the publication's prologue, Meg Taylor wrote: "As our young nation moves into the twenty-first century, we look for individuals that keep us rooted in traditional values and those that challenge us in the transition into a modern Papua New Guinea, embracing modern education, knowledge, and maintaining our values" (2004:5).

Santana's efforts to paint his country fit Meg Taylor's description of visionary nation-making. As discussed earlier, his narratives of Papua New Guinea society and culture include images of the mythical and historical past, the modernizing present, and perspectives on the future. But they also represent challenges and predicaments to record that national culture and identity are contested processes on both a collective and personal level. Like other contemporary PNG artists, Santana has to manage conflicting demands of his wantoks, his job, and his own art practice. Unfortunately, his personal difficulties in advancing his career have been exacerbated by government corruption and national fiscal crises, which brought him to insolvency and homelessness.

Santana is not, however, a victim of his difficult circumstances but has used his art to actively comment on the dislocations affecting traditional PNG lifeways. In seeking to promote his art in the United States, he has been advised to paint beautiful pictures that appeal to western stereotypes of Papua New Guinea as a primitive "Paradise", but he has resisted compromising his critical vision. Instead, he believes that a PNG artist must create images that make Papua New Guineans and people of other nations aware not only of the beauty of his country, but of the destruction of its land and resources affecting the well-being of its people and generations to come. One of his students at Tusbab High School admired that integrity:

> I really appreciate he is teaching us because I regard him as a true culture man who promotes PNG art and culture in all his paintings. (Sisii 2004:35)

Nevertheless, in a globalizing art world, Santana knows the realities of business where success depends on managing the unpredictable. Like most of his fellow artists, his professional life has been a struggle because he lacks the basic resources and government support to sell his art at home and overseas. Santana and other national artists also want to tap lucrative foreign markets. Locally, high prices can only be obtained from the government or expatriates. With more artists being trained, Santana faces competition from a new generation of talented men and women, and he recognizes that his reputation can fade if he does not exhibit regularly.

In the early seventies, Ulli Beier gave a lecture at the recently established University of Papua New Guinea, where he called contemporary PNG artists "cultural outsiders" (Beier, n.d.) because their new work had no value for village people or urbanized "grassroots" migrants. It was dismissed as "samting nating" as opposed to "samting tru" — i.e., connected to rituals and ceremonies (Berman 1990:61). Yet, thirty years later this situation has changed as contemporary art has diversified to include a variety of work promoted to different market niches, all reflective of the nation's modernizing culture melding old and new. Today, popular arts include designer t-shirts, a dazzling assortment of woven bilum bags and bilum fashions, and colorful printed laplaps. Fine arts include painting, sculpture, glazed pottery, photography, and jewelry inspired by indigenous motifs now made in silver and gold. To raise their incomes artists also sell to a variety of consumers. Santana's primary focus is selling large paintings but, when these sales were stagnant, he designed t-shirts and small drawings to sell in tourist shops and at the market. For trendy fashion shows, he has painted designs onto models' bodies, where flashing strobe lights and rock music heighten aesthetic effects.

Santana's professional ambition is to organize an exhibition of his paintings in the United States. There are, currently, indications that the western art world is beginning to take an interest in seeing and understanding contemporary arts of the Pacific. Two block buster shows were recently exhibited in New York and London; two University galleries in California mounted exhibitions of contemporary Pacific art in 2006 and 2007 (including works by Santana and Daniel Waswas); and vital for exposure and education, the Jolika Collection of the de Young Museum of Francisco initiated a program of art residencies for Pacific artists.

In 2008, the East-West Center Gallery in Honolulu exhibited *Altogether: Contemporary Papua New Guinea Art*; in 2009, *Hailans to Ailans* was exhibited with critical acclaim and a substantial catalogue at the Rebecca Hossack Gallery, in London, and Alcheringa Gallery, in Victoria, Canada. In 2010, The River Project of the Campbelltown Arts Center, New South Wales included a series portraits of people from the Sepik painted by Jeffry Feeger, one of PNG's most talented younger artists. Whether Larry Santana will benefit from this widening window of global interest in contemporary PNG art to create a solo exhibition of his work in Papua New Guinea or abroad is an open question. It will depend on the management of his resources to create a body of art and institutional support for the expenses involved in mounting exhibitions and selling art. As Fred Myers describes as "the traffic in culture" (Marcus and Myers 1995), modern artistic success does not depend just on artistic creativity and aesthetic power to bring this about. It requires operating an "art world" bringing together artists, buyers, gallery owners, curators and critics working in a socio-political context, mediated by art institutions and conditioned by the cultural values and contingencies of world capitalism.

As symbolized in his self-portrait *Pain and Sorrow at the Six-mile Dump*, Santana career's has been entangled and buffeted by these forces. When the young journalist students at Divine University nominated him as an inspiration model of national leadership, it was for his persistence in struggling with his problems. They regarded this struggle as his badge of honor whose predicaments were shared by many other Papua New Guineans in the contingencies of nation making. When Santana paints narratives of his country, he is helping to make this dynamic process visible in a repertoire of work that includes Papua New Guinea's heritage of village societies and customs now being lost, and the socio-cultural and economic dissonances accompanying the country's rapid modernization. Beyond the inadequate resources and institutional support hampering the marketing and sale of Santana's paintings is the need for better public understanding of their nuanced meanings and styles. As the artist stated in 2007, his work is intended to be much more than decoration. It is deeply spiritual. [27]

> Art to me is my life... I have used my artistic talent to translate, expose, describe, and record the heritage of my past, present, and future... the cultures and generations coming before and those to come. My hope is that one day my paintings will have a place in the National Museum of my beautiful country Papua New Guinea. As long as I live and paint, I see myself as a faded image on my own canvas hoping the world can see and appreciate the inner spirit of my feelings and not the quality of my materials.

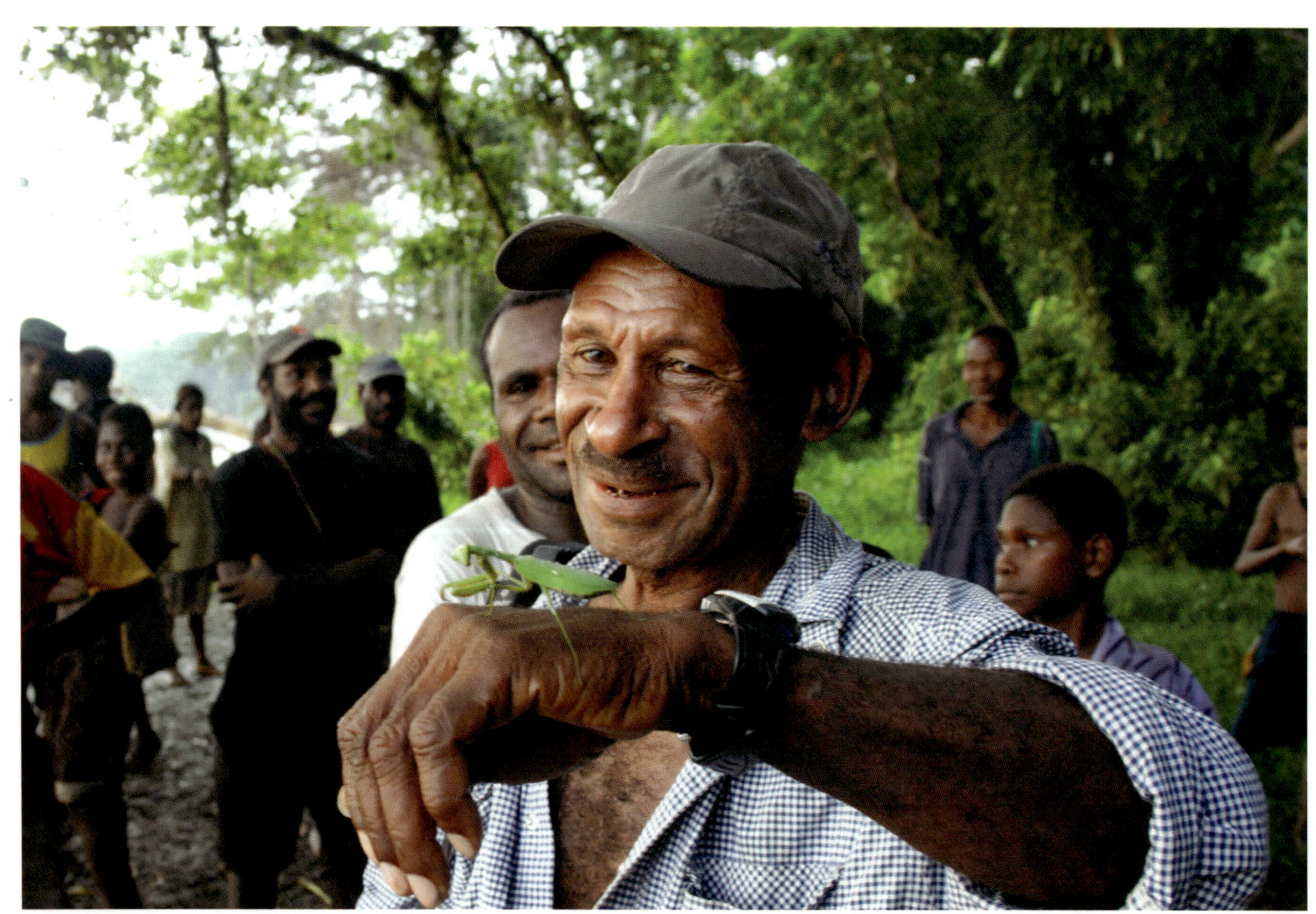

Figure 6.1. Cletus Maiban Smank our friend and guide on many Sepik adventures, beginning in 1984. Photograph by Dan Lepsoe, 2008.

Pacific Artists in the Fine Art Market

Elaine Monds

The aim of this paper is to describe the development and methods of a gallery that exhibits and markets artwork created exclusively by contemporary indigenous artists from the Pacific Rim. The art we are privileged to display ranges from wood and metal sculpture through a wide array of graphic work on paper and canvas. Here, I will discuss the various avenues we have explored to showcase the work, educate the public about it, promote it in the fine art market, and ensure that art-making is an attractive and sustainable livelihood.

The gallery's geographical position on Vancouver Island, home to the great artistic traditions of the Coast Salish, Kwakwaka'wakw, and Nuu-chah-nulth nations, has made it possible to create a gallery that works solely with aboriginal cultures. Our efforts are focused on the Pacific and the Pacific Rim, and are aimed at representing these artists by showing their work with dignity, respect, and attention to cultural protocol. The vibrant cultural and artistic revival that has happened along the Northwest Coast (NWC) of Canada during the past thirty years has demonstrated that traditional arts can be given a contemporary face. During this time, Canadian First Nations artists have experienced a revival of ceremonial life, which in turn has necessitated creation of finely made sculpture and regalia. The corresponding demand for individual artistic excellence has made it increasingly inappropriate for outsiders to view their creations as artifacts rather than art. There has developed an established audience in Europe and North America who appreciates and collects these works.

Over a similar time frame, the gallery has worked to alter the common perception that contemporary arts from tribal societies are remnants of the past rather than dynamic creations from living and vibrant cultures.

Which Cultures to Represent?

I was born in Australia, and spent my early years in East Africa. The experience of growing up there has enriched my life and heightened my awareness and interest in aboriginal peoples wherever I have lived. My interest in Oceanic art began thirty years ago, when I had the opportunity to see, and subsequently exhibit, Sepik artwork from a private collection in Vancouver. In those days, the public paid little attention to any kind of indigenous art, but the fascination I felt for these artworks led me to visit Papua New Guinea in 1984. During my travels, I visited the Sepik River in Papua New Guinea (PNG), and was fortunate to meet Cletus Maiban Smank [fig. 6.1]. Originally from Tambanum village, Cletus was an excellent guide and a carver with a wide knowledge of the varied artistic styles of the Sepik region. Since this visit, I have returned many times to Papua New Guinea. With the invaluable assistance of a network of master carvers, Alcheringa Gallery has assembled collections from a number of Sepik artists. On subsequent trips, ongoing relationships were established with traditional carvers in New Ireland and urban artists in Port Moresby (Lincoln and Monds 1993, Monds and Tutton 1996). The gallery has curated over thirty exhibitions including PNG artists to date. Alcheringa is most strongly associated with wood sculpture, but the importance of paintings and fine art prints of virtually every technique imaginable has been steadily developing.

In an effort to broaden the viewing audience and maximize exhibition space, we have on occasion hosted exhibitions in collaboration with other galleries who usually exhibit mainstream artists. Further expansion of our client base occurred from 1989 to 1997, when Derek Simpkins Gallery of Tribal Art, a leading private gallery in Vancouver, hosted exhibitions of the work of Sepik and New Ireland carvers that Alcheringa Gallery had selected on field trips. Prior to the development of the Internet, these exhibitions presented important opportunities to educate the public about an art form that was new to them. These collaborations were a key success factor in developing the market.

In 1989, Aboriginal Australia became part of the gallery collection. Gordon Grimwade, an anthropologist friend working with Aboriginal and Torres Strait artists at the Tafe College in Cairns, suggested that Alcheringa and The Gallery of Tribal Art co-host an exhibition of their paintings. Andrew Williams, one of the participating Torres Strait artists, was able to attend and conducted a workshop for children. Although the artists were disappointed by relatively poor sales of their work, the show created enormous interest and a base for the future. Spurred by this introductory exhibition, I satisfied a long-held desire to explore remote places in the land of my birth. In 1990, I travelled by air and four-

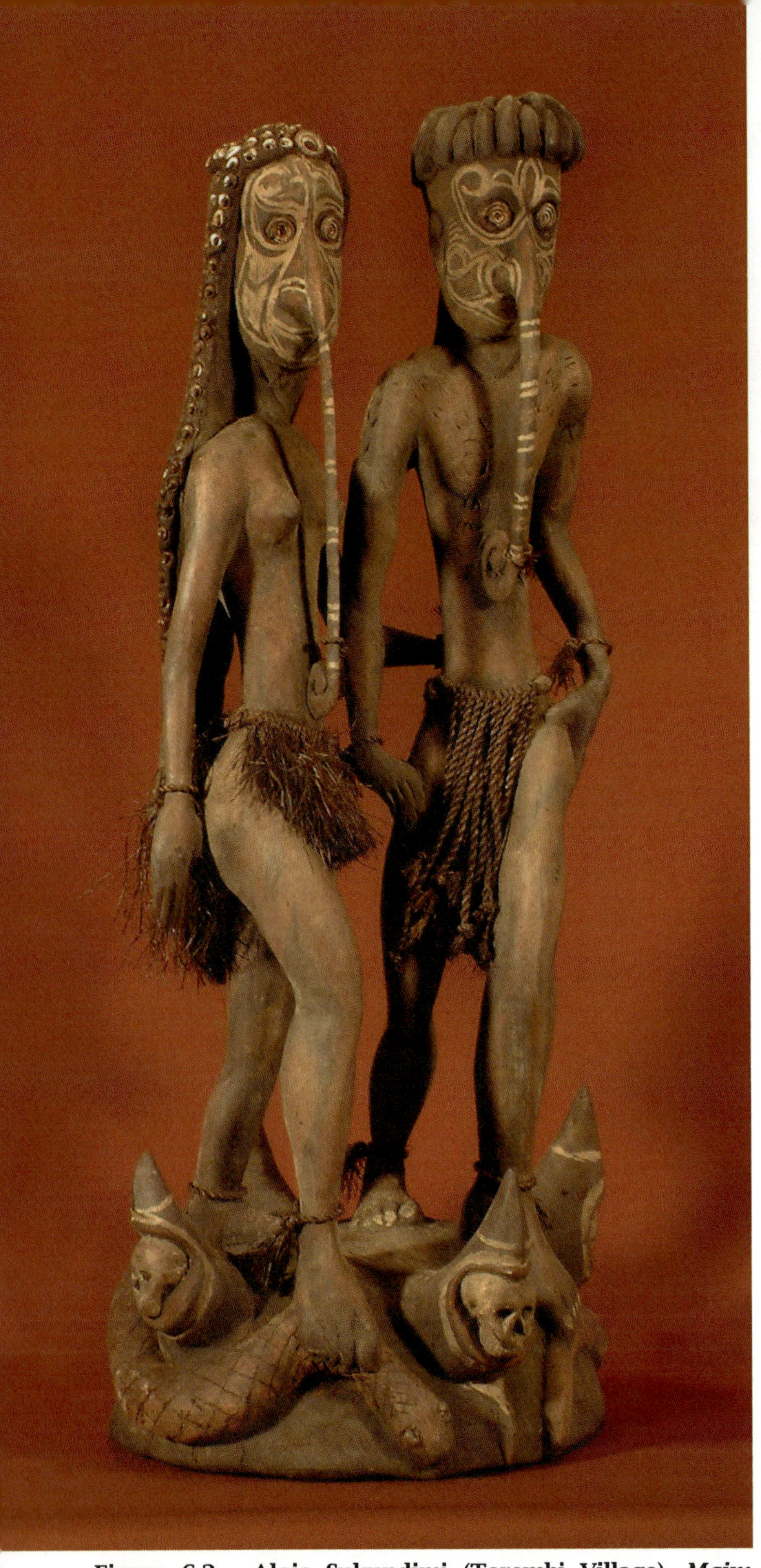

Figure 6.2. Alois Sukundimi (Torembi Village), *Maim.* Wood, cowrie shells, bush fibre, natural pigments, 2004. Alois describes this couple as former butterflies who lived in the sago swamp. He told me the parts of the story that he was free to share. Photograph by Dan Lepsoe, 2004.

wheel drive vehicle through remote settlements in the Western Desert, Arnhem Land, and the Cape York Peninsula. The network established as a result of this journey made it possible to respond to a request in 1994 from the Art Gallery of Greater Victoria to curate an Aboriginal Australian exhibition as part of the cultural festival associated with the Commonwealth Games.

Northwest Coast art has also been a core part of the gallery since 1989. Its inclusion was a natural choice, given our location and the many exciting artistic developments accompanying NWC cultural revitalization.

Though we represent some artists from other traditions (the Solomon Islands, Vanuatu, Métis, and Cree) and are often approached with opportunities to expand our portfolio, our small staff has found it necessary to focus on a few core regions in order to be able to represent them well.

Who Collects Indigenous Art?

The number of people who are both interested in and financially able to buy fine art is very small. The number who chooses to collect indigenous art is even smaller. Thus, our challenge has been to find a way to connect with this exclusive group of people. Our client base has grown considerably and on a global scale over the past fifteen years since we launched our website (www.alcheringa-gallery.com). Because our clientele is distributed worldwide, we use detailed online catalogues and regular mail outs (electronic and print) to ensure that distance is not an impediment to enjoying what the gallery has to offer. About half of our clients are from the United States, a third are from Canada, and most of the rest are from Europe, Asia, and Australia.

We have discovered that desert paintings from Australia and sculptural work from the Sepik appeals to clients who are attracted to contemporary abstract art. We sometimes work with interior designers to place these pieces in private collections. Many of the clients who are attracted to the work are emotionally drawn to it. Some are visual artists themselves.

Collectors of Northwest Coast art can roughly be divided into those who enjoy acquiring pieces without needing to view the work in any kind of aesthetic setting, and those who see the work as adding a dimension to their daily lives as home decoration. We have a number of clients who are passionate about their collections, but have made them with the long-term view of bequeathing the works to a museum rather than enjoying them every day hanging in their homes.

A few years ago, most gallery owners assumed that collectors of Northwest Coast native art were collectors of antiquities — old works made mainly for ceremonial use. But on the coast of British Columbia, making art for sale is not a new phenomenon: it has occurred

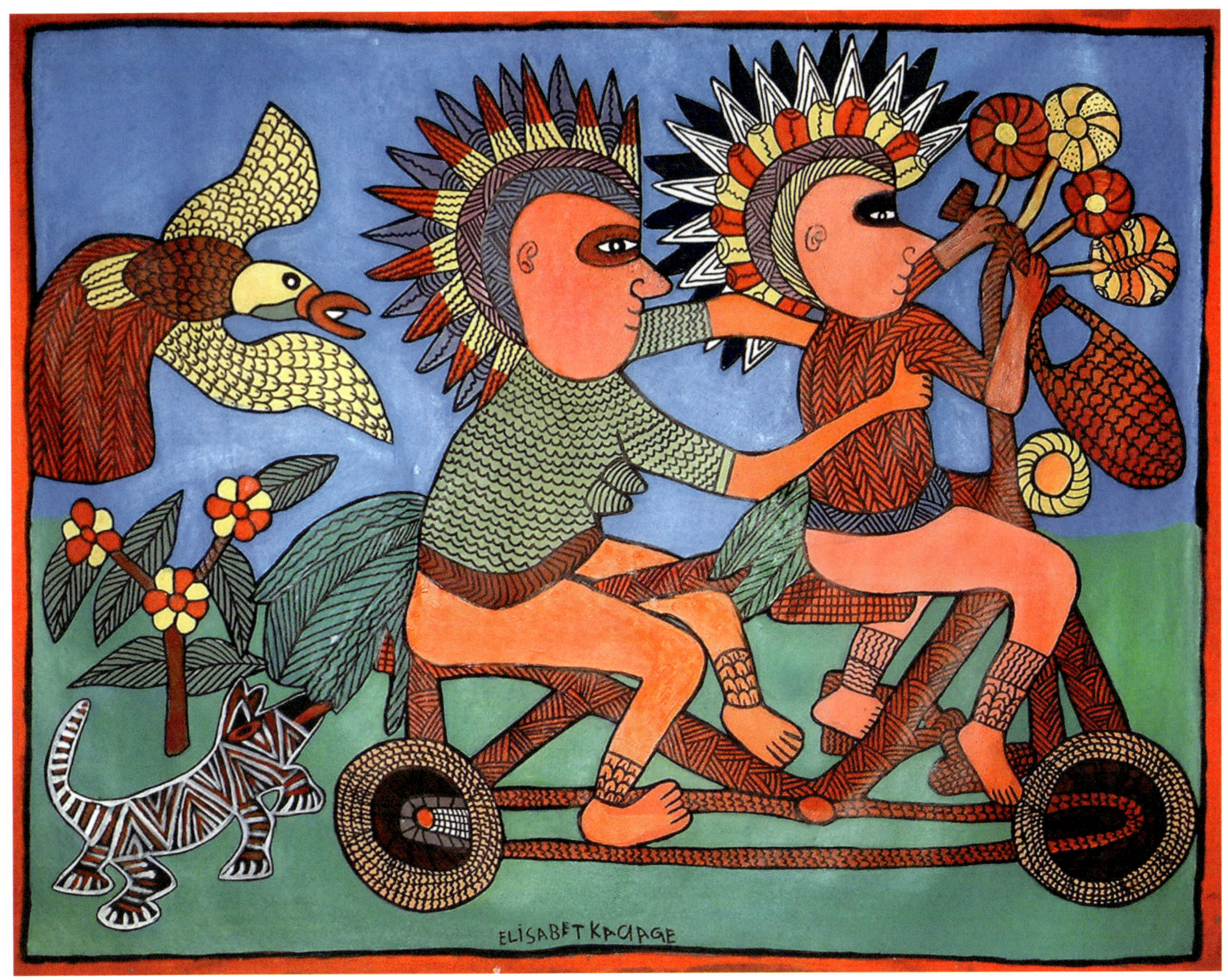

Figure 6.3. Elisabet Kauage (Chimbu) widow of the late artist Mathias Kauage, celebrates Mother's Day in her painting, *Going Shopping on Mother's Day*. Photograph by Dan Lepsoe, 2004.

since the early 1800s, when pieces were collected as curios by explorers and early settlers (Macnair 1994). More recently, however, there has been no difficulty convincing the public of the validity of recently created work from the Northwest Coast. Many contemporary carvers on the coast have developed international reputations. This increased appreciation has contributed to the ready acceptance of contemporary work from other aboriginal traditions in the South Pacific.

What is Authentic Now?

When first visiting carvers on the Sepik River in the early 1980s, I wondered why recent carvings that had obviously been painted in bright ochres appeared to be so ancient. It soon became clear that the market they were supplying only valued works that appeared to be old. Old and authentic traditional art was expected to be by an anonymous carver. The idea of honouring the creator of an artwork as a contemporary artist did not exist. To assist these carvers in establishing their own identities as artists, we had to find some way for their work to be recognized as the artistic creations of individuals. At that time, questions of authenticity were often raised about new works that were almost always referred to as artifacts rather than art. In the minds of most collectors, such pieces could only have relevance if they were old and had been used in ceremonies. The obsession with age inevitably encouraged the proliferation of fakes on the Sepik River. The creators of these fakes were not driven by a desire to deceive or to engage in criminal activities: they were merely trying to please dealers who would give them small amounts of money in exchange for carvings that had been smoked to appear old.

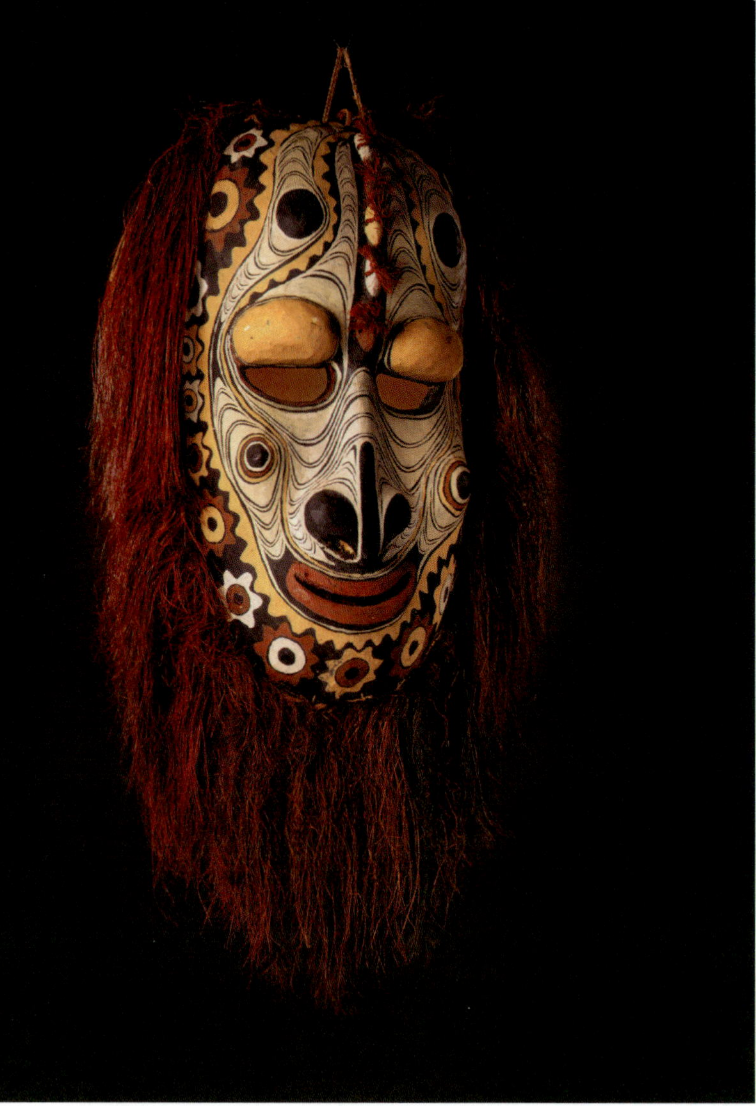

Figure 6.4. Joseph Timbin, deceased, master carver from Palembei Village, Middle Sepik. This *Victory Dance Mask* was selected by Coca Cola for inclusion in their global yearbook to represent their business interests in Papua New Guinea. Photograph by Janet Dwyer, 1996.

Today, our collectors rarely raise the question of authenticity, as they have little reason to doubt that the exquisitely carved object, which bears the carved signature of the artists — accompanied by his photograph, biographical and contextual information (like the artist's own inspirational references in life and mythology), and sometimes a video interview — could be anything else. They are delighted to own a piece of beautiful and emotionally engaging art created by a contemporary Sepik artists. Artists frequently provide background stories to their pieces. Some parts of the stories are secret and cannot be shared [fig. 6.2.]. Nevertheless, we pass on whatever can be told to our clients, allowing artists to provide a small window into the inspiration for their works.

Few collectors deny the authenticity of works created from new and traditional stories being told on paper with oil and acrylic paint, or by various printmaking methods. Master carvers on the Sepik are attempting to prove that the same can be true for wood sculpture. These practices support the premise that, as Haidy Geismar comments in this volume, "categories of authenticity are essential to the constitution of indigenous identity".

Through our growing involvement with artists from the Northwest Coast of British Columbia, it became evident that the contemporary art movement developing in Northwest Coast communities since the late sixties had managed to emerge from the label of "curio" to enter the fine art market. This shift was due to the vision of a handful of artists who had caught the attention of curators and private galleries. They presented their work in an exhibition context rather than as a display of traditional carving in a shopping mall or department store, as was common in the 1960s.

Commercial galleries close to Papua New Guinea tend to place highest value on sculptures that are old or have been used in traditional rituals. By contrast, Alcheringa presents PNG art within the context of a well-developed market for Pacific Northwest Coast art. Our clients tend to approach PNG art in a similar way to Northwest Coast art: with a keen appreciation for contemporary forms of indigenous artistic expression. In our gallery, collectors who follow artists from one culture are often surprised to fall in love with artists from another. We encourage these leaps in our exhibition planning.

The reactions of our clientele in western Canada to artworks created from new materials by 'urban artists' has been more supportive than those in Germany, as described by Marion Struck-Garbe in this volume. Our audience on Vancouver Island has been exposed to myriad styles of graphic work from many resident First Nations traditions. Their response to contemporary expressions from PNG [fig. 6.3.] has been along the lines of "It is wonderful to see these artists using modern media to illustrate their culture!", "We have borrowed from them for so long- why should it not happen in reverse?" and "So delightful to see our world through their eyes!"

Why the difference in response? I believe it is simply because here, indigenous people are part of mainstream society, so the use of cross-cultural means of expression is no surprise. Despite this welcome reception, however, sales of PNG graphic works have been impeded by the poor quality of the paper used. Also, the age of the earlier prints has caused the condition of the work to be less than pristine. Our audience is sophisticated and aware of the value of acid-free paper and quality painting materials. These are still hard to get in PNG: they need to be accessed from outside the country, and are beyond the available budget of most urban artists

Using Education to Develop a Clientele

Education is a top priority for Alcheringa: it's one of the most important strategies we've used to develop a core of enthusiastic collectors. Biographies with photos of the artists are offered to clients in the gallery and through our web site. Photographic records of past works — updated portfolios for each artist — are always accessible. It is not unusual for a client to make two or three visits before a major piece is chosen, and during this time, they become more familiar with the artist's work and the context for it. We keep track of our clients' individual interests so that we can let them know when new works arrive that they may like. Our clients appreciate this personal service. Many buyers become friends of the gallery. One long-time collector regularly enriches our library by sending us a volume of every major work on Northwest Coast contemporary art as it comes off the press. Our artists, clients, and staff use our library as a reference.

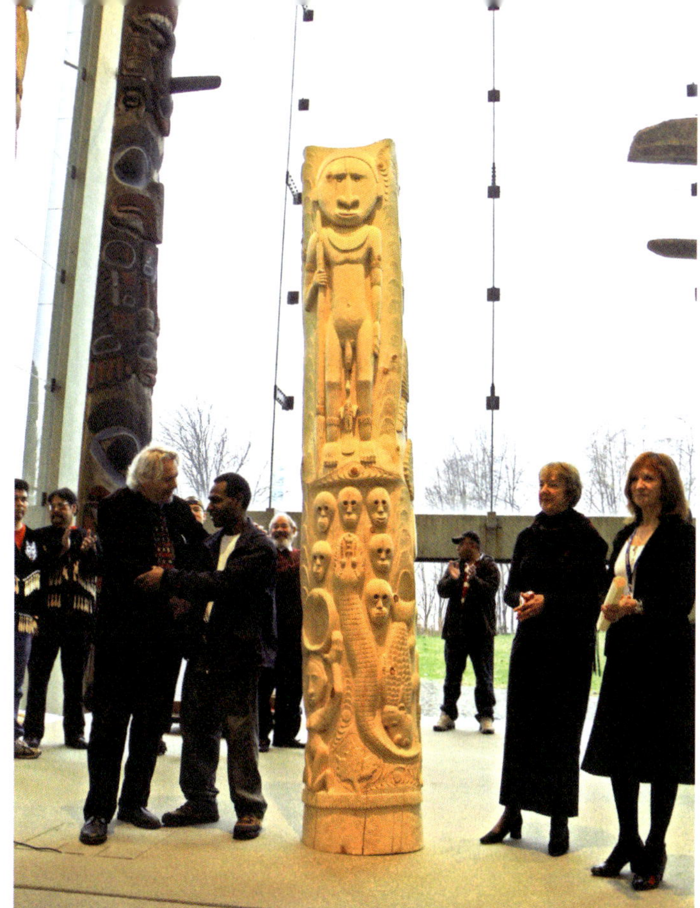

Figure 6.5. Ceremonial raising of *Tuwatmeri*, house post carved by Teddy Balangu for the collection of the Museum of Anthropology University of British Columbia, during his residency there in 2006. Balangu is seen with museum Director Dr Anthony Shelton, Dr Carol E. Mayer and Elaine Monds. Photograph by Dan Lepsoe, 2006.

We've published several print catalogues (e.g. Monds and Tutton, 1996) and dozens of web catalogues about the artists and their work. These efforts have been valuable as a way of introducing the artists to clients. But of equal importance, catalogues and documentation give the carvers an opportunity to show visitors to their villages evidence of the attention paid to their work overseas, demonstrating that while their careers may be village-based, their sculpture is highly regarded by serious collectors globally. This in turn empowers them to achieve better prices for their work, enabling them to provide their children with the education that is increasingly important as Papua New Guinea further integrates with the global economy.

In recent years, anthropologists, art historians, and directors of commercial galleries have documented the careers of indigenous artists from the Pacific Northwest. Over the past several years, there have been no fewer than three major exhibitions in prestigious New York art institutions that have featured contemporary aboriginal artists from the Northwest Coast (Macnair et al 1998, McFadden 2005, and Whiteley 2004-05). Because of this attention, many of these artists have become household names in North America, and their cultures have also become more widely appreciated [1].

Prior to our first exhibition of Aboriginal Australian Art in 1989, there was little knowledge in our region about the contemporary Aboriginal art movement. Thanks to our early exhibitions and extensive networking in Aboriginal Australia, we were asked in 1994 to co-curate an exhibition at the Art Gallery of Greater Victoria (MacNayr 1994) as part of a cultural festival accompanying the Commonwealth Games in Victoria that year. It was followed by a commercial exhibition at Alcheringa. While the public show was well received, our exhibition was well attended but not very successful commercially, much to the disappointment of the six artists who attended. Subsequently, illustrated invitations and extensive online catalogues have encouraged growth in our client base for Aboriginal Australian art, and many scholarly texts offer our clients further opportunities to learn about the work (e.g. Sutton 1988, Ryan 1989).

The Pacific Northwest is fortunate that the Seattle Art Museum is home to the distinguished Kaplan/Levi collection of Australian Aboriginal Art. Part of this collection is on permanent display at the museum and works are regularly loaned to other institutions. As

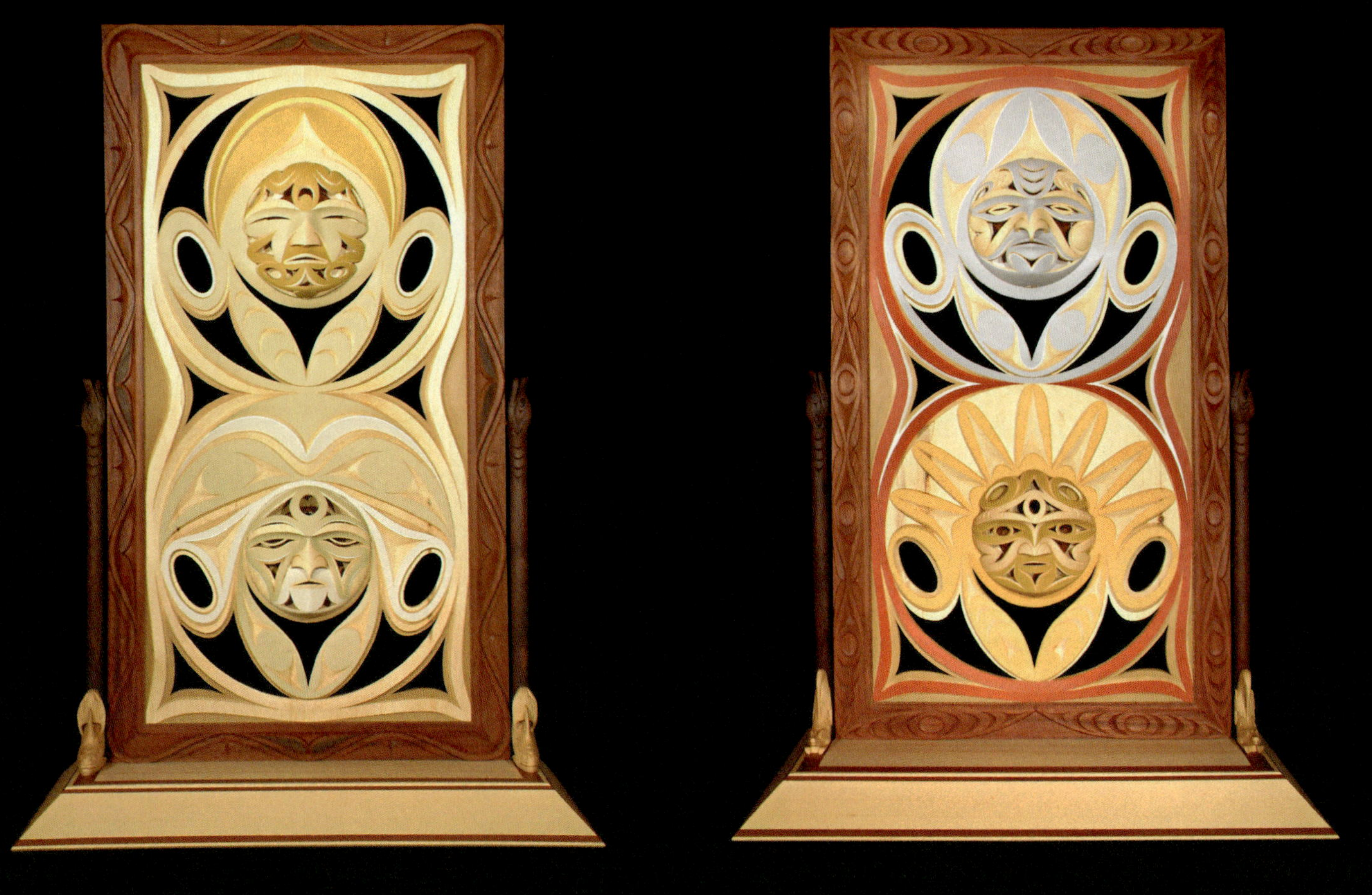

Figure 6.6. John Marston (Coast Salish), *'ehhwe'p syuth* (To Share History). Yellow cedar, Sepik rosewood, black walnut, ebony inlay, 2007. This monumental sculpture is one of several tributes to the Sepik art and culture John experienced as part of the Alcheringa Gallery's 2006 trip to Papua New Guinea.. Photograph by Dan Lepsoe, 2007.

Konau (2006) comments, public exhibitions increase client confidence in buying artwork. Also, the attention given by the academic community, both in terms of publications and public exhibitions, enhances the general public's confidence and knowledge in Indigenous arts.

Awareness of Copyright

There is a growing understanding of the value of copyright among artists of the Canadian Northwest Coast. These artists are frequently approached to sell the copyright of their images. These days, artists recognize that once they do so, they lose all control over its future use. Many commercial publications featuring First Nations artwork, such as calendars, journals, and diaries, do not pay for the use of the images, offering instead a small reimbursement in kind. Many artists feel honoured to have their work chosen for inclusion, and feel that any financial loss is offset by the value of being seen by a wide audience.

We are often approached by members of the public for suggestions for Northwest Coast tattoo designs. People seldom realize that must obtain permission from the artist, and should also be prepared to pay for that privilege. Upon learning this, many lose interest, but in the occasional case, a design has been commissioned from an artist. Our South Pacific artists — especially those in remote places — have no control over the use of images of their creations. There seems to be a growing understanding (no doubt influenced by fear of litigation) among large corporations and film companies that permission must be sought from artists when using images of their work. It was encouraging when the Hong Kong office of the Coca Cola Company contacted us recently to purchase the right to an image of a mask by Joseph Timbin that they had seen in one of our catalogues [fig. 6.4.].

Facilitating Travel & Exchange

Opportunities to work abroad and interact with other cultures do much to further artists' careers. The support given by the Australian government over the past few years to Aboriginal and Torres Strait artists has made it possible for artists to travel overseas. In 2001, four artists and a storytelling elder from Mua Island

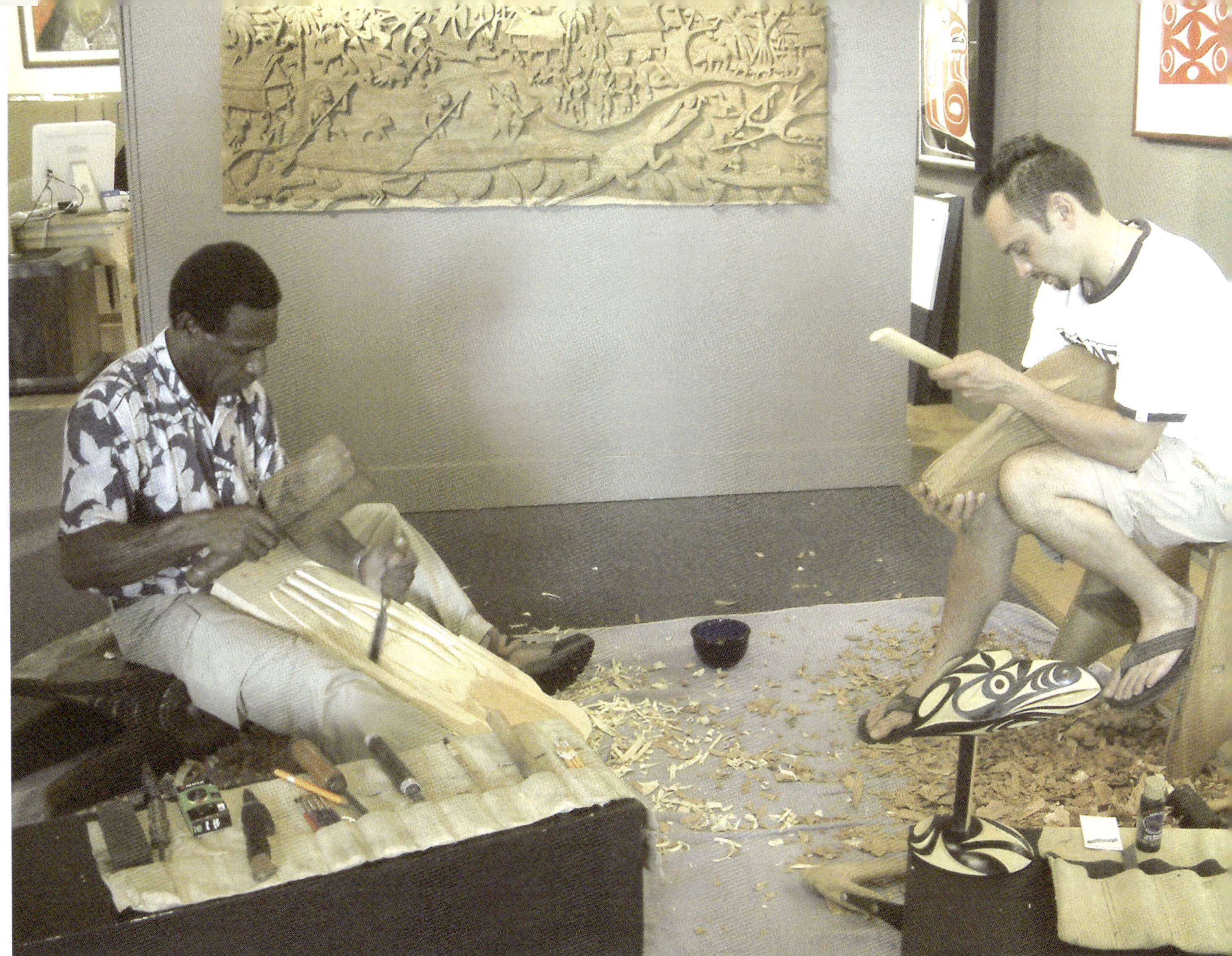

Figure 6.7. Teddy Balangu (Iatmul) and John Marston (Coast Salish) carving together at Alcheringa during Balangu's residency at the University of British Columbia. Photograph Dan Lepsoe, 2006..

in the Torres Strait were able to attend the opening of an exhibition of their intricate linoprints at Alcheringa. They stayed for three weeks in Victoria, spending many days in the gallery talking to clients and other artists. Subsequently, they travelled to the Rebecca Hossack Art Gallery in London.

In 2006, John Marston, a Coast Salish artist from Canada, came with me to meet and work with the master carvers of Palembei Village on the Sepik River. Later that year, Teddy Balangu travelled to Canada at the invitation of Carol Mayer from the Museum of Anthropology, University of British Columbia, to create a house post for their collection [fig. 6.5.]. Alcheringa Gallery had worked with Teddy for many years and our knowledge of his work, coupled with familiarity with the Sepik region, made it possible for the gallery to assist with his selection for this experience, and later to facilitate his visit. John Marston called the exchange between the two carvers "a life-changing experience". His artwork now reflects not just his Salish heritage, but an expanded design palette and use of some of the exotic woods he discovered on his journey [fig. 6.6]. A creation by Teddy Balangu [fig 6.7.] featuring both a killer whale and a crocodile, symbols of his and John's cultures, was part of Hailans to Ailans (Mel and Rosi, 2009), a major international exhibition held at Alcheringa and the Rebecca Hossack Art Gallery in London, in 2009.

Bravo! Canada commissioned filmmakers to document the exchange between Teddy and John, resulting in *Killerwhale and Crocodile* (2007). Since its release in August 2007, the film has been selected for inclusion in many international film festivals throughout the Pacific and North America, and has recently been

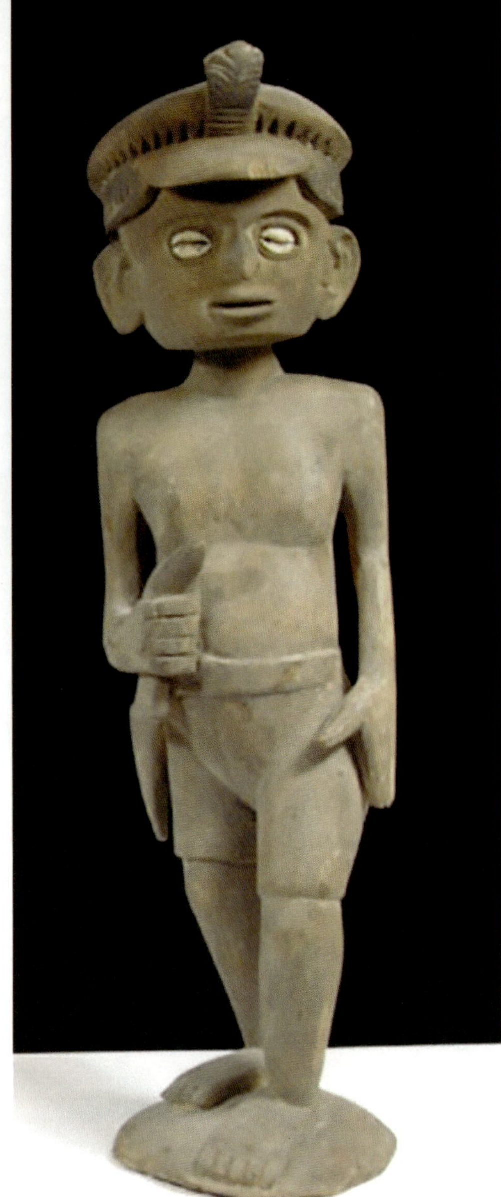

Figure 6.8. Plasios Asapi, deceased (Maramba Village), *Sepik Policeman*, Garamut wood, cowrie shells. Photograph Emma Monds-King, 2009.

purchased by the Australia Broadcasting Corporation. Although Australia is a former colonial administrator of PNG that still provides foreign aid, little is known there of the contemporary master carvers from the Sepik. In fact, Australian media feeds commonly held views that PNG is too dangerous to visit. ABC's purchase will give their audiences a distinctly different impression.

The recent introduction of a residency program to assist artists (mainly Papua New Guinean) to spend a month or more at the de Young Museum in San Francisco has provided them with valuable opportunities to broaden their knowledge by studying early works from their own culture (catalogued in Friede and Peltason, 2005), and also to demonstrate their own contemporary skills. This program is made possible through the generosity of Marcia and John Friede, and is also supported by the Embassy of Papua New Guinea.

In collaboration with the de Young and other institutions, and with the support of the Christensen Foundation, five Papua New Guinean artists went to London (UK), Victoria (Canada), as well as other destinations in the United States as part of the touring exhibition Hailans to Ailans (Mel and Rosi, 2009; hailanstoailans.com). Although the show focused on contemporary PNG art, other Pacific artists participated to enrich the examination of common issues such as cultural sustainability, colonization, and exchange.

Working with Artists

Most mainstream commercial galleries work with a stable of artists who consign works. If these works are not close enough to be personally viewed, they are chosen from photos. The gallery director may not need to travel to conduct business with artists. We have a somewhat different approach because we work with artists scattered around the Pacific Rim, many of whom live in remote places without access to photographic equipment. In order to represent their work to best advantage, we travel to meet them, as they cannot usually come to us. I also like to travel to meet artists because I have never felt comfortable showing works of art that I have only seen disembodied from their cultural background. Our Northwest Coast artists are geographically closer to us, and many visit the gallery regularly, bringing their work for us to see. Those further afield are often able to communicate by email.

My travels in Australia have taken me to a number of remote areas in the Tanami Desert, where the Western Desert art movement began in the 1970s, north to Maningrida, Oenpelli, and Aurukun in Arnhem Land, and to the Munupi painters on Melville Island. I've met many artists and purchased works with the assistance of the art advisors in each area. Connections and experience gained during those trips have made many of the gallery's exhibitions possible. But this way of collecting, enjoyable as it is from a personal perspective, has required extended periods away from home and the gallery and an investment that was beyond our capacity. In order to continue showing the work, some more direct and less financially onerous processes needed to be found. In the last few years, the increased support of Aboriginal artists by the Australian government has enabled us to work at a distance, but it has also made it possible for artists to visit us here in Canada. We have hosted three exhibitions of graphics with the cooperation of the Aboriginal Art Print Network, based in Sydney. This group documents and publishes etchings, linocuts, and silkscreen prints using the highest quality hand-made papers, drawing together artists, community workers, academics, and printmakers for exhibitions that explore diverse themes of Aboriginal culture.

It has been exciting to witness the influence new technology is having upon the lives of artists from the Pacific Rim. As long ago as 1996, I was given sleeping quarters in the video theatre in the Tabar Islands. On the Sepik, many villages now have access to DVD players, and most recently, cell phones. It is still difficult to call landlines in Port Moresby from North America but I have no problem reaching my friends in Angoram on their cell phones. I recently had an email from one of our artists, Elias Samba, from Kaminibit village, over a hundred kilometres along the river from road access. Emailing from Wewak, the regional centre, he had been surfing the net, and was delighted to see his recent work on Alcheringa's website. This powerful connection made over such distance was thrilling and gratifying for us, too.

While these changes expose people — especially young people — to the Western world, often with negative effect, they have also given those in remote areas, such as the Sepik, knowledge of a world formerly outside their experience. Sepik art is evolving to encompass new forms and ideas between the Sepik and the outside world. These increasingly innovative artworks tell of the exploits of mythic heroes, but also show the musculature and stance of real Papuan New Guineans [fig. 6.8].

The pace of life is changing globally, and we see this with each succeeding trip to PNG. As my colleague Dan Lepsoe (2008) observed of our last Sepik trip:

> Young men are incorporating new masks and dances into ceremonies that include traditional songs and regalia. Young women are weaving bilums (string bags carried by every Papua New Guinean) with cell phone pockets [fig. 6.9.], anticipating the technology's advance along the river this year... Museums around the world are starting modern collections to complement historical ones that have long been seen as representative of a more or less static culture... [These collections include] bold variations on traditional flute designs, deeply carved storyboards that conflate multiple visual and narrative perspectives, body sculpture that stretches traditional bounds of realism and abstraction, life-like woven animals, mesmerizing dance masks [fig. 6.10.] and a large cast of characters ranging from mythological heroes to contemporary politicians [fig. 6.11.] [2].

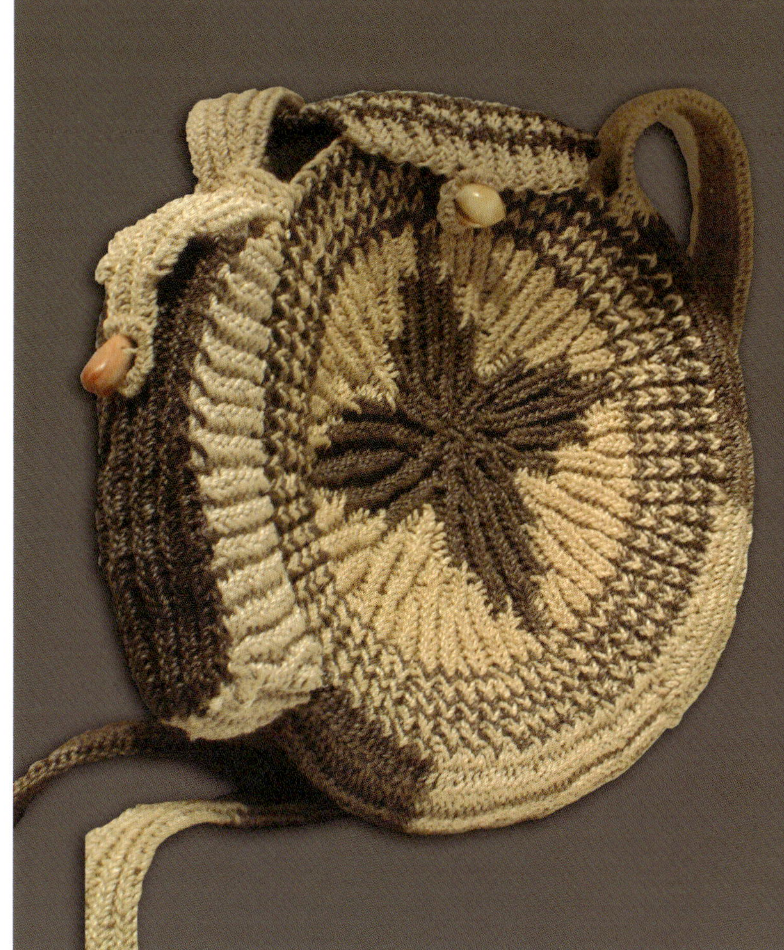

Figure 6.9. Mrs. Camillus Waybenang (Kambot Village), Bilum, Natural fibre (mangus) and dye, cowrie shells, 2008. Note the cell phone pocket, a stylish innovation on this traditional Papua New Guinean form. Photograph by Sarah Stein, 2008.

Changing technology has also influenced artists from this side of the Pacific Rim. The adaptation of mainly three dimensional art to silk screen printing has served to increase awareness of the culture and has also made it possible for younger people to become involved in collecting. Haida artist Robert Davidson and Salish artist Susan Point have experimented and successfully translated their original woodcarvings into laser-cut steel and etched glass. As a result of his experience working with Sepik master carvers, Salish carver John Marston incorporates tropical woods in some of his new work.

Accessing Remote Areas

All of the Sepik artworks are purchased in the field, and the process of collection is expensive. The costs of transportation of people, packing materials, and artworks all have to be included in the final retail value. I explain to artists what is involved in a gallery markup while we discuss purchase prices. For the younger carvers, at least, these prices always exceed their asking prices. Among carvers with whom we have worked consistently, there is a growing understanding of what

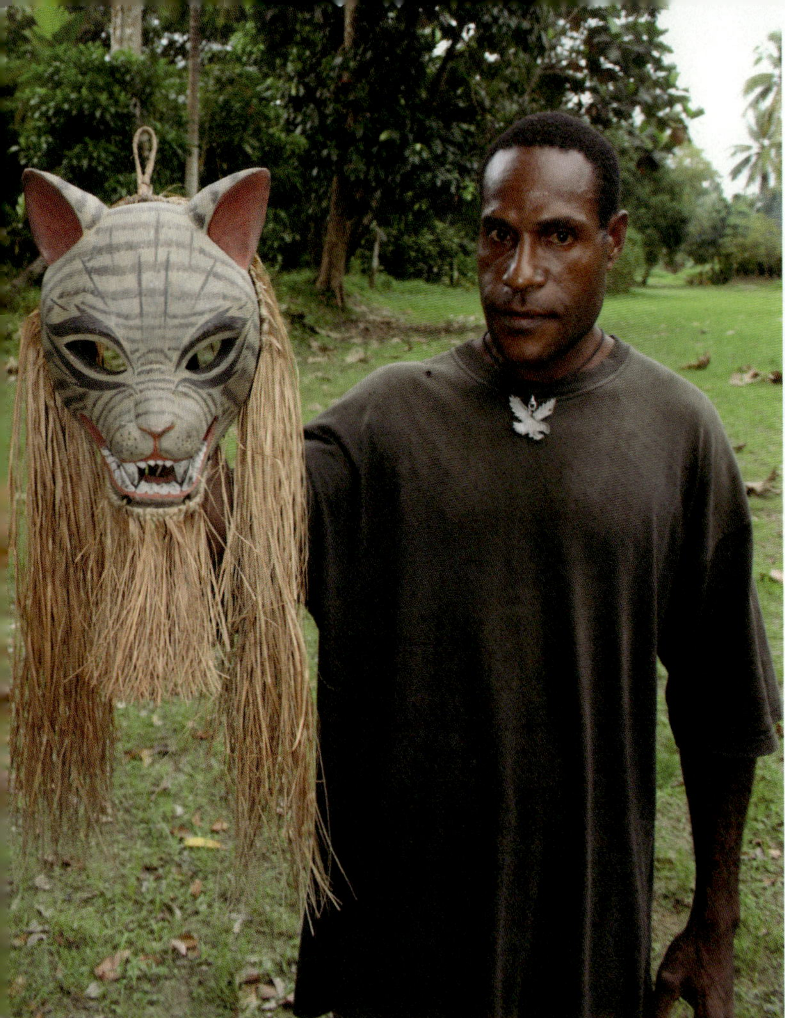

Figure 6.10. Edward Dumoi (Palembei Village), *Cat Dance Mask.* Wood, fibre, natural pigments, 2008. This mask was worn by a young dancer as part of a ceremonial welcome for us.. Photograph by Dan Lepsoe, 2008.

their work is worth in the Western world. Good carving tools are scarce in PNG, so on each visit, the gallery takes a range of chisels for master carvers in a number of Sepik villages.

Because of the high costs involved, each trip must furnish work for at least three exhibitions, and it is difficult to finance these in advance. As these artists receive more recognition for the contemporary expressions of their culture it will be possible to make these trips more economically viable by purchasing works for other galleries at the same time. There are many "artifact" dealers, some of whom could be persuaded to market the best of the work by identified artists. Growing recognition by the academic world will give them confidence to take some degree of financial risk in order to market the work as fine art.

There have been many attempts by aid organizations to introduce Western-inspired projects to assist people living on the Sepik River, but surely there is no better way to achieve sustainability than to harness traditional means to live in the modern world. The creation of magnificent carvings for the fine art market results in cash creation, but it also reinforces the culture, as has been clearly illustrated by the experience of contemporary artists from the Northwest Coast of Canada. Although institutional recognition has been slow to come for Papua New Guineans, the number exhibiting the work of identified, contemporary Sepik carvers are growing.

Marketing

Most of our advertising budget is directed to our mailing list of about 3500 individuals. Printing and mailing costs make this an expensive endeavour, but it is important for the artists to have their works documented in print, and most of our clients are so bombarded with email that we find it best for them to have an invitation to hold in hand. These invitations often ignite interest in a very direct way. They have a longer life and are often kept or passed on to friends. The PNG artists particularly enjoy them, as they lose all contact with their artwork once it has left the village.

Northwest Coast exhibition openings are festive occasions. Artists can easily be present, and dancing, drumming, and singing illustrates the ceremonial context of works on display. There is a psychological advantage in creating an aura of anticipation around selling artworks at an opening. For major Northwest Coast exhibitions, the works may become available for sale at a specific time on the morning of the opening, and the evening is then committed to a celebration of the culture with friends, family, and clients.

The gallery has published several print catalogues documenting artists from the Northwest Coast and several cultures of PNG (Lincoln and Monds, 1993; Alcheringa, 1994; Monds and Tutton, 1996; Mel and Rosi, 2009). These publications are circulated among ethnographic book suppliers and museum libraries. Besides furthering the careers and work of artists, catalogues help artists market their work in places as remote as Ambrym Island in Vanuatu and the Sepik River in Papua New Guinea. One of our clients met artist Douglas Solomon from Ranon village on Ambrym Island in Vanuatu. After paddling out to meet him, Douglas showed him a copy of our exhibition catalogue, which featured one of his tam tam drums. On his return to Vancouver, this man came to the gallery and told us that the encounter provided the reassurance necessary for him to pay Douglas a substantial sum for a major piece in this remote place. A collector of historical work found himself also drawn to contemporary work after seeing Alcheringa's *Life of the Copper* (Macnair, 1994) in the library of the British Museum. I believe that a substantial catalogue is the single most valuable promotional and educational tool for both individual artists and galleries. We would like to be able to afford to publish this kind of record more frequently.

Membership in a Gallery Walk Association is part of our local promotion efforts. The other galleries represent mainstream non-native artists of international stature. We have chosen to be part of this group because our artists are part of this same global fine art market. After many years of experimentation, commercial print advertising is confined to one magazine targeting our local clientele to keep them apprised of current events in the gallery, and to one tourist publication that is distributed through major hotels. The gallery appears regularly in two magazines directed entirely to the visual arts. One of these has a circulation close to home, including the western United States; the other targets Canada's prairie provinces.

The best kind of advertising is the kind that does not require payment. As Victoria is a tourist mecca, we have benefited from inclusion in some prestigious travel guides, including the French-language Michelin Guide and Frommer's Guide to Vancouver Island. The gallery regularly attracts the attention of freelance writers, and their articles have had wide circulation in arts-related magazines.

In 1995, Alcheringa launched www.alcheringa-gallery.com. Since then, the growth in our use of this medium has proceeded at an extraordinary rate. Initially, the majority of our clients did not have personal access and would visit the library to look at our site. In those days, the medium was mainly of use to direct existing clients to new works as they came into the gallery. Despite the site's value, reliance on services outside our own staff made updating it expensive and inaccurate. To remedy this, we switched to a database-driven model so that staff with little technical expertise can easily make additions and changes. All new arrivals are posted on the web as they arrive into the gallery. Periodic email updates inform clients of current and coming events. A comprehensive online catalogue accompanies each exhibition [3]. Clients appreciate the educational material relating to the cultures represented, including information, photos, and biographies of the artists. Many of our clients seem to require instant gratification; the advent of quality digital photography has allowed us to satisfy their needs. We have also discovered that no matter how fine a website may be, unless people can easily find it, it is irrelevant. To this end, we conduct periodic reviews of search engine rankings and try to improve them. These efforts have resulted in many new clients — even from Papua New Guinea!

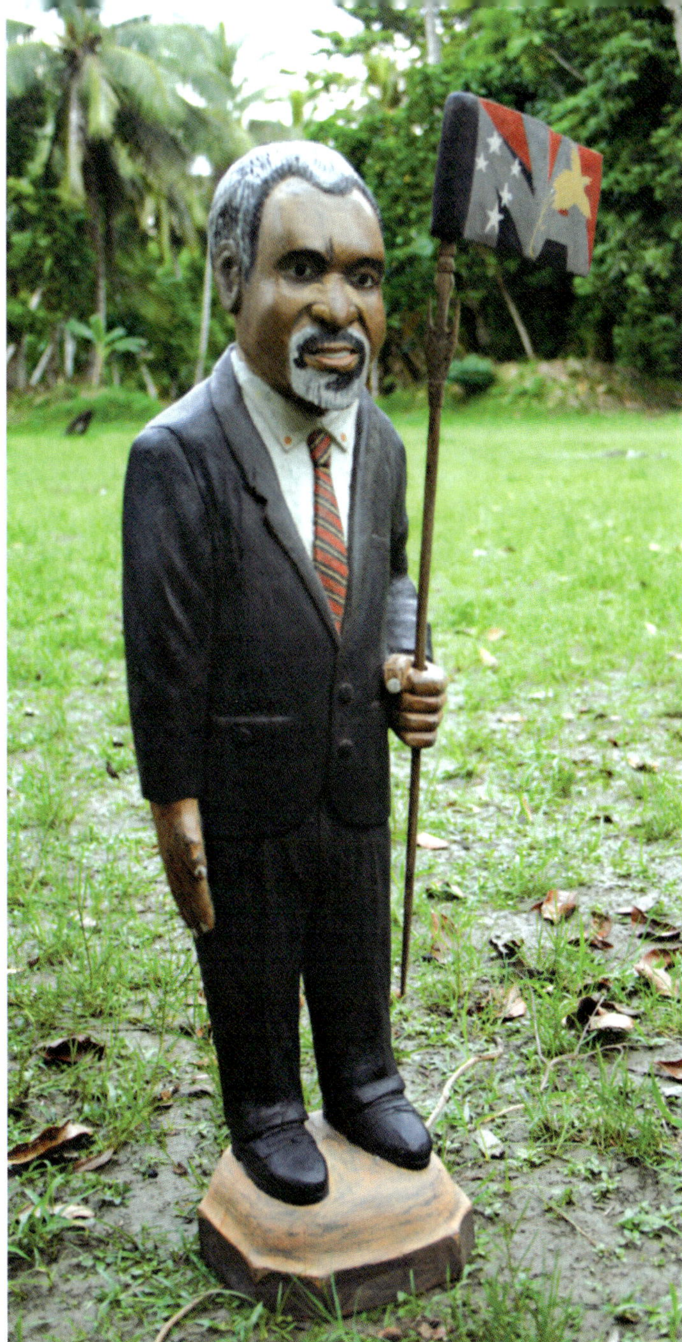

Figure 6.11. Edward Dumoi (Palembei Village), *Prime Minister Michael Somare*, wood, paint, 2008. Photograph by Dan Lepsoe, 2008.

Conclusions

A global market for contemporary indigenous art from the South Pacific can grow using similar methods to those used to develop the market for Native American art. The so-called "commercial" galleries need to be acknowledged for — and assisted in — the role they play in creating income for the artists by promoting, exhibiting, and finding a clientele for their artwork. Indigenous artists from wealthier countries such as Australia, Canada, and New Zealand frequently receive funding to enable them to attend arts events in other parts of the world, but there is little funding available in developing countries for artists to travel. At Alcheringa, we have proven the value of travel and cultural exchange to further artists' careers [fig. 6.12].

There is an equal need for more venues devoted to marketing indigenous fine art. Artists need galleries to show their work, and it would help the artists a great deal if there were more opportunities for public institutions and private galleries to work together to both celebrate and sell the work.

I am privileged to be in the pivotal role of establishing relationships between artists and art lovers from such distant contexts. The challenges that must be faced when working from within a private gallery such as Alcheringa are outweighed by the satisfaction of witnessing the growing confidence and self-awareness of artists as their creations and cultures are more widely appreciated.

Afterword: On New Voyagers & the Benefits of Collaboration

When first preparing this text, it was in response to an invitation from anthropologist Pamela Rosi. She invited me, as the director of a commercial gallery, to be a member of a working session about contemporary indigenous art in the Pacific. This discussion was part of the ASAO (Association for Social Anthropology in Oceania) conference held in Vancouver, Canada, in 2003. These meetings culminated in a symposium in 2005. Further time elapsed between then and the publication of this volume, necessitating an updating of some of the material in my essay. However, as I began that task, I realized that so many of our gallery activities had grown and altered, and that this paper needed to reflect the value of that networking.

Partly as a result of 'New Voyagers', the range of artists represented at Alcheringa has grown. Communications have improved between artists and between the institutions, public and private, that work with them. Prior to the first meeting in Vancouver in 2003, it seemed that the few galleries around the world that worked with indigenous artists from developing countries in the Pacific did so in a vacuum. There was little communication internationally between artists or those of us representing them. The value of cross-cultural and international exchange has been growing steadily ever since.

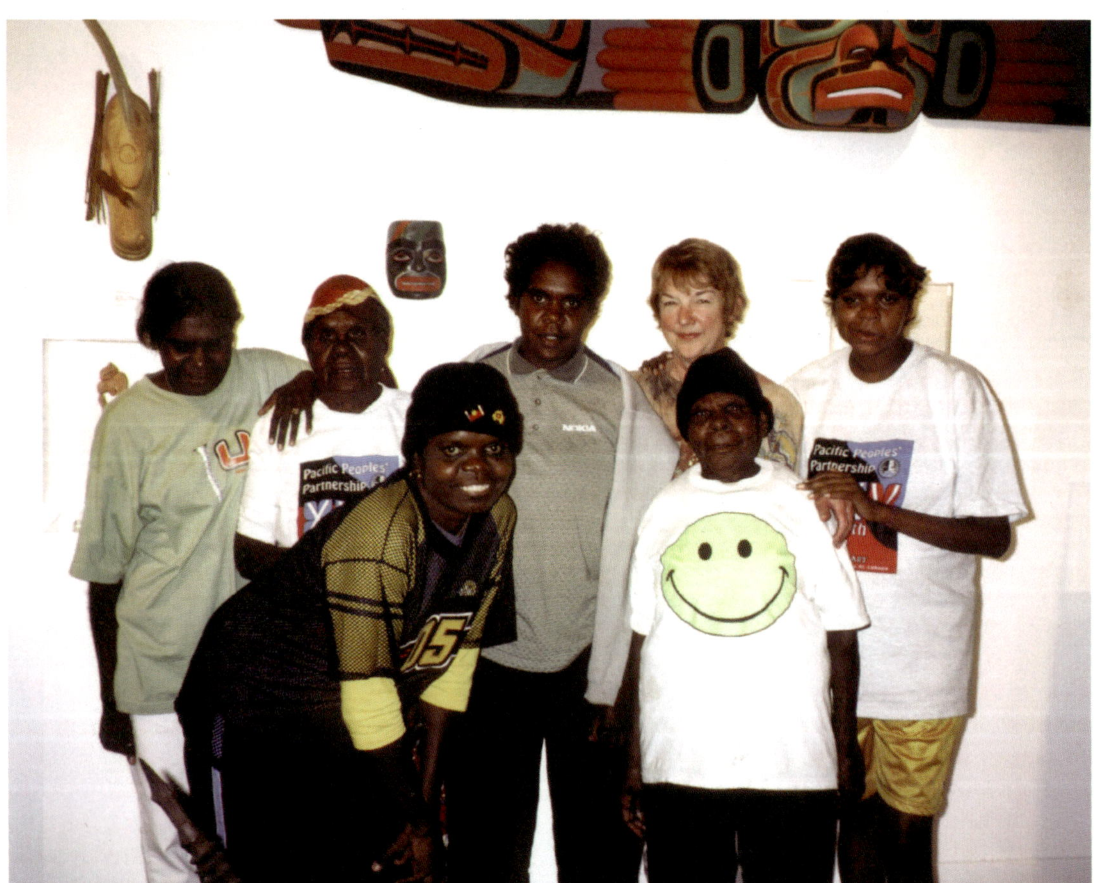

Figure 6.12. With the artists from Balgo, Northern Australia, during their visit to Alcheringa Gallery in 2001. Photograph by Troy Hunter, 2001.

Expressions of Continuity and Reflections of Rupture: Contemporary Pacific Art in an Anthropology Museum

Carol E. Mayer

When Alfred H. Barr Jr., former director of the Museum of Modern Art, tried to persuade Gertrude Stein to leave her collection of contemporary works to the museum she quipped "You can be a museum or you can be modern, but you cannot be both" (Mellow 1968). The comment, although made more than 60 years ago, still resonates for those who persist that the central function of a museum is to collect, preserve and display only those objects that have withstood the test of time.

In this paper I will explore some of the issues and challenges facing an anthropology museum that has recently decided to collect and exhibit contemporary works from the Pacific. The Museum of Anthropology (MOA) at the University of British Columbia is particularly well known for its scholarship, publications and exhibitions relating to the collection of objects made by the First Nations peoples of British Columbia, Canada. Lesser known is the fact that the museum also holds significant collections from around the world, particularly the Pacific. In order to provide a framework for this exploration I begin with a discussion about the legacy of earlier collecting practices of anthropology museums. I continue with a brief description of the Pacific islands' collections at MOA and the exhibition *Pasifika: Island Journeys*, and then talk a little about what limits the museum's commitment to collecting contemporary works from the Pacific. As this has been a new direction for the museum, I examine our practices and decision-making processes associated with the collecting and exhibiting of First Nation's contemporary art to ascertain whether and/or how the issues and challenges associated with contemporary collecting practices in British Columbia might inform contemporary collecting in the Pacific. I was interested in whether those of us who work in anthropology museums distinguish between collecting works viewed as remnants of authenticity — that symbolize the continuity of what museums already have in their collections and co-exist, even comingle, with historic collections — or collecting works that challenge continuity, reflect rupture and change, and compete for the contested spaces occupied by Western contemporary arts. We seem to be generally comfortable with, and have the experience and knowledge to form an opinion about the first; the question is whether we can do the same for the second. In order to examine this question I will look at some examples of how First Nations' contemporary works have been critiqued and examine how copyright law, which protects the rights of Canadian artists, has been applied to contemporary works from the Pacific. I conclude with a discussion about how the purchase of a contemporary mask from Vanuatu, intended for display in a Canadian museum, provided the opportunity to perhaps contribute to the discussions and critiques related to collecting practices, how we define and interpret the rights of the artist and how we look at and categorize art in anthropology museums

Anthropology and Collecting

There is a generally held view that museums emerged from anthropology, a discipline formed by colonial practice. This practice was underpinned with the belief that indigenous peoples were on the road to extinction and would disappear. [1] Objects belonging to their tangible heritage were collected in great haste, poorly documented and warehoused in museums where they were re-presented as remnants of a still and silent ethnographic past (Phillips 1993:99). Although the objects collected were usually contemporary at the time of collecting, they were immediately historicized by their role as the concluding representatives of a disappearing heritage. Their authenticity was based on them being uncontaminated by Western influences — yet Pacific Islanders and First Nations here in British Columbia had been creating objects for sale or exchange long before the frenetic collecting began. [2] These objects entered museums as remnants of authenticity — trophies of colonialism — isolated from their cultural context, stored according to western museum management systems, [3] and detached from their makers, who invariably remained unnamed. They were displayed either as artifacts, *memento mori*, or as primitive art, isolated, spotlighted, and glassed in.

When portents of doom proved to be wrong and indigenous artists continued to make objects, both for cultural use and for sale to tourists, notions of authenticity became muddled. Art historians denounced tourist art as inauthentic, shoddy and unworthy of study. Museum anthropologists invested authenticity only in those works (artifacts) that showed evidence of use — something easily rectified by the canny maker (Jules-Rosette 1984). Museums were entangled in notions of their unique ability to display the artifact as

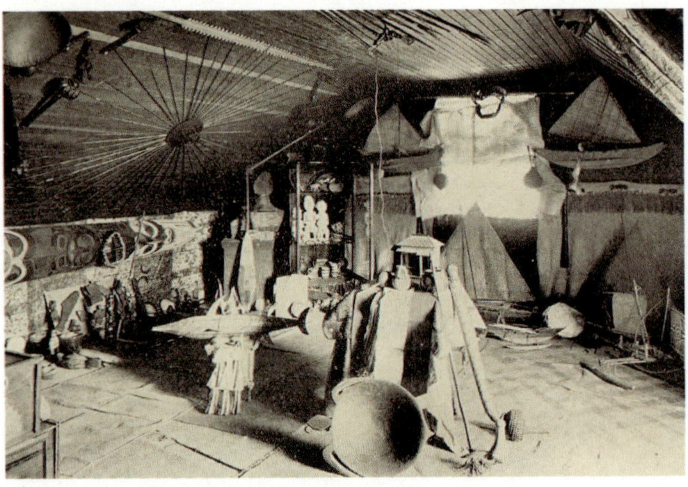

Figure 7.1 Frank Burnett's Collection of South Seas artifacts. c. 1910. . Photograph courtesy of the University of British Columbia Museum of Anthropology.

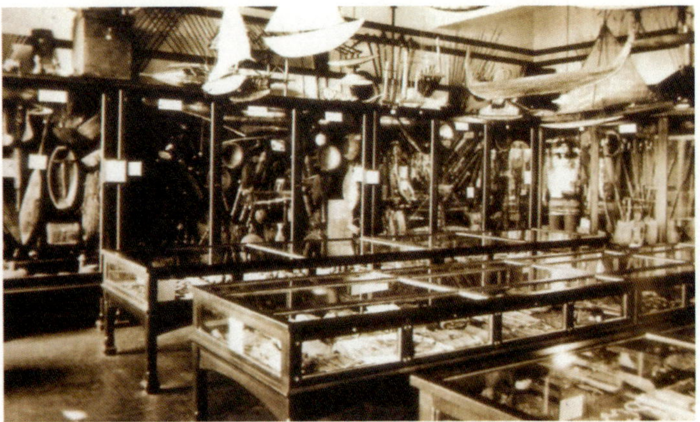

Figure 7.2 Burnett Collection in Main Library, 1929. (UBC1.1/1255). Photograph by Frank Leonard.

the 'real thing' and the realization that they didn't really know what they meant by 'real,' whilst art historians embraced notions of primitivism in exhibits of works, displayed as art, that were undoubtedly made for the market. Some progress has been made, as evidenced in more recent exhibitions, but many of the questions and inconsistencies that have arisen from these earlier viewpoints still need to be addressed (Jules-Rosette 1984). It is not the objective of this paper to provide the answers but to embark on an examination of how past practices have shaped the questions and opinions held by Anthropologists and Art Historians.

MOA

The Museum of Anthropology was founded on a donation of about 1500 Pacific Islands' objects collected between 1898 and ca 1923 by Frank Burnett, Canadian writer and traveler. There is no doubt that his collecting motives and practices were driven by his belief that "it can only be a matter of a few years before his island home will know him no more, and he will form a part of antiquarian lore, and rank among the extinct races of mankind" (Burnett 1910:6). The objects were displayed both as curios and authentic representations of past, or soon to be past, cultures. The collection remained in Burnett's curio room until 1927 [fig. 7.1] when it was donated to the university and displayed for twenty years in a room in the library [fig. 7.2]. In 1947 Dr. Harry Hawthorn came to the university to create a new department of Anthropology. His wife Audrey Hawthorn took over the curating of the collection and used it primarily as a teaching tool for early anthropology students. This interest waned as the museum's focus shifted to the works created by First Nations of British Columbia. It wasn't until 1976 when the museum moved to a new building that some of the Pacific Islands' collection was made accessible to the public. [4] The objects were organized in an open storage system, along with the rest of the worldwide collections, and grouped according to type and geo-cultural distribution [fig. 7.3]. Over the years this system, initially promoted as a move towards the democratization of the museum, was soundly critiqued by students, scholars and visitors. The large number of objects (about 20,000) stacked on shelves was viewed by some as an opportunity to discover and by others as a disorienting experience. There was no interpretation, objects were not displayed singularly as art or grouped by any specific cultural context. When contemporary works were added they were not adequately distinguished from the older works and so for many visitors the collection remained historic and static. To some extent this was rectified by a temporary exhibition program, and related public programs, that showcased the contemporary works of First Nations' artists. However, there were no exhibitions about the Pacific Islands' collection, no public events or education programs. It was never formally exhibited until 2003 when the museum celebrated its 50th anniversary and the decision was made to focus on the founding collection — those objects from the Pacific collected by Frank Burnett. [5] This resulted in the temporary exhibition *Pasifika — Island Journeys* (June 2003 — March 2004). The exhibition was well received by visitors but perhaps more importantly the research associated with its implementation served as a catalyst for new partnerships with cultural centres, museums, scholars and artists in the Pacific. Connections were also made with the local communities of Pacific Islanders, many of whom did not know there was a Pacific Islands collection at MOA, and the descendants of Frank Burnett who were extremely keen to contribute to the re-knowing of their ancestor. In

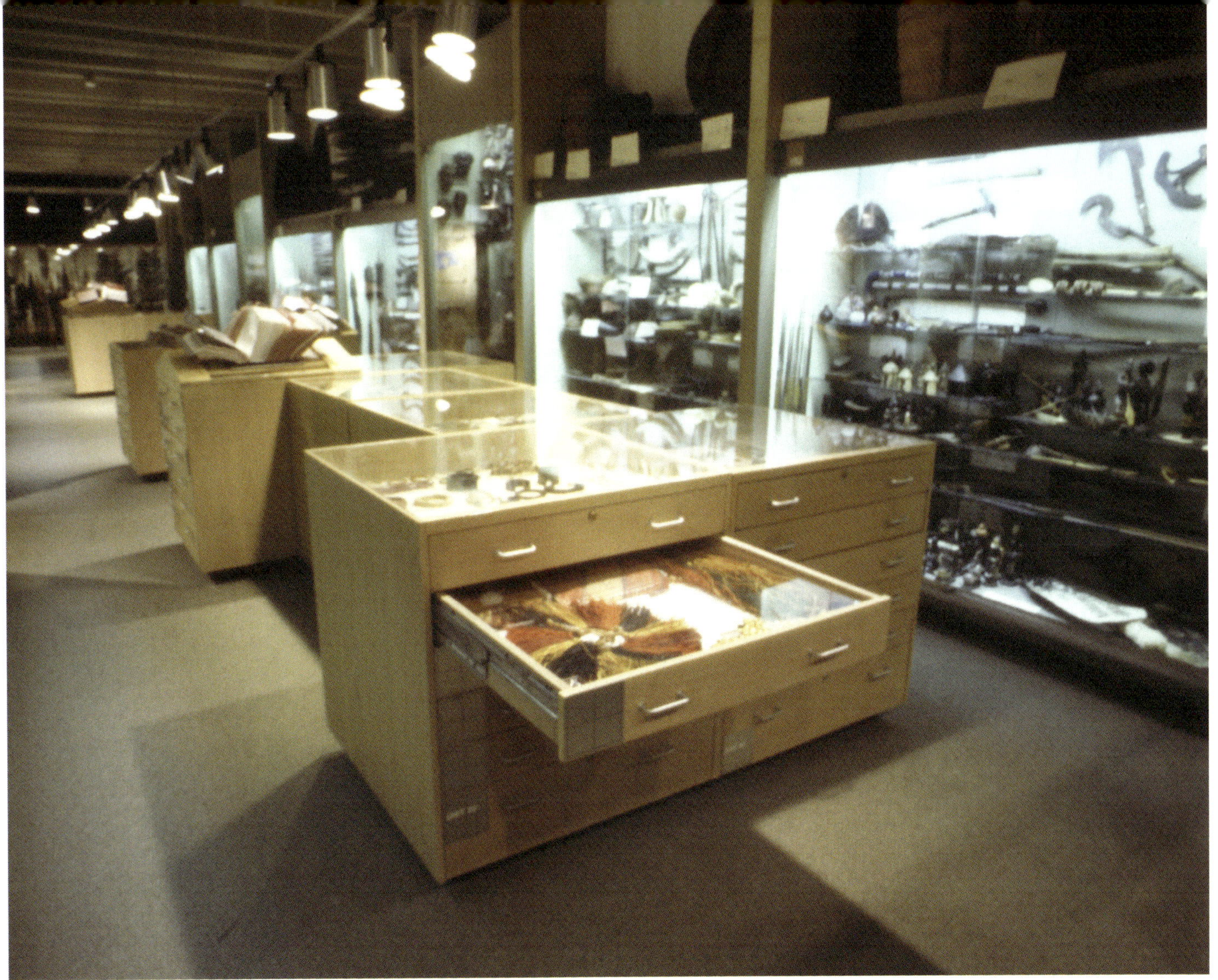

Figure 7.3 Visible Storage at the University of British Columbia Museum of Anthropology, 1995. Photograph by Ken Mayer.

Pasifika — Island Journeys the objects collected by Burnett were removed from storage, cleaned and displayed in their own right [fig. 7.4]. They were also identified and named where possible by Pacific Islanders and scholars working in the Pacific. This privileging of indigenous terms over western counterparts grew from a conversation with Mali Voi, UNESCO Subregional Advisor for Culture in 2000. He said "You don't know the significance of an object until you know [the] language in which it was created." [6] Photographs and contemporary narratives, including poetry served as counterpoints to narratives derived from Burnett's writings. [7] For the first time since they had been collected the objects were, where possible, re-attached to their names and displayed in an environment that honored their agency. [8] Members of the Pacific Islands' community officiated at the opening and Laurence Foanaota, then president of the Pacific Islands Museums Association, formally opened the exhibition. Relationships forged during the planning of this exhibition have continued and have culminated in a number of projects. However, for the purposes of this paper it is important to note that the exhibition was the initial stepping stone towards raising the profile of the Pacific Islands collection, and the move towards more research relating to the collection as well as the acquisition of contemporary works. This added a new facet to our collecting practices and the recognition that there would be more competition for the funds held in our limited acquisition budget.

Before discussing collecting practices at MOA it might be useful to think about who is doing the collecting of contemporary works for museums and how their different priorities and practices influence what is collected. The 'who' are anthropologists, curators and dealers/gallery owners. James Clifford and others have noted that writing, rather than collecting, has emerged as central to what anthropologists do in the field and thereafter (Clifford 1986:2). Yet it was the

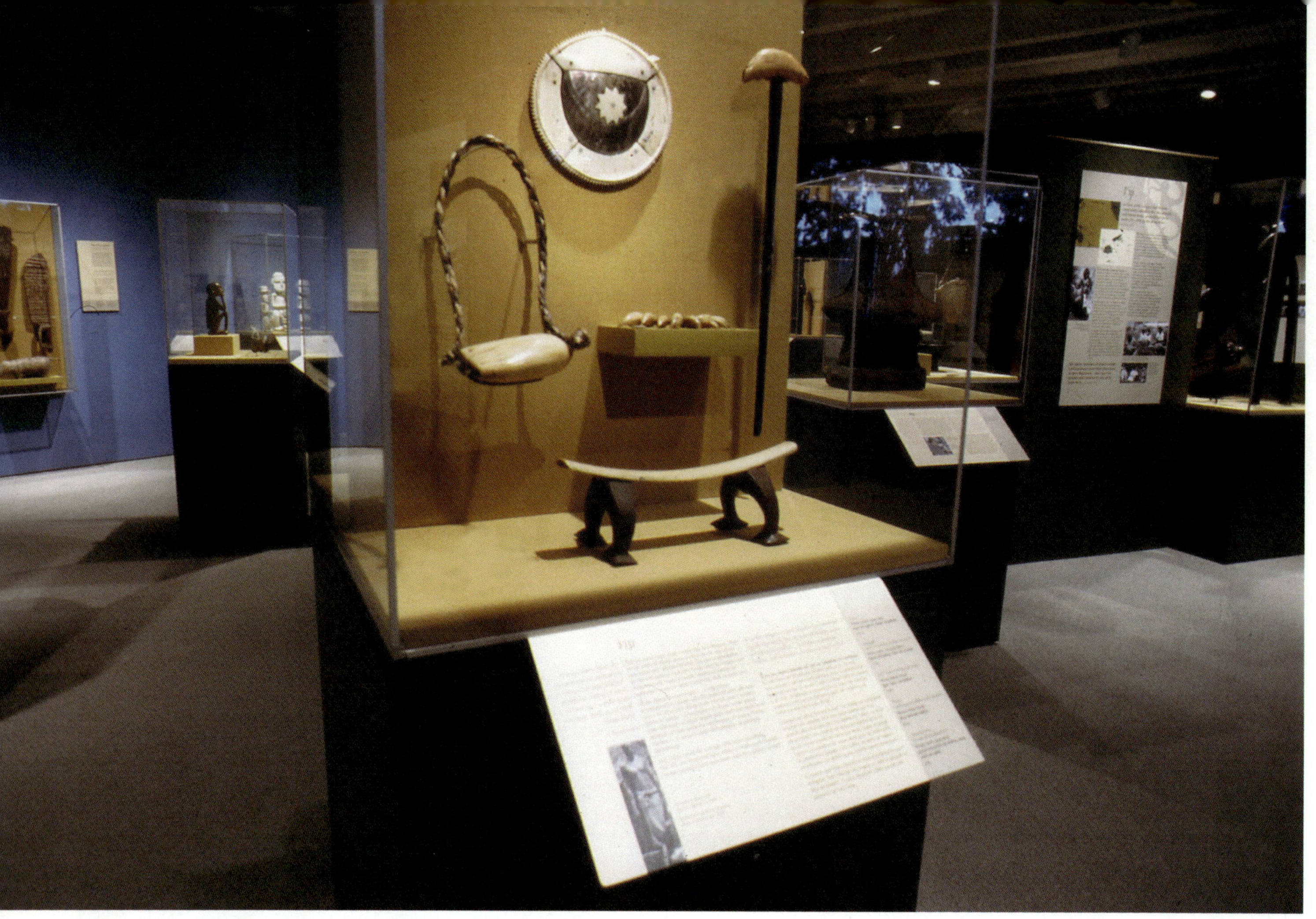

Figure 7.4 'Pasifika: Island Journeys' (Fijian case). Exhibition at University of British Columbia Museum of Anthropology, 2004. Photograph by Ken Mayer.

early 20th century anthropologists, mostly sponsored by museums and all driven by the presumption that cultural extinction was inevitable, who built some of the early Pacific collections now found in museums in Europe and North America. Today, anthropologists are well entrenched in the discourse that addresses the commodification of cultural material and the associated issues of ownership and copyright, yet the study of contemporary visual arts and what Jacques Maquet defined as aesthetic anthropology is yet to be seriously embraced by mainstream anthropology (Maquet 1986:2). Few anthropologists have written about contemporary art, which leaves the role of critique to art historians who are less interested in the anthropology museum as a place to study or contain contemporary arts. The building of contemporary collections is usually the responsibility of the second type of collector, the curator (see Raabe, this volume). While historic collections continue to enter the museum by the usual routes of bequests, donations and purchases, contemporary works are acquired by those curators who, over the years, have developed relationships with artists, auction houses and private galleries and through these relationships have developed the knowledge and skills to collect and write about contemporary arts. The third type of collector of contemporary arts for museums is the dealer or gallery owner — a person who is knowledgeable, has a vested interest in the success of the artist and who situates the art in the fine art market (see Monds and Hossack, this volume). Anthropology curators have encountered some dealers who use unscrupulous, sometimes illegal, strategies when buying and selling historic ethnographic objects. This has resulted in an arms length policy, and some degree of suspicion, between dealer and curator. Great care is taken not to be perceived to be close enough to suggest the possibility of a conflict of interest. This air of suspicion is less prevalent when working with owners of galleries of contemporary art. They can work closely with curators; share with curators an interest in the development of artists, and the promotion of contemporary art within the gallery and museum setting.

At MOA, as with most anthropology museums, collection development has focused on both historic and contemporary objects and, because of its geographic location, MOA's primary collecting, research and exhibiting foci have been and continue to be the tangible

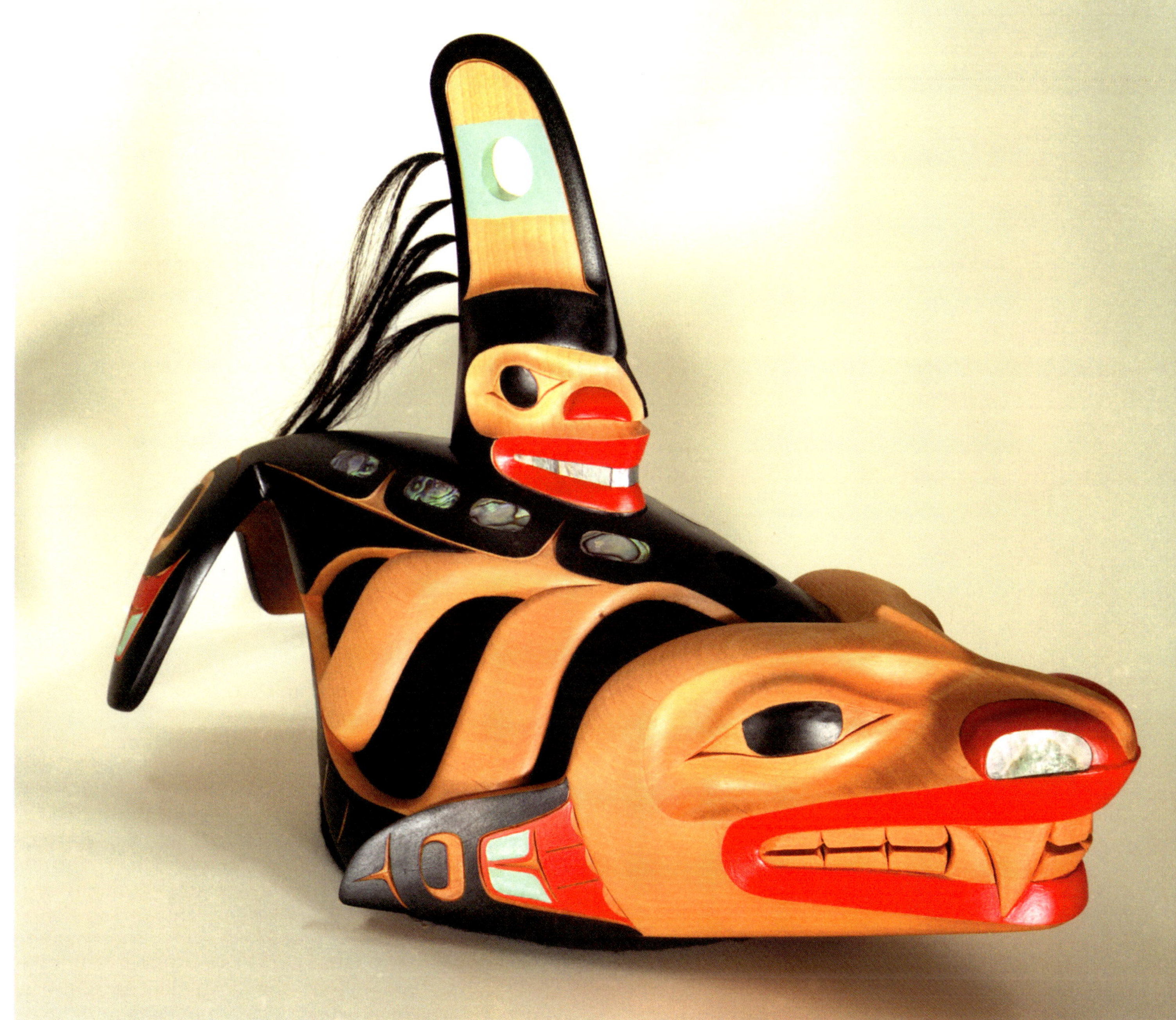

Figure 7.5 Bob Dempsey (Tahltan/Tlingit), *Whale headdress*, Alder wood, paint, 31.0 x 22.0 cm, 1987. (Nb22.79) Photograph by Bill McLennan.

heritage of indigenous peoples, First Nations, of British Columbia. The collections in this area are considered significant and account for 25% of the museum's total worldwide collection; the Pacific Islands' collection accounts for about 14%. [9] The history of collecting contemporary works began in the 1950s when the first curator, Audrey Hawthorn, purchased a series of paintings by George Clutesi, of the Tseshaht band. [10] She noted that this was a time when "the artists and craftspeople of the Coast, in spite of their great tradition, were now producing very little and for a very unsatisfactory market" (Hawthorn 1993:7). Enthusiasm to do further collecting was, as always, tempered by financial restrictions, storage capabilities, copyright issues, and available expertise. However, the growing presence of contemporary First Nations' work contrasted with the lack of such a presence anywhere else in the collection, including the Pacific. Some of this was due to the same challenges faced during the acquisition of First Nations' work — shortage of money and storage capabilities — but the main differences were to do with collecting priorities, staff resources and the dearth of locally available work by Pacific Islanders. [11]

In the late 1990s the Acquisition Policy was revised to give more priority to the collecting of contemporary

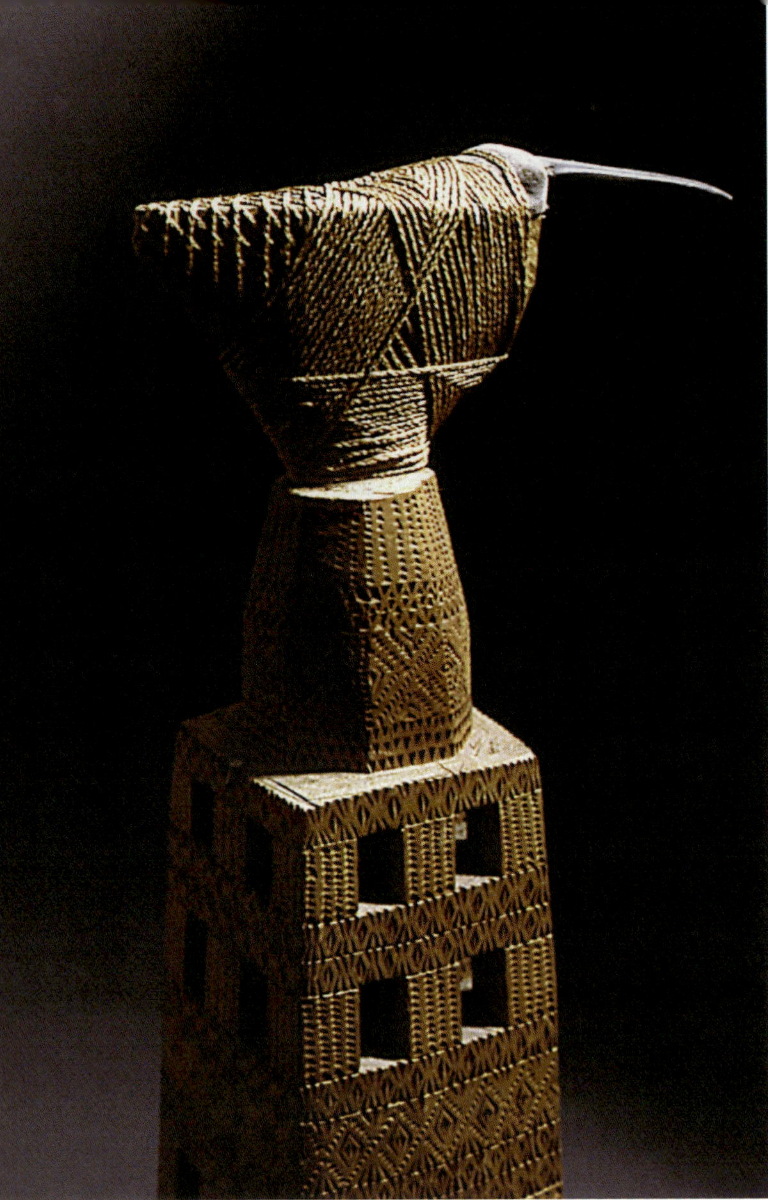

Figure 7.6 Mangaia, Cook Islands, *Adze*, Wood, stone, sharkskin, 47.0x 19.0x11.0 cm, ca 1902. (C45) Photograph courtesy of the University of British Columbia Museum of Anthropology.

works created by First Nations' artists. This revision was in response to a number of factors: since the 1970s artists had been advocating for the recognition of their work as art, and for the institutional support of their new work; there was an increase in artists creating new works, a growth in public awareness of contemporary art, and changes in the funding structure at Canada Council that enabled museums to apply for acquisition funds. [12] At the same time there was a pragmatic recognition that only a finite number of historic pieces were available and that these demanded prices often exceeding the museum's purchasing budget. Most museums, aware that the legacy of their own histories of collecting practices has left them with poorly documented collections subject (and rightly so) to repatriation requests, will only purchase objects that have well documented histories — or histories yet to be developed, such as contemporary works. Also, in the current climate of change most museums view the acquisition of contemporary works as a positive action that aids in the casting off of the negative connotations associated with historic salvage collections.

To date the practice at MOA has been to collect contemporary First Nations' works that are inspired by familiar forms of the past, expressions of continuity, paralleling the existing collection and demonstrative of a continuity of form and design, perhaps learned from elders or inspired by museum collections [fig. 7.5]. Also, there is still an emphasis in communities on strengthening threatened cultural knowledge and in reintegrating "art" into cultural practice on their own terms. Such works meet the expectations of the popular art market, a significant portion of which continues to believe that authenticity is dependent on the work being based on traditional forms. Such works occupy a lucrative niche; they demonstrate the power and continued presence of traditional ideals; they are safe in their authenticity and critiques are usually confined to technical virtuosity. [13] Geismer, (this volume), quoting Linda Tuhiwai Smith, refers to a notion of authenticity as deriving from a time before colonization when indigenous people lived in a universe of their own making. Anthropologists and museum curators know the majority of museum collections postdate colonization and do not use contact as a necessary criterion when considering new acquisitions. However, the search for criteria that determines authenticity and value — rarity, quality of material, historical association, authenticity, technical virtuosity, age, aesthetic quality and knowledge quality — has dogged many an acquisition meeting (Pearce 1995:354). There is no doubt that late 19th century collectors such as Frank Burnett collected only those contemporary works considered authentic in those terms and that he, like his contemporaries, believed it was necessary to preserve these remnants of authenticity before they disappeared. For example by the time he collected the Cook Island adze [fig. 7.6] it was no longer being used and was probably made for the traveler market. It retained all the traditional components that Burnett, and others, would have looked for as evidence of authenticity. There is little doubt that these early collectors viewed the Pacific as an unchanging place of clearly defined histories and simplistic worldviews that would not be able to stem the tide of European influence. He and many others did not think of the past in the Pacific as being multifaceted and as open to interpretation as the present. Nor did he recognize that traditionalism was not fixed but contested. When he acquired the adze he was actually acquiring notions of an uncomplicated past and the belief that traditionalism was fixed and based on

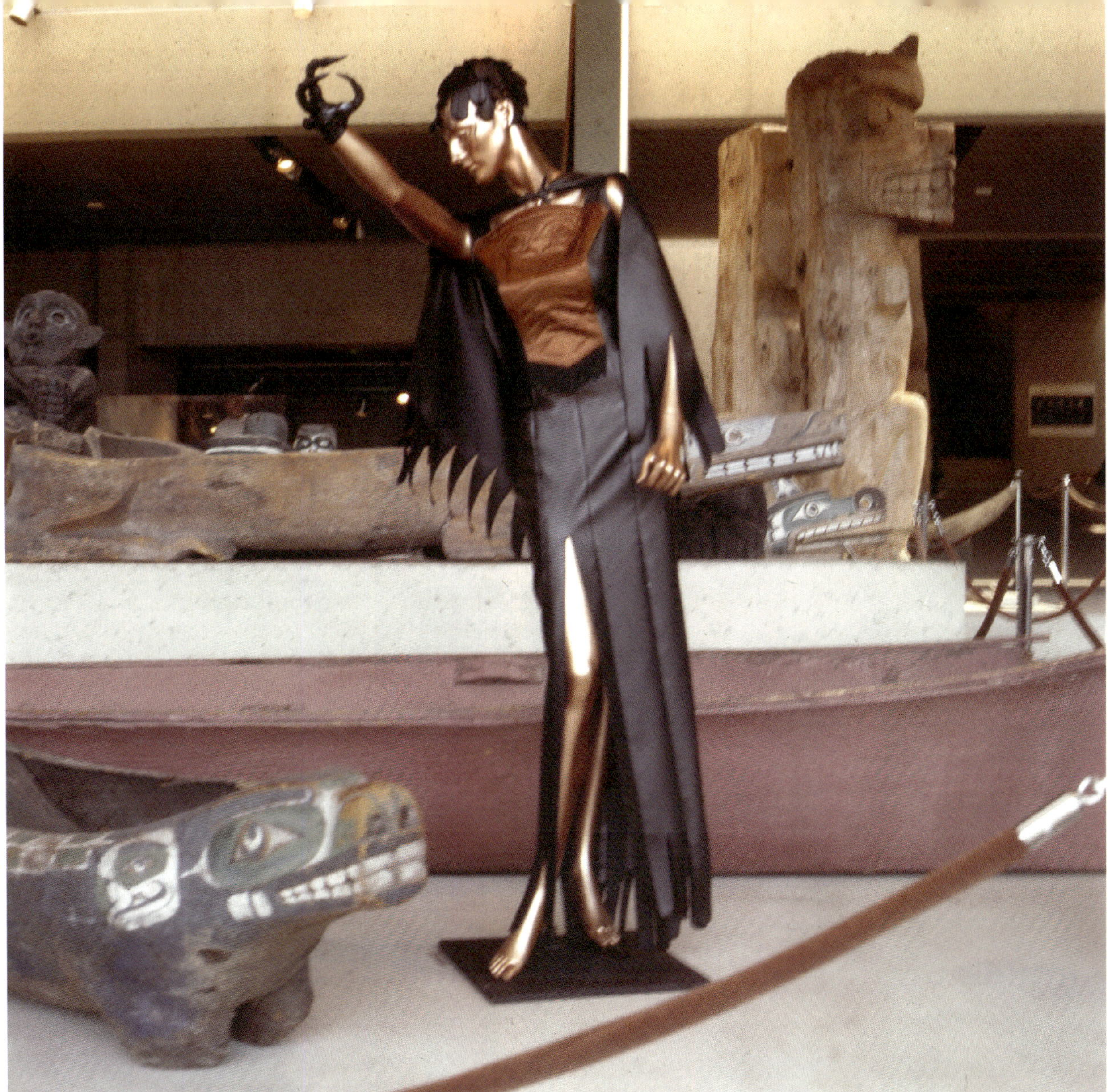

Figure 7.7 John Powell (Kwakiutl), *Metamoravinyl,* in Raven's Reprise. University of British Columbia Museum of Anthropology, 2000. Photograph by Bill McLennan.

consent. The adze would continue to be made for sale for as long as he, and others, supplied the demand or until the material was no longer available.

Critiquing Contemporary Indigenous Art

In a 1953 catalogue of an exhibition of Pacific Islands' art Paul Wingert, the curator, said "the art stands on its own merits and must be judged by its own criteria. Since all art is an expression of a culture, it is obvious that a culture so different from our own will have a very different art" (Wingert 1953:12). In the Pacific some artists have moved away from the repetition of existing forms and have adopted new media, including painting, sculpture and printmaking. They blend indigenous symbols and artistic styles with Western material. Some of their art reflects a reclamation of traditions lost in urban relocation, missionary fervor and colonial regimes — it also explores social and political issues that face artists today. Museums and cultural centres in the Pacific, who have acquisition budgets, are adding these works to their collections. European and North American museums have been slower. There are a number of reasons for this. The most obvious is one of availability. Pacific arts are not well marketed in the west. Here in British Columbia there are only two galleries that sell contemporary Pacific arts alongside First Nations' art. [14] Both gallery owners have a personal interest in Pacific arts and both recognize that Pacific arts are in competition with the more well-established market for First Nations' arts. Second, budgetary restraints prevent museums from developing long term collecting strategies and thirdly training in anthropology does not prepare future curators to assess objects of art that exist outside existing conservative frameworks.

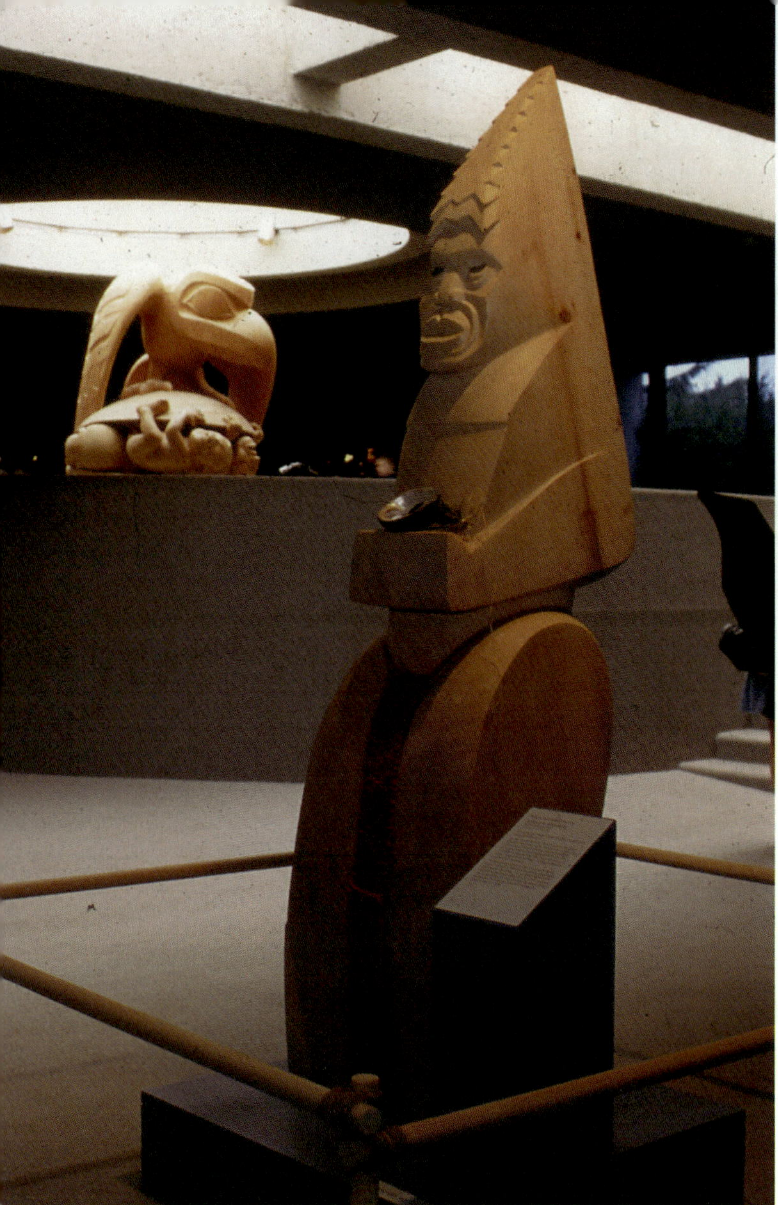

Figure 7.8 View of 'Maui-Turning Back the Sky'. In the foreground is Rocky Ka'Iouliokahihikolo'Ehu Jensen (Hawaii), *Lono*, Wood, 1997. In the background is Bill Reid (Haida), The Raven and the First Men, Yellow cedar, 1.9 x 1.9 m, 1980.. (Nb1.481) Photograph courtesy of the University of British Columbia Museum of Anthropology.

In the catalogue for the exhibition "Paradise now?: contemporary art from the Pacific" Karen Stevenson notes that "an acceptance of the fact that Pacific cultures are alive, thriving, and producing art has moved previous discussions from the museum to the islands and have moved the islands to the art galleries" (Stevenson 2004:23). This is a situation yet to be realized in Canada, where the question of whether contemporary works belong in anthropology museums or whether they are better housed in gallery settings continues to be debated. In his book Cannibal Tours Michael Ames, past director of MOA, talks about what he calls the formalist and contextualist approaches to the display of objects. The formalist approach is based on the presumption that aesthetic knowledge exists among all people and therefore anything made by anybody can be subjected to formal analysis. The contextualists on the other hand maintain that taking objects out of context is somehow immoral. Needless to say, all is well as long as the formalists remain in the art gallery/museum and the contextualists remain in the anthropology museum. Ames notes that it is when boundaries are crossed that "people get agitated or confused. If a museum of anthropology displays the material workings of a tribal society as fine art, then a boundary is violated, categories become mixed, and people are likely to become disoriented and upset" (Ames 1992:53). There are those curators who believe that challenging boundaries is a compelling and defensible approach to exhibitions in museums, whether or not the subject matter is contemporary or historic. Then there are those who would argue that such an approach reveals more about the curator's thesis and the designer's sense of aesthetic than it ever can about the artist. This was well articulated for me by the Ni-Kiribati artist and poet Teweiariki Teaero when we spoke about the museum exhibiting its Micronesian collection. He argued that if we displayed objects in the collection as art pieces then art critics could only base their observations on the finished product, and such an approach does not take into account that it is "the process, the production, who makes it, who you give it to, [that] is important; it reinforces kinship, and place in society." [15] So the conversation continues.

Art critics are, however, beginning to view museums as places to look at contemporary works. A certain validation takes place when critics and curators pay attention to contemporary indigenous arts — the curio assumes the attributes of an art object. Sarah Milroy who writes for the major Canadian newspaper Globe and Mail critiqued works by Jane Ash Poitras, a well-known Cree artist and, in Milroy's words, "every inch a market phenomenon." Poitras has a national reputation and what Milroy refers to as a "feverish media following." Milroy asks "What, exactly, is it that audiences are responding to?" She goes on to say (2001:R1)

> As a white viewer of art by First Nations' artists, I come looking in all sincerity for insight into what that experience might really be, hoping for newer, sharper tools of understanding. When I look at some installations I feel that I have connected with something outside of my experience, and I am grateful for the authenticity of that. But when I look at these paintings, I feel talked down to, as if more nuanced and personal truths would be beyond my understanding.

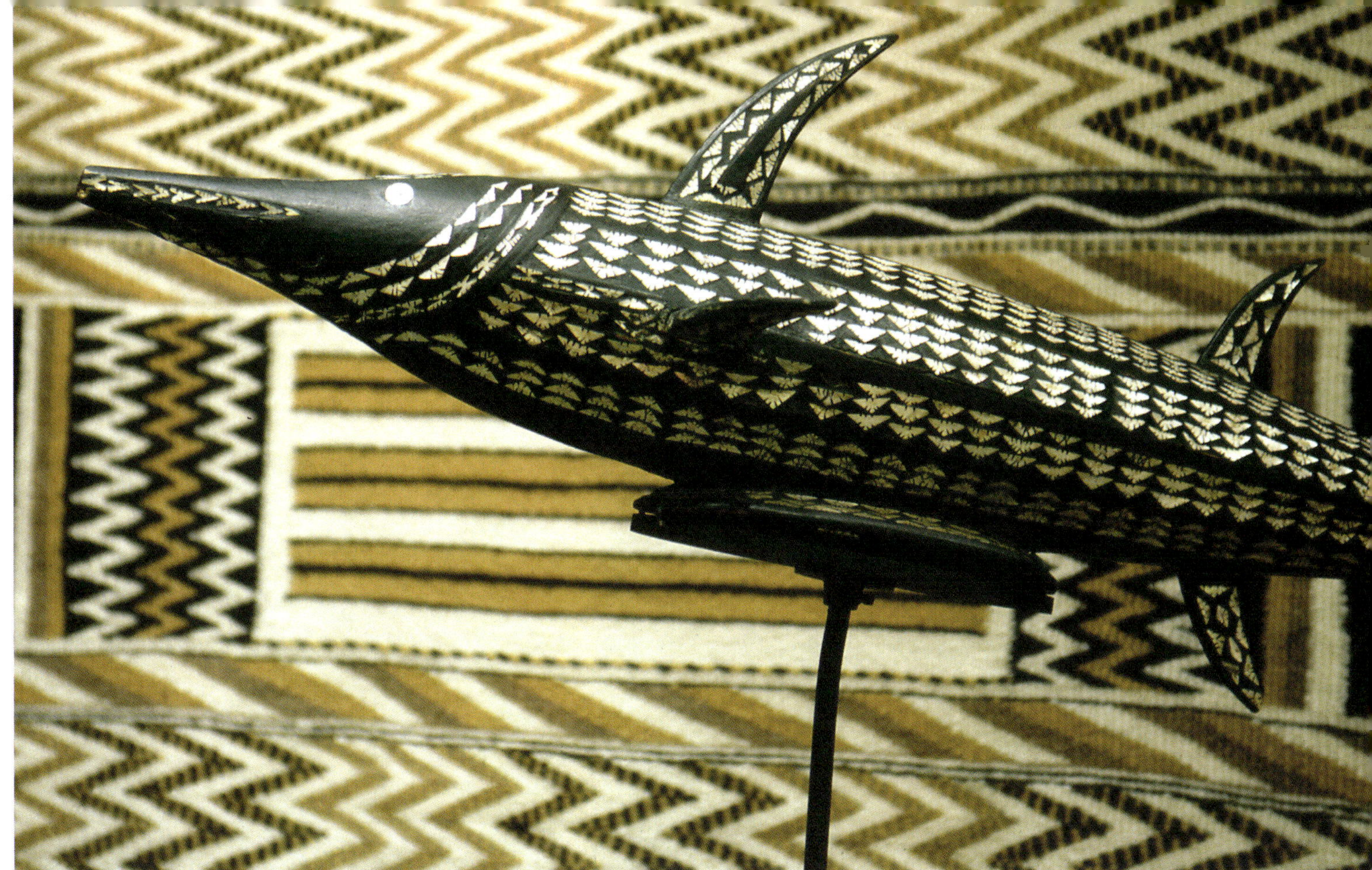

Figure 7.9 View of 'Objects of Intrigue'. In the foreground is *Bonito fish carving* from New Georgia, Solomon Islands. Milky pine wood, pava shells, 93.5 x 36.7 x 19.0 cm, c. 1909. (C378). In the background is Debra Sparrow and Robyn Sparrow (Coast Salish: Musqueam), Blanket, Wool, tea dye, madder root dye, 168.0 x 155.5 cm, 1991. (Nbz 841) Photograph courtesy of the University of British Columbia Museum of Anthropology.

Milroy provides one of the few critical comments on contemporary First Nations' art and she, in turn, was criticized for not contributing to any analysis of the artist's work. Jamelie Hassan, Canadian artist and activist, writing in Fuse Magazine, referred to Milroy as being prejudiced against artists who are "giving voice to their immediate, political histories." Hassan accused Milroy of exposing her own "Euro-Canadian values and her rigid ideas of what constitutes First Nations' art." She continues: "When will the outdated idea of the critic, cloaked in the claims of her 'sincerity', dispensing, through the power of mainstream media, the stamp and measure of 'authenticity' be finally put to rest?" (Hassan 2001). Reading Milroy's critique it could be argued that it wasn't contemporary indigenous art that left her unimpressed — it was specifically the formulaic nature of the artist's work that deserved critique instead of automatic acceptance and celebration. No critique can truly disentangle the complexities of cultural knowledge, political histories and concepts of aesthetics that inform First Nations' art and many critics air on the side of political correctness and produce non-critical and essentially descriptive essays which leave First Nations' art immobilized, stuck in some kind of primitive paradigm. However, it would seem that the artist and the art benefits more from those, like Milroy, who will initiate the dialogue, be as effusive as she is critical, and raise the ire of those, like Hassan, who disagree with her.

There has been some considerable movement away from notions of primitive art and the importance of the authentic and traditional towards the acceptance of indigenous arts as a new category of art with its own vocabulary, and a recognition of the agency of the indigenous voice (Stevenson 2004:21-23). These ideas have broadened to include issues of ownership, value, and representation. At MOA we have experimented using the temporary exhibition as an avenue of introduction to contemporary art that reaches beyond the traditional form. Lynn Hill, an Iroquois curator, installed *Raven's Reprise: Contemporary Works by First Nations Artists*, in 2000. The contemporary works in this exhibition were installed throughout the museum amidst the permanent collection. This placement enabled the artists to create a visual dialogue between the contemporary and historic pieces. These juxtapositions provided the viewer with visual references and established the context from which the contemporary works stemmed. The exhibition was not meant to disclaim past artistic traditions or scholarly explorations, but rather sought to offer some insight into current art practices that ventured beyond an analysis of traditional forms and genres. One installation, Metamoravinyl by Kwakiutl artist John Powell, married the themes of transformation and garment designer [fig. 7.7]. A female mannequin painted copper colour was dressed in a pleather (fake leather) outfit and placed amongst the historic feast dishes in the museum's Great Hall. The copper colour symbolized wealth and nobility echoing bronze statuary of antiquity; the black pleather clothing illustrated how technology imitates nature — the black representing the mystery surrounding the supernatural worlds of transformation. The artist stated that positioning pieces amongst the ancient pieces in the Great Hall was not intended to be presumptuous or offensive; its purpose was to bring attention to the fact that Kwakwaka'wak people still exist in today's larger contemporary context and like their ancestors the contemporary artist continues to be innovative and feels the same need to express himself in what the majority culture terms art. Other pieces in the exhibition did not produce as much criticism as Metamoravinyl which received numerous complaints from visitors; most were offended by the 'jarring' presence of this painted mannequin. Research at MOA has shown that visitors, including First Nations people, expect to see the arts of the Northwest Coast stored and displayed respectfully and the juxtapositioning of contemporary works was, for some, disrespectful. Gloria Cranmer Webster, Kwakiutl elder and activist, said of this exhibition

> It is an exploitation of the worst kind. I am particularly incensed when these urban Indians mangle the orthography. There is such a phoniness about it. It is as if they think that, if they throw in a few kwakwala words or phrases in their pathetic presentations, the audience will think, "These are real Indians." It's all so superficial and offensive. [16]

She goes on to say "when individuals try to portray something that is not community-based then they're doing a 'White Thing." Others might argue that the installation was demonstrative of the idea that we live in "an epoch of simultaneity... an epoch of juxtaposition, an epoch of the near and the far, of the sideby-side, of the dispersed" (Foucault 1986:27).

Other exhibitions have been less contentious — more about continuity than rupture. Earlier, in 1997 the museum hosted an exhibition *Turning Back the Sky* that included works by contemporary Hawaiian artists. One carving *Lono* by Hawaiian artist Rocky Ka'Iouliokahihikolo'Ehu Jensen was displayed in juxtaposition with Haida artist Bill Reid's sculpture *Raven and the First Men* [fig. 7.8]. When Rocky and Bill, artists from different cultures, met side by side in this space the far became near, and they talked to each other about their work. Both works offered simultaneous interpretations of origins, different yet similar. The difference between these works and those by Jane Ash Poitras and John Powell was that these were not driven by a political agenda; they were expressions of continuity, not rupture. They were carved with recognizably traditional imagery, even though both bore the distinctive style of each artist. Clearly, they existed in a comfort zone of conservatism not enjoyed, or even sought, by those indigenous artists working with western media. There were no negative critiques, no public complaints.

In an exhibition called *Objects of Intrigue* a contemporary weaving by Musqueam artist Debra Sparrow was displayed with a historic bonito fish carving) from the Solomon Islands (collected in 1906). Again juxtapositions — one in front of the other [fig. 7.9]. Debra Sparrow speaks of design being universal. "I believe that where the spirit is moved, the creative process follows" (Webb 1999: 37). The First Nations' artist speaks of universality yet the Solomon Islands' artist who made the bonito fish was unable to speak, unable to agree or disagree. The curatorial decision to display these two works together could be viewed as an act of misappropriation or, conversely, as an act that enabled artists to share space and "coexist with parity of esteem in which meaning is made in the space between, not locked mysteriously into the artifact" (McGonagle 2004:25). Alternately, the decision also provided a place for "a dialectic that created multiple points of entry" (ibid). All of these exhibitions, in their different ways, exposed the tensions, complexities and possibilities associated with museums' adding contemporary works to their ethnographic collections. Another, worthy of singular attention is that of copyright.

Copyright

When MOA purchases work from contemporary artists they are required to sign a Statement of Agreement based on the Canadian Copyright Act (known as Bill C-60) that seeks to strike a balance between two interests: the rights of the creator or copyright owner and the reasonable demands of users of copyright materials. All Canadian artists are protected by this Act (there are no specific laws for indigenous artists) as are treaty members of the World Intellectual Property Association (WIPA). Fifteen Pacific Islands' nations are members. In 1988 Bill C-60 was amended to include more succinct definitions of moral rights. Museums are interested in copyright because it bestows certain rights on the authors of works that have financial implications. Put simply, earlier works were purchased (or donated) and the museum acquired full ownership and authority over those works. Changing the law changed that presumption. Today, artists have the legal right to be paid for the exhibiting of their creations (according to a national fee structure), and to negotiate conditions of purchase that might include moral rights that can determine when, where, and how their works might be exhibited. For the museum this means that the relationship between the institution and the artist is not severed at the time of purchase — negotiations are ongoing. This, of course, is not as straightforward as it seems. The Act is constantly being revised and Copyright Agreements can become outdated very quickly. Many artists and museum staff are not conversant with the terms of the Act and few can keep up with the changes. This calls into question the amount of protection the Act actually affords.

In a 1999 Kamala Purim, Professor of Law at the University of Queensland, and president of the Australian Folklore Association said "Generally, the Pacific Island nations only provide a limited amount of protection for indigenous peoples' expressions of culture and traditional knowledge through their intellectual property laws" (Purim 1999: 6-34). Laws are written but are extremely difficult to enforce. The focus is on the notion of cultural appropriation — considered to erode or degrade cultural identity by those who have no right to do so — and the `exploitation of traditional knowledge, indigenous customs and expressions of popular culture. Copyright legislation in the Pacific is based on The Berne Convention for the Protection of Literary and Artistic Works, created in 1886, which refers to 'authorship,' a concept that is generally based on single ownership and difficult to apply to cultural property that is community owned, or when the ownership can be transferred temporarily for specific occasions. Ralph Regenvanu, director of the Vanuatu Cultural Centre, about the development of copyright legislation:

> subsequent to the meeting at the Secretariat of the Pacific Community (SPC) in Nome where Kamala Puri was a key resource person, the Pacific Island States through the SPC have come up with a "Model law for the Protection of Traditional Knowledge and Expressions of Culture" with the intention that each Pacific Island State can then adopt this model law nationally. It is a good model in terms of addressing issues of communal rights, perpetual ownership and moral rights… We will meld it with another model law concerning protection of traditional ecological rights before doing consultations with communities around Vanuatu about the overall law to protect custom. [17]

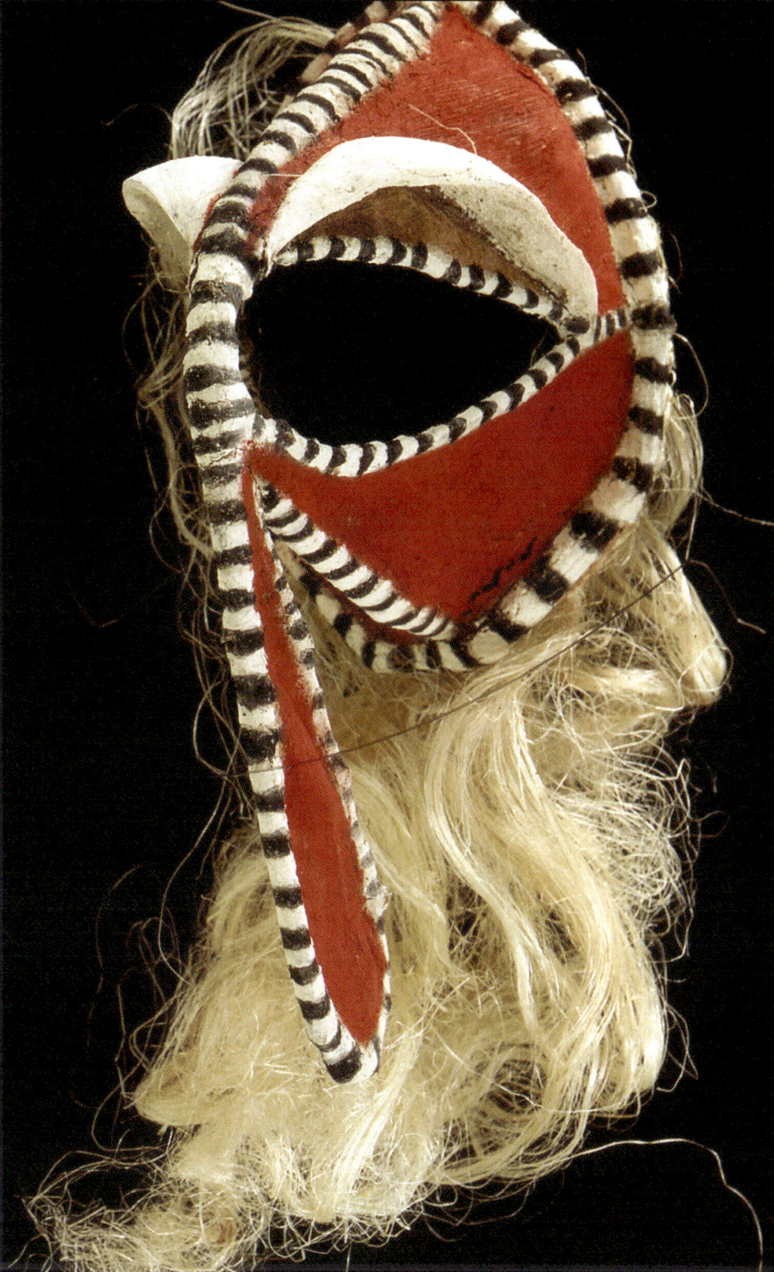

Figure 7.10 Johanin Bangtor (Ambrym, Vanuatu), *Rom Bacco Mask*, Coconut husk fibre, paint, 49.5 x 26.5 x 23.0 cm, 2000. (2523/1 Photograph courtesy of the University of British Columbia Museum of Anthropology.

Existing protection for intellectual property rights gives priority to individual ownership, imposes strict interpretations of invention, and has a limited life. In contrast, traditional knowledge and expressions of

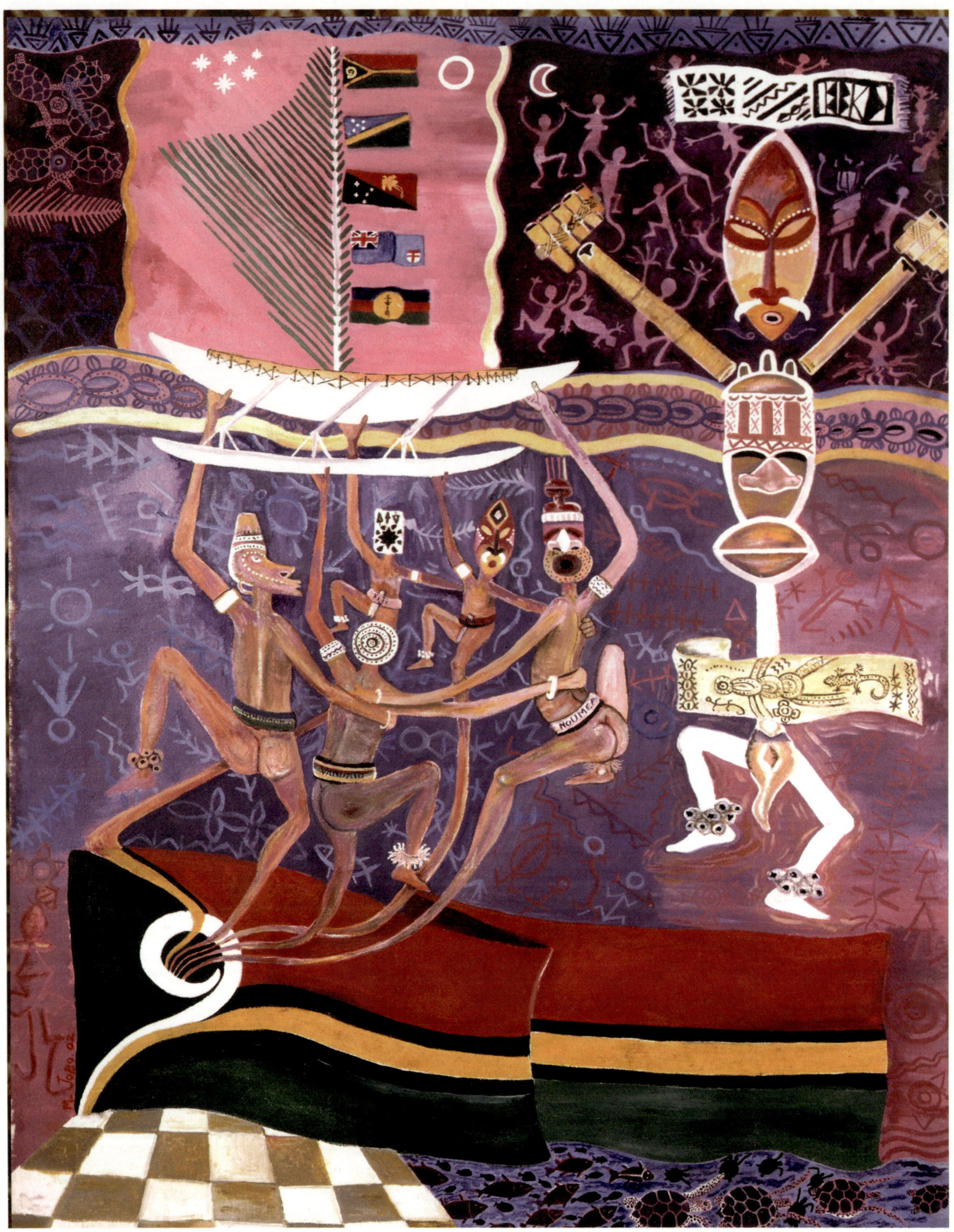

Figure 7.11. Moses Jobo (Vanuatu), *Melanesie*, acrylic on canvas, 118 x 88 cm, 2002. Photograph courtesy of Ken Mayer.

culture are characterized by collective ownership, are normally held in perpetuity from generation to generation, and are incremental, informal and subject to change over time. We are familiar with this concept in British Columbia as it often applies to First Nations' art.

Rom

It was during research visits to the Pacific in 2000 and 2002 that I had the opportunity to think about the impact of intellectual property right on the acquisition of contemporary works. I purchased a number of works by Vanuatu artists to add to MOA's small Vanuatu collection. The first, and the most complex, was made in 2000 when I acquired a contemporary Rom Bacco mask during the Festival of Pacific Arts held in New Caledonia [fig. 7.10]. This was, as I soon discovered, a mask that had gained its own history, adding layers of meaning and associations with the passing of time and circumstances. It is a tabu ritual mask used during a ceremony called Rom or Ole, practiced on the island of Ambrym, Vanuatu. It was, I was told by the exhibitors, made for the market by Chief Johanin Bangtor and considered to be an accurate reproduction of a traditional work. Such masks should not be shown to the Ambrymese public, and after the Rom ceremony it would have normally been burned.

> As legend has it, a local girl made the first costume to seduce a young man from her village. She enticed him into the bush where she revealed how the costume was made. Once he knew the secret he killed her and sold the rights to make copies to other men. It is still tabu to see a Rom costume being made. If someone transgresses this rule they must pay a fine (a pig) to the chief, then have their backs whipped with the leaves of a stinging plant called the naggalat, the poison from which burns the skin like fire for several days. (Forsyth 2003: 7)

According to the vendor this particular mask was made for the opening of the cultural centre in Port Vila in 1995 along with other cultural works that now reside in the permanent collection. The artist had purchased the right to make the mask from the owner of the right. My first question was 'who should I credit the work to?" The Canadian Copyright Act states:

> Where the author of a work was in the employment of some other person under a contract of service or apprenticeship and the work was made in the course of his employment by that person, the person by whom the author was employed shall, in the absence of any agreement to the contrary, be the first owner of the copyright. [18]

However, there was some confusion over payment. The artist retrieved the mask from the Cultural Centre and sold it to the Himford Museum, part of an artist cooperative run by a fundamentalist Christian group where it was viewed as a work that belonged to *kastom* no longer followed by the members of the co-op — all members having converted to the teachings of this group. In other words, it was viewed as a replication of a traditional work, not a tabu piece. The co-op took the mask to New Caledonia in 2000 during the Festival of Pacific Arts where it was exhibited at the city museum alongside other contemporary works. At the end of the festival the co-op offered to sell the pieces and I purchased the Rom mask and other pieces for my museum's collection on the presumption it was reasonable to do so because these were contemporary works on public display, offered for sale. Also, the purchase echoed others we had made of First Nations' work in that these pieces were also based on familiar forms of the past. It was during subsequent interviews with Wendy Himford, director of the artist co-op, and Ralph Regenvanu, director of the Vanuatu Cultural Centre, that the complexity associated with the ownership of this mask was revealed, as was the probable reason why it was moved from Vanuatu, away from possibilities of being penalized by kastom restrictions. Himford viewed the mask as a contemporary piece that was made for the market, not for ceremony, that would help promote Vanuatu arts overseas. When I asked Ralph Regenvanu about ownership rights he said,

> One has to purchase the right to reproduce a particular piece like the Rom Bacco mask. This is different from the right to use the piece, which you have to obtain (including purchase) through a different system. So you can have the right to carve or construct of the piece — but may not have the carving skills, so you pay a craftsperson to make the piece. The craftsperson does not have the independent right to make the piece; he can only make it for someone who has the right. The person who sells the right to reproduce the piece does not himself then lose that right, rather both he and the person he sold it to now both have the right to make the piece. And once you have the right, you can sell it to someone else as well..." [19]

Both Himford and Regenvanu agreed that the Rom Bacco mask was made for the market and had no power so it could be photographed, published and exhibited. Was it therefore a remnant of authenticity? If made for a ceremony it would be authentic... if made for sale it would be inauthentic... so what if it was made for a ceremony associated with the opening of the cultural centre... .not a 'real' ceremony but a western derived ceremony? Given that the right to make such a mask could be bought and sold then it could, if made by a different artist, be a tabu piece to be used in a specific ritual. Should it therefore be treated as a culturally sensitive object and if so, should we display it? [20] There are Coast Salish masks in MOA's collection of types that are still used in secret ceremonies. Such ceremonies were once attended by outsiders; the masks appeared for sale and found their way into museum collections. More recently the ceremonies have been restricted to those who have the right to attend and masks are no longer made for sale. When a mask is to be retired it is usually destroyed and replaced by a new version. At the request of the Salish people all versions of these masks in our museum's collection, whether they had evidence of use or not, have been removed from display, treated according to the procedures associated with culturally sensitive material, and made accessible only to those who have the right to view them. This was possible because we are geographically situated on the traditional territory of the Coast Salish Musqueam people and have, over the years, developed strong relationships that resulted in collaborative exhibitions and programming. Working closely with First Nations communities has enabled us to recognize what questions should be asked prior to the acquisition of new works. This becomes exponentially less possible when the homelands are thousands of miles away and opportunities to travel are very limited.

In Canada, the Rom mask is protected by the Copyright Act. However, this does not contain any solutions to the complexity of ownership uncovered during its acquisition (see Geismar, this volume). How can we, for example, ensure that the relationship between the artist and his or her work is not severed at the time of purchase, especially when we are not sure who can claim authorship? How can we justify purchasing a contemporary work when there is the possibility we may not be able to display it, especially when there are limited financial resources and no government funding for collecting art outside of Canada. We do know that appropriation of expressions of traditional culture is reaching pandemic proportions in the Pacific and we also know that little can be done, at this time, to stop it. Laws are only useful when they can be enforced. This is exacerbated by the procurement of images of historic objects held in western museums that have no documentation and the memory of their ownership has disappeared. All of a sudden there are traditional designs that no one owns, and with no mechanism to protect them they can both add to the repertoire of the artist, which is positive, and be open for exploitation by anybody who want to reproduce them on t-shirts or whatever. It is in this complex climate that contemporary artists in Vanuatu are functioning. They have formed loose associations such as the Nowata cooperative, created in 1984 with the goal of "heightening people's awareness of the contemporary arts in Vanuatu through self promotion — usually exhibits" (Port Vila Press 2004). Another group formed in 2005, the Red Wave Vanuatu Artists Association, hopes for "self-governance for our artists, we act to protect artists' rights and copyright, and promote the interests of fine artists who draw on traditional culture in their contemporary arts." Sculptor Eric Natuoivi, added "Revisiting our cultural histories, looking at what they represent to us and making sense of that in a modern context, is our role as art educators. There is a new wave of artists coming through as art education becomes more important in Vanuatu. We will see more artists, and we will represent their rights." [21]

On a later research trip to Vanuatu I purchased an acrylic painting on canvas "*Melanesie*" by the artist Moses Jobo, a member of the Nawita cooperative. [22] The painting depicted the coming together of the Melanesian nations for the 2002 Melanesian Cultural Festival held in Vanuatu [fig. 7.11]. It was a celebratory work, a combination of understandable realism, national flags and symbols, underpinned with stories about travel and origins. Jobo said "It means that they had to come to one agreement for this gathering. On the right I tried to assemble all the elements of the five countries... along with the spirit of our ancestors." [23] *Melanesie* was the first non-traditional work that MOA purchased from the Pacific. It contained complexities of cultural knowledge, political histories and concepts of aesthetics that I knew could never be completely understood, the painting was very accessible and a good first step into the world of contemporary art. The acquisition of works that are traditional (marked by a style that emulates an older culture) alongside those that move beyond the prescribed form and that can be assimilated by the art world suggests a simultaneity that marks both the survival and dynamism of indigenous cultures as well as an indigenous refusal to be excluded from the projects of modernity and cultural critique. As John Stanton has noted "The notion that a distinction can be made between 'traditional' and 'contemporary' art in today's setting risks insulting present-day practitioners, as well as a means of dichotomizing the 'remote' from the 'urban', 'near' from the 'distant'" (Stanton 2004:72). Epeli Hau'ofu, comments "we are not interested in imitating (western art) and asking our artists to perform dances for tourists. It is time to create things for ourselves, create to established standards of excellence which match those of our ancestors" (Hau'ofu 2000).

At the beginning of this paper I said I would explore some of the issues and challenges facing an anthropology museum that collects and exhibits both historic and contemporary arts. At the end of this paper I am reminded of a professor who once commented on a rather dense paper that I had written about the contributions of Durkheim to the discipline of anthropology. He said, "This is rather like going for a swim but only succeeding in paddling." I've never forgotten this comment and although I'm still paddling around Durkheim, I still think of it as an interesting metaphor when I am trying to understand and make sense of ideas that involve reaching beyond known territory. In this paper I have explored and sought to understand the issues and challenges associated with collecting practices, concepts of authenticity and ownership, and interpretations of copyright as they pertain to the understanding, exhibiting and promoting of the contemporary arts of the Pacific. There is no final word or no finite conclusion, and nor should there be — but the exploration so far puts Gertrude Stein's assertion that you cannot be both a museum and modern in jeopardy.

Acknowledgements

Many thanks to Karen Duffek, Elizabeth Johnson, Ulrike Rademacher and Ralph Regenvanu for their comments on an earlier version of this paper.

Reclaiming Our Heritage
Vince Reyes

Unlike many Pacific Nations, Chamorro cultural dance from the United States territory of Guam has only recently seen a resurgence of interest. As a result of over 300 years of colonial oppression, this art form was lost. Only in the last 25 years has there been a serious effort to reconnect with this aspect of our culture. Because it is a fairly new idea, many young people feel that this particular art form is strictly for performance purposes and fail to see its connection with their island's culture. This is why many instructors are forced to market Chamorro cultural dance in the same way a company would market its product.

This essay will discuss the history of Chamorro cultural dance. In particular it will focus on the youth of Guam and the efforts that have provided them opportunities to embrace their culture. I will then discuss the issues surrounding my efforts in bringing culture to the youth of Guam in the hopes of perpetuating these traditions. In this process I discuss how Western marketing techniques are applied to attract young Chamorros to learn about their heritage. I will also discuss the programs I have developed and conclude with insights from other Dance instructors. My goal is to provide some insight into Chamorro cultural dance, its challenges, successes, and it's overall importance to my island's culture.

The History of Chamorro Cultural dance

As in all Pacific Islands, Chamorro cultural dance was an integral part of our daily way of life prior to colonial contact. By the early 1800s this particular art form was lost. Only a few clues remained; common dances were only those from Spanish and American influences. By the 1970s Polynesian cultural dance from Tahiti and Hawai'i were introduced to the island and became the dominant forms of entertainment in Guam's tourism industry. A shift in this type of dancing occurred in 1984 with the creation of Taotao Tano. According to Frank Rabon, its founder, the organization was created because he felt the need to promote and teach the art of Chamorro dance as little was known or done about it at the time. [1] Through his research he was able to re-create and reinvent many of the cultural dances that are seen today. Throughout the years, he has "created a basic foundation for any person interested in teaching and formulating pre-contact Chamorro dances for presentation." [2] His travels throughout the Pacific region and around the world "assisted (him) in comparing, connecting, borrowing, and eventually re-creating our past" through dance. [3]

Taotao Tano continues to be the leader of the movement to perpetuate Chamorro culture. Since its inception, many groups were created, focusing primarily on Chamorro cultural dance performances. Two elementary Schools, four middle schools, and one high school now offer cultural dance as an elective course. In addition, a handful of community-based programs on Guam, the Commonwealth of the Northern Mariana Islands (CNMI), and the United States have also been established.

Although formalized Chamorro dance is a fairly new concept [fig. 8.1], there have been some efforts to organize it as a formalized discipline. The creation of Pa'a Taotao Tano, an organization consisting of various Chamorro folk artists and dance groups, was established to collaborate efforts among cultural practitioners. A Chamorro cultural dance manual of Chamorro dance has been written by Frank Rabon and is now available. In addition, two radio stations are now devoted to the promotion of Chamorro music. One instructor stated that through all these efforts, "People are now embracing cultural dance, and are constantly demanding it. Many times people request for shows specifically in Chamorro." [4]

Attitudes Towards Cultural Dance

In many societies, cultural dancing is considered an integral part of a peoples' heritage. These dances are a medium in which cultural practices, stories, and traditions are handed down through the generations. Because cultural dance on Guam is a fairly new idea to our youth, I wondered if students knew of its importance. I surveyed 200 students attending Inarajan Middle School (IMS), a local middle school on Guam, to determine the general attitude and perceptions of cultural dancing from children, ages 12 to 14, who have never experienced it before, and compared it to those who are currently attending a class. The results of this survey follow.

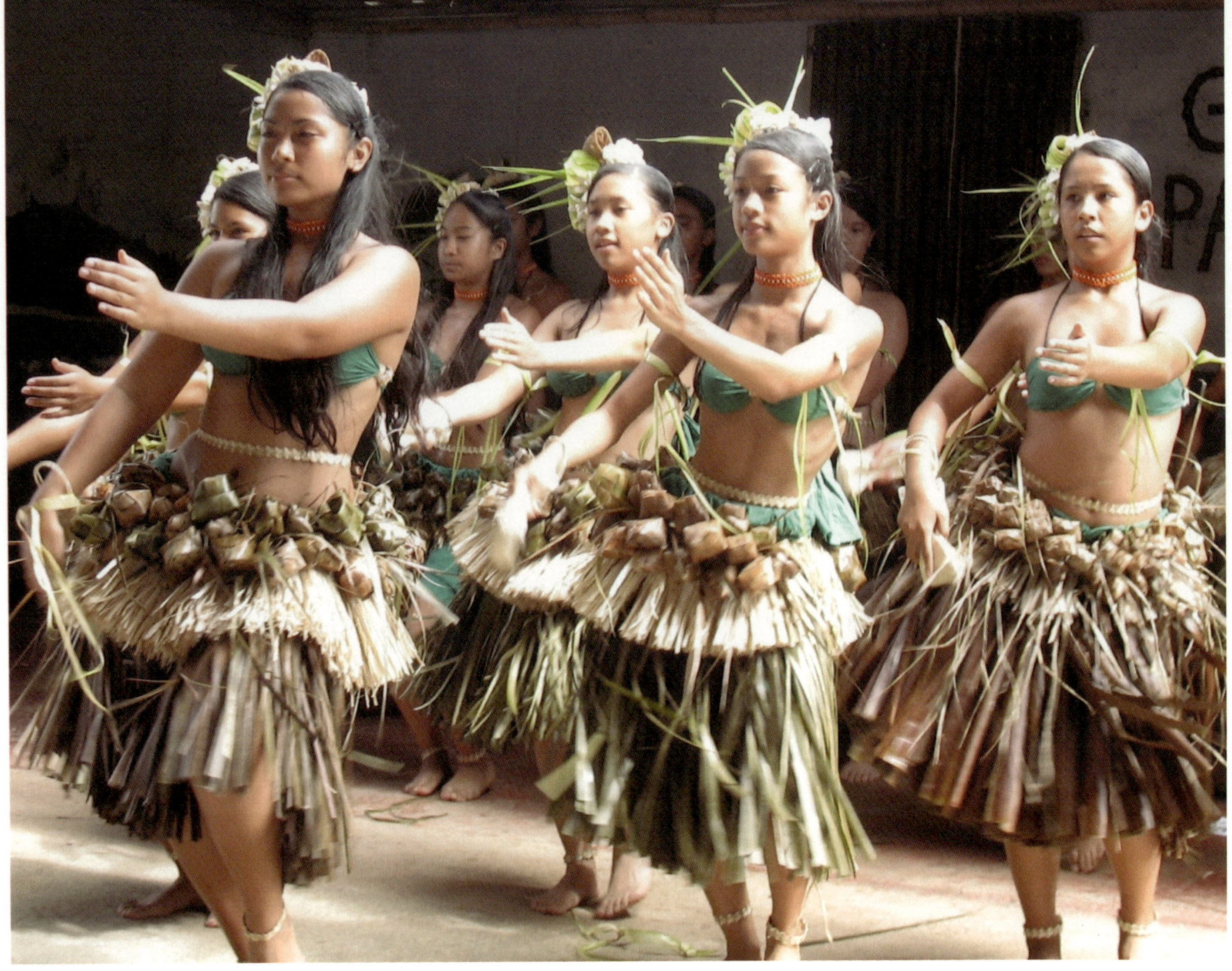

Figure 8.1 Dancers perform at the 2007 Dinana Minagof Cultural Dance Competition. The katupat or woven basket was said to be used as a form of percussion in precolonial Chamorro dances. Here the ladies use this implement to tell of this story of the Legend of the Coconut Tree. Gef Pa'go Chamorro Cultural Village. Photograph courtesy of Inetnon Gef Pa'go, 2007.

When asked if the students understood the meaning of cultural dance, 64% of those individuals who have never danced before viewed it as a performance for entertainment only. However, 70% of those already attending a class stated that although it is for entertainment, it was also a way of telling a story, promoting and reenacting the way of life of our ancestors. Therefore, if most students, who have not been involved in cultural dance, see it only as a performance and not closely related to them, how can they relate to the dances being portrayed?

To answer this question I needed to determine why they felt so disconnected when thinking of cultural dance. A second question was then asked to determine if they understood the dances and the messages being conveyed; and 64% of those who have never taken a cultural dance class stated "no". Unfortunately, the percentage remains the same for those individuals currently attending the class. When asked why, most stated that they do not understand what is being said. It is safe to assume, therefore, that the main reason for this disconnection is due to the inability of our young people to comprehend the Chamorro language.

The next step was discovering the underlying fears that students have as they consider being part of a cultural performing group. When surveyed, 54% stated that wearing the costume was the biggest concern, and 23% stated that performing in front of others was difficult [fig. 8.2]. These students like the idea of cultural dance but were not as willing to participate. 88% of students currently attending the class believed these fears were not an issue. When asked if they would consider continuing in cultural dance, 91% said "yes". Most stated that it was "fun" and expressed their happiness of performing in front of others. Few made any comments that dealt with cultural perpetuation or pro-

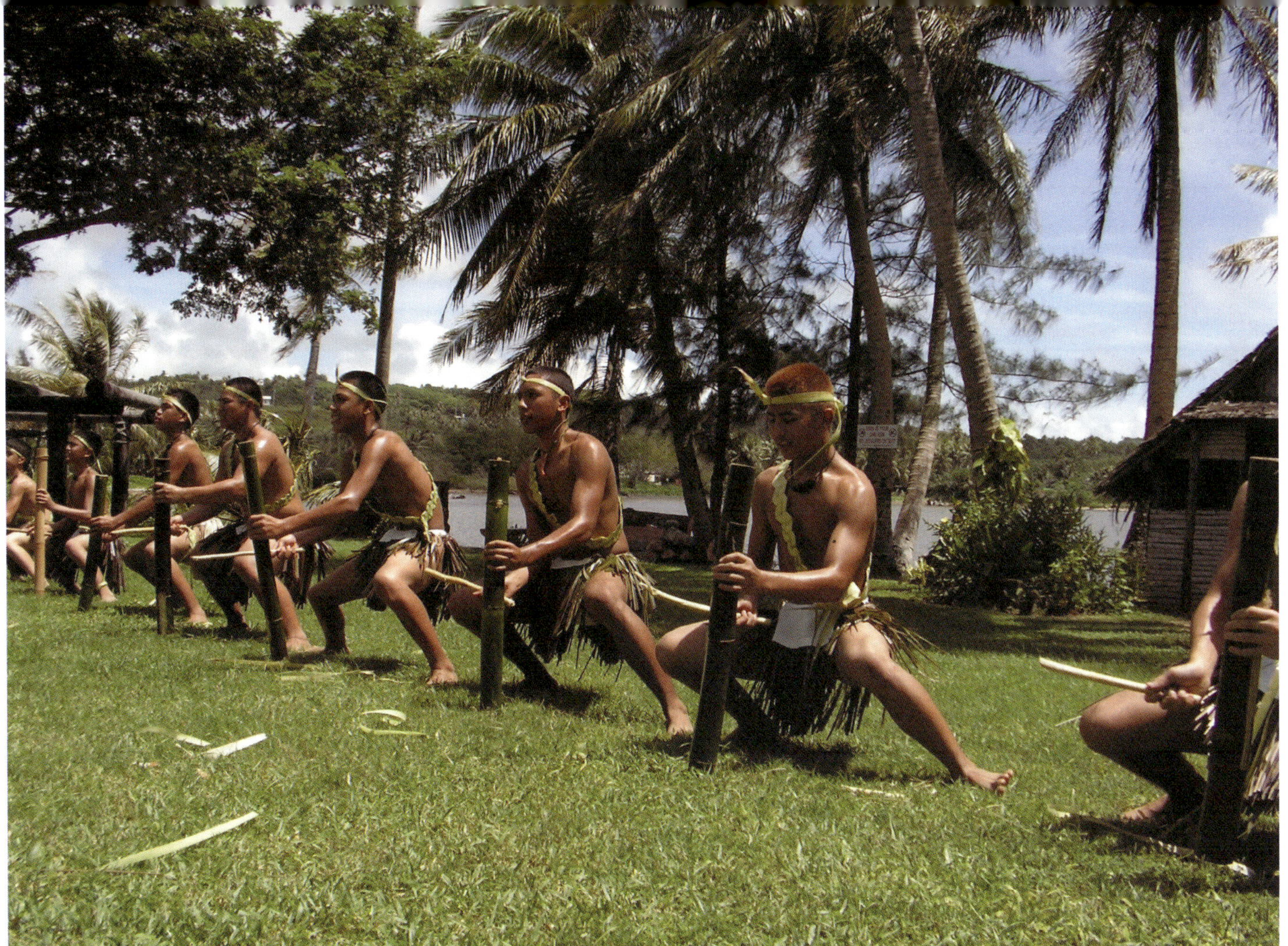

Figure 8.2 Male Bamboo Dance telling the story depicting a written account about the spiritual practices of the "Makana", or traditional healer. Gef Pa'go Chamorro Cultural Village. Photograph courtesy of Marcella Takai, 2007.

motion, which can be attributed to their age and maturity level.

At the same time I asked four dance instructors what they believed to be the challenges students face when considering cultural dance. All agreed that the fear of the unknown is the biggest obstacle. One instructor observed; "most of them are not very knowledgeable of what it means to be involved in, or to belong to a group of cultural agents and the main purpose behind this belonging." [5] Also, many do not "realize the concepts behind perpetuating culture." [6] "Kids may want to join but are afraid because they don't understand enough about it." [7]

Western stereotypes of cultural dancing and peer pressure are other prominent factors in their decision to either join or not join a group. One instructor commented, "the average male considers dance as something feminine and not macho." [8] In addition, "during adolescence, the fear of not conforming to what peers expect of them or, what they think is cool may hinder an individual from joining a group." [9] Another stated that, "many kids worry about what people will think of them and how their body will look when performing." [10]

Another key issue is Family support, or the lack thereof. Many children want to participate, however, "sometimes they don't get the support or the positive reinforcements from their family members." [11] In addition, the financial requirements may also prevent a child from entering into a group as some "groups require a tuition fee in addition to payment for costumes, equipment and so forth; many parents opt not to have their child participate because they cannot afford it." [12]

Those who have been able to overcome these barriers have decided to take part in dance, face obstacles that impede their progress. As one instructor states, "several times, an individual may have the potential to continue and progress in the program; however, because their friends don't have that, he feels more obligated to follow his friends and not be so good. At this age,

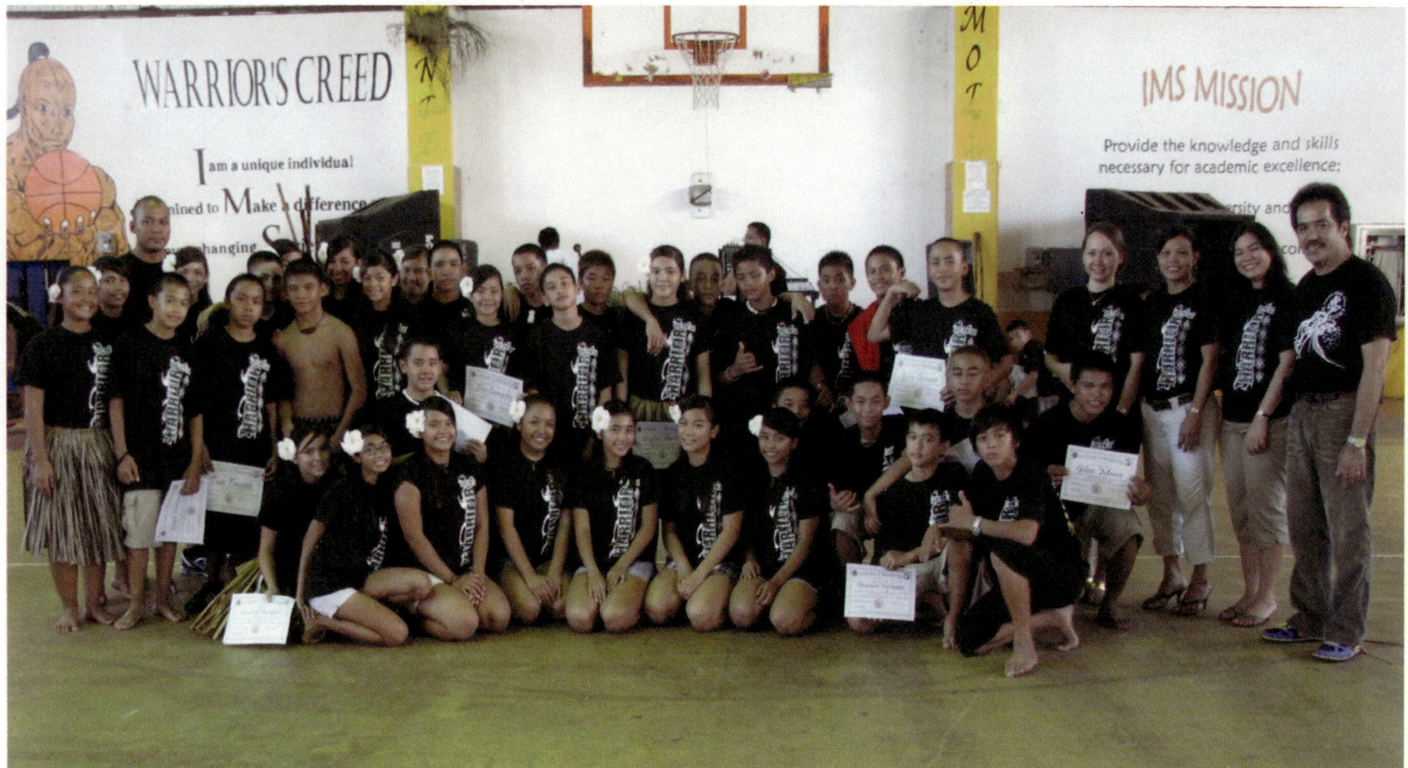

Figure 8.3 The Newly Inducted "Traveling Group" selected at the school-wide assembly, Inarajan Middle School. Photograph courtesy of Inarajan Middle School, 2008.

being in the spotlight is not a big issue." [13] Another instructor reiterated; "these kids would rather be a subtle follower and not necessarily be in the limelight." [14] Not achieving hinders the progression of both the individual and the group. This may discourage many, as they are not challenged.

Marketing Cultural Dance to Students

Because the art of Chamorro cultural dance is a fairly new subject, many students approach this class with trepidation and fear. Through both my observation and research, many students feel that this particular art form is strictly for performance purposes and fail to see the connection it serves to our island's culture. This is why I am forced to market this class in the same way a company would market its product. I have surrendered to the idea that I must "sell" my product — the product being cultural dance. This is one of the major challenges that I face as an instructor. In doing so I do not devalue my culture, as I believe I must do whatever is necessary to create the interests for student success.

To entice students, a variety of marketing tools such as trendy t-shirts, brochures, posters and an appealing dance presentation are used. To maintain their interest, promises of fieldtrips, off-island travel, and dream outings are also used. The most successful inducement is the creation of a safe and nurturing family for students. The students then focus on developing an intrinsic value of Chamorro dance and its role in the perpetuation and promotion of our culture. My first priority is to teach them the value of our culture and identity and then teach them how to convey that pride through dance.

A performance group of the 'best' dancers provides and promotes an elite status for the class. These select few make it hip, cool and fun; and students want to become a part of that. For example, out of 240 students enrolled, a selection process is undertaken to determine who will comprise a performing group of 30 dancers. For one month, each student must go through a series of interviews and auditions. A semi-final list of 60 students is then announced in the daily bulletin and throughout the school. From there, a final selection is made and announced during a school-wide assembly [fig. 8.3]. It is gratifying to know that what started out as a novel idea to provide a practical approach to Chamorro dance and chants has blossomed into a vibrant and popular class. Although the class began in 2000 with only a few skeptical students, it has now become the performing sensation of IMS.

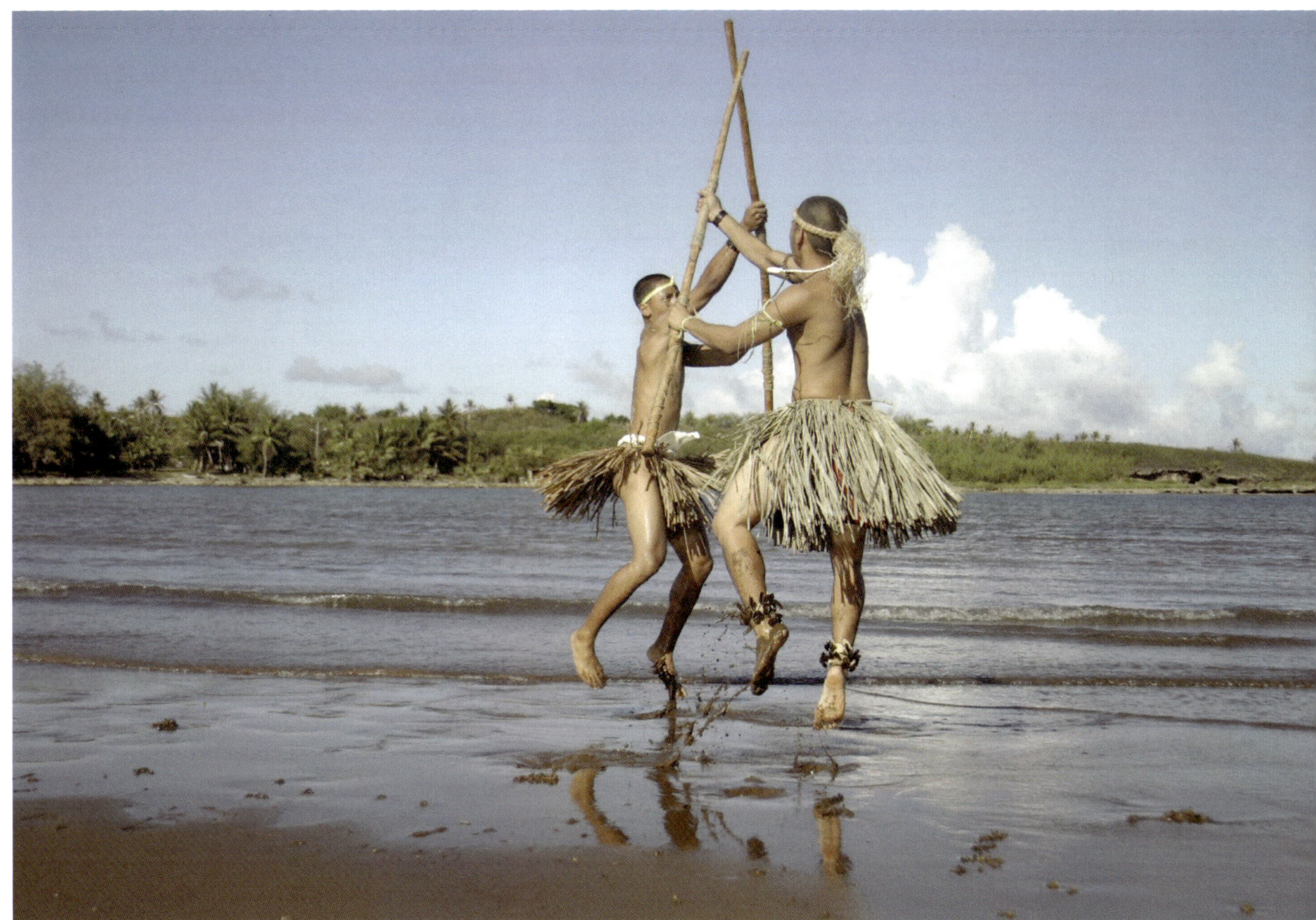

Figure 8.4 Bailan Tunas or Warrior Stick Dance. Gef Pa'go Chamorro Cultural Village. Photograph courtesy of Pa'a Taotao Tano, 2007

Accomplishments

Over the years I have developed a passion for the perpetuation and promotion of my island's culture and identity. For the past nine years, I have channeled this passion as a teacher of Cultural Arts at IMS. I pioneered and solidified the first cultural arts program at IMS and achieved a notable reputation for the perpetuation of Chamorro culture through dance [fig. 8.4]. IMS has also established a working relationship with Gef Pa'go Chamorro Cultural Village. Gef Pa'go Cultural Village is a living museum of crafts and demonstrations that portray the lives of native Chamorro people in the early 1900s. It also serves as a tourist venue for visitors. Together with the executive director, Dr. Judy Flores, we have created a curriculum that provides students the opportunity of learning from the master crafts persons based at Gef Pago. [fig. 8.5]

We received a grant from the Administration for Native Americans in 2004, which established a community-based cultural dance program. Inetnon Gef Pa'go was created to provide opportunities to those students graduating from the middle school program who wanted to continue learning about their culture. Approximately 60 students, ranging from ages 14-21, are utilizing this program. That same year, I traveled to meetings of the Association of Social Anthropologists of Oceania in Massachusetts in 2003 and Kauai, Hawaii in 2004 to discuss this program. [15] There, I had the wonderful opportunity to meet and collaborate with other Pacific artists and scholars. I was also able to bring a small group to perform at the ASAO meetings in Hawaii. We also took this opportunity to perform at various venues across O'ahu. These experiences enabled my young dancers to blossom into true ambassadors of our culture. This was especially so during our cultural exchange with the students of the Kamehameha School and in our performance at the Polynesian

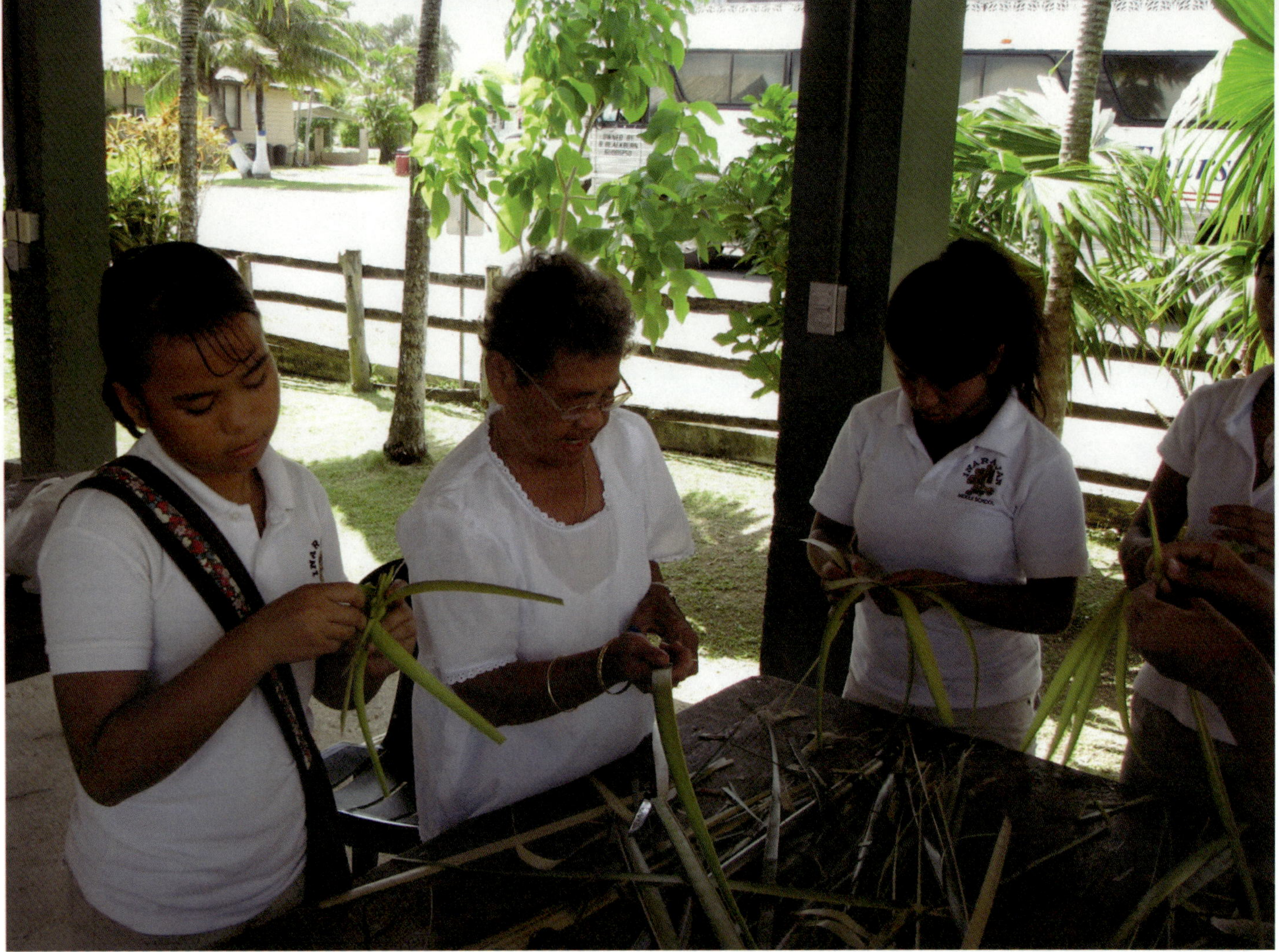

Figure 8.5 Students learn traditional weaving from Master Weaver, Floren Paulino, November 2008. Photograph courtesy of Historic Inalahan Foundation. 2008.

Cultural Center. [fig. 8.6] As they were asked questions about their culture, they began to search for information about their history, and to ask about words and meanings in the Chamorro language. Since then, we have been able to provide numerous cultural exchange opportunities in our neighboring islands of Saipan and Tinian, as well as Australia, Japan, Hawaii, mainland United States, New Zealand and Europe. In collaboration with the Guam Visitors Bureau, we were selected to promote Guam in various locations in Japan, Korea, Hong Kong, and Macau. With these experiences and a wider acknowledgement of Chamorro dance, we finally broke through Guam's tourism industry (in 2008) by providing the only nightly full-Chamorro Show at the Sheraton Laguna Guam Resort.

It has been overwhelmingly fulfilling to share my passion; not just "to" my students, but "through" them. I hope these experiences have planted a seed to further their cultural awareness and assist them in developing a long-term interest in cultural perpetuation through dance.

In 2004 I was awarded the Traditional Teacher of the Year Award by the Guam Humanities Council. In 2005, Inetnon Gef Pa'go was invited to perform at a conference, "Culture Moves! Dance in Oceania" in Wellington, New Zealand, where I also served as a discussion panelist. In 2006, the program received the Excellence in Tourism - Hafa Adai Spirit Award by the Guam Visitors Bureau and was nominated for Program of the Year by the Guam Humanities Council. In 2008, I was invited as a presenter at the International Organization of Folk Art (IOV) World Youth Congress in Bountiful City, Utah and was elected Representative for Oceania in the IOV Youth Commission on Preserving Intangible Cultural Heritage.

As I continue to define and redefine my role as an artist, I have realized that my passion focuses on cultural promotion, preservation, and perpetuation and through my art I am able to channel this passion. It is not just professional, but personal as well. This deep and abiding concern for our youth and our culture forces me to continue to explore and research ways to entice and appeal to students so they may learn more

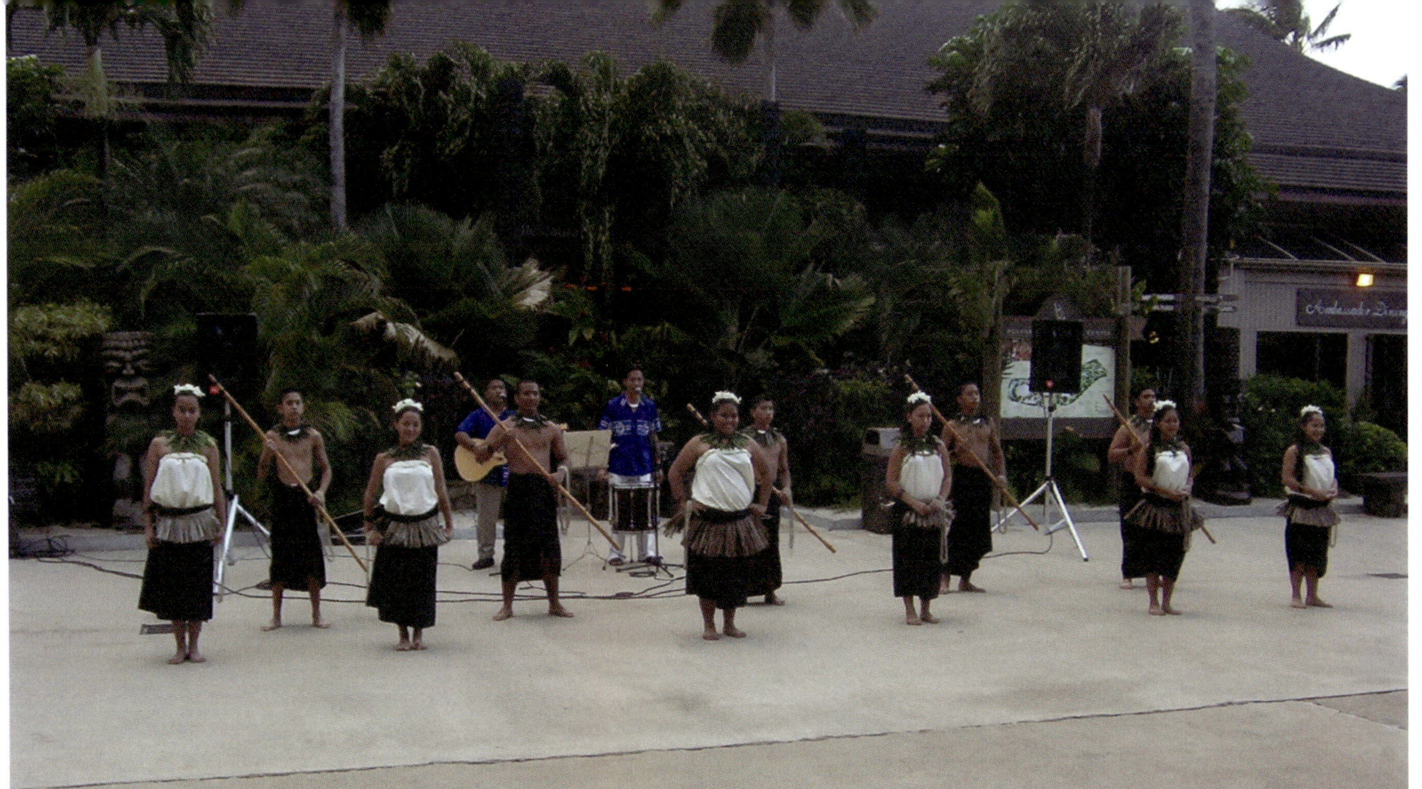

Figure 8.6 Inetnon Gef Pa'go Performance at the Polynesian Cultural Center, February, 2004. Photograph courtesy of Inetnon Gef Pa'go, 2004.

about their heritage. This will provide them opportunities to become true cultural agents of the island.

Challenges

There have been many challenges along the way for the success that we have gained. The lack of a public venue to perform on a regular basis has hindered the acceptance of Chamorro cultural dance. But differing opinions as to how cultural dance should be taught, lack of community support, and problems associated with reinventing these dances have also placed large obstacles in our way.

In contrast to Hawaii, with it's Polynesian Cultural Center, which was established as a venue for Pacific cultures to showcase their dances on a daily basis, Guam only has special events such as the Micronesian Island Fair, village fiestas, and other island-wide activities, many groups here do not have that kind of consistent outlet. The only such venue is the Wednesday Night Market at the Chamorro Village in our capitol of Hagatña.

Although many efforts are being made, instructors have all agreed that more collaboration is needed. Both Frank Rabon and Pa'a Taotao Tano have worked hard to create a unity and consistency among all dance groups. However, an underlying sense of hesitation still exists amongst some group leaders that prevent a full sense of unity. Two instructors frame this unease; one states that there is a need to dissolve the constant "pulling of ranks among (some) dance teachers," [16] another suggests that there "needs to be an understanding that we are all working towards the same product."[17]

Attendance at ASAO has made me aware of the sensitive issues of cultural borrowing. Unfortunately, the research of pre-colonial Chamorro dance can only be found through Spanish records where information is minimal, one-sided, and underwhelming to anyone wanting to know more about this art form. Clues can be found in current cultural practices, but this leaves much room for interpretation. As many of our instructors began their journey in cultural dance by learning Polynesian dance, there are many elements of movement and instrumentation that are influenced from this area of the Pacific. The lack of information and research contributes to the issue of authenticity. However, efforts are being made not to authenticate, but to substantiate Chamorro dance, which emphasizes the unique aspects of our own culture. My reconstructive efforts, in particular, infuse a choreography and instrumentation that first and foremost attempts to embody the unique essence of my people's culture and identity. [fig. 8.7]

Funding and community support is another issue. Most groups rely on simple fundraisers to purchase much needed supplies and equipment. Many dance instructors resort to using their personal income to help support their groups. The community needs to be aware that programs and presentations of culture are very

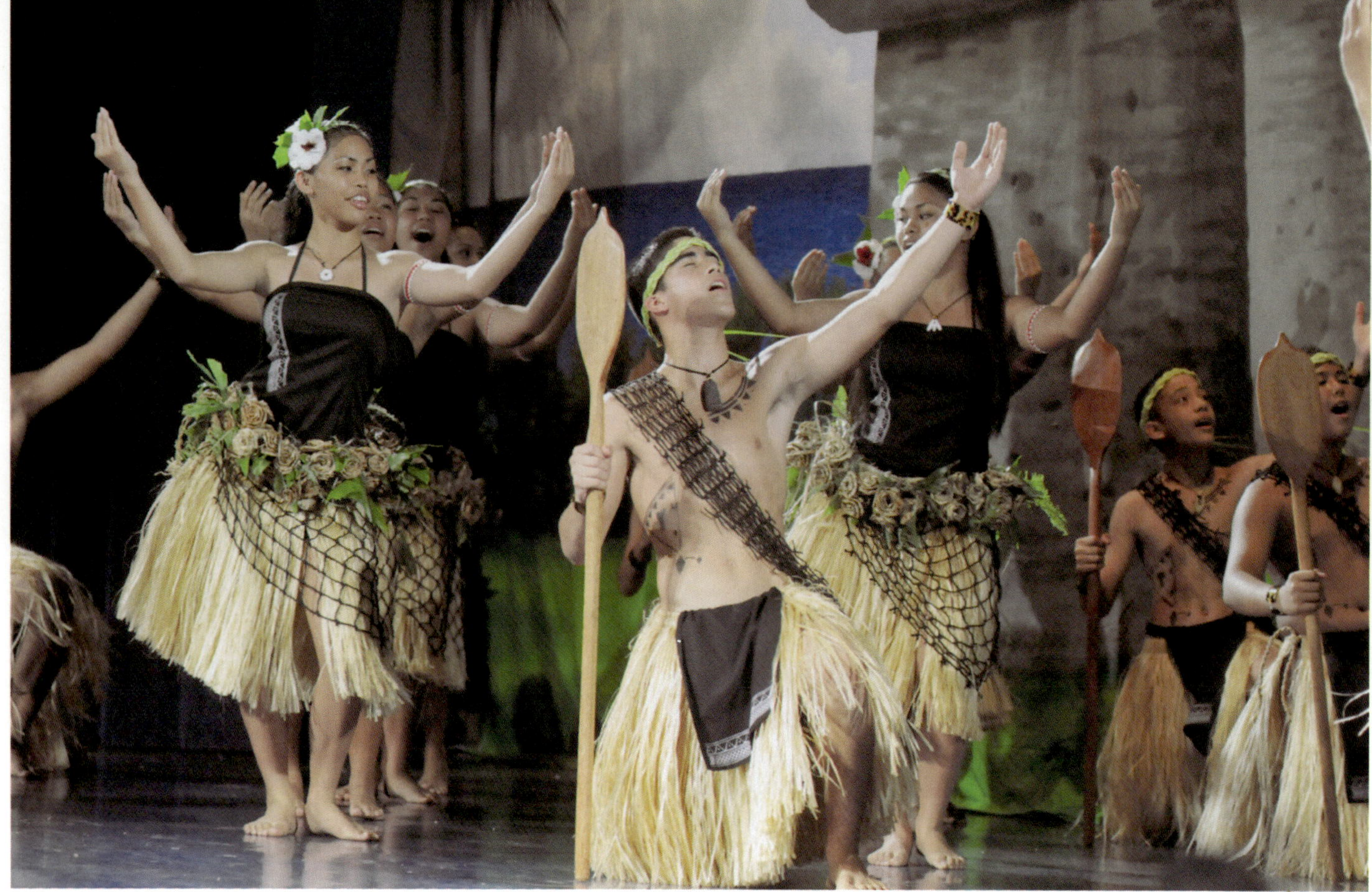

Figure 8.7 Inetnon Gef Pa'go Performance at the Dinana Minagof Cultural Dance Competition, Guam June, 2009. Photograph courtesy of Pa'a Taotao Tano, 2009.

important. "There needs to be more support from the local business and community." [18]

Despite these difficulties and challenges, I asked each instructor what motivates them to continue. One stated; "the fact that I know that there is more out there. There is more room to create and we have only touched the surface in creating what is Chamorro."[19] He continues, "We have only opened the lid half way. Through the medium of the kids, there is so much more that I can do to broaden their horizons."[20] Another instructor states; "my stimulus is the kids."[21] Planting the seed for further cultural awareness continues to be the driving force.

The uphill battle continues for cultural dancing in Guam. It is evident that continued education for our kids and community is important. Consistent schoolwide programs in culture should be integrated into every school curriculum. Through education, the students are able to gain the experience and knowledge of appreciating cultural dance, which is not readily available for them outside of school. It is my goal to stimulate long-term interest in the arts through cultural promotion. Cultural dancing will continue to represent who we are as a people. Through this medium, our children will continue to enhance their knowledge about the rich history and practices of the Chamorro people. The pride that this will instill will be the necessary tool to ensure that our Chamorro culture remains vital for future generations.

"*Ai Bilong Meri*": Making and Marketing the Contemporary Vision of Papua New Guinea Women Artists

Marion Struck-Garbe

> It is obvious that art can fulfill the enduring needs of the mind and spirit of every individual and of the most varied situations. [1]

Papua New Guinea is famous for its many diverse cultures and their varied artistic expressions, styles, decorations, and patterns. For most Germans, art from Papua New Guinea continues to imply the objects displayed in ethnographic museums or in specialized antique shops. If produced today, only objects such as masks, storyboards, sculptures, and shields, will be judged as contemporary examples of traditional art or perhaps as "primitive art." All other forms of artistic creativity, such as contemporary painting and sculpture, are viewed as inauthentic, non-original, and not genuine. PNG art, per se, is of little interest in a Western country like Germany; interest emerges from the countries traditional past. However, what is considered traditional may differ between professionals, scholars and museum personal, as well as the general public.

As an anthropologist and an artist, I worked with a group of woman artists in PNG and organized three major exhibitions of contemporary art in Port Moresby, the capital, between 1998-2000. Because of the stunning success of these exhibitions, I was also encouraged to curate Papua New Guinea art in Germany. However, curating an exhibition in Germany proved problematic, largely because most art gallery owners refused to exhibit contemporary Papua New Guinea art. Instead, I was forced to find exhibition space in churches, local cultural centers, and educational institutions. Based on these experiences I frequently ask: What problems do Papua New Guinea artists face by creating contemporary art for two audiences, one at home and one abroad? What obstacles are keeping German art professionals and the public from recognizing and appreciating the aesthetic qualities of contemporary Papua New Guinea art? What is necessary to deepen and broaden the acceptance of these new artforms in overseas countries like Germany?

It has become clear that the West requires a better understanding of contemporary Papua New Guinea art, *particularly if it is to be positioned in the international art scene.* Contemporary PNG art must move out of ethnographic museums and into art museums and art galleries. By saying this I do not mean to suggest that Papua New Guinea art does not need contextual information (see Raabe this volume), but in ethnographic museums "the exotic" takes precedence over the art. This essay will address the conflicts between the primitive and contemporary, authenticity and the exotic, the position of Papua New Guinea art, and most importantly the position of the women who create it. It will assert that Papua New Guinea art needs to be recognized as Art, not as evidence of the exotic other (see Rosi this volume). Placing contemporary art in art galleries and public galleries, where it may achieve commercial success is a necessary step towards enabling Papua New Guinea artists to make a living from their art (see Castro this volume).

My Involvement with Papua New Guinea Art

Contemporary artists in Papua New Guinea are not easy to find. No one keeps a list of who and where they are, and there is no organization that represents them. No records are kept of the artwork produced, not even with the National Cultural Commission. Contemporary art is a neglected field left to foreigners who generally live in Papua New Guinea for limited periods before returning to their own homes in Australia, North America, or Europe. Through their support contemporary art blossoms for a time, but when they leave the developments they have initiated often collapse. Even internationally known artists like the late Mathias Kauage (1944-2003) were left sitting in front of hotel entrances selling their work to make a living.

For the more then thirty years after independence (1975), successive governments have failed to recognize either traditional or contemporary arts as important. In fact they have gradually stopped or weakened their support for cultural and art institutions (see Rosi this volume). This situation is worse for women artists as there is no clear role for them in contemporary Papua New Guinea.

My personal involvement with the PNG contemporary art scene began while I lived in Port Moresby between 1996-2001. Early on I recognized that at the monthly arts and craft market only men were selling contemporary art. This led me to investigate whether there were

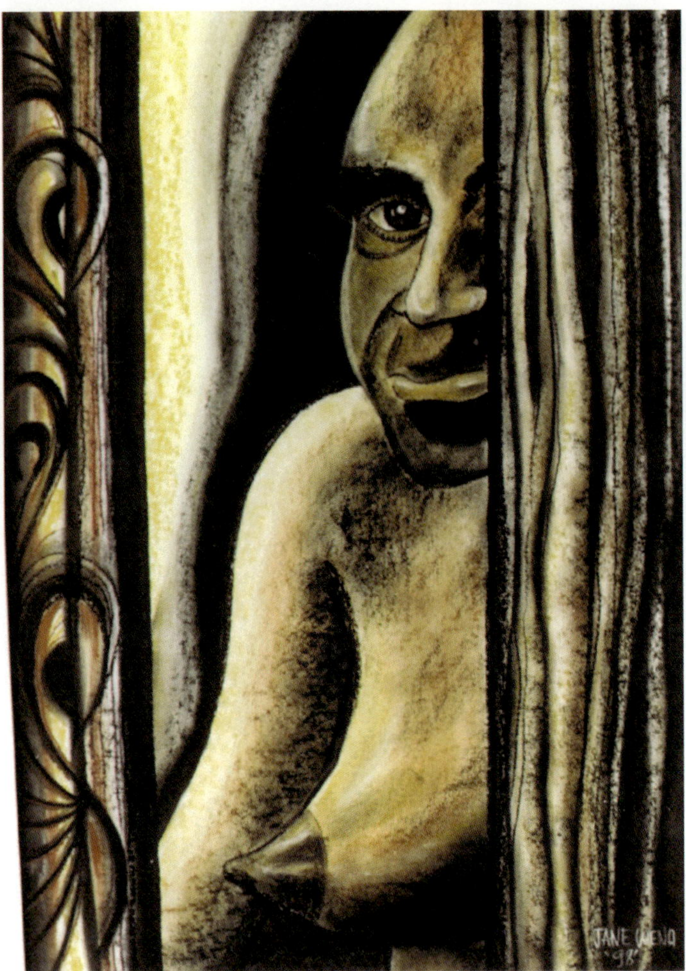

Figure 9.1. Jane Wena, *Behind the Fence*, charcoal/crayon, 40 x 57 cm, 1998. Photograph by Marion Struck-Garbe.

women producing artwork. I learned that five women had studied at the School of Creative Arts, but they seemed to have disappeared. After some weeks looking for them I finally met four: Jane Wena, Gazellah Bruder, Winnie Weoa, and Julie Mota.

Soon we organized weekend workshops in my house and we set up our first exhibition, showing only female artists, at the end of 1998. A top executive of the German Development Service, who was in Papua New Guinea during that time, was so impressed that he organized a small exhibition in Berlin. He invited Jane Wena and Gazellah Bruder to work in Berlin for three weeks and while there they took part in two small exhibitions. I returned to Germany to organize the opening of the main exhibition. The tremendous public success of those exhibitions led to the idea of exhibiting Papua New Guinea art in other places in Germany.

When I returned to Port Moresby several male artists approached me to promote their work as well. I agreed to help them and working jointly with the National

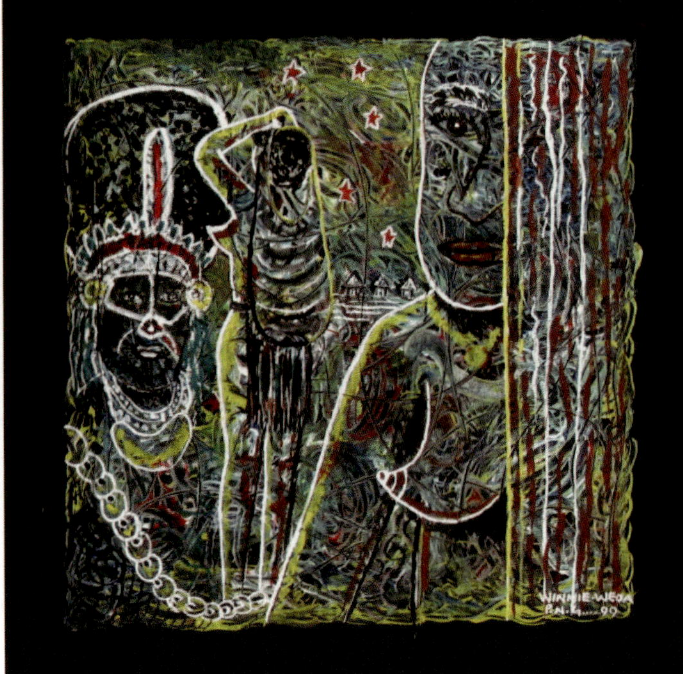

Figure 9.2. Winnie Weoa, *Behind the Fence*, gouache/crayon, 13 x 18 cm, 1999. Photograph by Marion Struck-Garbe.

Museum and Art Gallery, I curated two more exhibitions in Papua New Guinea. After leaving Papua New Guinea, however, few Westerners seemed willing to promote contemporary art in their homelands, resulting in only a few public contemporary art exhibitions. Since my return to Germany, I have curated more than twenty exhibitions. My aim is to show contemporary Oceanic art in galleries; I want to present it as something that can stand on its own merit.

Working with Women Artists

From 1998-2000 I worked very closely with the four women artists mentioned above, all of whom except for Winnie Weoa were brought up in Port Moresby and still live there. We met every weekend (for almost a year) to draw and paint together at a studio room in my house. One problem that all artists in PNG face is the shortage of material for their paintings. Sometimes the artists use whatever they can find to paint, such as the reverse side of old maps or plastic tablecloths, or they use children's paints. Proper materials are either not available in town or the artist can not afford to buy them. I was able to provide them with different kinds of art materials. Usually we worked all night Friday till Saturday morning. Sometimes one or another of them stayed and painted till Sunday afternoon. In this creative atmosphere these women developed the courage to experiment with different techniques and styles. Sometimes they painted the same motifs with different styles or materials. In the end they all developed

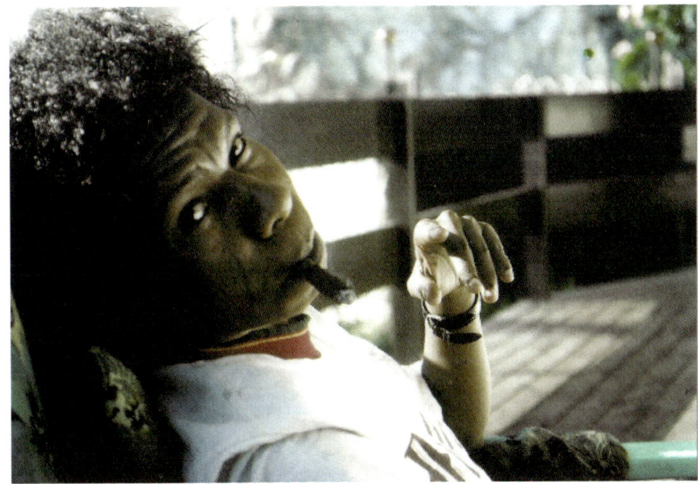

Figure 9.3. Jane Wena shown during a weekend working session at our rented house at Tuaguba Hill in Port Moresby in 2000. Photograph by Marion Struck-Garbe.

their very own personal way of depicting motifs, a fact best illustrated when they all chose the same motif.

At first a favorite theme was "faces of Papua New Guinea"; later they chose "behind the fence," a theme depicting the situation of many women in Papua New Guinea, who were kept isolated from modernity and excluded from access to services and development resources. In post-contact PNG many women are cut off from decision-making about the development process of the country. The "behind the fence" theme also emphasizes the situation of women artists in the art industry [figs. 9.1 and 9.2]. Each artist produced two or three variations of this theme. The styles, patterns, designs, and motifs these women used were always very different from the artwork of their male colleagues. It seems that women are not only inspired by different things, but they also have their own ways of feeling and expressing these sentiments. It goes without saying that their works clearly reflect their educational, local, and tribal backgrounds.

The Artists

Jane Wena [fig. 9.3] (born 1970) is from Kerowagi in Chimbu, an area where a lot of Papua New Guinea's artists and painters come from. Her late uncle, John Danga, was also an artist, her role model and mentor. Jane visited the National Arts School in 1988 and holds a degree from the School of Creative Arts at the University of Papua New Guinea. Belonging to a family of seven, she stays in touch with people in her home village in the remote Highlands, but lives on the coast in Port Moresby. Jane has been trained as a graphic designer and specializes in pen illustrations. She earns a living with one of the national newspapers and both

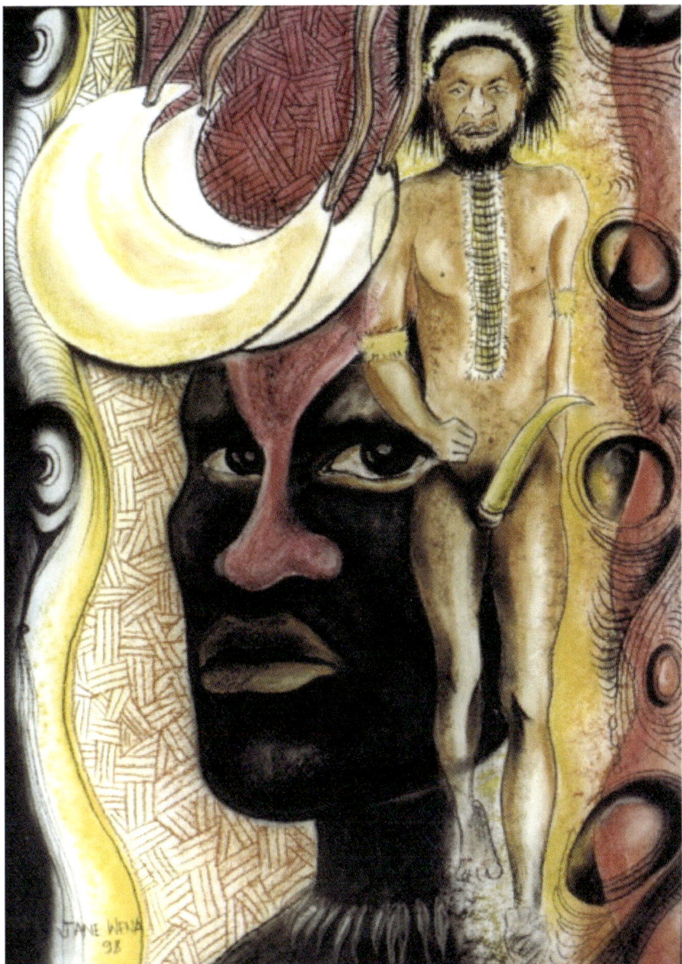

Figure 9.4. Jane Wena, *The Power of Men*, gouache on paper, 40 x 57 cm, 1998. Photograph by Marion Struck-Garbe.

her rural origin and modern profession influence her art.

Jane considers her artwork as "just straight forward and not based on legends, stories or myth." [2] She depicts people from the Highlands in traditional costumes and ornaments [fig. 9.4]. She has the conviction that Papua New Guinea's cultural heritage might vanish and she wants to preserve it through her drawings.

Winnie Weoa [fig. 9.5] (born 1971) comes from the even more remote Enga Province, and was the first woman artist to graduate with a Diploma in Fine Arts from the University of Papua New Guinea in 1993. Her regular income derives from different jobs as a graphic designer. Winnie is deaf. For over a year she shared a flat with Jane Wena living a rather independent life. In her artwork Winnie developed her own exceptional style of dot painting. She has won several awards and has received recognition overseas. Winnie's paintings were first shown in the Islander Hotel in Port Moresby

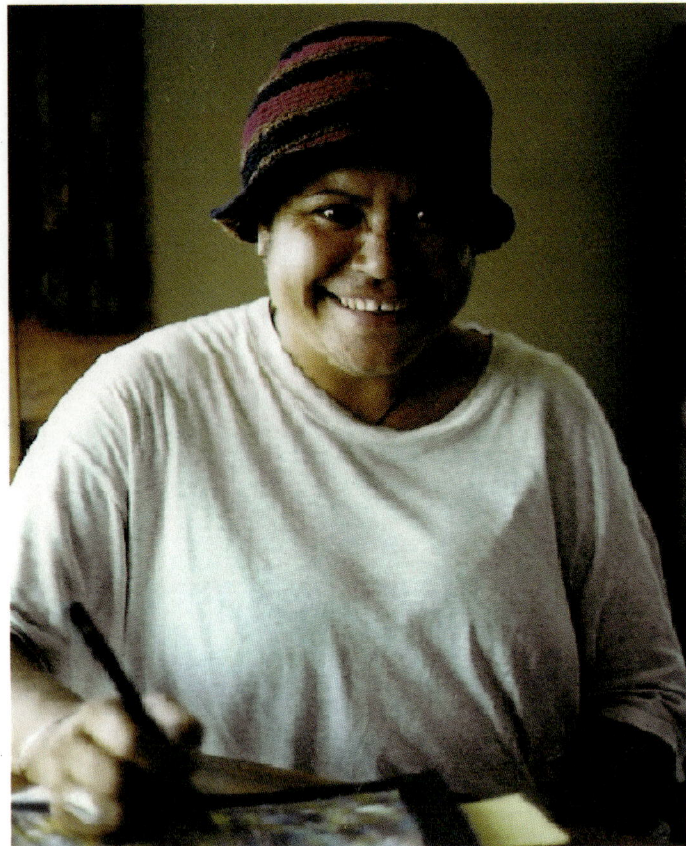

Figure 9.5. Winnie Weoa shown during a weekend working session at our rented house at Tuaguba Hill in Port Moresby in 2000. Photograph by Marion Struck-Garbe.

in 1987. She draws most of her motifs from PNG's traditional cultures and lifestyle [fig. 9.6].

Winnie says she wants to show love for her country in her paintings, and she wants to express what she thinks in pictorial form.

> As we know words are expressive — fear, hate, loneliness, cheer, excitement, happiness, love, wonder, and many more will show in words. Similarly, colors possess expressive qualities. They can be described as warm and cool, light or dark, hard and soft, strong or weak, gentle or violent. Selective combinations of colors and words can produce specific feelings or moods. Therefore, all my painting donates a personal mood or feeling. Most of my paintings are traditional in nature and when viewing, it stimulates the emotions that encourage interpretation, that lead to personal statements, which evoke immediate impact of the viewers. [3]

Gazellah Bruder [fig. 9.7] (born 1977) was born in Port Moresby of mixed New Britain and Central Province origins. She earned her degree in Fine Arts in 1997 specializing in printmaking. At the time I met her Gazellah lived together with her husband and daughter in her parents' house, sharing one room. She did not have a job. Her paintings and prints very rarely show items and objects from traditional culture. In her early work the figures seem to float, much as Kauage's did, and they often appear as dream-like figures with no individual faces or other individual traits [fig. 9.8].

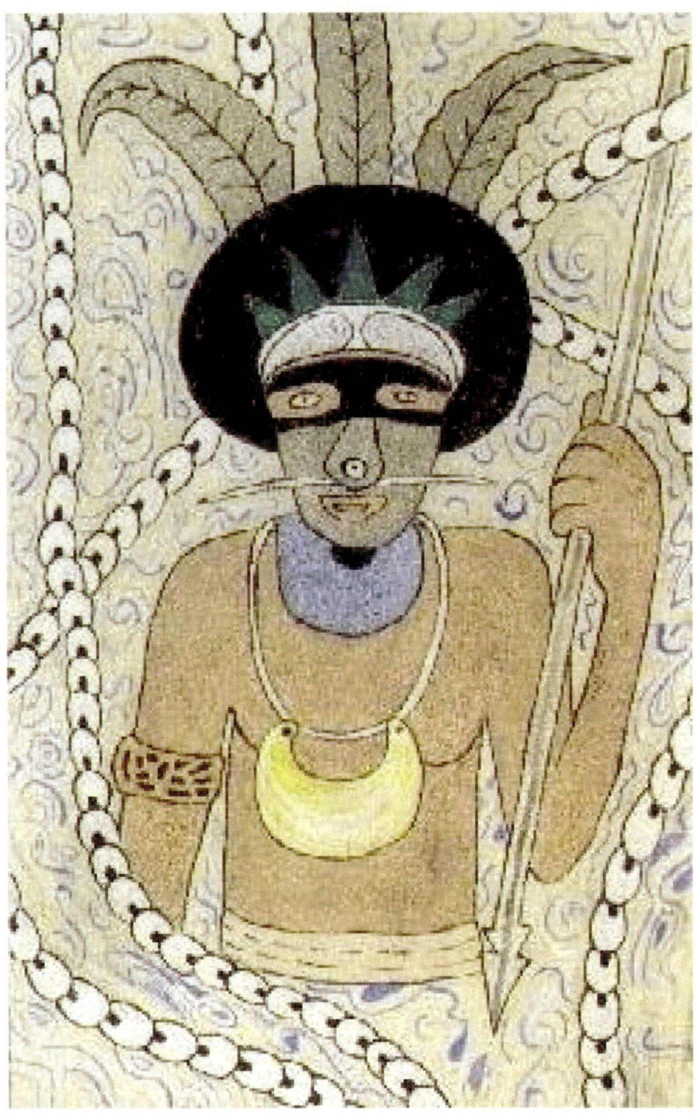

Figure 9.6. Winnie Weoa, *Man from Enga*, sand on paper, 39 x 52 cm, 1998. Photograph by Marion Struck-Garbe.

Gazellah explained [4]:

> Art to me is not just color and beauty of the image. Art should tell a story. I honestly believe that a painting is meaningless without a story line. In my art, I express how I feel as a woman in this day and age living in our Papua New Guinean Society. I get inspiration from how I feel about the most important aspects of my

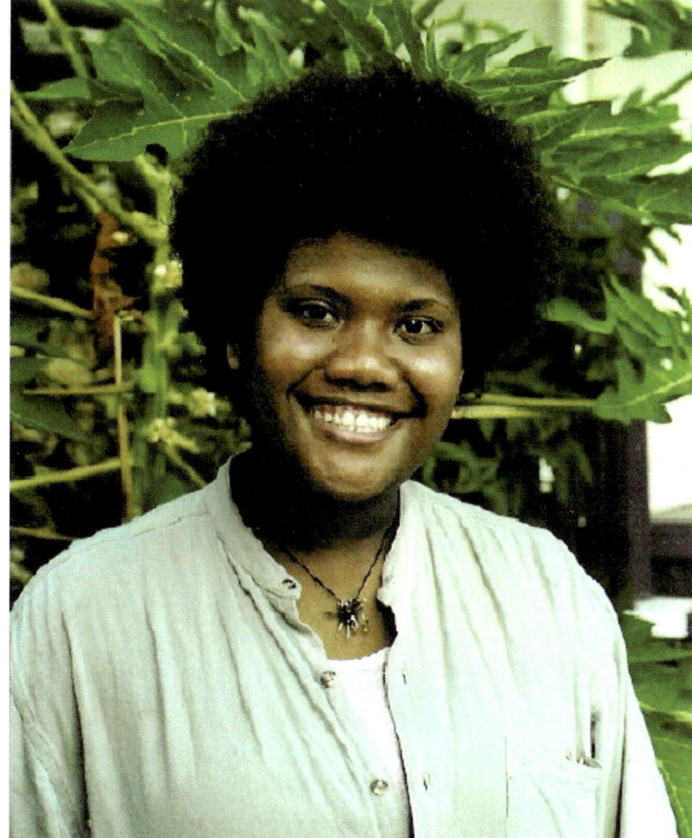

Figure 9.7. Gazellah Bruder shown during a weekend working session at our rented house at Tuaguba Hill in Port Moresby in 2000. Photograph by Marion Struck-Garbe.

> life and this is motherhood and my marriage. I paint and draw from the inside out.

Julie Mota [fig. 9.9] (born 1978) is from Oro Province but has lived in Port Moresby since 1995. She took one art class while she studied drama and play scriptwriting at the University. She stayed with her parents and took classes in commerce while she worked as a finance officer. Julie is very concerned about the changing role of women and the threats of urban life. A lot of her work depicts this social concern as well as showing something from her inner world [fig. 9.10]. Her work consists of pencil drawings and collages in a more abstract style with slender figures. Sometimes Julie illustrates mythological stories. She wants to continue what her grandmother did when she painted on tapa cloth.

Julie comments [5],

> My work is influenced by traditional legends and stories told by my grandparents. Most of these are in our songs and dances. They talk about how a supreme being called Foroga created the first man and how the first village began. For me to follow my great grandmother's and grandmother's footsteps and put ink on paper instead of bark and make my mark in history is a tremendous and privileged task. Instead of using the family, tribe or clan style I use my own style incorporating both traditional and western ideas. Thus establishing an individual identity.

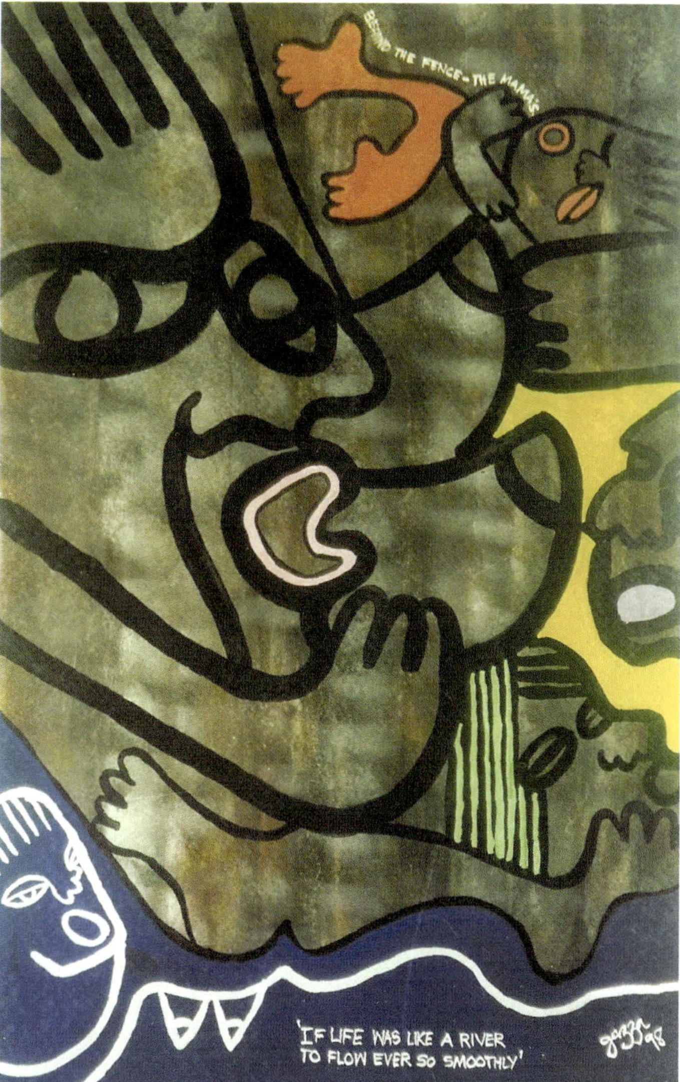

Figure 9.8. Gazellah Bruder, *If life was like a river to flow ever so smoothly*, acrylic on paper, 52 x 70 cm, 1998. Photograph by Marion Struck-Garbe.

Living in the city allows these four women to feel and act as individuals. Here they have freedom to experiment and draw upon what they find useful from any traditional Papua New Guinean culture. The city also provides clients, predominantly expatriates (Beier 1976). Despite its possibilities for freedom and excitement, Port Moresby still does not offer women artists a recognized place in society. Isolated from each other

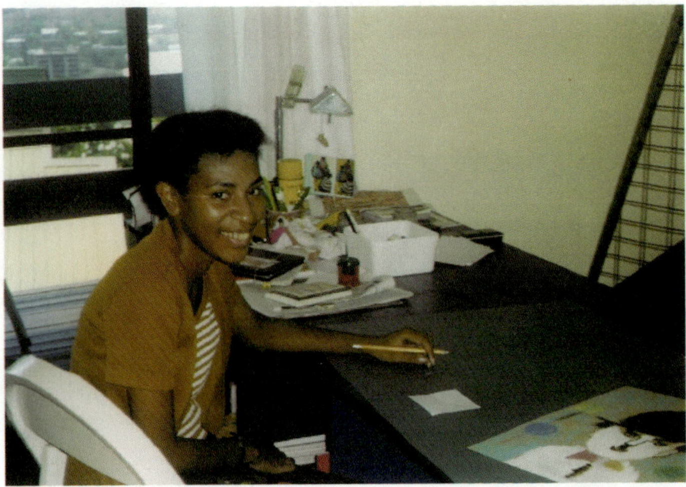

Figure 9.9. Julie Mota shown during a weekend working session at our rented house at Tuaguba Hill in Port Moresby in 2000. Photograph by Marion Struck-Garbe.

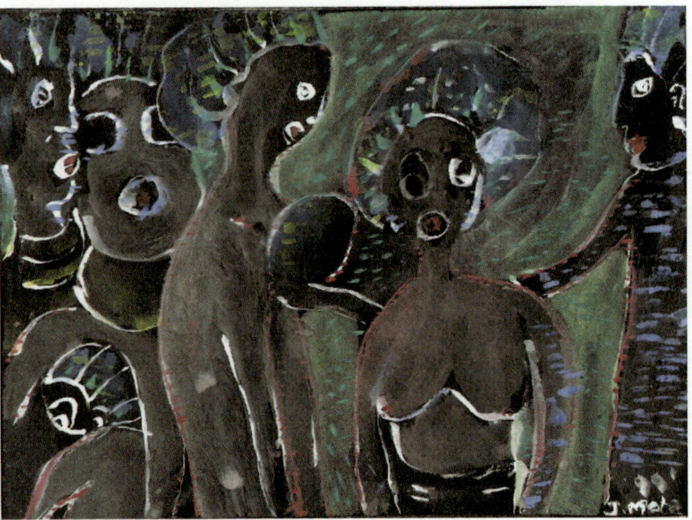

Figure 9.10. Julie Mota, *Pricetag of Woman*, gouache on paper, 13 x 18 cm, 1998. Photograph by Marion Struck-Garbe.

they worked in silence almost unheard and unseen. In their traditional cultures there was a role for women to make useful items, just as they helped with subsistence, cooking, and childcare. But generally speaking there was no role for women as artists in the modern sense. Professional women in contemporary Papua New Guinea are still seen and perceived as a threat to male dominance and represent a contradiction to the traditional woman's role model (Rosi 1995). This attitude, among men, has lead to efforts to suppress women's activities and independence rather than supporting them. This situation is changing as women work collectively and emulate the few role models for women available. This however is a slow process.

These four artists strongly asserted that PNG society is not fair as it ignores and denies their talents. They felt despised, isolated, and unrecognized; their work neither understood nor valued. They believe that the government should encourage women artists, and that more recognition would keep them motivated and inspire others. The women see themselves as important voices in a changing society, and they believe they are as capable as male artists. They believe that their art is as vital and valid as men's art.

> The failure to develop and recognize the wider role of women artists to date is the fault of successive governments since independence. This failure is evident within our formal education system. Our education system does not focus and highlight the work of traditional and contemporary women artists and their contribution to this country. [6]

These women need government support to market their work both at home and overseas (see Rosi, Raabe, and Monds this volume). They have challenged the government and national organizations to provide them with an appropriate venue, such as a well-funded gallery or a serious institution that focuses on and provides all artists opportunities.

"Art is not for the elite and man. It is for everybody," Gazellah Bruder said in a personal conversation. [7] She believes that contemporary art from Papua New Guinea needs to be accessible to her fellow countrymen and women as it is an expression of a living culture.

Organizing Exhibitions in Port Moresby

The first big exhibition presenting female artists in Port Moresby was in 1998. Two more exhibitions followed over the next two years that included works of both male and female artists, but highlighting female artists as important to the Papua New Guinea art scene. Middle-class local people from business, media, churches, diplomatic, and political circles attended the opening events for these exhibitions. Some artists brought their friends and relatives. These exhibitions were well covered by the PNG media (newspapers, magazines, radio, and even TV) prior to the opening with special articles and stories about individual artists. The first exhibition *PNG Meri Artists Soim Piksa (Women artists from PNG show their paintings)* was set up in the Waigani Arts Centre. The National Cultural Commission was not interested in supporting this exhibition, and as such sponsors were sought to defer costs (rental fees and framing).

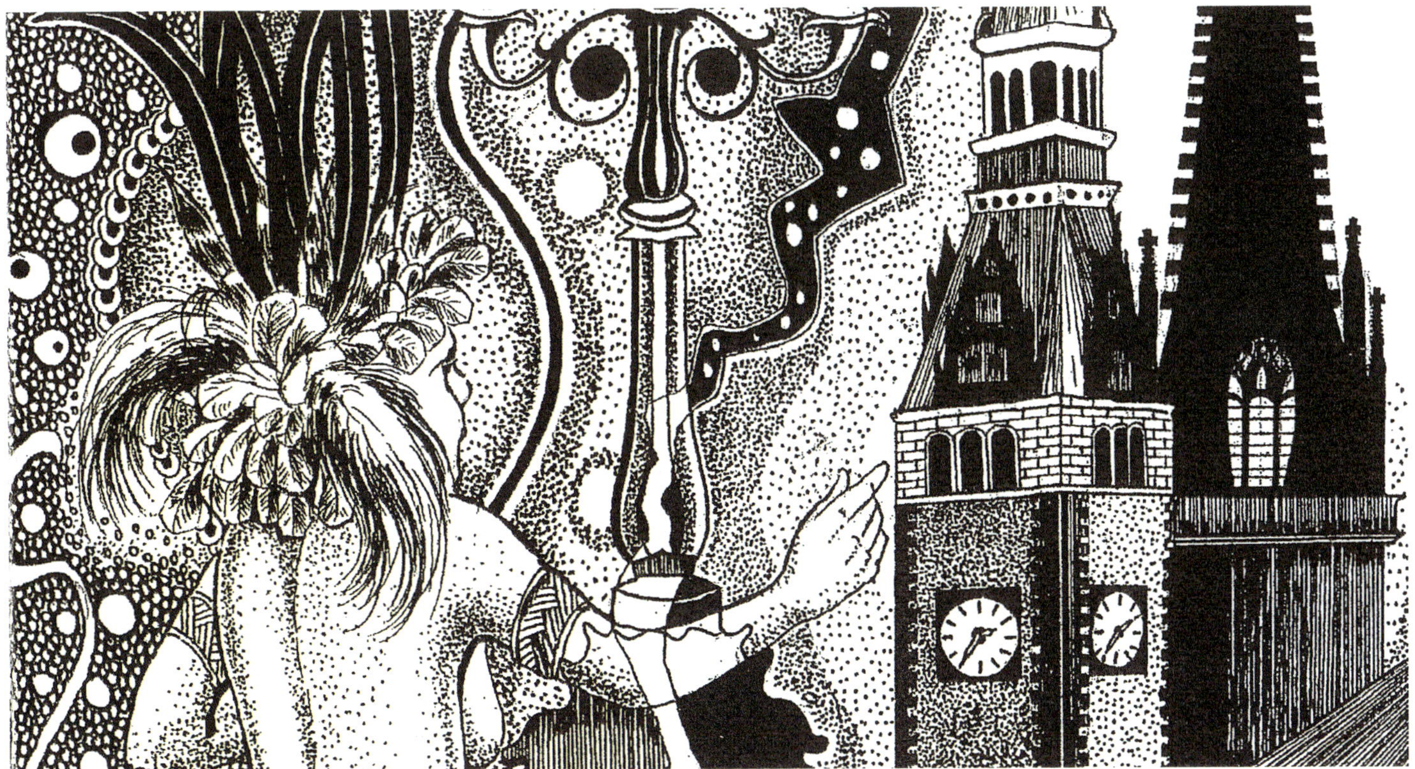

Figure 9.11. Jane Wena, *Hamburg*, ink on paper, 30 x 20 cm, 1998. Photograph by Marion Struck-Garbe.

The exhibition was comprised of 50 contemporary works by five women artists. These paintings and drawings depicted culture and traditions, traditional face paintings, and the changing lifestyle of the people in Papua New Guinea. The aims of the exhibition were; to educate the public that there are female artists in PNG producing important contemporary art, to expose the artists to the market, and to build their confidence. The exhibition received good coverage in the newspapers (including seven feature articles) and two radio shows focused on the lack of opportunity to exhibit and develop a professional career for female artists. In an interview Jane Wena made the point that, "although, I graduated in graphic art at the university, society still has no confidence in our ability as professional artists." [8]

About 70 people attended the opening, and the artists sold twenty works, none of these to their fellow countryman. The exhibition lasted a week, with just a few people attending during work days. For the artists it was an economic success, and the first time that they had experienced the public's appreciation.

The "Meri Artists" Exhibition Empowered the Women

Gazellah Bruder commented, "For me personally it was a success, not because I sold my paintings but more because I have gained so much confidence out of the exhibition [9]. Two months later Gazellah Bruder and Jane Wena traveled to Berlin and Hamburg. Upon their return they were once again in the newspapers. Their trip was described as an "artistic milestone, because it was for the first time that their work has been taken out of the country for exhibition". [10]

These two women embedded their experiences and impressions of Germany in a few outstanding paintings and drawings. Bruder's art expresses her loneliness and fear of the unknown mass of people while she was in Germany. Wena's painting depicts herself in a dancing costume in front of a townhouse in Hamburg, thus pointing to her encounter with a foreign world while reflecting on her national pride [fig. 9.11]. Her ornaments connect the two worlds.

This led to the idea of staging an exhibition about *Images of Germany*, in which other artists, both male and female could take part. The German Embassy agreed to sponsor the month-long event (June-July 1999) together with the Papua New Guinea National Museum and Art Gallery who provided the venue. Fifteen artists [11] depicted their ideas, concepts and images of Germany. This was not an unusual theme for most of the artists as Germany was once a colonial power in the islands and in the Northern part of the country. A special interest in Germany has persisted ever since in Papua New Guinea. The artists submitted seventy paintings and drawings for the exhibition.

The works in the exhibition were multifaceted, some documenting current events, such as when the Berlin wall came down or Germany's aid for the victims of a tsunami. The Charge d'Affairs of the German Embassy opened the exhibition, attended also by high-ranking guests including Government Ministers, Heads of Departments, and Members of Parliament. The biggest success, however, was that the exhibition had the support of and was held on the premises of the National Museum and Art Gallery, the very place that should be holding such an exhibition. After the show, the artists met at the Museum to discuss the establishment of a permanent exhibition in one of the rooms of the museum. A dialogue began but nothing achieved. There is still no permanent contemporary art exhibition space.

Before leaving Papua New Guinea in 2000, I wanted to dedicate one last exhibition to the hardworking and enduring women of Papua New Guinea. Advertised in newspapers and on the radio, thirty artists provided ninety artworks for the exhibition *Laip Bilong Meri (Everyday Life of Women)* held at the National Museum and Art Gallery. The artists included the woman artists I had been working with; Jane Wena, Winnie Weoa, Gazellah Bruder and Julie Mota, as well as Mathias Kauage, Martin Morububuna, Apa Hugo, Daniel Holland, Larry Santana, and others. Gickmai Kundun contributed sculptural work, and Maria Santana included some of the T-shirts she makes collaboratively with her husband Larry. [12] The artwork showed a strong sense of identity characterized by both the continuity as well as the changes in women's lives. Dame Carol Kidu (a Member of Parliament and role model for Papua New Guinea women) opened the exhibition. Lady Morauta (wife of the then Prime Minister), dignitaries, officials, diplomats, and many guests attended the opening. A few works there sold.

Neither of the exhibitions at the National Museum had the intense media coverage as the first one at the Waigani Arts Centre, nor were the number of paintings sold as high. Nevertheless, during both exhibitions artists appealed to attending government officials for increased support for contemporary art. Unfortunately, (as underscored by Rosi's paper, this volume) the Government has done little to support contemporary art production.

Expatriates and foreign visitors to Papua New Guinea are impressed and surprised that "these far away third-world artists" are able to create stunning contemporary artwork. This attitude reinforces suspicions about this genre and questions its authenticity vis-à-vis the conventional handicrafts available at the Port Moresby Ela Beach Craft Market, hotels, or airports throughout the country. Artistic authenticity is often associated with objects perceived to be traditional art. "True" art and therefore more precious and valuable things are from the past. There is a sense (amongst Westerners) that contemporary artists will never be able to produce works equivalent to the traditional ones, or as Victor Totu stated:

> "The artist is then condemned as 'non-traditional' by the fine-art market because of his increased sophistication in ways of the dominant culture, or because the art he produces reflects new experiences as well as 'traditional' forms. The artist is thus not given the freedom to develop in the way he wishes. And, at the same time, it is assured that by definition he can never produce the fine works of uncontaminated old art that his father made." [13]

Contemporary art has not yet found an audience amongst Papua New Guineans, even though this art expresses a national consciousness and pride as well as concerns about its future development. This art is as vital as traditional art and gives expression to a living culture. It tells of the feelings, emotions, conflicts, and stories of people in a rapidly changing country. Yet, little is done to promote it. Despite their rhetoric, those in power do not consider contemporary art important enough for government support, even though, if fostered, this art could contribute a greatly to PNG's emerging and much needed sense of national identity. The artists feel this disinterest bitterly. Gazellah Bruder comments [14]:

> They [Germans] treat art as a priority and they look after their museums and art galleries very well and with much pride. After seeing this I feel it is a shame and very sad that our rich and vast cultural heritage is dying slowly and we are being negligent and not doing anything to save it. I urge our Government to do something now before Western influences destroy our culture forever.

Julie Mota argued, that without sponsorship from outside Papua New Guinea, women artists would still be in the "silence of male dominance of the artistic profession." [15]

The "sorry state of art" is one problem, enhanced by the lack of a market, except for resident expatriates or tourists just passing through. Rarely does the new

Papua New Guinean elite buy contemporary Papua New Guinea art. Instead, they buy cars, which are prestigious symbols of modernization (Rosi 1998). Price is also a problem. The 'market' allows works to be valued for several thousand Kina. [16] However, need comes into play and artists undercut their own prices to suit their needs. Frequently a painting demands 700 Kina one day and 200 Kina shortly thereafter. Prices also depend on the locations where paintings are sold. Prices are considerably lower at the monthly craft market than at the National Museum and Art Gallery. Unlike other commodities, bargaining is not common with contemporary art and the artists often reject such attempts. As such, neither the artist nor the buyer has a real sense of the works 'market value'. Despite the difficulties facing the promotion of contemporary art, it provides a platform for local PNG issues and worldviews that would otherwise remain silent. To promote an emerging national identity PNG contemporary art requires more venues where ordinary citizens can readily see and experience it.

Papua New Guinea Art in Germany

Ingrid Heermann installed the first exhibition of contemporary art from Papua New Guinea, called *Ting-ting Bilong Mi*, at the Linden Museum in Stuttgart in 1979. Georgina and Ulli Beier, who had lived in Port Moresby and had promoted artists there during the 1970s and 1980s, continued with further exhibitions. From 1990 to 1995 the Beiers exhibited the work of Mathias Kauage, Barnabas India, William Onglo, and Akis at the Iwalewa House Bayreuth, an institution that specializes in presenting art from non-Western cultures, especially Africa. Eva Raabe (1998, 1999, and this volume) as curator of Gallery 37 at the Museum of World Cultures in Frankfurt held exhibitions in 1997, 1998 and 2000. Another important promoter of Papua New Guinea art in Germany continues to be the Lutheran Church. During the past twenty years, the Church has exhibited paintings from Kauage and Joe Nalo. In 2002 the Church invited sculptor Gickmai Kundun as well as Kauage to work and present their art in Neuendettelsau, a small town in Southern Germany.

These exhibitions neither presented nor even mentioned the art of female artists from Papua New Guinea. Even though female creativity was recognized with painted tapa and bilums (traditional arts), this was not acknowledged in Germany until recently when Eva Raabe included art from women artists in her Frankfurt exhibitions.

Of the over twenty exhibitions I have curated in the Northern part of Germany only two of them were solely with female contemporary artists. Each exhibition was accompanied by a small catalogue and lectures helped to contextualize the work. As I am not a gallery owner substantial volunteer input from friends is necessary to make these exhibitions possible. Friends' help to store the artwork when not being exhibited, to frame the paintings, write labels, to keep the records about each piece, and to do the accounting. They also help transport and install the artwork. All work connected to these exhibitions is done voluntarily and in places that usually serve another purpose.

At all of these exhibitions, visitors could buy the artwork. Artists want to sell their art because "making art" is also "the art of making money" (Matbob in Rosi 1998). They also aim to make their living from selling their art. However, Western buyers need to be educated about the meaning of the art and the constructs of its imagined identity (just as they need this for appreciating contemporary western art). Given the context they become attracted to the art and interested in it beyond its exotic character (see Raabe this volume). Most sales come directly after an introduction to contemporary Papua New Guinea art, and the art scene in Port Moresby is given. The criteria for setting prices generally follows the prices that the artist asked for at the National Museum and Art Gallery, which depended on the size of the canvas and it's quality. Pricing the artwork is as difficult in Germany as it was in Papua New Guinea, and anything higher than 500 Euro is hard to sell. We attached prices to each of the paintings and drawings. All income from sales was sent directly to the artists in Papua New Guinea.

Obstacles to the Recognition of Contemporary Papua New Guinea Art in Germany

Most of the contemporary Papua New Guinea artwork shown in Germany today, and probably all over Europe, still refers to 'traditional' art and 'traditional' life. The artists see themselves as "keepers of traditional culture and environment" by depicting ornaments, body decorations, house styles, and birds. In addition, traditional customs and mythological topics are also depicted. They are inspired by and use styles, ornaments, and mythology from cultures all over PNG, sometimes all in the one painting. This both aids and hinders the acceptance of contemporary PNG art as it balances perception and acceptance.

Most contemporary artists now live in the larger towns and are no longer restricted to symbols and patterns derived exclusively from their home villages. As such, their work crosses borders (tribal boundaries). By constructing new symbols, they promote a new national identity. As contemporary writers in the Pacific see their work as (re) writing history, artists are seen as

Table 1. The Prevalence of Certain Motifs in a Sample of Papua New Guinea Paintings

Motif	No.
Motifs involving people dressed traditionally with traditional face paintings of village life	73
Paintings with ornaments and traditional wealth	32
Paintings showing local Papua New Guinea animals	16
Motifs about personal issues, depicting topics that matter to the artist	18
Paintings taking their motif from myths and legends	7
Other motifs	22

"(re) painting history". Art, therefore, is just another mode of discourse (see Rosi this volume) — one subject to debate.

Honoring the past and traditional culture is a key trait of contemporary arts as most artists draw their inspiration from the traditional concerns of village life. Out of 168 artworks chosen at random from more than 300 in the collection in Hamburg, the following motifs were most important (Table 1).

Yet, a handful of artists choose to address important contemporary issues, such as the conflicts and changes in daily life. Motifs and messages may be similar yet the styles used to depict them may differ profoundly. Some artists have used the same personal style for many years, while others often try new and different ways of painting or delight in choosing innovative subjects. It seems that certain styles go in and out of fashion. Artists take up a new style because it sells. When Kauage, for example, created his painting technique, many others imitated his style, and many still use this way of painting. Recently a more realistic style and the first landscape paintings have appeared. Larry Santana (see Rosi this volume) and Laben Sakale John are two of the artists who are painting in this new realistic style. Switching between different styles is also an indicator that the artists are still experimenting and trying to find their own and special way of painting their country. [17] In contrast, women artists do not follow fashion. They assert their personal style, yet also tend to experiment more with materials.

Contemporary art provides a view of both the past and present of Papua New Guinea even when foreign materials are used. Artists have taken up the Western way of expressing themselves through painting. Unfamiliar with Western artistic canons they have not followed them. They choose the style they prefer. A problem remains, however, in that the West, with its desire for the 'exotic' (which the traditional motifs reinforce) does not see this contemporary expression as authentic. However, contemporary artists do not want to be dictated to by the West. A balance between contemporary and traditional is necessary, as is a 'dealer' who provides didactic information to potential buyers.

Some Aspects of Perception of Papua New Guinea Art

Distant people and places have fed the European imagination for centuries. Yet, they have never been viewed in their own terms. Their works of art were never recognized as such, nor were they accepted as being valuable enough to be considered as art at all. The "other" became the backdrop of European longings. The yearning to return to one's "roots" manifested itself in the myth of all that was wild, exotic, and primitive, acting as a counterweight to bourgeois society. "Primitive art" was (and is) only acknowledged when it feeds these expectations. This was indeed true for the early workshop style of PNG art because it was tropical, colorful, fresh, fun, exotic, and 'childlike'. Most visitors to the exhibitions in Germany appreciated this genre.

However, contemporary art remained secondary to traditional Papua New Guinea art. One person commented, "For me, art from Papua New Guinea is traditional art. Contemporary art has no meaning; it is not earthy [from their original state]." [18] Nevertheless, many visitors liked this art because it radiates something positive and it mediates the exotic images and visions that are often related to a "Pacific Paradise." Thus, contemporary PNG art fits well into the expectations of the public about the Pacific Islands, but not as fine art.

As Papua New Guinea paintings became more realistic, gallery owners rejected them as did Western art historians, who consider contemporary works as being far too similar to European art in technique and style to be truly Papua New Guinean. They have judged these paintings as copying Western style, as outdated and old-fashioned. Such paintings do not fit into the aesthetic mould of European modernism. Art historians do not give it a second glance. Even if a motif is foreign and unknown, the style of presentation is much too familiar to be exotic. If a painting is neither "exotic" nor in fashion, then there is no place for it in Western galleries. If the art world's greed for the "new" is not satisfied, then foreign artwork has no chance to gain access. When I displayed such different, innovative works as Alexander Mebri's *Heritage*, Laben Sakale John's *Wealth*, and Julie Mota's *Disco Lights*, one art historian commented, "That's nothing new," meaning, it is not worth showing.

Apparently, drawings incorporating traditional ornaments or motifs more closely fit European images and expectations of the mysterious "other." Gallery visitors are fascinated by their secret/hidden images and fictitious meanings. They see the mystery rather than its disclosure as the art in an artwork. Here the unknown creates a special charm, and the symbols touch everyone even if they do not understand its indigenous meaning.

Some of the exhibitions I have organized in Germany did emphasize the work of women artists. Their artwork has been well appreciated, and it sold well because customers liked the idea of supporting PNG women. Guests and buyers liked Weoa's and Wena's works because of the "exotic" motifs and their unusual style, and as such they sold very well. Bruder's and Mota's paintings, however, have not been commercially successful because they look too much like contemporary Western art. Sometimes they provoke outright rejection. European customers want art from Oceania to be immediately different; its "otherness" should not have to prove itself. Thus, contemporary artwork from PNG is best received when it depicts the exotic and it fulfills these European expectations by relating directly to Western images and myths of the South Seas.

People react to contemporary PNG art in two ways. The first is an attitude of superiority that places non-Western artworks as inferior. The second attitude is sympathetic towards non-Western art, and as such is positively viewed and not open to criticism as a Western work would be. Both are patronizing attitudes. For many, the idea of Papua New Guinea art immediately conjures up images of ancient masks and sculptures. They associate Papua New Guinea with museums and artifact shops, which focus on selling the idea of the primitive. Let me share just a few of many remarks I heard while walking through exhibitions [19]:

Wife to husband: "Let's go, this has nothing to do with us!"
Man to companion: "It's only Third World art, not real art!"
Head of a Gallery: "The artists are like obedient pupils, they follow Western materials and styles. It's not authentic."
Art historian: "It resembles too much of our art. We know it already."

Art galleries and art dealers jump to conclusions by following market criteria, and by understanding the prejudices of their clientele. They are mainly concerned about the monetary value of art. Unfortunately, there are no widely shared parameters for evaluating Papua New Guinea art. As one owner of a gallery puts it, "Sorry, I am unable to tell my customers how much a piece of art from this area will increase in value over time. And that is what customers want to know." [20]

Attitudes are slowly changing, yet art from Oceania figures rather low on the European agenda. Contemporary Pacific art from New Zealand is attracting critical attention with important exhibitions recently shown in New York and Berlin. [21] In some cases, contemporary Papua New Guinea art has been displayed in ethnographical museums, for instance in the Museum der Weltkulturen und Galerie 37 in Frankfurt or within a church context. [22] If it is dealt with in art magazines, it is because of its exotic place of origin, and not for the sake of the art itself.

The works of artists from Papua New Guinea are seldom shown in the context of international art. [23] They rarely have the opportunity to exhibit their works along side Western artists. As Eva Raabe has pointed out, anthropologists are much more closely associated with art from the Pacific region than are art historians. Anthropologists often have a different gateway into the topic, focusing on the ethnographic context. They do not tend to discuss the aesthetic aspects of contemporary art. This too is changing as Pacific art historians, such as, Karen Stevenson, Caroline Vercoe, Terri Sowell and others are focusing on the ethnographic context as well as discussing the aesthetics of contemporary Pacific art.

As in colonial times, primitive art is still only acknowledged as an inspiration for European artists rather than as something aesthetic in its own right. In Germany, contemporary Papua New Guinea art has no place in museums of art. Instead, it is only shown in anthropological and ethnographic museums. These venues exclude it from intercultural communication within the global art world today. This reflects Western attitudes more than the qualities or the importance of emergent PNG art. The globalization of the art world has not led to a critical look at, or dialogue with, contemporary art from PNG although a small number of Papua New Guinea artists have achieved regional recognition within the Pacific. What is clear is that traditional Western categories are incapable of explaining current Oceanic art when it is still considered bastard art, ethno art, tribal art, exotic art, hybrid art, airport art or even as kitsch. Ironically, the break with established traditions by PNG artists and their search for a new emergent identity is often seen as simply a product of Western development and not as a dynamic movement of a rapidly modernizing nation.

Artistic innovation is thus seen as the exclusive preserve of Western artists. What appears to be of positive value for a Western artist — such as vision, a search for identity, tackling the problems of the past and the present, being innovate, creative, different from the rest of the society they come from — seems to have a negative connotation when attached to non-Western artists; at least in traditional art circles. The word avant-garde is still reserved entirely for Western artists. Contrary to all the talk about the globalization of art, double standards still apply. Unless artists are granted value and acceptance in their own countries, then their existence at home has little or no meaning. Such work is then often reduced to status of a curiosity, considered exotic just as it is in the Western world.

Conclusion

Western audiences have a limited understanding of non-Western art because they only view it through a Western lens. At recent Papua New Guinea art exhibitions in Germany, nearly all my interviews with viewers, buyers, and owners of art galleries demonstrate that for Western audiences, and even for most art professionals, contemporary PNG art is seen merely as exotic, colorful, or amusing. In other cases, when it is seen as neither traditional nor primitive art, it is regarded as having no value and therefore as inauthentic. In other words, if the predominant feature of a contemporary artwork is its exotic otherness, then it is accorded some appreciation. However, if viewers can see no appreciable difference between what PNG and Western artists create then, ipso facto, Papua New Guinea art has no value.

Furthermore, it does not seem to matter what media are utilized. PNG artists engage with issues of contemporary life, thereby coming to terms with its realities. Artists are part of the changing fabric of Papua New Guinea national culture, but they do not have a voice in the current discourse about PNG national life. This is because new art forms are perceived as lacking the power and agency of the traditional arts. As a result, they sell very few artworks to their fellow countrymen. Occasionally, the government and local businesses buy work, but most sales are made to western expatriates. However, it is not just a lack of interest and understanding that deters Papua New Guineans from buying contemporary art. Artists compound the problem with their high market prices.

Lacking popular appeal or the support of a professional art association, contemporary artists seldom make it into the public limelight. This is demonstrated by the break up of the group of women artists I had worked with in Port Moresby. Once I left, the women no longer worked together or supported one another. Instead, they work separately, giving up the empowerment that the group was providing them. By doing this, they have also given up the opportunity to build a lobby group that can seek support from the government. They have withdrawn and simply present and sell their artwork at the monthly craft market.

Papua New Guinea contemporary artists strive not only for recognition in their country but they want to be acknowledged in the international art scene. They want to be part of that scene. However, the international art scene and the global art markets function as a rigid system of inclusion and exclusion. The global art markets restrict entrance to a lucky few. PNG artists are cut off from the discursive process of the global art scene, unless promoted by Westerners.

Papua New Guinea's contemporary art is committed art and aims to advance emancipatory processes of constructing national identity. The women artists I have worked with exemplify this. Their work focuses on the central issues of human interaction and should therefore flourish within the international context. Contemporary PNG art is not an object, or a thing, but rather it is a medium, a means of transferring thoughts and feelings to canvass or paper. It demonstrates the contradictions between the past and the present, highlighting PNG's struggle as a developing nation. We need to respect and to acknowledge these thoughts, feelings, and processes. The global art world must put aside its prejudices and embrace these new artistic voices.

Individualism and Tradition, Curating Contemporary Art from Papua New Guinea

Eva Ch. Raabe

'The language of art is universal. Good quality art does not need to be explained.'

These are lines you will very often hear from an art audience in Europe. In my experience as a museum curator, this opinion is often expressed by those gallery visitors who do not seriously reflect on the meaning of an artwork. Educated visitors to galleries and museums were taught about European art history, style development and the life of famous European painters at primary school, high school and college. They utilise this familiar scholarly knowledge when viewing art regardless of the artist's ethnic or national origin. Seldom do they reflect on the fact that their own interpretation is influenced by their European origin, which may be contrary to the intended message of the artist. This essay suggests that a new approach is necessary for European viewers to understand artworks from different cultural backgrounds. I will demonstrate that it is necessary to learn about the artist's own cultural background to acknowledge his/her individual creativity. Without any knowledge about the artists' cultures one will not understand how their ideas are transferred into form and colour and will not be able to appreciate their artworks for their aesthetic qualities.

Offering knowledge to the museum visitor is a curatorial task. To do this, however, a curator must mediate between the museum (the director, sponsors, and staff), the artist and the viewer. This essay will focus its attention upon four artists from Papua New Guinea. It will illustrate the complexities of introducing new art forms and styles to the European public and demonstrate how curatorial input provides a better and fuller understanding of these art forms.

In Europe, studies in Pacific art have traditionally been the domain of anthropologists, while the discipline of art history exclusively dealt with European and western art developments. This has impacted strongly on curatorial practice. For a long time Oceanic art was placed in a traditional context and labelled 'primitive art'. Because 'primitive' creativity was believed to be ruled by firmly established artistic and religious rules it was never connected with the Western idea of the development of art leading to contemporary forms. In the experiences of western museum visitors' Pacific art exhibited at ethnographic museums included masks, ceremonial shields, and ancestor figures. These were exhibited with text and were explained as ethnographic documents of Pacific cultures and religions while European art was exhibited solely on aesthetic qualities. According to an European art tradition, which claimed that art could speak for itself, museums of fine art displayed works of art without any explanatory text or other sources of information. When non-western art objects were discovered by modern European artists during the height of cubism, expressionism and surrealism (as sources of aesthetic inspiration), the European public learned to appreciate masks, shields and ancestor figures as primitive artistic expression.

Today, traditional material culture from the Pacific may be presented in an ethnographic museum or in a gallery of fine arts. The western beholder will see a mask or sculpture as an example of superior 'primitive' craftsmanship and as art, which is authentic because it is rooted in cultural traditions. But the character of a contemporary painting is not what western audiences are used to from visiting museums of anthropology. Contemporary painting is produced by an artist who does not work in a traditional village but in town, who was educated at school and university and who employs western styles and techniques (e.g. oil/acrylic on canvas, watercolour or drawing) for his artwork. Very often a contemporary artwork is denied its 'Pacificness' by the European audience because it seems not foreign enough (see Struck-Garbe and Geismar, this volume). Pacific arts have changed, but not the habits of the European beholder. The European viewer recognises the painting with oil, acrylic or water colour on canvas or paper as familiar western techniques and classifies the artwork automatically as an offshoot of western art. Without any understanding of the themes and motives depicted by the artist his/her work is therefore not accepted as authentic Pacific art in spite of all its relations to the artist's Pacific culture background (Raabe 1995:96- 104, 1997a: 7 ff., 1999:21). Many European viewers, not realizing how vague the concept behind the term 'authenticity' really is, use this term without second thought.

When I began the contemporary collection for the Oceanic department of the Museum of World Cultures at Frankfurt, [1] I was met with a dilemma: What kind of public reaction will be provoked by explaining the meaning of artworks to an audience that believes in

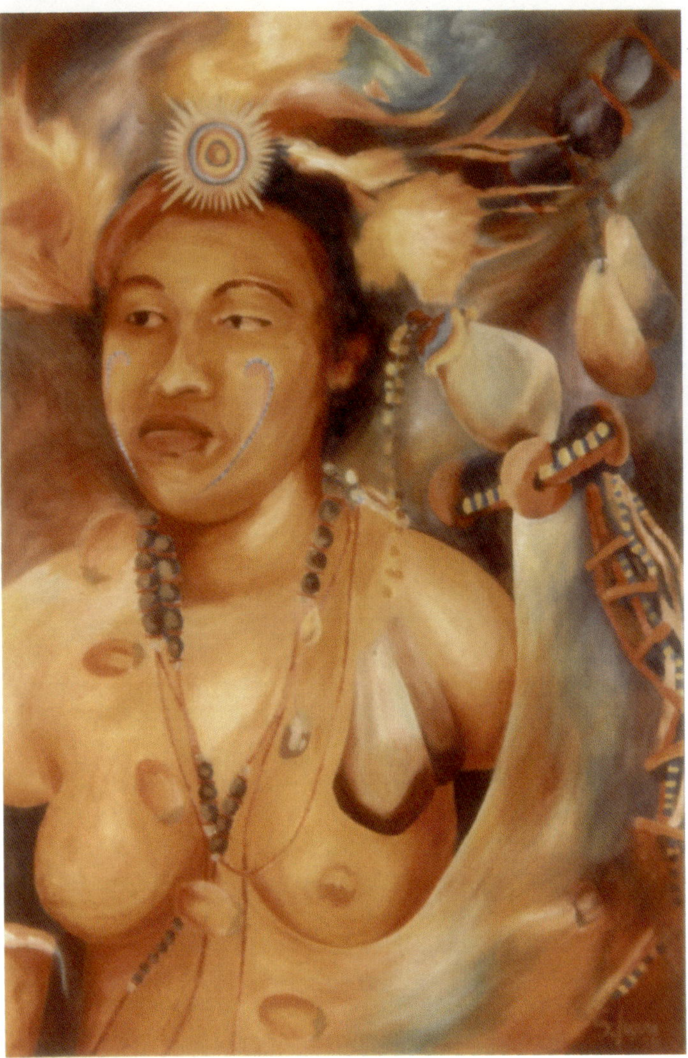

Figure 10.1. Samuel Luguna, *Meri Trobes*, 1998, acrylic on canvas, 117 x 161 cm. Photograph by Stephan Beckers, Museum der Weltkulturen, 2000.

the universality of art and uses this as criteria for the judgement of artistic quality. I (Raabe 1999:21) have summarized this problem elsewhere:

> Contemporary paintings without obvious traits of Pacific traditions are not accepted by the public as authentic Pacific art works — but as soon as they incorporate an ethnographic element they are not regarded as being contemporary or modern. In the first case the art work is not seen as genuine and therefore as not good enough to be included in any art show, in the second case the work is classified as ethnographic or folk art and is therefore excluded from modern art exhibitions.

For this reason many non-western artists resist showing their work in ethnographic museums. Curators must negotiate between artists who demand to be treated as members of a global art world on equal terms with their European contemporaries and a public who need to be educated. Situated in between the European point of view and the demands of non-Western artists, curators must play a twofold role — that of translator and diplomat. They must reconcile the intellectual dissonance between the Pacific artists, who constantly develop new means of aesthetic expression, and the stagnant habits of the European art audience. Marion Struck-Garbe (this volume) reinforces this dichotomy when she states that "PNG art is something that can stand on its own" and does not simply reflect "only a part of cultural development".

To assert that contemporary Pacific art is 'contemporary art' and not ethnographic, Struck-Garbe believes that PNG art must get out of ethnographic museums. However, museums of ethnography need to find other solutions to the problem if they do not want to leave the display of contemporary New Guinean art, exclusively, to commercial galleries. As a consequence the Museum of World Cultures changed its attitude towards contemporary art during the last twenty years. The somewhat naive approach of interpreting contemporary art as a document of cultural change has to make way for the detailed study and presentation of non-western art in all its aesthetic diversity.

In 1997 the Museum of World Cultures opened a special gallery where contemporary Art from Africa, South America, Asia and the Pacific is exhibited on a changing schedule. With this gallery the museum initiates dialogues between different art worlds and educates an European audience. Art that has not originated in Europe cannot be explained from within an European context. Using ethnographic models, as opposed to European art criticism and history, the context of non-European cultures and cultural histories, can be better understood (Raabe 1997a: 7-12). Different from commercial galleries, museums are non-commercial institutions with educational tasks. They provide basic knowledge and information and, in such a way, offer support to the developing market of contemporary Pacific art. Elaine Monds' comments (this volume) on her work at the Alcheringa Gallery demonstrate that a western audience provided with the necessary information learns to appreciate New Guinean art not as anonymous 'tribal art' but as works of art by named individual artists. One important way to increase such kind of appreciation is, of course, to initiate a direct dialogue between the artists and their audience. But the occasions on which European art viewers and Pacific artists can meet each other for art discussions are rare. Even if artists from the Pacific attend openings, are invited to hold symposiums or to take part in educational programs in Europe, they will depart again, often, leaving their art work behind as part of a long term display or as an object in a permanently hold collection. Curators then find themselves alone with the artwork and an audience without much knowledge about Pacific cultures. In such situation the curators at the art gallery of the Museum of World Cultures found it necessary to provide didactic information to pave the way for understanding the diversity of cultural identities in non-western art.

PNG painters, in particular, have developed contemporary genres, which differ from their European counterparts because they are based not on western but on Pacific aesthetic concepts. However, the reception by the western art audience shows that the European viewer judges Pacific art in comparison to images already known to them. The lack of cultural knowledge by the European art audience does not allow them to reflect on the artists' own culture. This becomes problematic as an artwork conveys only what the beholder is able to detect depending on his prior knowledge, his personal and social experiences, and his personal and social prejudices. For the contemporary public a medieval altarpiece stems from another completely unknown culture. Looking at van Gogh's sunflowers, cornfields or skies no viewer today is able to comprehend the revolutionary effect these had on the painter's contemporaries. Yet, every European viewer understands that the altarpiece depicts different scenes of Jesus Christ's life and death, and that van Gogh struggled for a new artistic way to paint his impressions of landscape. However, when it comes to Pacific art, there is no school subject the viewer can recall and no piece of general education that will enable him to identify the meaning of a painting.

In 1997 I coordinated the opening exhibition of the gallery, which included Papua New Guinean paintings. A year later I curated a show that presented exclusively contemporary art works from Papua New Guinea (Raabe 1997a, 1998). During these projects it was necessary to provide detailed analysis of every artwork to convincingly convey their aesthetic qualities to an European audience. From the Papua New Guinean artwork I collected and documented for the museum in 1991 and 1999 I would like to choose examples to demonstrate the cultural determination of the application and reception of artistic images. The analysis shows how one piece of art may combine a whole world of complex cultural ideas, images and visions. It demonstrates that one must understand the Pacific cultural background to be able to judge how skilfully the artist converted his message into form and colour.

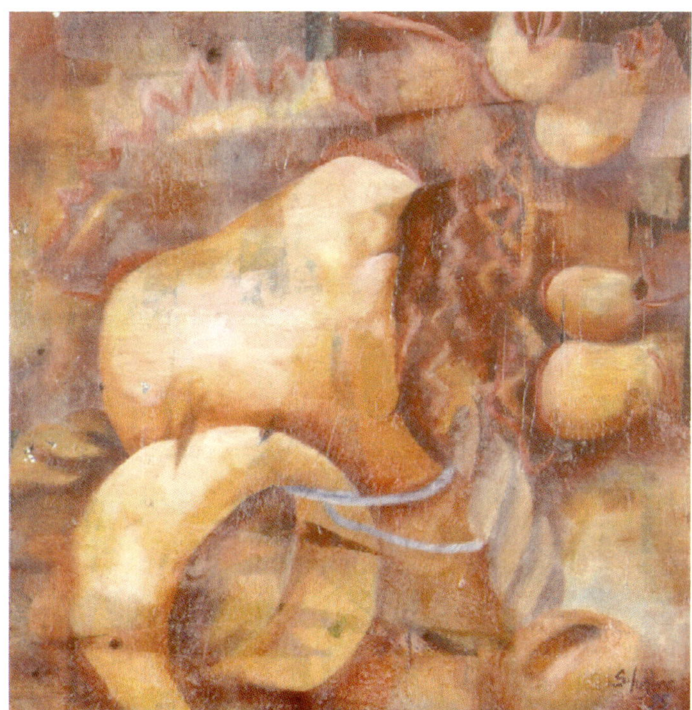

Figure 10.2. Samuel Luguna, *Mwali Abstraction*, 1998, acrylic and mixed media on canvas, 120 x 120 cm. Photograph by Stephan Beckers, Museum der Weltkulturen, 2000.

The Cultural Meaning of Colour

The young artist Samuel Luguna was born on Kiriwina. After finishing high school he stayed at home for a year to learn traditional carving and gardening. He, then, joined the National Arts School to study visual arts and finished with an university diploma in painting and printmaking. Today he works as a teacher of visual arts. Samuel Luguna's work deals with the cultural traditions of his Trobriand Island home Kiriwina. The main subject of his paintings is the Trobriand kula trade and the objects that circulate from island to island — mwali arm rings and soulava necklaces. [2] The artist's style has developed from detailed realistic depictions of kula items in early woodcuts into abstract images in later acrylic paintings.

Meri Trobes, 1998 [fig. 10.1] shows a young girl from the Trobriand Islands wearing a kula soulava necklace. The pearl shell is depicted as the prominent image in the foreground. It is still not an abstract painting but the usage of dominant red and orange shades leads to the colour symbolism found in Luguna's abstract images. Mwali Abstraction (1998) [fig. 10.2], on the other hand shows an arming. The canvas surface is build up from tissue, silica flour and marble dust mixed with glue, then painted over with acrylic colours. In his artwork Luguna depicts kula ornaments again and again. But these depictions are far more than the mere repetition of the same motive. The title Mwali Abstraction

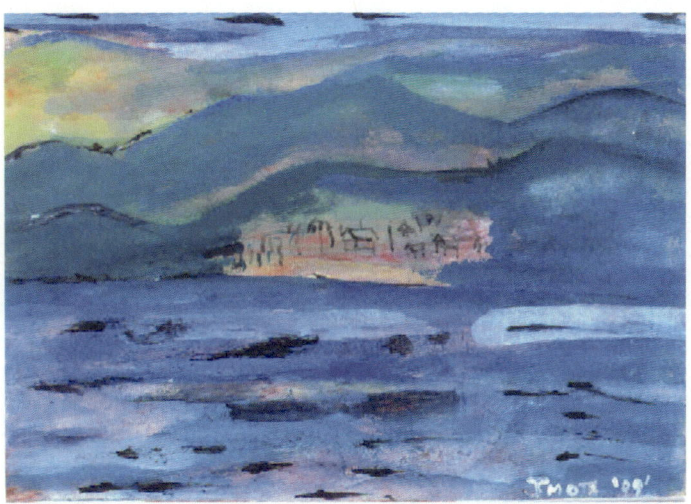

Figure 10.3. Julie Mota, Kiki — *How the first village came up*, 1999, watercolour on carton, 11 x 15.2 cm. Photograph by Stephan Beckers, Museum der Weltkulturen, 2000.

indicates that the artist did not simply intend to execute a still life showing a mwali but rather wanted to visualise an abstract cultural concept.

As in the painting *Meri Trobes* the dominant colours are warm shades of red and orange. However, the kula arm rings consist of whitish shells and are not at all of bright red material. Nevertheless, bright orange-red is an important colour in traditional Trobriand colour concepts. It is used for painting the front of yam houses and the splashboards of kula boats. Young unmarried girls wear short red skirts made from banana fibres. A widow who is allowed to leave her enclosure after a period of mourning and is now allowed to marry again will be given the red skirt of the unmarried. Skirts dyed with red colours are also important exchange items for the women. In short, red was and still is an important symbolic colour in ceremonial life.

The artist explained to me that he combined European colour theory and traditional colour concepts in his painting. [3] European theory categorises red as a warm colour, in Trobriand colour concepts the red used ritually is endowed with power and therefore has 'hot' qualities. In the painting different shades of red with their shining, somewhat heat radiating quality expresses the powers of kula. During the interview it became quite clear how fascinated the artist was with the kula. To him — and to many other Trobriand Islanders — the kula ornaments stand as symbols of cultural identity. Kula is inspired by a certain power — a driving force in the whole of Trobriand culture.

The alteration of the mwali's original white into bright red tones is not simply an artistic effect of alienation. With the mwali shape the artist employs a local image. The combination of local shapes and warm shades of red and orange presents a broader message to the viewer: an expression of cultural power and the visualisation of an abstract cultural force. Many European viewers reacted emotionally to the red shades. They felt the power of the radiating colours. But they had never seen kula ornaments and were not able to identify the depicted object. They could not associate the red colours with the kula ritual and were not able to see the abstracted kula items as expressions of cultural identity. Although the symbolic use of colours is, in general, a worldwide concept you have to know the cultural determined meaning of colours to understand their particular symbolism. European viewers might like the painting for its expressive red shades but without any knowledge of Trobriand culture will not fully understand what the painting stands for and will not be able to appreciate the skilful interaction of images and colours.

Landscape and Layers of Meaning

In European art history it is an accepted fact that in many genres the depiction of natural sceneries or landscapes served a symbolic purpose. In spite of this knowledge, many Europeans do not reflect that this might be the same with non-western art. Very often they take landscape paintings from Papua New Guinea as naïve attempts to depict a realistic scene. Using the watercolours of the young artist Julie Mota I will demonstrate that, far from being naïve, New Guinean landscape paintings embed different layers of meaning.

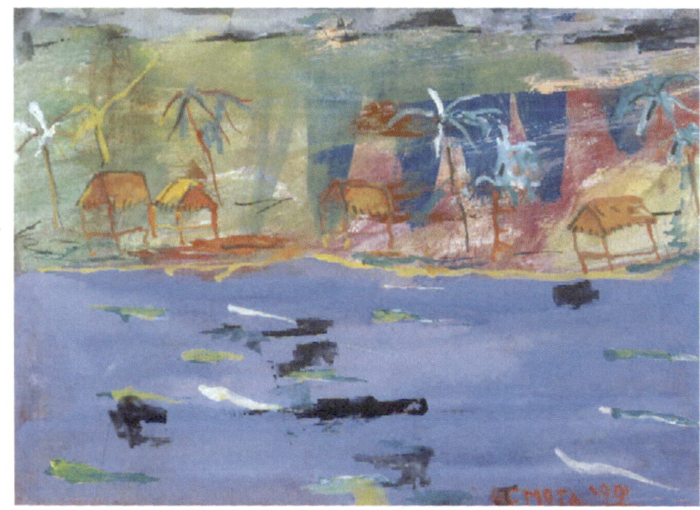

Figure 10.4. Julie Mota, *Papua Peles*, 1999, watercolour on carton, 10.7 x 15.4 cm. Photograph by Stephan Beckers, Museum der Weltkulturen, 2000.

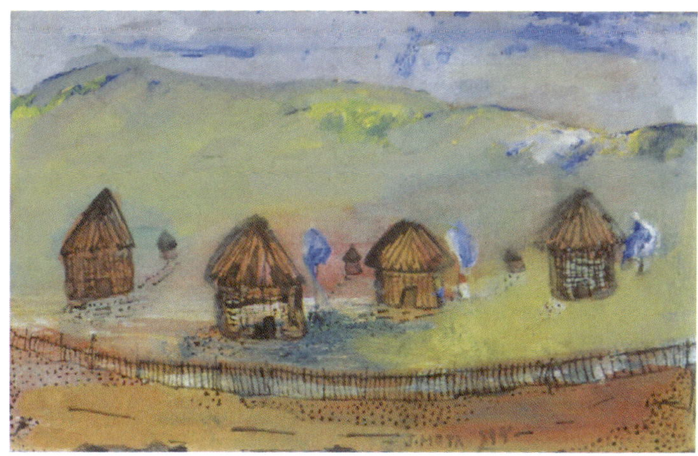

Figure 10.5. Julie Mota *Highland Peles*, 1999, watercolour on carton, 10 x 15.4 cm. Photograph by Stephan Beckers, Museum der Weltkulturen, 2000.

Mota was born in Lae. Her family of Tufi/Oro origin moved later to the capital where Julie attended Port Moresby National High School. When Julie entered the Faculty of Creative Arts at the National University she was interested in theatre design. Unfortunately no lecturer was available and the course had to be cancelled. Julie enrolled in visual arts and finished with a diploma in drama and play writing. After that she pursued business studies and worked for a bank. She sees herself more as a self-taught artist because she never underwent formal training in the techniques of drawing and painting. [4] Mota belongs to a group of female artists who struggle for acceptance in a male dominated art scene in the country's capital Port Moresby. These women are all of different ethnic origins but live in the city under similar circumstances. Every day they experience cultural diversity and ethnic conflicts. As migrants from across Papua New Guinea settle in Port Moresby people from various regions of the country live side by side, and frequently act out their differences with interethnic fighting. Increasing social and cultural conflicts cause people to consider the diversity of cultures and to compare customs. This leads, especially amongst young people towards reflection of one's own way of life. Girls and young women going through the educational system of Port Moresby experience the differences between patrilineal male dominated Highland societies and matrilineal organised groups of the coast and the islands. It is not surprising, then, that these differences have become one of the prominent subjects in the work of female artists (Struck-Garbe 1998).

In 1999 I purchased, for the Museum of World Cultures, a series of twenty postcard sized watercolour paintings by Julie Mota. The subjects of these miniature paintings include traditions, cultures and landscapes not only from Mota's own ethnic background but from all over Papua New Guinea. At first sight I was attracted by the paintings because they seemed to depict very charming little scenes. On second sight I realized that many of the miniatures were related to each other by a similar subtext. Throughout the varied themes the contrast between high and low country was as striking as their depiction in both a realistic and symbolic manner. To demonstrate that these miniatures are not only depictions of scenic landscapes but also a reflection of a young woman's experiences of cultural and social differences I choose five of Mota's watercolours for discussion and arranged them in a sequence like successive parts of one narrative.

Kiki — How the first village came up, 1999 [fig. 10.3] was inspired by a genesis story sung to Mota by her

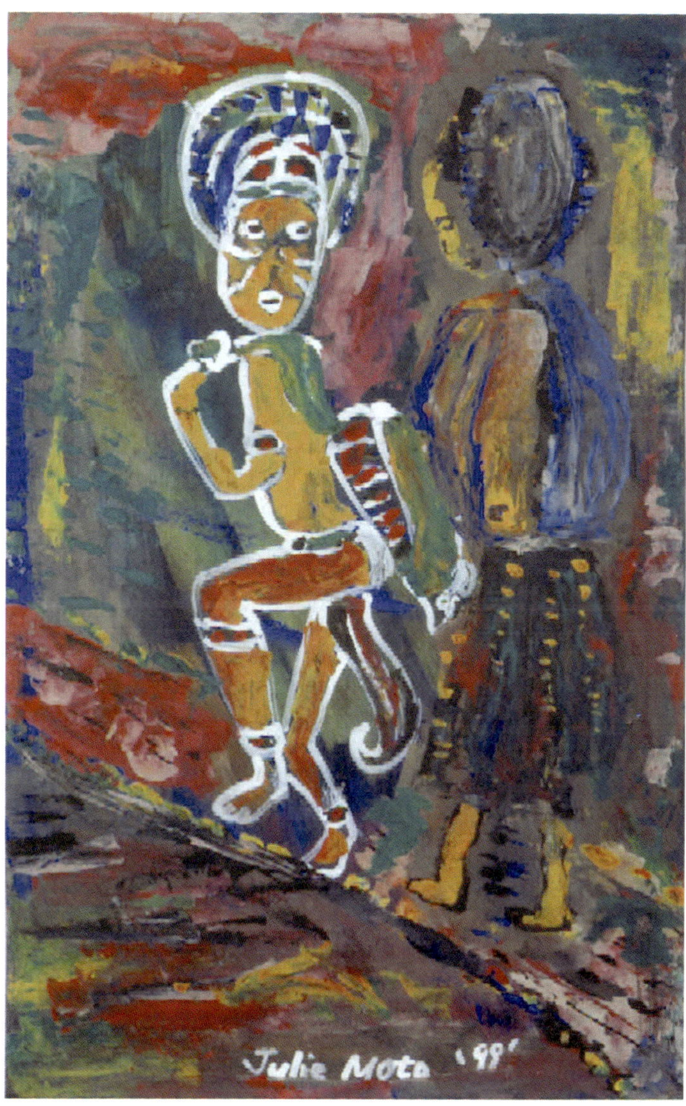

Figure 10.6. Julie Mota, *Walkabout*, 1999, watercolour on carton, 16.4 x 10.5 cm. Photograph by Stephan Beckers, Museum der Weltkulturen, 2000.

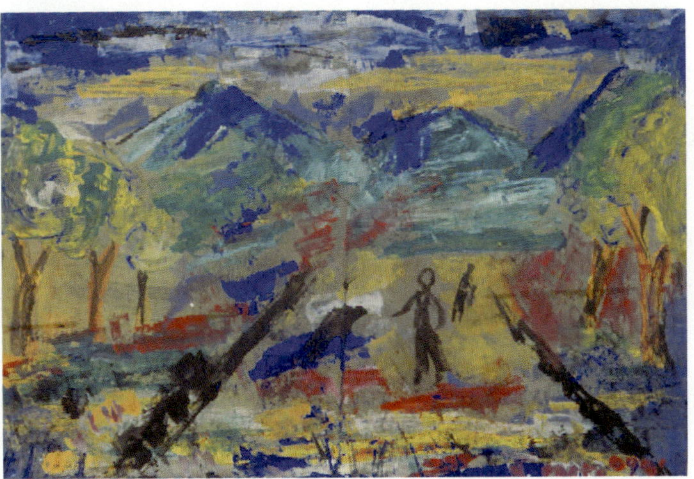

Figure 10.7. Julie Mota, *Crossroads*, 1999, watercolour on carton, 10.4 x 15.4 cm. Photograph by Stephan Beckers, Museum der Weltkulturen, 2000.

grandparents. Her grandmother used the local language mixed with Pidgin and English words. Because Mota was not completely familiar with the local language she was not able to understand every detail, but did get the gist of these stories: The moon goddess banishes one of her sisters, the rain woman, from the sky. The rain woman then descents to the sea where she meets the sea god. She gives birth to a fish — the only being in the sea. Out of his loneliness this fish being comes up to the land where he creates a village and marries. The miniature watercolour depicts the sea and a mountainous coast. Blues and greens of water and mountains merge. Only the lighter coloured village in the middle of the coastal line is easily identified. It seems as if Mota tried to catch the moment after a storm on the sea when the sky starts to clear and one can glimpse the first moments of clear sight across the coastal landscape. The first village emerges from water, storm and mist in front of our eyes.

Mota explained that the paintings titled *Papua Peles*, 1999 and *Highland Peles*, 1999 [figs. 10.4 and 10.5] were a pair of opposite scenes. [5] One is the depiction of a Papuan village with houses build on stilts along the shoreline. Palm trees and houses are arranged loosely along the shore. The coastal landscape is painted in bright green and yellow with a bit of blue and red while the calm sea of light blue develops a light swell of green, white and black. It is a light and colourful landscape — the atmosphere seems delightful and merry. Its counterpart depicts a place in the central highlands. Here the round and conical roofed houses of a highland village are lined up in a much stricter order. The whole village is fenced. In the foreground the village is separated from the street by a garden fence made from wooden poles typical for the Highland areas. In the background high mountains block the site.

Another painting in the series of miniatures titled *Walkabout*, 1999 [fig. 10.6] is executed in much stronger and darker colours. It shows a man from the Highlands, identified by his head dress and long apron, and a Papuan woman wearing a net bag (bilum) and a grass skirt with long dyed fibres (as is usually worn by women from the coast). They seem to ascend a steep trail — the man in front turning around to look straight at the woman, while the woman behind him lowers her eyes to the ground. The artist's explanation is that this painting expresses gender inequality in Papua New Guinea. [6] The oppression of women is often connected to gender relationship developed in highland cultures while the position of women in coastal societies is regarded as freer and more independent. Here the repressive attitude of Papua New Guinean men towards women is expressed in the positioning of the figures In this painting the landscape forms a remote background, while the contradictions Highland/Papua, male/female are symbolically expressed by typical dress elements.

The painting *Crossroads*, 1999 [fig. 10.7] is executed in similar strong colours to Walkabout and is dominated by complementary colours (blue/yellow and red/green). A road lined with trees like an alley leads towards the mountains. Two shadow-like figures walk along but seem to be lost on the broad road. One turning to the right, one to the left they seem to have difficulties with orientation. The artist symbolically expresses the difficult choice of lifestyle on the way towards modernity in Papua New Guinea. [7]

The five paintings together are miniature illustrations of one narrative — the history and origin of gender inequality and difference in contemporary Papua New Guinea. At the same time they are autobiographical — the life history of a young Papuan woman torn between modern education and village tradition. A native homeland emerges from the mist over the sea. Leaving one's own village opens one's eyes to the different cultures in Papuan and Highland villages. People migrate to the modern suburbia of the capital — the melting pot of New Guinean cultures — where Highland and Papuan cultures mix. The dominant male still bound to local village traditions and the oppressed female searching for liberation in a contemporary nation must negotiate their lives. They face crucial decisions about how they can live side by side and what their future may be. Crossroads may be read as the last of the five paintings described here. It depicts a landscape of vague distinction, not clearly identifiable as mountain or plain: an adequate way of life for all citizens of Papua New Guinea is still to be found.

Within this series of watercolour miniatures Julie Mota uses the genre of landscape painting to reflect upon the issue of Papua New Guinean gender inequality. Mota develops a symbolism that consistently juxtaposed the New Guinean Highlands and Papuan lowlands. The differences between mountainous and coastal scenes stand for cultural differences in Highland and lowland societies. On another level the cultural determined differences of gender roles associated with Highland and coastal cultures are symbolic of gender inequality as a general social problem.

To someone who does not know the cultural differences between Highland and lowland societies 'Highland' and 'Papua' are simply terms for regions or landscapes. European viewers who are not familiar with Papua New Guinean cultures will not discover the symbolism expressed in these island and village scenes, nor will they understand the complex layers of meaning. Without background explanations European viewers will simply miss why the artist meant the two watercolours Papuan Peles and Highland Peles to form a pair of counterparts or why she chooses a title like Crossroads. They might regard Mota's watercolours as skilfully executed miniatures but would still see them as products of naïve art not recognizing how the artist developed her own sophisticated way to turn the depiction of landscape into social commentary.

Decorative Elements and their Symbolism

As European viewers will not accept New Guinean landscape painting as an art genre in its own right neither will they regard decorative ornaments incorporated in New Guinean art as meaningful elements. Today, in the European art scene, ornamental decoration is associated with products of arts and crafts but not with contemporary painting. Using two drawings by Jane Wena it will become clear that in New Guinean paintings decorative elements are much more than mere ornamentation.

Jane Wena was born in Kerowagi in Simbu Province. Like Julie Mota she also addresses the subject of gender roles by comparing Highland and coastal custom. Wena has developed a style that is characterised by filigree ornamental detail. She earned a certificate in visual arts and an university diploma in graphic design. Wena has worked as a graphic artist for the daily newspaper, *The National.* Executed in a naturalistic manner, the ornamental elements in her fine ink drawings resemble the patterns on incised bamboo containers or painted barkcloths, which are found in many Highland regions as well as the valleys of Ramu and Markham. Traditionally, ornaments on these objects are not only of a decorative character they are abstractions of flowers, leaves, animals or their tracks. Jane Wena has taken up this tradition of New Guinean decorative art and developed it into a contemporary genre that, as a trained graphic artist, she masters distinctively.

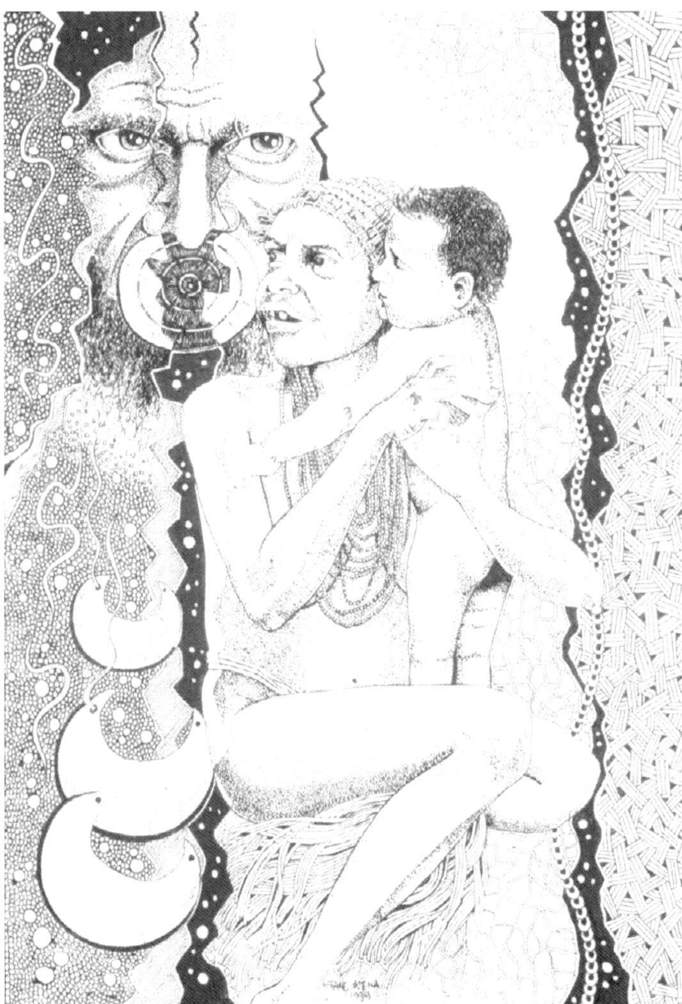

Figure 10.8. Jane Wena, *Women subservient of man particularly in Highland society,* 1999, ink on paper, 34 x 23.6 cm. Photograph by Stephan Beckers, Museum der Weltkulturen, 2000.

The museum collection contains a pair of Wena's ink drawings, which were created in 1999 for an exhibition on Papua New Guinea women's life. One drawing is titled *Women subservient of man particularly in Highland society,* 1999 [fig. 10.8], the other *Features of beauty,* wealth and love from the Trobriand Islands, 1999 [fig. 10.9]. Each drawing depicts a woman in her local traditional attire surrounded by typical shell valuables of the cultural area. Traditionally decorated male faces look out from the background of both.

Choosing the tradition of her Highland home area, Jane Wena expresses the repressive aspects of women's lives. The woman in the picture holds her child

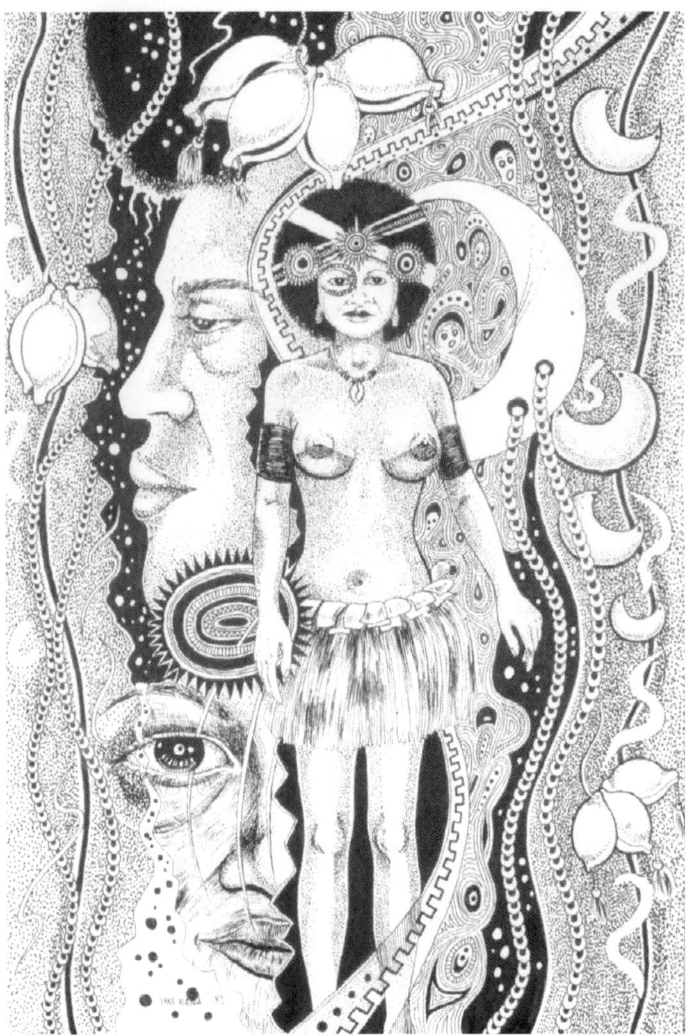

Figure 10.9. Jane Wena, *Features of beauty, wealth and love from the Trobriand Islands,* 1999, ink on paper, 34 x 23.6 cm. Photograph by Stephan Beckers, Museum der Weltkulturen, 2000.

on her lap while glancing with fearful expression at the grim looking male behind her. The background is covered by a network of patterns, partly like the structure of woven walls or fences, which are used in highland villages. In the foreground Wena depicted kina shells [8], which are typical bride price valuables in the Highlands. The young Trobriand woman is dressed for dancing. She wears the short skirt of the unmarried and is decorated with bracelets, necklace and hair ornaments. Around and behind her are strings of shells, big white egg cowries, and pearl shells that are both components of kula necklaces and kula armlets.

The two drawings are meant as an opposing pair showing differences in gender roles in highland and island societies. It seems that Wena tries to visualise the subordinate female position in the highland societies by the strictness of ornamental patterns. She depicts the woman, as mother, being 'fenced in', controlled by dominant males and reduced to her role as wife and mother. The kina shells in the foreground stand as both a general indicator of Highland society as well as important bride price valuables. As such they may indicate not only her position, but also her situation — married into her husband's family she always will be a stranger among related clan members. The scene from the Trobriand Islands seems much more relaxed. The young woman seems proud and independent and well aware of her attractiveness. During dance festivals young women may wear their maternal uncles' kula shells for display of wealth and status. The depicted kula valuables symbolize the women's freedom to express themselves. Unlike in the highland scene there is no strictness in the arrangement of ornaments. The shell valuables are in a constant flow up and down the drawing. [9]

In both drawings the background dissolves into ornamental elements, which are not just decorative patterns but motifs that establish a relationship to women and their social position. Unfamiliar with Papua New Guinean culture and society the European viewer will not be able to understand the symbolic meaning expressed in these works. He may be able to admire the technical qualities of the drawings but his lack of knowledge will not allow him to reflect upon the cultural connection of shell valuables, body ornaments and gender roles. He will not understand that Wena did not simply repeat traditional patterns but developed her own symbolism based upon the traditional meaning of shell ornaments not only as body decoration but also as markers of wealth, status and cultural identity. To appreciate Wena's individual interpretation of traditional ornaments the European viewer needs background information about the depicted cultures.

Whose Voice? The Curator as Translator

Contemporary painters in Papua New Guinea express their Pacific identity by means of an artistic medium that very often constitutes an intersection of the local and global art world. In their paintings many artists communicate local traditions. They incorporate mythical stories, objects of indigenous material culture, and ceremonies or body decoration in their artistic images. The message may be found in many different pictorial elements. It may lie in a stylistic device, in the depiction of a certain object, in the way an artist paints nature or landscape. Samuel Luguna established the link between local image and broader message using colour, Julie Mota embedded the subject of gender inequality in the depiction of cultural landscape, while Jane Wena addressed the same topic by using traditional objects. Their message may be hidden beneath the surface and as such it is necessary to reflect upon Papua New Guinea's cultural traditions to understand their meaning. Comparing these paintings to images known from European backgrounds is not helpful. In her essay, on the painter Larry Santana, Pamela Rosi (this volume) demonstrates how the artist's work and career is shaped by the political and social history of his home country. Therefore, his practice must be analysed in connection with the national culture of Papua New Guinea. What the mentioned artists have in common, is, that; they develop their art in a local context, they communicate aesthetic messages to an art market on national and international levels, and they work in highly individualised artistic styles (Thomas 1996:17). They are, as Miller (1995:15) categorises their position, local artists in world art.

Yet, curators are often reluctant to explain contemporary artwork in cultural terms because they assume that would deny the artist's individual creativity. It is true that within the disciplines of anthropology and art history scholars of Pacific art have moved beyond the debate on definition, function or classification (Welsch 2002:1), but the scholarly debate has neither reached art historians working outside Pacific studies nor has it developed beyond the pale of the academic world. Scholars of Pacific art came to use different approaches to art studies and no longer indulge themselves in whether ethnic art is undisturbed in its tradition, whether tourist art may be degenerated, or if contemporary art is authentic. Outside the grove of Academe, museum visitors continue to question the authenticity and the quality of contemporary Pacific art. When it comes to representation certain branches of contemporary Pacific art, like the paintings I analysed above, have not profited from academic criticism. Even though curators take part in scholarly discussions they are reluctant to transfer art analysis into the public debate on aesthetic quality. European curators of non-Western art are confronted with the question of how to explain art from another cultural background. Curators with an anthropological training are unwilling to employ their own discipline to interpret a piece of art because they fear the accusations of not communicating the artist's intention and of depriving the artists of their right to speak for themselves. Even more they fear that museum visitors and Pacific artists could regard their explanations as a disparagement of the artwork's quality because the widely held opinion that 'good art always speaks for itself' is still such a popular idea.

I would like to counter these fears with the following argument. Just as you have to explain foreign ideas and ways of life to achieve the respect for different cultures you have to explain an artist's cultural background to enable the European public to establish a respectful relationship with his/her artwork. A deeper understanding of an artwork's meaning can lead to the appreciation of its aesthetic qualities. To improve comprehension the curator must provide an analysis of the different elements in the picture. The curator does not simply translate the artist's verbal statements about the work but must translate, to a European audience, the artistic language embedded in the art. As I demonstrated above the curator negotiates between the artist, painting and viewer. To do this, I have drawn upon different sources of historical and anthropological art writing. To explain artistic creation and the messages underlying art works from different artistic periods, the art historian Michael Baxandall uses the term "intention" not for a construction of the declared aim of the artist but for a description of the relationship between an artwork and its "circumstances" (1985:41f.). Nicholas Thomas discusses the exchange between western and indigenous art in settler societies. In his book, *Possessions*, he shifts between a "discussion of particular works and their situation" (Thomas 1999:18), and describes his method as a "kind of intellectual exchange, between anthropology and art history (Thomas 1999:17). Another example of fusion of historical and anthropological art writing is Howard Morphy's work *Aboriginal Art* (1998) in which he combines the description of historical development, the discussion of the artists' cultural and social backgrounds and the analysis of aesthetic elements of particular art works. These three authors define artistic meaning as the interplay between the artist's intended message, the conditions of artistic production and the artwork's reception.

These examples of art interpretation may not only inspire academic writing about art but may also be a useful guideline for curatorial practice. The curator choosing an artwork for display must concern himself with the intended message of the artist and with the context in which it was created. At the same time he has to be aware that in presenting the work he initiates critical judgement by an European audience. In most European exhibitions the display of art means the separation of the artwork from its original place of creation and from its creator. Like Baxandall, the curator has to explain aesthetic concepts and their structural conditions in reference to "pictures rather more than to painters" (1985:42). In this situation the curator becomes a translator to bridge the gap between the artist's cultural experiences on which his/her art work is founded and the European understanding of art. That means that the Pacific artwork on display in Europe enters a history independent of its origin and

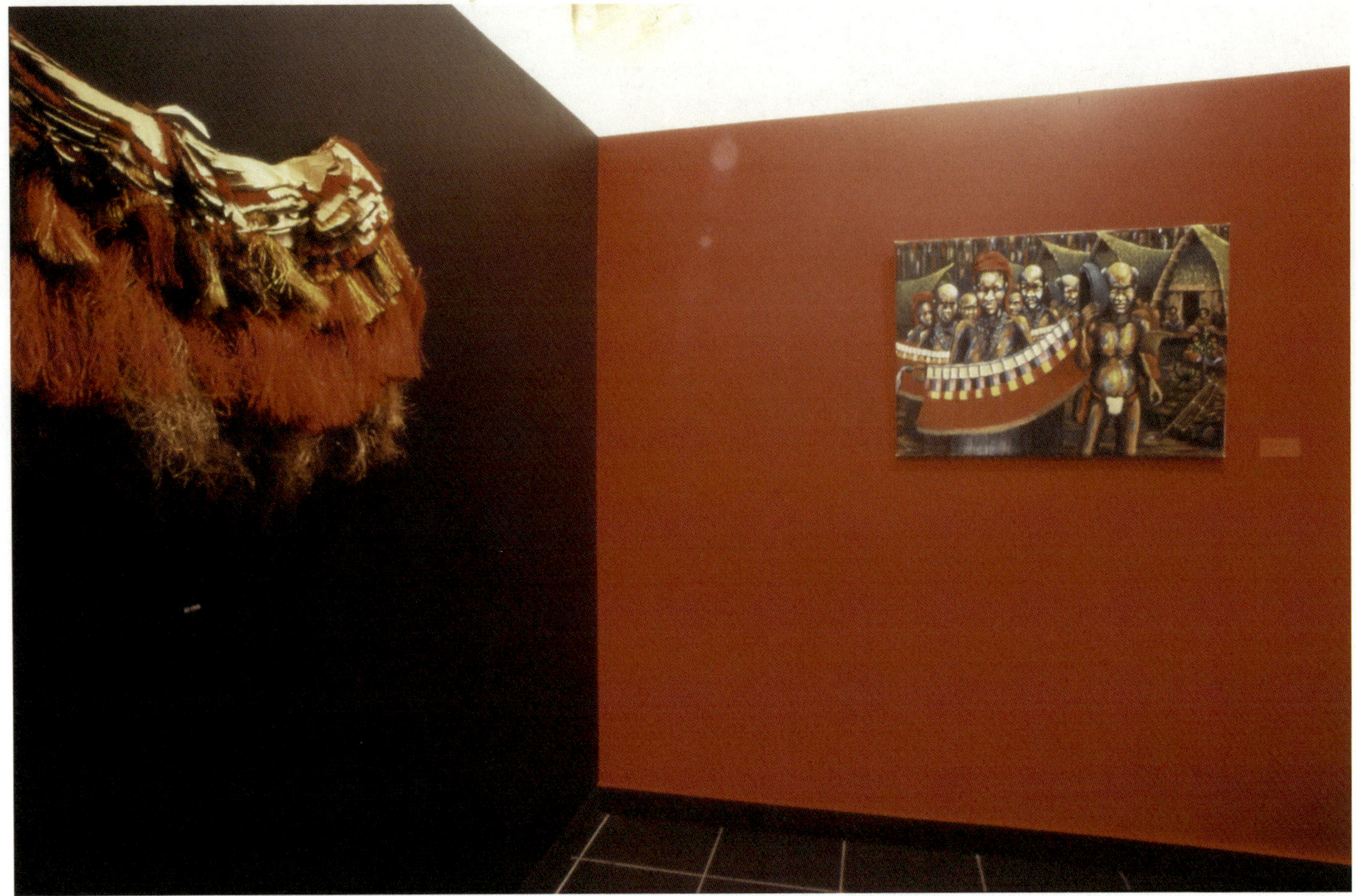

Figure 10.10. Martin Morububuna, *Sagali* 1991, oil on canvas, 83 x 109 cm. On display at the Museum of World Cultures. Photograph by Michael Wiener, 1998.

the message intended by the artist. Therefore, the curator planning an exhibition attaches great importance to the analysis of the audience he will address. In addition to being a translator between different art worlds, he must also become the advocate for the arts he curates in an European environment. He learns what the viewer of Pacific art already knows (without a cultural explanation), and what must be translated (as it lays far beyond the experiences of an European art audience).

How one visualizes art interpretation and analysis within the context of display remains an important problem. Exhibition design should help to explain the art works on display and should therefore reflect their contents. In museum practice the development of such design never lies in the curator's hands alone. Exhibition design which provides a special context to every work on display is costly and time consuming. It requires field research, intensive communication with the artists' involved, long-term preparations and the production of expensive exhibition architecture. Therefore, the curator must convince those in charge of the museum finances — the directors, the administration and the sponsors of the importance of the exhibition. The exhibition design is developed and executed in co-operation with architects and designers who do not belong to the museum's permanent staff. Most designers are not trained in anthropology and therefore discussions concerning cultural context are essential. To enable them to develop an adequate exhibition design every artwork intended for display is discussed with relevant ethnographic and historic details. This constitutes the first stage of cultural translation. The second stage of translation is the negotiation between the designer's mode of display with both the artists' messages and the viewer's habits of seeing. I have written elsewhere about my attempts to mediate the meaning of Papua New Guinean paintings to an European audience. Successful strategies that I have employed include; using a background of coloured walls to emphasize colour symbolism, placing artefacts next to paintings in which they were depicted, and providing photographs of the Papua New Guinea landscape (Raabe 1999:21f.).

One example is the painting *Sagali*, 1991 [fig. 10.10] by Martin Morubuna. It depicts a specific part of the mourning ceremonies from the artist's home region, the Trobriand Islands. When I collected the painting for the museum I was intrigued by its clearly recognizable ethnographic details (Trobriand skirts and pots). I also knew that the Frankfurt museum audience would question the work — its execution in a realistic manner with dominating colour contrasts of dark grey and orange red would not be judged as 'authentic' Papua New Guinean. Because this audience is not familiar with the details of Trobriand culture they would not understand that the artist had transferred his culture's traditional colour symbolism into a contemporary painting.

In Trobriand culture black and red are an antagonistic colour pair. Black is a mourning colour and symbolizes death, illness and decline while red stands for life, sexuality and sexual activity. After a period of mourning a widow is allowed to marry again and is given the red skirt of unmarried girls. Morububuna depicts this final stage of mourning: relatives and friends walk up to the house, where the widow stays, bringing red skirts and black clay pots as gifts. Afterwards, the widow is dressed in a new red skirt and is allowed to step outside and start her new life. The colours in the painting indicate this transition from grief to joy. In an explanatory note the artist refers to the well-known lines from Ecclesiastes; 'there is a time for everything, a time to weep, a time to laugh, a time to mourn and a time to dance.' He also uses the depiction of the Sagali ceremony and the combination of symbolic colours to express his own feelings of being torn between mourning and joy. [10]

To reinforce the central role of colour in Morobubuna's *Sagali*, the Frankfurt museum designers prepared coloured walls for the display. The painting was placed on a red wall while a red Trobriand skirt, like those shown in the picture, was positioned on a black wall. Museum visitors were overwhelmed by the impression of contrasting black and red as they entered the space. Most visitors immediately understood that the painting transferred symbols and connected human feelings into colours -- an understanding which led to an appreciation of the painting's expressionistic qualities (Raabe 1999: 21f.)

The Trobriand artist Samuel Luguna was also aware that an European audience may not understand his depictions of kula valuables. In an interview [11], he suggested that placing a collection of traditional kula items next to his paintings would enable the viewer to compare the objects and their images. This idea corresponded with the museum's concept and presentation. It is a first step in exhibition design, which allows the specific meaning of an artwork from another cultural background to be readable to a European audience. As many see this kind of curatorial practice as an intrusion upon the artist's individual creativity, I would like to compare exhibition design to the translation of poetry. To transfer a poem from one language to another one must not only translate word by word but must transform structure and rhyme as well. To translate poetry one creates an adequate poetic expression in the language the poem is being transferred to. The result will always contain a great amount of the translator's interpretation. The translator, as well as the European curator of Pacific art, provides a context of presentation, which translates the context of origin.

In Europe modernism represents the break with classical traditions and the individual search for a new identity. This is in contrast to contemporary Pacific art. In her analysis of the Vanuatu art market, Haidy Geismar (this volume) distinguishes different categories of contemporary art objects that are connected with different concepts of indigenous authenticity and national identity. Vanuatu artists are aware of the tense relationship between tradition and modernity in their country. They not only reflect contrasts and tensions in their artwork but also make use of them as vital forces for an art market at the national level. However, the European audience is seldom aware of the interconnections between traditional and modern in Pacific art. In many Pacific art forms it is not the breaking with but the transformation of traditional contents that determines modernism. Also, the assertion of a Pacific identity combines individual self-awareness with regained ethnic and newly found national identities (Raabe 1997b: 61f.). To position tradition and modern art in a contradictory relationship hinders the detailed interpretation and critical analysis of art works from Papua New Guinea. Without enough knowledge to relate to the many diverse ethnic and historical backgrounds Pacific art embraces the audience in Europe continues to search for cultural authenticity of an imaginary Pacific culture. In this respect the anthropologist's explanations are more helpful to the fuller understanding of an artwork than any discussion by European art critics.

In an early version of this paper I wrote: "Criticism of contemporary Pacific art still needs to be developed". More to the point, art criticism and analysis should be transferred into curatorial practice. At the moment the European art scene has no fundamental knowledge of

Pacific art. Art historians and anthropologists must join in an effort to develop a practice of art presentation, which takes into account that tradition and modern artistic expression are linked. As anthropologists and curators we need to discuss the individuation of tradition in contemporary Pacific art. It is this individuation, which leads -- not to cultural authenticity so often claimed by European art audiences -- but to artistic authenticity valued by all. The way we represent Pacific art will shape the development of an European art criticism, which will judge, value and appreciate Oceanic art.

Acknowledgments

To the artists Samuel Luguna, Julie Mota, Martin Morububuna and Jane Wena I would like to express my deepest gratitude for their kindness and patience while discussing with me their works in detail. I would like to thank the Australian Research Council and the Centre for Cross Cultural Research, ANU, for funding my research on contemporary PNG art in 1999.

Full Tusk Maiden Aotearoa: Ramblings of a New Voyager in Words and Visions

Rosanna Raymond

To Chase A Tuna

To chase a tuna to
Sasina
Savaii,
Samoa

In a pond more costly to women, I walked as Sina, salt not battered, awash in deep water pond, spring into life, refreshed revitalised, realised, attitudinising

I was going with the flow with my bros' in a land, fa-fa away, when a sudden, reflection, direction, diversion, excursion, emersion, slipped through time and space offering protection as we just landed lactating lava lavaciously in lalolagi

Grounded sitting with mountains, head in the sky, getting the massage with hands on assimilation, migration, integration, instigation

Eyes thick with vision, decisions, descriptions,

Choking on lava

Good reef we pierced the sky, departed divine inspired by my Turangawaewae

And in the lay of the land... lies, a plan plain to my mother land, the far north land, to my father less land, where burnt and bleeding coconuts, soak the sky, (there we cried, my sisters and i) to my homeland, auckland, tamaki-ma-kau-rau, te henga, i resided.

Where west coasting with kupe the connector, the shared ancestor, gives direct line, to my p.i's, re-prazent and wreckognise, as i stand in admiration and appreciations for the inspirational, affirmation, imagination, creations, transformations... sensational

Here i stand full tusk maiden aotearoa... kssss aue aue he full moons in my horizons, wandering clouds passing by, east to west with soft caress, stained rosey, steeling, the sea shines

and dusky softly i have spoken

As in two the night my home works, as reflective, subjective, objective, situations are in operation, too much moon shinning, as the sliver delivers...

Deep come the dark, colding
Longing the long the longest
The stars shine

Breathed i have bled, when the moon drops past my pants, i look at her in the eye, golden, slippering, it dropped into my mouth, dripping with fooled mooned horizons

Be aware, urban in fusion, do not be confused by this unison, a class 'a' injection, fraction, reaction, orator, orientator, defining, fortification, exploration, explanation, feet firm, mat laden. This is where my eyes doth landed, surrounded by eyeland cult'ya

In the late months of 1999, I moved to London with my husband and children. Moving out of the Pacific has affected how and why I work in so many different ways, good and bad. Living in a new environment with different cultural beliefs and many other cultures and histories has made me view my work very differently. Yet, I found that I have kept the fundamental kaupapa (ideals/beliefs) within the work [fig. 11.1]. The past has been the way to my future and has helped me adapt to living in new circumstances even when distance or my own diaspora has become an issue. It has changed but the core has remained intact.

The celebration of my cultural heritage is fused into my work as an artist, whether perceived as invented, revivalist, authentic, traditional, contemporary, identity based, gendered, or craft based. Whatever label you want to call it, or has been called, this is not how I and other *HYBRID* Polynesian artists view our role in producing art that speaks, and relates to living in Polynesia today in a modern urban environment.

I cannot produce artworks, write poems, and create costumes without the knowledge of my cultural heritage, and the experience of living it. Producing art works is my way of putting my culture into the future... not in past boxes — making it relevant to me as a *modern pacific person.*

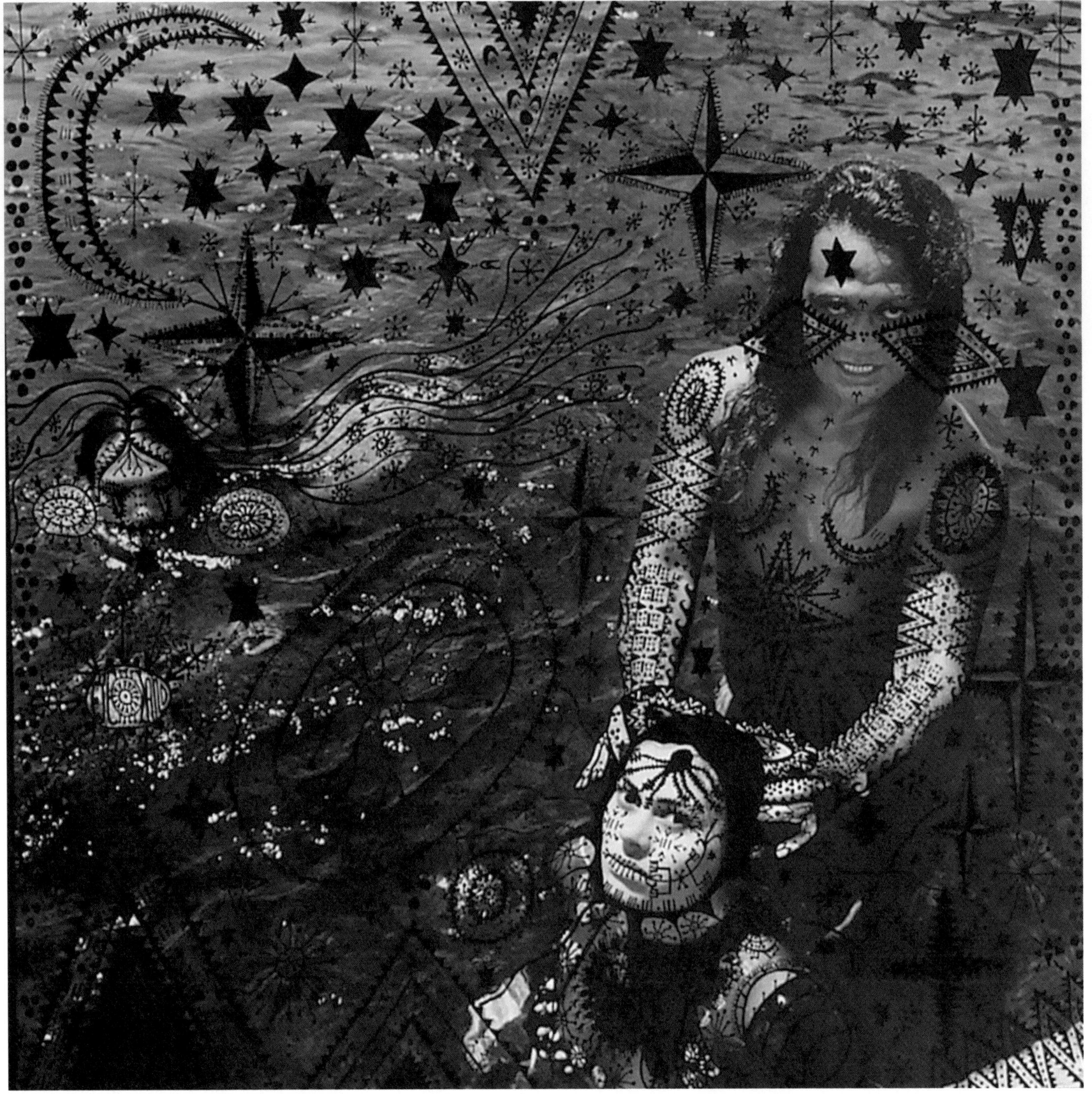

Figure 11.1. Rosanna Raymond, *La'a la'a luga o fanua o le mata,* Hand embellished photographic print: Rosanna Raymond. Photograph by Greg Semu, 1997. Collection of the Auckland City Art Gallery.

New modes of work and materials were needed in my new homeland. I could no longer walk down the beach and collect shells for costumes. The light was different, the stars in the sky, the birds, the trees, I had no community to rely on only an indifferent art world in a global market. These were some of the problems that I first experienced in my effort to settle in the UK. This was a great shock to me, as I had been living in an urban Polynesian setting, Aotearoa, (New Zealand), where systems of belief and appreciation were already in place. Practicing my art and cultural beliefs was a part of my everyday life.

Yet, I still produced work as an artist, which eased my sense of alienation. I had no room for a workshop, so words became my new material; I wrote and wrote.

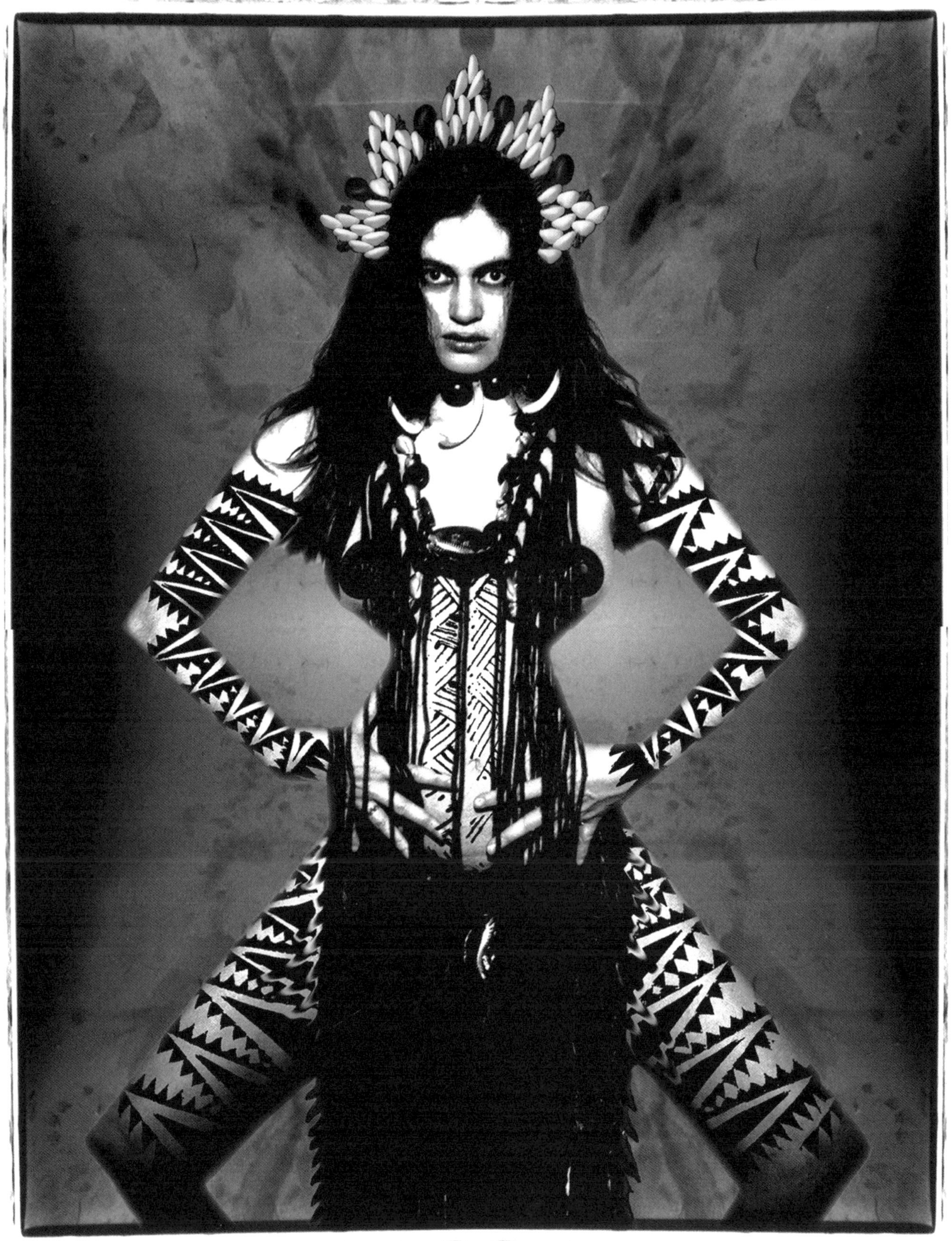

Figure 11.2. Rosanna Raymond, ***Full Tusk Maiden***, **Embellishments and Adornments: Rosanna Raymond. Digital manipulation: Damon Mangos. Photograph by Kerry Brown 2005.**

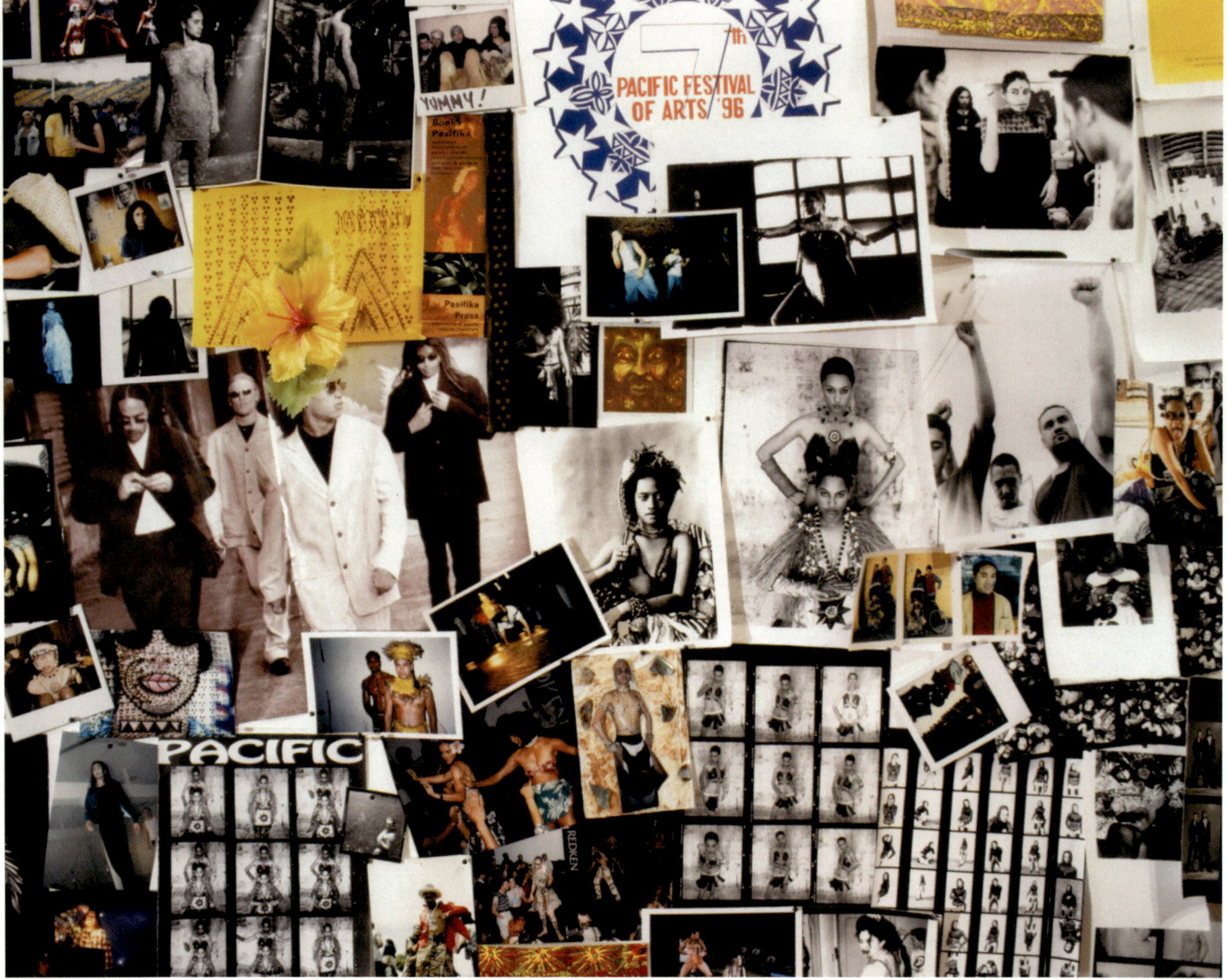

Figure 11.3. Rosanna Raymond, *Eyeland: Part 1*, Multi media installation for the Open Skies Divided Horizons exhibition, Auckland City Art Gallery. 1997. Images courtesy of the artist.

As I met new people with new creative skills, I started to work with digital technologies [fig. 11.2]. *Full Tusk Maiden* may have been created in Aotearoa but she has transformed into a digital artwork, and I became the virtual personification of a character I helped create and present to Te Papa with the Pacific Sisters — *21st Sentry Cyber Sistar.*

Auckland in the late 1980's was a hot bed of Polynesian empowerment through the arts, music and fashion. A new wave of urban Polynesians were finding new avenues to create their own visual landscape, telling new stories and creating new histories. I was part of this movement... it was a result of 2nd and 3rd generation NZ born Polynesians finding a place/space for themselves in a country that was learning to accept their presence and impact on the 'bicultural' society that it thought it was.

It was within this backdrop that I became a member of the Pacific Sisters, a multi-cultural collective of artists [fig. 11.3]. We were all New Zealand born Pacific Islanders: Maori, Samoan, Cook Island, Tongan, Rotuman and Fijian. We were defining ourselves as Pacific Island culture that had developed within New Zealand, using the arts, crafts, fashion, and music. Urban Pasifika was coined to describe this movement.

Academics started to creep into my peripheral vision at festivals and art galleries. My first impression of the world of academe (and anthropology) was based on the experiences I had with various academics and articles written *from a distance, by professionals with impartial views*?!?!?!? Apparently, they were the only credible way to articulate issues of cultural identity and heritage. I found some very staid views on what Polynesian culture should be, not about what it has developed into. Debates on hybridity, the effects of diaspora and the institutionalised telling of histories, challenge the legitimacy of our culture and how it has been maintained... a one-way dialogue... we were having our own debates on such issues.

The realization that we were been watched by 'others' outside our creative community (which was mainly but not exclusively NZ-born Polynesians), slowly dawned on us as we began to read published works by professors and journalist in art and fashion magazines and books published on Pacific Art. We were used to media exposure through the TV program *Tagata Pasifika*, which had exposed our work to new peoples in our own community. This had worked well for us, and we became a part of the visual landscape of the Pacific community — Urban Pasifika.

To read about yourself labelled as hybrid and having your authenticity questioned by people outside your community left me feeling disempowered. I was often frustrated at the many mistakes and misrepresentation that appeared in articles, especially by peoples who had spent very little, or no time, with us or within our community. Often our involvement as practitioners was welcomed but our analysis of what we were doing was not considered as important unless validated by an educated expert.

It left me feeling apprehensive about this world of *academia and its experts*, but since then a more balanced relationship has developed and anthropology, academia, institutions, have all become part of my working/creative process. I have been inspired to create new works of art and have worked in ways that I could not have contemplated in New Zealand. This process has been gradual and is still developing.

Through my contact with the academic world I have found myself in many new venues; Museums and their collections have had a big impact on me. I have meet, face to face, taonga (cultural treasures) from Polynesia. Being directly connected to these *objects* is like discovering whakapapa (genealogical links). It has also shown me how things are made and helped my techniques as a craft person and artist. This has been invaluable because in my leaving New Zealand, I left behind my most precious taonga...my elders, and peers, who helped me, nurture my craft and help develop my techniques and knowledge, kanohi ki te kanohi... face to face.

Silence of the Gods

A throng of gods
Assembled in silence

Accused of decadence
Offered out of deference

Emptied of resonance
Collected for reference

And now in idol consideration

Engaged in your estrangement
I gaze at you like a stranger

Enjoying your sing song
that fell on deaf ears

I give you my name
And you give me your number

To revive you
To revere you

Looking at taonga that is so familiar, yet very separated from its' original place and purpose can be a frustrating and painful process, especially if you feel connected to it, spiritually. I feel a strong bond to my ancestors when I meet artefacts. It is as if a direct line (whakapapa) opens up with my cultural heritage, the past becomes present. Academia and institutions have initiated new ways for me to explore my cultural heritage — working hands on and face to face with the taonga — whilst not living directly within its cradle.

One of my first forays into the this world was when I had the opportunity to work with the Forster collection at the Pitt Rivers Museum, for their website project *Pacific Pathways.* This project has opened an interactive relationship with their collections. With new technology, a two-way dialogue of sorts can begin.

The Forster collection was the starting point for an inspiration that manifested itself in words, vision, and sound. I found a series of tapa cloths that had come from Tonga on Captain Cooks 2nd voyage [fig. 11.4]. In his manuscript, 'The catalogue of Curiosities', George Forster had itemised and described this collection. Number 42 read "a piece of their brown cloth". This was the trigger, as I started to think about what tapa or siapo meant to me, I was pulling stories out of the taonga, smells, sounds... this project started a new working pattern for me, one which has brought much enjoyment and creativity [fig. 11.5].

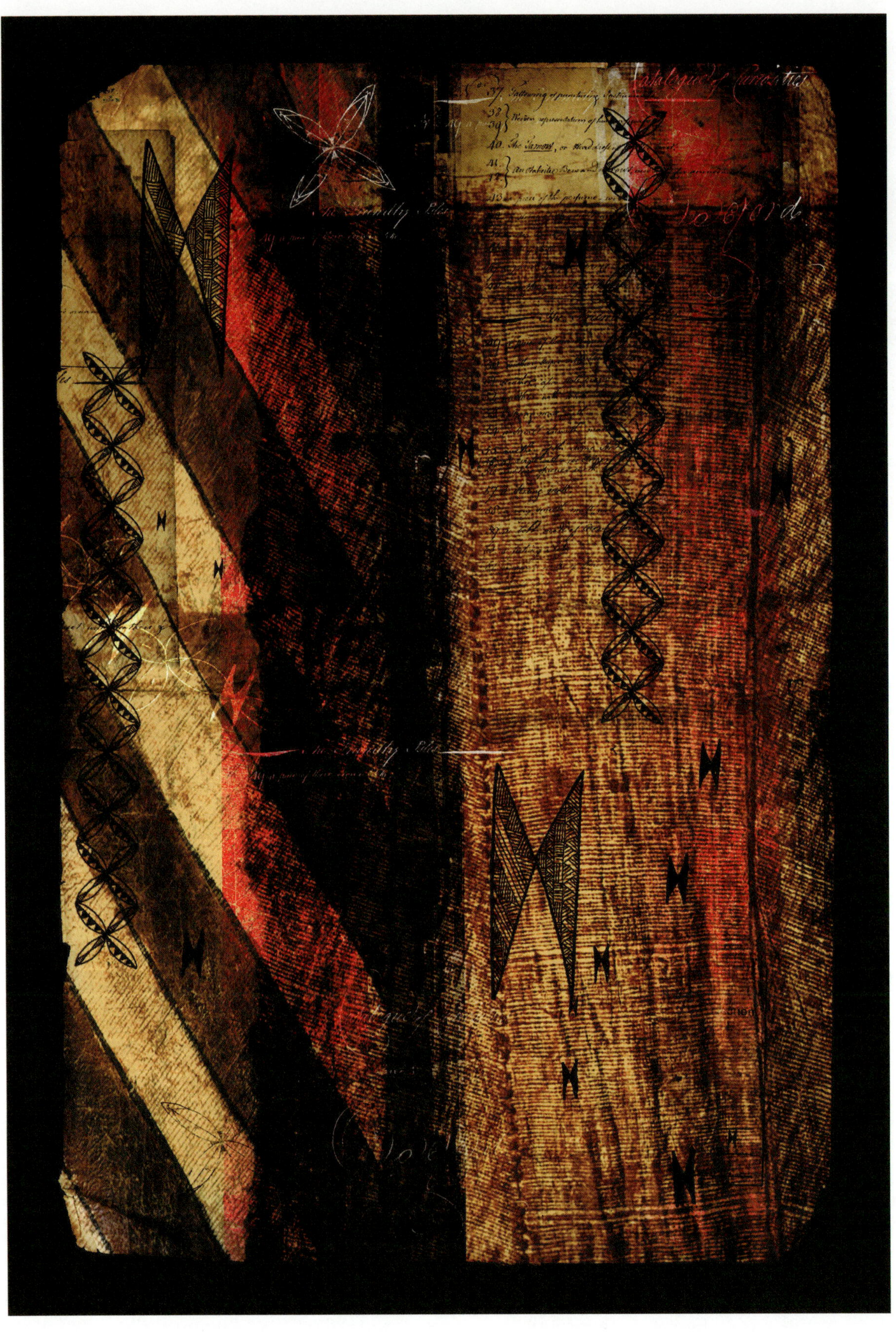

Figure 11.4. Rosanna Raymond, *A Piece Of Their Brown Cloth*: Digital barkcloth for the Pacific Pathways project, Pitt Rivers Museum, Oxford University, UK, 2003. Embellishments: Rosanna Raymond. Digital Manipulation: Matt Barron.

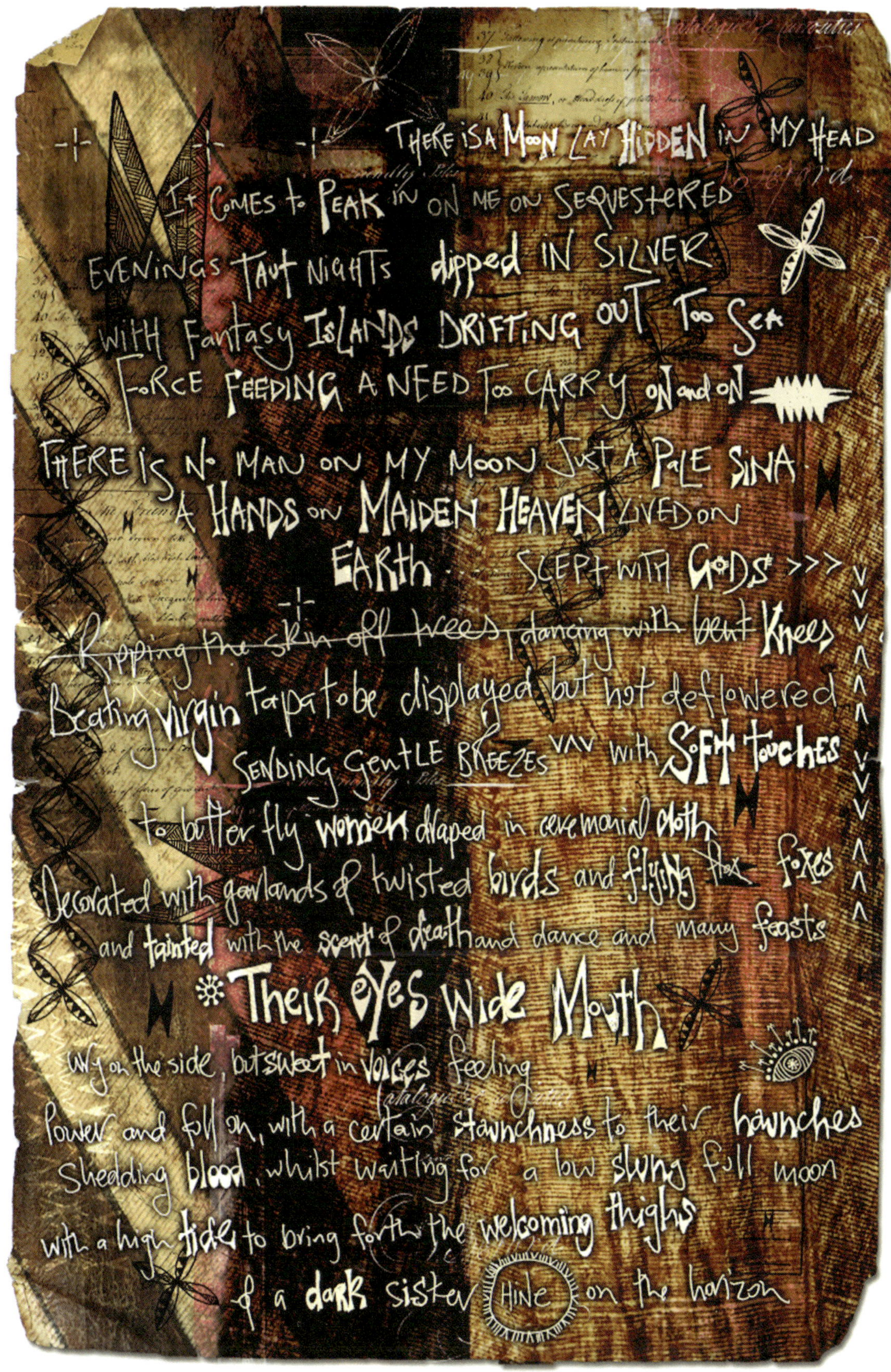

Figure 11.5. Rosanna Raymond, *A Piece Of Their Brown Cloth*: Visual Poetry, Pacific Pathways Project, Pitt Rivers Museum, Oxford University, UK, 2003. Embellishments and Poem: Rosanna Raymond, Digital Manipulation: Matt Barron.

Ode to a Pale Sina
(Beat Me and I Shall Fly to the Moon)

There is a moon lay hidden in my head, it comes to peak in on me

On sequestered evenings...... taut nights dipped in silver

With fantasy islands drifting out to sea and in the deed

Force feeding a need to carry on and on...

There is no man on my moon, just a pale Sina

A hands on maiden heaven lived on earth... slept with gods

Ripping the skin off trees, dancing with bent knees

Beating virgin tapa, to be displayed, but not deflowered

Sending gentle breezes with soft touches

To butterfly women, draped in ceremonial cloth,

Decorated with garlands of twisted birds and flying foxes

Tainted with the scent of death and dance and many feasts

Their eyes... wide... mouth

Wry on the side, but sweet in voices

Feeling power and full on, with a certain staunchness to their haunches

Yet shedding blood, whilst waiting for a low slung full moon with a high tide

To bring forth the welcoming thighs, of a dark sister, Hine on the horizon

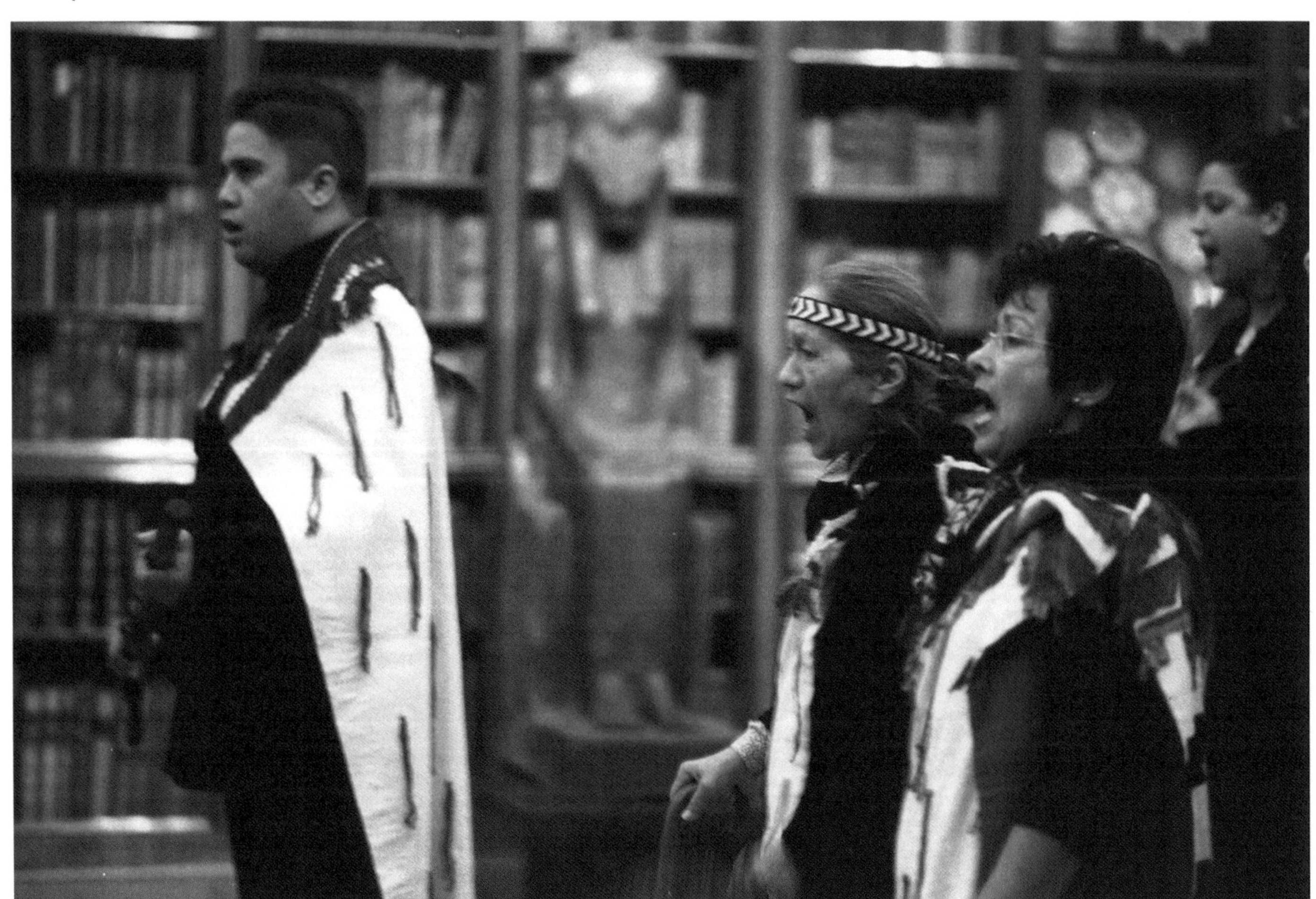

Figure 11.6. Ngati Ranana (Tribe of London) *Whakarite mauri* (The Enlightenment) Gallery, Kings Library, British Museum, 2004. Photograph by Kerry Brown.

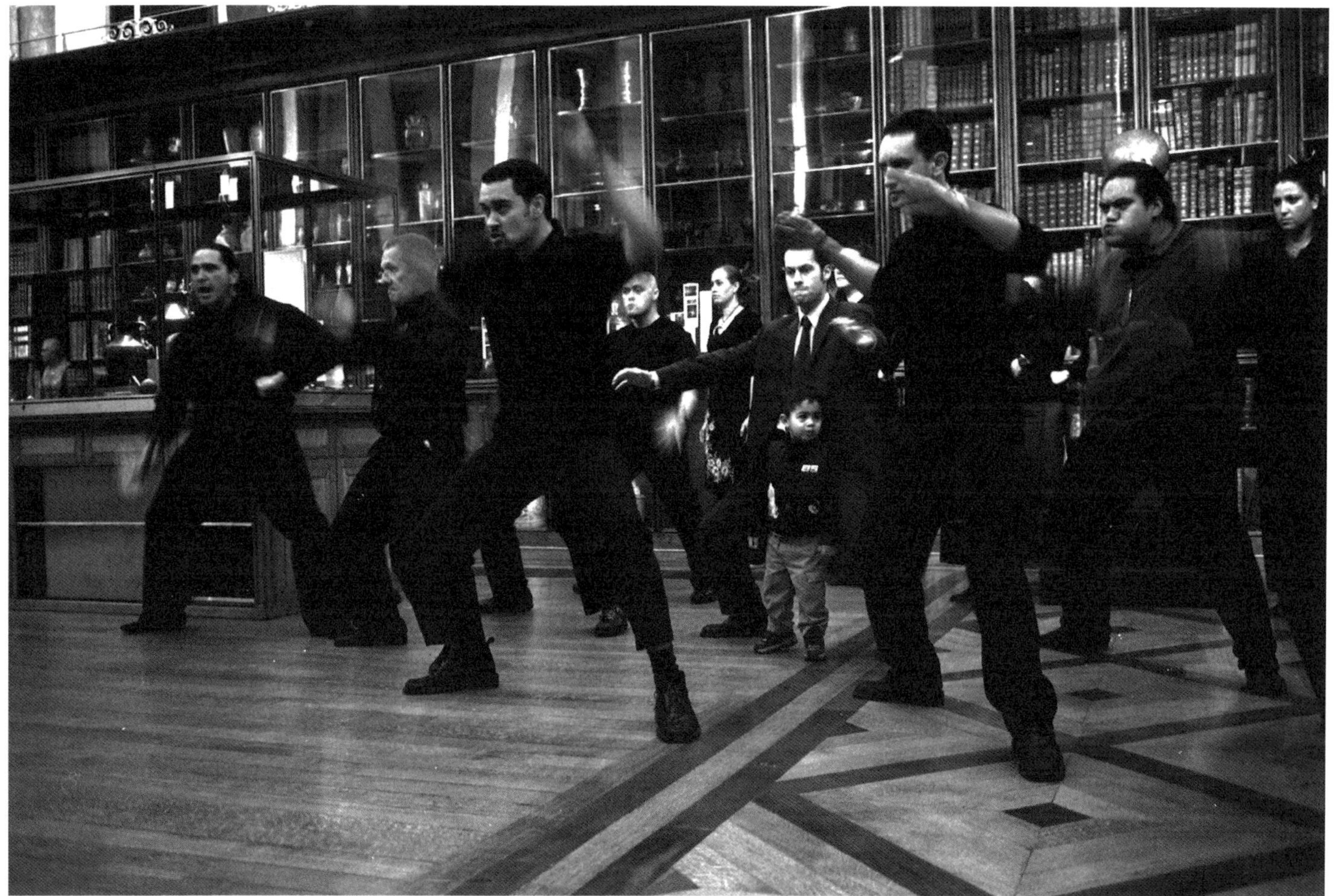

Figure 11.7. Ngati Ranana (Tribe of London) ***Whakarite mauri*** **(The Enlightenment) Gallery, Kings Library, British Museum, 2004. Photograph by Kerry Brown.**

However, artifacts alone are not enough to satisfy the cravings of this homesick Polynesian and for the last four years, I have been a member of Ngati Ranana, The tribe of London. The club has been going for over 50 years. We meet every Wednesday night we and learn kapahaka (aspects of Maori performance arts), but more importantly take time to Kotahitanga (come together), Whakawhanaungatanga (nurture relationships), and Manaakitanga (hospitality, kindness) each other. It is a transient group due to the nature of visa requirements and immigration laws, and has become an important way for me to express my Polynesian self in Ranana... It was through my relationship with anthropology that I was able to bring these two different worlds together.

I was actively involved in the setting up of the welcoming and blessing of the Maori taonga in the *Enlightenment* exhibition at the British Museum. This was a two-way dialogue between the museum and Ngati Ranana and it set a precedent for possible dealings with peoples that are related to the artifacts, both spiritually and physically.

We held a hui (meeting) and much korereo (discussions) was had on how and why this taonga was there and how we were to address our tupuna (ancestors) after such a long time of not being part of the "world of light"; re-connecting with its people, its people. Issues of ownership, appropriation and colonization came to the fore. New waiata and haka (song and laments, posture dances) were written by club member Che Wilson, as the healing process was addressed. Rehearsals bought us together — learning — it was a very productive time, and we were excited to meet the taonga.

The night was full of magic and the presence of our ancestors reveled in the room with us [figs. 11.6 and 11.7]. It touched the very souls of all who attended: museum staff, the security staff and Ngati Ranana. I feel the evening was an important milestone for both the Maori community of London and the British Museum in the context of preserving the spiritual conversation of the taonga. Even though the two parties have very different agendas in the preservation of the taonga, the night brought together three worlds, the past, present and the future. Again, I was moved to articulate my experience of this night through spoken word and this in turn inspires me to make costume and movement to adorn these spoken words. I now see working with institutions as a venue to help bridge the gaps that have evolved in the process of housing, collecting and writing about indigenous peoples over the past 200 years. I see the future of collections and museums becoming an arena for cultural exchange, going outside the boundary of space into everyday life... my life... and my new voyages.

Leaves and Song

Open the door

And call on the winds... to blow the dust from my eyes

Shake your leaves and lament

We can anoint each other with the past
And readdress my lost adornment

Come to me... share some air... let it quaver and reach far inside you

Breathe with perpetual emotion

Blow me... wrap your lips around me... I will release gods and call for my love ones

Sing me a song to take away this cold

Possess me... give me your skin to hang from stroke by stroke, we can evoke an affinity

Impress your essence, I will shine

Cling to me... give up your grieving, but don't deny those tears

Let them fall in tribulation

These plaintiff moments, will lull the pain, as you leave me behind

A..........I..........E

Without Boundaries: Contemporary Oceania Artists, A Movement Happening Now

Jewel Castro

I begin by focusing on an event that inspired the ideas covered in this paper. In July 2005, the Peabody Essex Museum (PEM) in Salem, Massachusetts hosted the Pacific Art Association's (PAA) VIII International Symposium, "Pacific Diasporas: People, Art, and Ideas on the Move." Dr. Carol Ivory, the PAA President [1] and Christina Hellmich organized the symposium [2]. It was like a grand rendezvous. Scholars of Oceanic art gathered at the PEM from all over the world with contemporary artists from all over Oceania. A spectacular performance event featured the New York based Mahina Movement whose Tongan member, visual artist Vaimoana Niumeitolu, caused a roar of appreciation when she instructed the audience in hip hop poetic style toward the correct pronunciation of her homeland, 'Tonga' not 'TONG-GAH.' [3] In juxtaposition, performance artist Rosanna Raymond, a 'Tusitala' (teller of tales), mesmerized the full house like a conduit for the ancients, with her beautifully rendered part visual, part dance, part poetry compositions. The Marquesan dance group, Te Pua O Feani from Hiva Oa honored the symposium with powerful percussive performances that seemed to emerge out of the belly of the earth [fig. 12.1]. Along with other attending visual artists, I had a painting titled, *Tales of a Fisherman II* [fig. 12.2], that was included in the PEM exhibition, *(Re)settled/(Re) viewed: Recent Expressions of Pacific Identity*, curated by Hilary Scothorn. It is part of my *Assimilation* series, which is about family members who migrated to the United States from Samoa in the 1950s and 1960s. The images represent their stories of assimilation or their resistance to it.

A handful of the other artists in the exhibition were New Zealand based wonders like Tongan artist, Filipe Tohi [4], and Maori/Cook Island artist Dr. Richard S. Cooper [5], and Samoan artist and curator Fonofale McCarthy. Feeling solidarity with all of the artists, I wondered, in what lofty halls of United States institutional bliss were their cutting edge works hanging, setting, and in collection? Where was the theoretical writing that provided discussion of these twenty-first century expressions of a contemporary world identity?

My reaction to that PAA symposium balanced between thrilled and challenged. Part of the beauty of the Pacific Art Association, in general, is that it brings forward discussion and transnational exposure to contemporary Oceanic art. Even now, the artists who attended speak of the important connections that happened in Salem. My challenges have to do with the sessions' combination of anthropological-type research mixed with presentations by living artists who represented the cultures of the researchers' focus. There was an interesting sense of intellectual ownership. I began to understand for the first time the link between Oceanic Art History and Anthropology, and the clash between that union, and contemporary art. Conversations I overheard that dismissed our work as "contemporary" as if that reduced or negated its authenticity amused me. This begs the question, whose voice should define what is 'authentic' about our work when it essentially represents our world experience? Cultural authenticity in contemporary art and the notion of the artist as a living specimen, are professional challenges that Oceanic artists must deal with as we push for transnational exposure. We must be aware that this exposure effects how our work is interpreted, exhibited, and written about. The problem is, however, that most scholarly attention brought anonymously to our ancestors' art is through western sciences. Today our art must no longer be categorized as anonymous examples of our culture. Today both the artist's cultural history and the contemporary issues that affect their communities influence contemporary Oceanic art. Formal aspects of culturally historic art, as well as all aspects of contemporary fine art practices inform their artistic processes. As we negotiate our niche within world art history, we still face professional colonization. In the United States, these issues are old battlegrounds. For decades, Chicano and Native American artists have been objectified and marginalized. Their experience and efforts are valuable information for Oceanic artists. For this paper, I interviewed eminent Native artist, James Luna [6], and Chicano artist, Richard Lou. [7] They have fought institutional racism in order to have their work recognized, valued, and reviewed. "We're still doing that," said James Luna, in December 2007. [8] Certainly, Luna has tackled objectification head on with his performances such as *The Artifact Piece,* and *Take a Picture with a Real Indian.* The strength of Luna's work is that it causes in his audience "reflection and change." Oceanic artists are also making work that challenges outsider concepts of a twenty-first century Oceanic identity.

Two months after that PAA symposium, Dr. Pamela Rosi [9], and Samoan artist and poet Dan Taulapapa

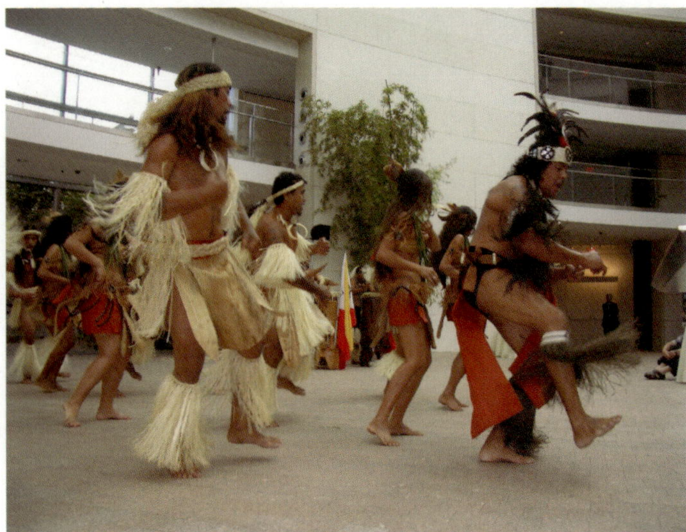

Figure 12.1. Te Pua O Feani in performance at the PEM in 2005. Photograph courtesy of Dr. Carol S. Ivory.

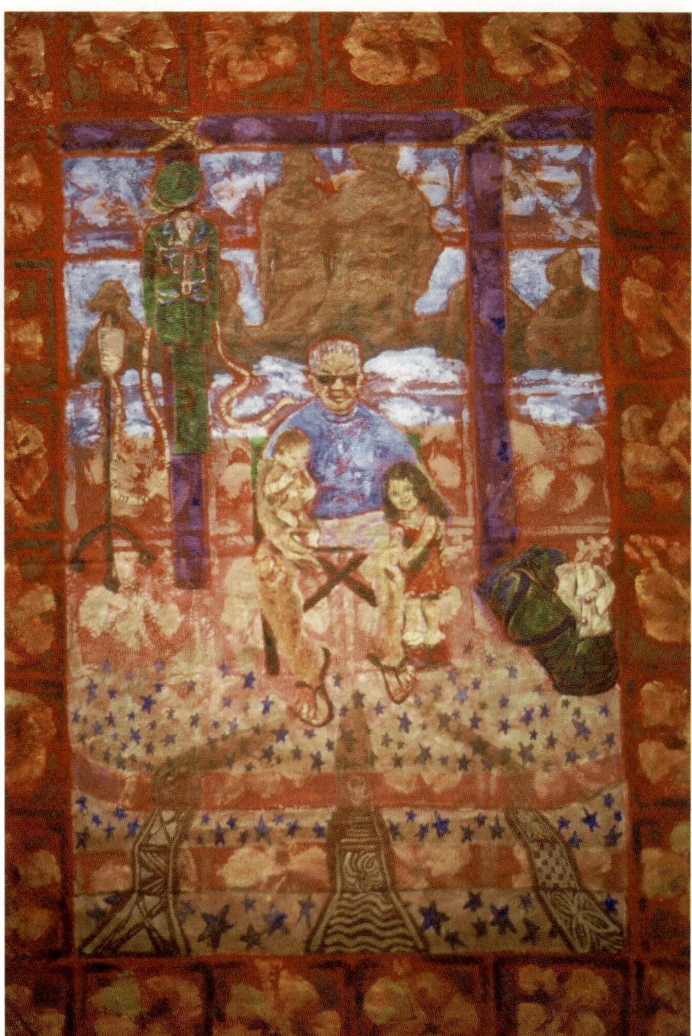

Figure 12.2. Jewel Castro, *Tales of a Fisherman II*, acrylic on canvas, 48" x 60", 2005.

McMullin [10], and I began co-chairing the session, "Gender in Oceania Art" for the Association of Social Anthropology of Oceania (ASAO) meeting in San Diego in February 2006. As artists from both New Zealand and Papua New Guinea were participants in our session, we thought it an excellent opportunity to organize a small exhibition and performance event. [11] Space and safety restrictions at the ASAO meeting venue reduced the exhibition to several pieces on easels in the corner of a ballroom. This is an indication of the difficulties contemporary Oceanic artists face as we enlist opportunities for transnational exhibitions. We have reluctantly accepted marginalized exhibits of our work since we need the exposure. It became clear during the ASAO meeting preparations that however well meaning the host, this activity had to stop. Oceanic artists and curators recognize the twenty-first century as a period of prolific artistic industry. There is a sense of collective achievement and advancement with the recognition of our individual artistic endeavors. Having our work haphazardly displayed marginalizes and disenfranchises this art. It is important that both Oceanic artists and curators protect the integrity of the work through proper exhibitions.

Dr. Rosi, Dan Taulapapa McMullin and I communicated our concerns to the other artists. A strong proponent for having a serious exhibition during the ASAO meeting was Fonofale McCarthy, who was bringing art from New Zealand and giving a paper for our session. McCarthy's email response to our growing venue difficulties was emblematic of the main dynamic responsible for the progress of the contemporary Oceanic Art Movement, self-reliance. McCarthy would have none of our defeat, reminding us that it was an "important opportunity for all of the artists." He encouraged us to "find another venue". [12] In the end, and with Dr. Rosi's collaboration, I organized an exhibition and performance event. There were the usual obstacles to contend with — no money, no time to write for any, no venue, and of course, very little art. Thankfully, we received enormous support from the Visual Arts Department at the University of California San Diego who gave us their graduate gallery and state of the art performance space, plus full access to their technical equipment and staff.

Now operating under the exhibition title, *Turning Tides, Gender in Oceania Art*, and having a gallery and black box type theatre space, my intention was to exhibit as many artists' work in as many different media as possible. A compelling aspect of the contemporary Oceania art movement is collaborative determination, an ancient Oceania mindset that has to do with community members working in concert for the success and celebration of the whole. I contacted some of the

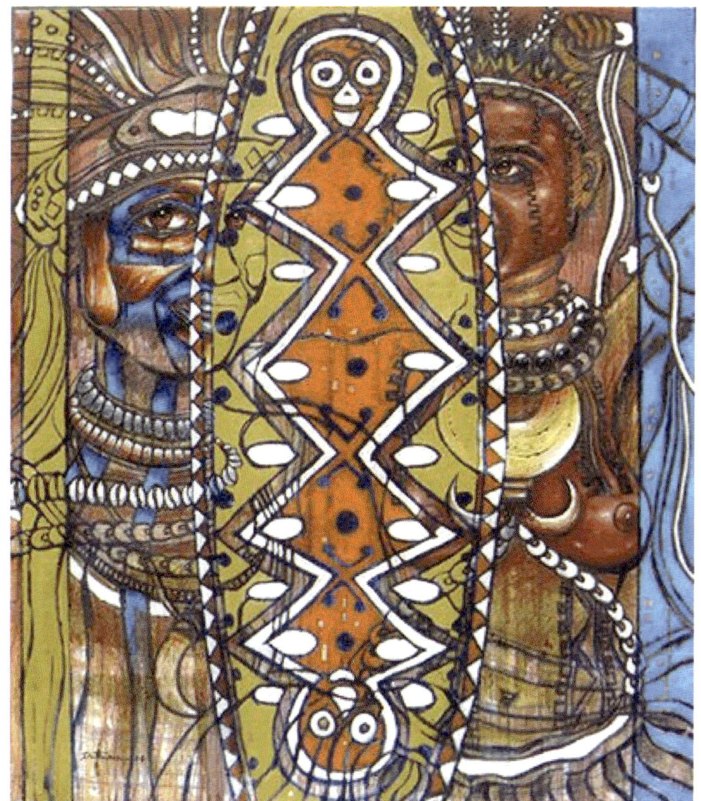

Figure 12.3. Daniel Waswas, *Shielding Our Women,* acrylic, oil sticks, and shellac on canvas, 40" x 48", 2005. Photograph courtesy of the artist.

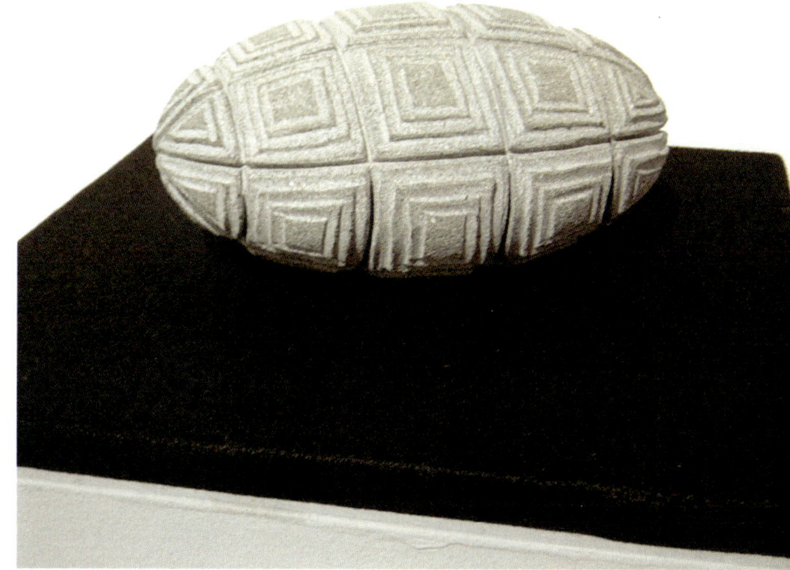

Figure 12.4. Filipe Tohi, *Untitled,* andesite, 12" x 10" x 5", 2004. Photograph courtesy of California State University Northridge Art Galleries.

artists that had attended the PAA Symposium. Each responded without hesitation, quickly sending one or more pieces at their own cost. In the end, the show included the work of Dr. Richard S. Cooper, Tupito Gadalla, Anne Keala Kelly, Shigeyuki Kihara, Fonofale McCarthy, Dan Taulapapa McMullin, Reggie Meredith, Julie Mota, the Otufelenite Tongan Community Group of Oakland, California, Rosanna Raymond, Larry Santana, Filipe Tohi, Daniel Waswas, Jane Wena, and me. Included in the show were paintings, sculpture, photography, performance, video installation, and traditional barkcloth. The breadth of the work speaks to the diversity of cultures represented and the range of media freely used in contemporary Oceania art.

Besides her invaluable expertise in the art and culture of Papua New Guinea, Dr. Rosi had paintings she could contribute for the show. One painting titled, *The House of a Thousand Tribes* is by well-established Papua New Guinea artist, Jane Wena. The image represents Papua New Guinea's Parliament House. Wena said, "It depicts PNG's vast cultural diversity… Its 800 plus languages… and a civilization that has only recently embraced modernization in all its forms and conflicts."[13] Dr. Rosi also contributed a series of 10 mixed media paintings by Papua New Guinean painter, writer, and theatre artist, Julie Mota. In Mota's words, they are "a series of paintings about the University of Papua New Guinea student protest in 2001 that resulted in four deaths and reportedly twenty-eight injured."[14] Mota's paintings are particularly interesting because her technique breaks with long held acceptable styles of PNG painting. These paintings are reminiscent of the groundbreaking paintings and teachings of Native American artist, Fritz Scholder, whose technique, informed by his university based art education, departed from the flat, decorative execution prescribed by outsider administrators of the Old Indian School of Santa Fe, New Mexico. Like Scholder in the 1950s and 1960s, Mota applies her media in expressive gestures that break with outsider expectation, and provide a new window to contemporary authenticity in Papua New Guinea.

Having Wena and Mota's art in the show became extremely meaningful for me. PNG women artists are rarely exhibited in their country and typically denied the right to be recognized. PNG artist Larry Santana stated "Papua New Guinean women suffer many kinds of discrimination… this includes rape, forced marriage for young girls, and frequent wife bashing."[15] With determination and risking personal ramifications, women like Wena and Mota are implementing change in their country by virtue of their art. And so are some of the men. An example is the painting, *Shielding Our Women,* [fig. 12.3] by PNG artist and curator, Daniel Waswas. In his artist statement Waswas explained, "In this artwork I'm trying to create a dialogue to provoke a shifting of our mind set… in giving women that respect they surely deserve." [16] It is noteworthy to mention that after our ASAO session, Daniel Waswas left for a residency at the deYoung Museum. Midway through the *Turning Tides* exhibition, *Shielding Our*

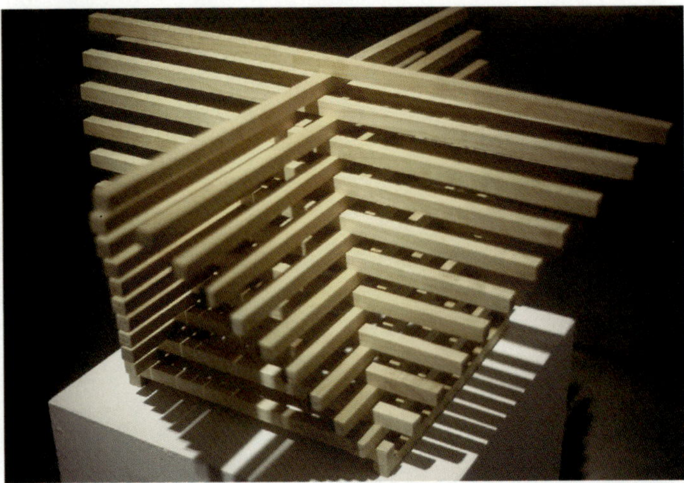

Figure 12.5. Filipe Tohi, *Lotomotua (Looking Inside and Out)*, pine, 24" x 24" x 24", 2006. Photograph courtesy of Jewel Castro.

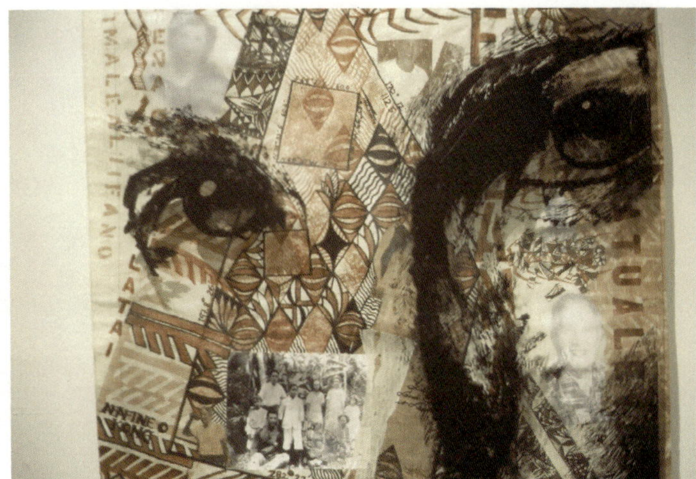

Figure 12.6. Detail of Reggie Meredith's, *Self Portrait*, mixed media, 36" x 36", 2005. Photograph courtesy of Jewel Castro.

Women sold, as did all of the art that Waswas brought during his visit to the United States.

Many of the pieces exhibited in *Turning Tides*, provided examples of how contemporary Oceanic artists integrate historic art making materials and processes with western art disciplines to communicate a contemporary identity. For example, Auckland based, Filipe Tohi, sent two sculptures, one untitled and made of andesite, [fig. 12.4] and the other, titled, Lotomotua (looking inside and out), made of pine [fig. 12.5]. Both sculptures are transmutations of the ancient lashing process called lalava. As indicated in his artist statement, Tohi first studied lalava, or sennit lashing, a traditionally masculine art form. Lalava was "an intrinsic component in (historic) daily life, used for canoes, fishhooks, adzes, and architecture. Mastering lalava brought a new perspective and moved (his) art into a minimalist genre that concentrated on sculpture..." [17] In his andesite piece, Tohi communicates the solid strength of lalava by subtracting its woven pattern from the surface of a perfectly balanced rock. Tohi's *Lotomotua* sculpture provides a stretched out, 3-dimensional view of the lalava pattern. Its wooden parts intertwining, like the sennit lashings, yet separated by airspace, the sculpture communicates both the simplicity of lalava, and its complex almost DNA like structure.

Reggie Meredith [18], a granddaughter of the late master siapo artist, Mary Pritchard, transformed the traditional art form into a mixed media self-portrait. [fig. 12.6] Meredith stated that her piece was "driven by loss and the consciousness of time." Her loss has to do with the passing of her Samoan father and the knowledge that he was the living link to her family heritage. She further explained that even in contemporary times, "...the handing down of family history, genealogy, chief titles, land, and personal possessions are key components to understanding how (a Samoan) fits into society." [19] The old photographs embedded into her traditionally made and decorated barkcloth provided a window to her memories and inner sense of place within the family. To complete her self-image, Meredith made a contemporary portrait on clear, colorless Plexiglas. It hung in front of the cloth, like a fragile skin that might shatter at the slightest provocation. Meredith's layered self-portrait communicated a time of mourning and her solitary, if not unsure, negotiation of the future.

In her artistic process, Rosanna Raymond freely weaves historic Oceanic traditions such as poetry, dance, chant, tattoo, and siapo design, with contemporary art practices such as performance, body adornment, lights, video, and sound. For *Turning Tides*, Raymond videotaped a new performance titled, *Sleeping with Mountains*, and provided three performance photographs titled *Beat, Twisted*, and *Flow* [fig. 12.7]. The physicality of Raymond's work expresses the feminine aspects of Oceanic cultures in her movements — the exacting arch and lift of her feet, the clap of her hands and movement of her arms. At the same time her words, stare, and toss of her head dare the audience to challenge who she is as a contemporary woman connected to her ancestors. In addition to her art, Raymond's professional outreach focuses upon creating opportunities. In 2006, she co-curated the successful *Pasifika Styles* exhibition and festival with Dr. Amiria Henare at the Cambridge University Museum of Archaeology and Anthropology. [20]

Samoan artist, Shigeyuki Kihara, sent two photographs from her outstanding *Fa'a Fafine* (In the Manner of a Woman) series, titled, *Tama Samoa (Samoan Man) and*

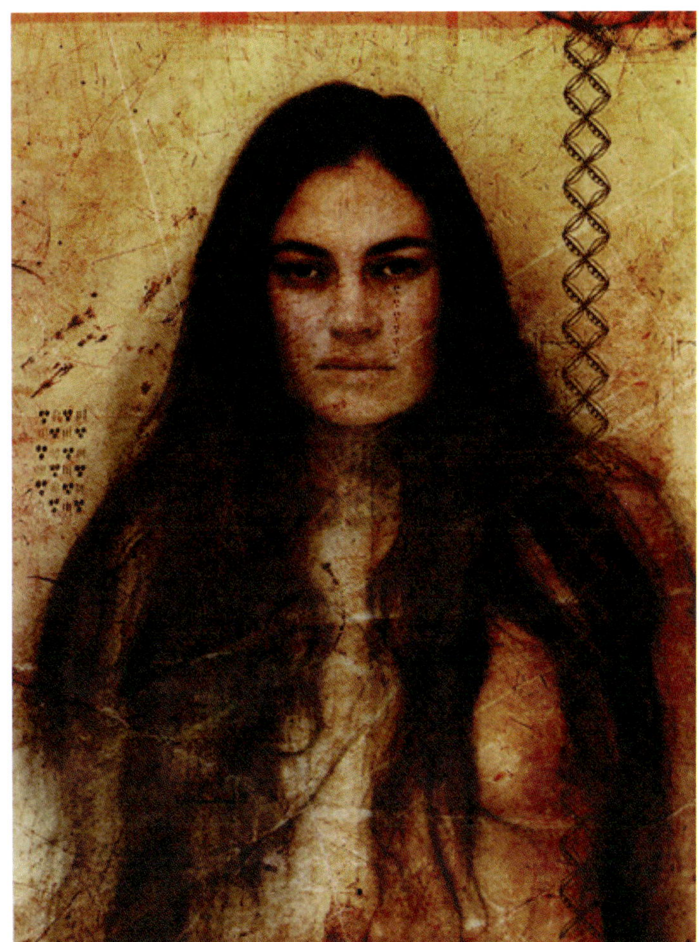

Figure 12.7. Rosanna Raymond, *Flow*. Photograph courtesy of the artist.

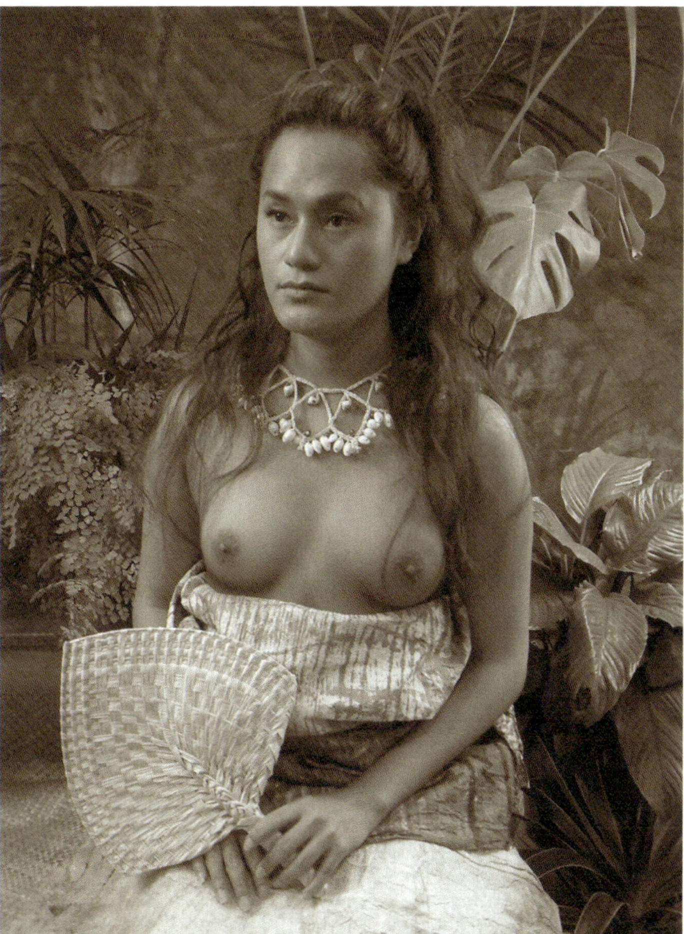

Figure 12.8. Shigeyuki Kihara, *Tiene Samoa (Samoan Woman)*, 80 x 60 cm, 2004-05. Post-production: Coylehall and Bronga Rhind Eglese. Photograph by Coylehall, courtesy the artist and Sherman Galleries, Sydney.

Teine Samoa (Samoan Woman) [fig. 12.8]. Kihara's striking images are photographic performances in which she and the background are dressed in historic character. But like Manet's, Olympia, Kihara strays from the conspired demure poses of nineteenth century ethnographic photographs and instead looks directly at her audience. The sepia toned images with complete sets and costumes beautifully present the era she is emulating while her confrontational gaze and physicality brilliantly challenge the notions of both voyeur and authorship.

Turning Tides was overwhelmingly successful and was ultimately extended. On its new closing day, art historian Dr. Peri Klemm of California State University Northridge visited the show. [21] Soon afterwards, Dr. Klemm and I began co-curating a new, expanded version of the exhibition for CSU Northridge. This new exhibition was held February-March 2007, and was called *Island Affinities, Contemporary Art of Oceania*. Among others, it included more works from Shigeyuki Kihara's *Fa'a Fafine* series. Filipe Tohi came to the gallery and created an additional sculpture, *Halakilangi (Stairway to the Sky)* [fig. 12.9], and my installation; *Red House/ The Daughters of Salamasina* was also included [fig. 12.10]. Thanks to Dr. Klemm, and the combined efforts of her Gallery Studies students and all of the Northridge Art Gallery staff, *Island Affinities* was a tremendous success.

The successes of these exhibitions as well as individual artistic pursuits are measured by their outcomes. Already mentioned are the sales made by Daniel Waswas and the curatorial projects by Rosanna Raymond. In 2008 Fonofale McCarthy opened the McCarthy Art Gallery in Auckland, New Zealand [22] and has since had a consistent flow of back-to-back solo and group exhibitions featuring emerging and established contemporary Oceanic artists. Another result was the deYoung Museum purchased five of Julie Mota's ten paintings shown in the *Turning Tides* and *Island Affinities* exhibitions. This was a significant event not only for

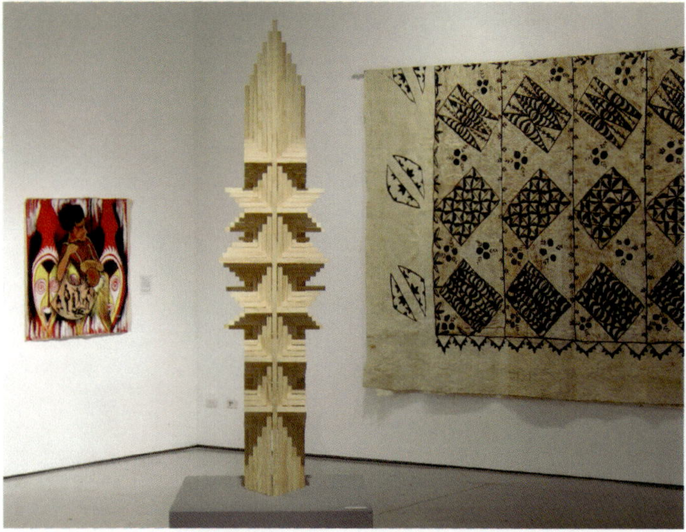

Figure 12.9. Filipe Tohi, *Halakilangi (Stairway to the Sky)*, pine, 72" x 18"x 18", as seen in Island Affinities, at California State University Northridge Art Gallery, 2007. Photograph courtesy of California State University Art Galleries. Also visible are Larry Santana's, *Bilum I Hevi Tumas (The String Bag is Too Heavy)*, (left) from the collection of Dr. Pamela Rosi; and the Otufelenite Tongan Community Group of Oakland's, *Ngatu 'o 'Otufelenite* (right).

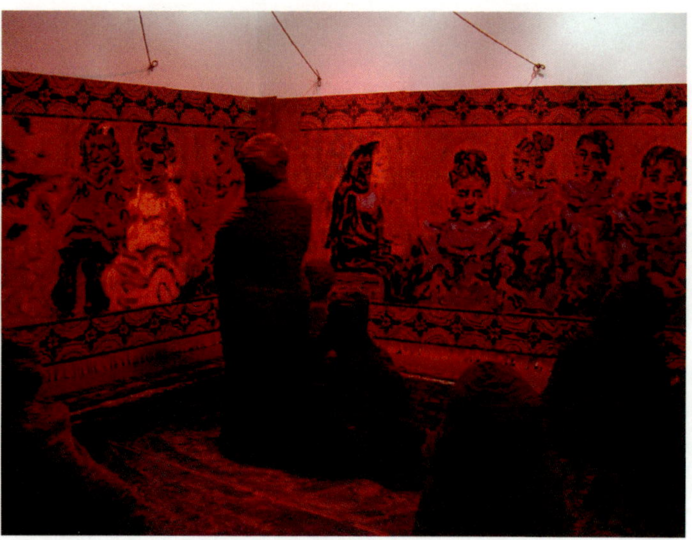

Figure 12.10. View of Jewel Castro's *Red House/The Daughters of Salamasina*, as exhibited at the California State University Northridge Art Gallery in 2007. Photograph courtesy of the California State University Northridge Art Galleries.

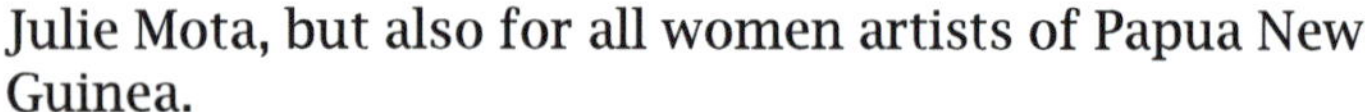

Julie Mota, but also for all women artists of Papua New Guinea.

Through her own negotiations, two of Shigeyuki Kihara's photographs were shipped at the close of *Island Affinities*, to the Southwest School of Art and Craft in San Antonio, Texas and were included in the 2007 exhibition, Te Taitanga/Bind Together; Contemporary Art of New Zealand. Later that year Kihara performed for the Pacific Art Association Symposium held at the Musée du Quai Branly, Paris. Subsequently the Metropolitan Museum of Art (MMA) acquired two photographs from the *Fa'a Fafine* series. In 2008 Dr. Virginia-Lee Webb, then MMA curator in the Department of the Arts of Africa, Oceania, and the Americas, organized a showing of Kihara's performance, Taualuga; The Last Dance, in conjunction with an exhibition titled, *Shigeyuki Kihara; Living Photographs.*

With this recent concentration of both individual successes and collaborative projects, it is certain that the contemporary Oceanic art movement is gaining great momentum. We have a lot of work to do to properly carve out our place in the arena of contemporary world art. James Luna provided us with troubleshooting points related to current obstacles that Native artists face: "...number one is that we don't have enough writers. We do not have enough curators. We need them in order to validate the work in the eyes of western people." [23] Luna indicated that today more Native peoples are achieving advanced degrees, which has resulted in a few gaining employment with key museums in the United States. Luna would now like to see these curators take on non-native projects because he feels that will increase their respect within the western art hierarchy. He also noted that a move from Native 'group' shows to solo exhibitions brings mainstream credibility to the work. These are important observations and Pacific Islanders and western museums and galleries should take note. Western museums and galleries should also recognize that Pacific Islander curators provide valuable expertise and alliances. Co-curation between western galleries and museums and Pacific curators will increase the profile of contemporary Oceanic art. In an interview, Sean Mallon [24] commented,

> I think these exhibitions and institutions can benefit from involving Pacific Islander curators who can bring artists from their locality together and know their work, but also understand the politics and relationships between these people... (Pacific). Pacific Islander curators need to work with people in the host institution who know their local audience/market and how the institution itself works...(Pacific) Artists and curators need to understand how galleries and museums work as much as museums

> and galleries need to know who and what they are exhibiting. [25]

To combat marginalization, the appropriate display of our art must be resolved. It is important to remove cultural specimen indicators and instead contextualize the work in terms of its significance within a global art history. To that end, I caution the overuse of visual directions such as explanatory signage and maps. In response to this activity Richard Lou, who is one of the original founders of the Border Arts Workshop in San Diego, California said:

> I would not provide a map unless it was important to the artist and their work. Nor would I provide a map if the artist was from France.... Your question I would interpret as coming from an understanding that Whiteness is race neutral and culturally centered so anyone outside of the hegemony would need translating and citing in the broadest sense. I prefer that the audience moves towards the center of the artwork in order to understand the work rather than the other way around. [26]

Finally, as James Luna suggested, we need more Pacific Islander writers who are knowledgeable about our art and share our life experiences. We need their voices in periodicals, books, and on the gallery walls. Shigeyuki Kihara feels that it is good for everyone to talk about our work but adds, "....the system in place is not giving equal opportunity for people from the Pacific to speak and contribute to the conversation. So everyone needs to shut up for awhile until we can have our say." [27]

Artist Statement
Ake Lianga

My parents are from the weather coast side of Guadalcanal. I was born in a village and grew up in various parts of the island. Growing up, I was fortunate to have a mixture of traditional and modern living. No matter where I lived, my parents held close ties to their village life and provided guidance in the traditional ways. It is to their credit that I have been able to retain knowledge of my culture to the extent that I can share it with the world.

In the Solomons, there is a spoken language that is unique to each island- nearly a hundred in all. Only three in our family of six children could speak the language of our village, myself included, although all of us could understand it. As the cash economy developed, my family moved from the village to the city; we now use only the Pijin that is spoken across the Solomons. The only time that the village language is spoken is when we don't want others to overhear.

When I was in school, the village languages were discouraged in the education system; even Pidjin was not allowed. We would be fined $0.50 for speaking a language other than English in the school compound. For my family, this was a large fine.

I learned to carve growing up in a community surrounded by villages where all traditional activities, including carving, were very strongly practiced. Carving was like a hobby to us kids because we didn't have toys. There were no toy shops nearby. When we returned from trips to town, we'd start right away carving our own versions of the toys we'd seen there. We'd sneak into the kitchen to borrow Mum's knife, then run out into the bushes and start carving things like little canoes and cars. So carving became a part of growing up.

I was introduced to other art forms when I moved from the village to town- to Honiara. At school I used paper and coloured pencils. I was always scribbling in class. A teacher from New Zealand had a strong influence on me. Most of the artwork I saw in town was painting and drawing, and I was curious to try it. That love for experimentation is with me still.

I apprenticed as a mural painter after I left school, working in collaboration with other artists through the Artists' Association of the Solomon Islands (AASI). We were quite well known in the city. It was through this work that I was commissioned to do a couple of murals on my own, then people started to know who I was. AASI would create exhibitions and promote the tribal aspect of the art. I encouraged the art community and the artists who were eager to learn.

The first international exhibition I participated in was held in 1995 at the University of New South Wales in Sydney. Artists came from all over the South Pacific to participate. During that time I not only had the chance to meet other artists (well-known artists who were all much older than me), but also to experience the potential of presenting my own work and representing my culture to an international audience. My piece was bought by the Jean-Marie Tjibaou Cultural Centre in New Caledonia: a great encouragement!

In 1996, I was very lucky to win a Commonwealth Scholarship. I chose to study in Courtenay, British Columbia, Canada. I nearly fled back home shortly after I arrived, because the cultural differences were so enormous. I put aside the traditional style of work I'm used to and immersed myself in the theory and practice of modern art. It was quite a learning process for me; it allowed me to grow by experimenting in different media and seeing how they can work with my tribal art.

Being away from home, I have come to realize the importance of my identity. When I first came to Canada it bothered me a lot that people would assume that I was from Africa or the Caribbean. I first thought it was a judgment based on my skin colour, but I soon came to realize that there was a barrier in peoples' geography that caused the misunderstanding.

I'm very fortunate to have learned from other artists I went to school with. I met a local native student who carved, David Jacobson Hunt, and from him I learned about local woods. We had an exhibition together, called Two Islands; it helped a lot of people to realize that there are many similar beliefs between our cultures. It was a shocking experience to return home in 2002. The country had been engaged in civil war for four years, and was totally demolished. The lifestyle of society was ruined. The people had lost pride in their culture. Most of all, I was saddened to see young people growing up knowing only violence.

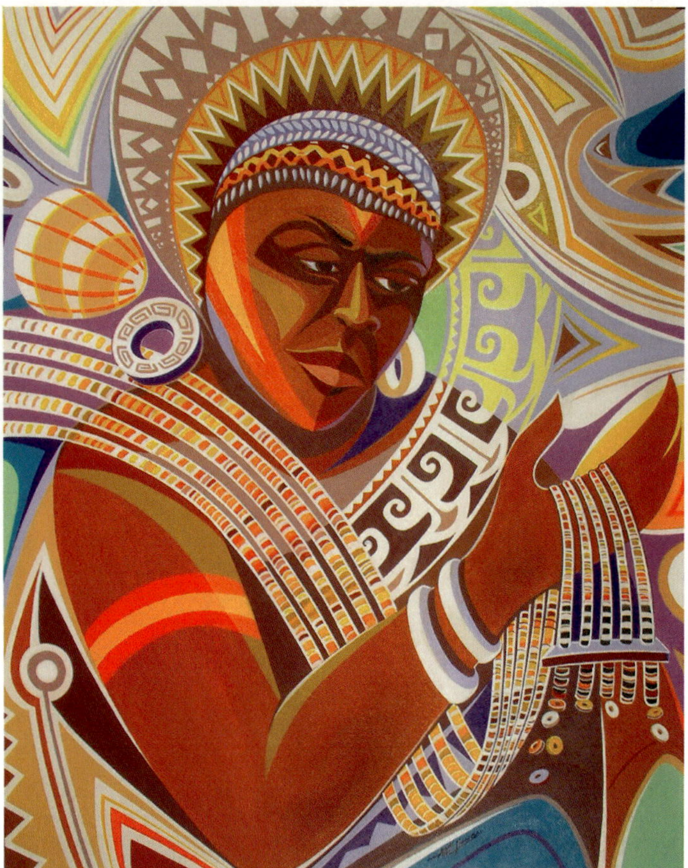

Figure 13.1. ***Shattered Value*****, acrylic on canvas, 30" x 24", 2006. Photograph by Dan Lepsoe, courtesy of Alcheringa Gallery.**

When I made a trip to the cultural centre itself, I saw all the totem poles, all the precious commissioned pieces, lying all over the place, chopped and demolished. It saddened me that society nowadays doesn't have any regard for its own historic values. I felt that I had to take responsibility and show the traditions in another way that would keep them strong.

I have always been proud of my Melanesian heritage, and I am honoured to show the world my culture and to explain the differences in my upbringing and traditions. I think many artists have the same ambition: to share a piece of their history through their art. It is an attempt to restore lost heritage, which has diminished as generations have moved forward, becoming more Western.

There has never been a practice of capturing the stories or legends of the Solomons in print. Continuity has always depended on the oral transmission of tradition from generation to generation. Unfortunately, as the stories are retold there are pieces that get lost, sometimes through changes in storytelling and language over time, sometimes through the loss of elders.

As I create each painting, I start with an ancestor story or legend and build that story as I go. I typically do not sketch a piece first but rather spontaneously paint what fits [fig. 13.1].

> This painting is about traditional shell money, once the common currency of the Solomons. I chose to use shell money as a subject because while it is still in use, it is frequently misinterpreted. During the headhunting days, shell money was used to settle conflicts between two parties. It was a way of showing respect and fairly compensating for wrongdoing. It was also used for bride-price, given from one tribe to purchase a bride from another. Shell money was passed down through the family traditionally from mother to daughter. Nowadays, it is mass-produced and it has lost its significance. It is sold in bulk and given out as souvenirs because it is pretty. I hope on the one hand that this painting will serve as a reminder of the true value of shell money, and in the broader sense, will capture the importance of maintaining the culture in print.

I respect what I paint. Some people express themselves through language or performing; I express myself through painting. Every piece is special to me and I feel very attached to it. The creation of a work feels almost like a meditation. I never forget any piece that I have created and always remember the special meaning that each one held for me. Because I manage my work as it develops, it is difficult for me to create a painting in a short time. I complete the work in stages.

At my first major solo exhibition in 2001, I concentrated on introducing the Solomon Islands to a community that had very little exposure to the Solomons before. In 2002, my first solo show at Alcheringa Gallery focused on the water and the significance it holds for my culture. The next exhibition was about the stature and cultural importance of sharks.

So far, I have focused on symbolism and colour to attract an audience; as yet, I have not put enough of myself into my paintings. In the future, I would like to expand the focus and move in a more contemporary direction. I want to show more of the current culture, as well as the history. I feel that I am bringing the art from the past into the present using the materials and resources that are available to me today. Art is not a static thing.

I have been very fortunate to be able to travel and study in North America; however, to achieve this success, I have had to leave the Solomon Islands, and it saddens me that there is so little encouragement for artists still working there. I was happy to return to Honiara in 2007, where I was able to speak to groups of artists, and also to work with school children during one of their art classes in a middle school. Art is part of the curriculum in school now, which was not the case when I was growing up. I feel a sense of responsibility to return home, and at present, am applying for funding from numerous sources to enable me to return to Honiara to conduct workshops to teach specific skills, like printmaking.

Details of my paintings have appeared on websites in the Solomons. The issue of copyright is one of the things that I should like to address through an artists' workshop, because I don't think it is understood that permission should be requested before a work of mine can be reproduced.

I have learned so much since I came to North America and have benefited from the technology that is so accessible here. It makes me even more aware of how few of these facilities exist in the Solomons. I feel very strongly that I want to bring about change and to act as a mentor to artists there.

Many of my works relate to ceremonial gatherings. In my culture, there are ceremonies for almost every occasion. They provide an opportunity for people to get together and keep cultural values alive.

Art in North America is viewed differently than in the Solomons. At home, art is created for ceremonial purposes and to keep the continuity of stories throughout generations, whereas art is made for pleasure and investment in North America.

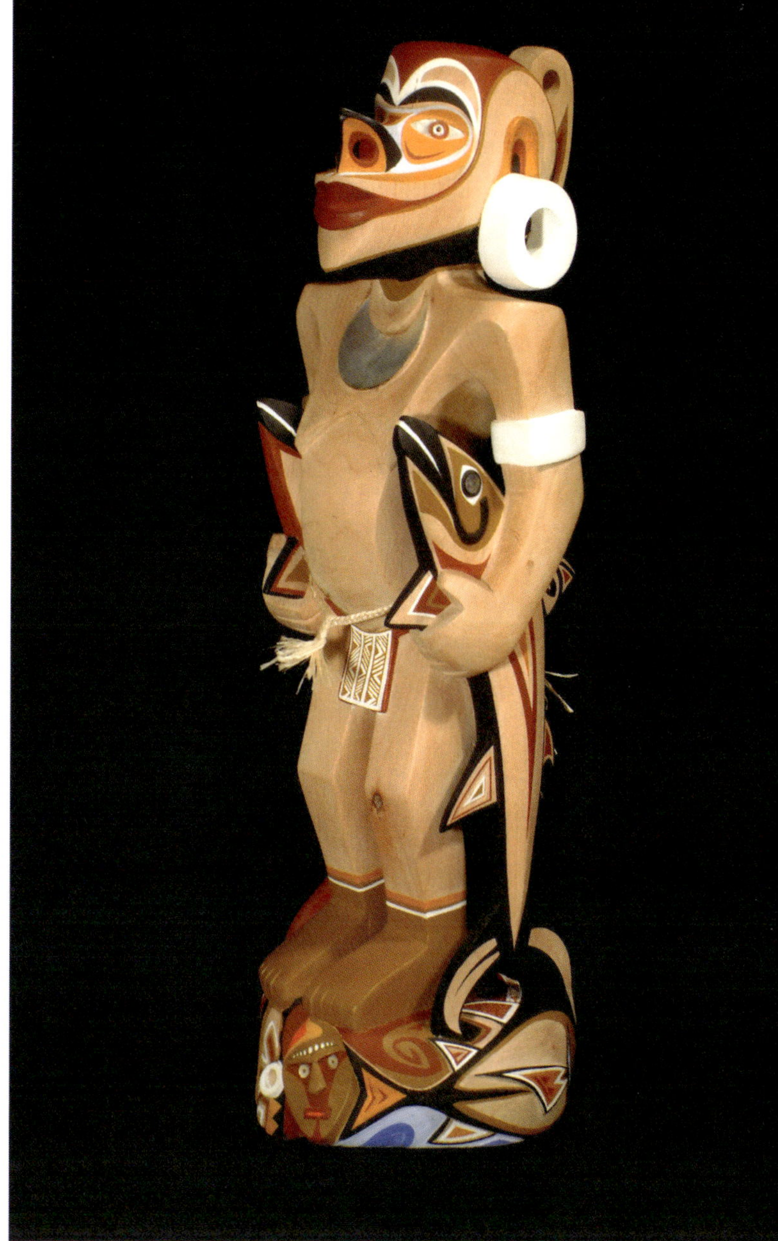

Figure 13.2. *Shark God*, Alder, abalone, mother of pearl, and paint, 26.6" x 8.5" (diameter at base), 2008. Photograph by Dan Lepsoe, courtesy of Alcheringa Gallery.

Through my studies in Canada, I have learned different techniques and approaches, and these are reflected in my work. However, when I create my art, I feel strongly that I am making it not just for myself, but also to help promote and protect my cultural values.

Wood carvers surround me where I live on Vancouver Island. As a result of their influence, I have recently been drawn back to carving, the art of my ancestors [fig. 13.2].

> Throughout many islands in the Solomon Islands, early history is told through myths and legends. In the early days, the coastal people depended on the ocean for survival and seafaring activities. It is believed that they held special connections with the sea and the spirit it holds within. Many tales tell that shark worshipping was a common practice among the islanders.
>
> This sculpture represents the totem of a shark tribe, which you would see in the waters or on the beach outside of the village. This totem would warn any outsiders of the tribe's connection with the sharks and the protection the sharks provide.
>
> Animal totems are important to the people of the Solomon Islands. A tribe will hold special ceremonies to show their appreciation and allegiance to their totems. There are very few tribes who consider themselves the descendents of

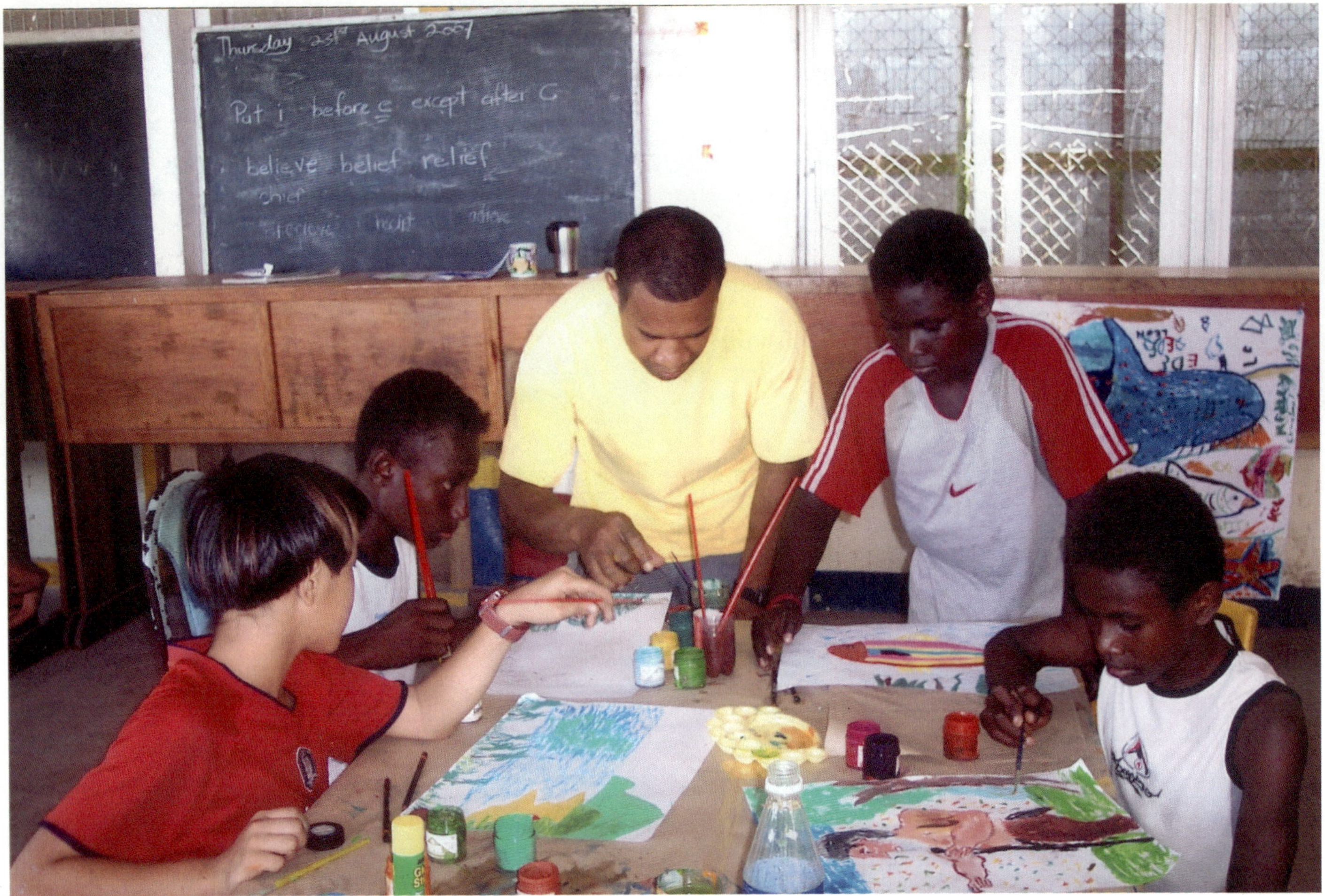

Figure 13.3. Ake Lianga with students in Honiara. Photography courtesy of the artist.

sharks. Tribes will hold sacrificial ceremonies where they will provide an offering before asking the sharks to assist them with a special task, such as protection from another tribe. On his deathbed, a chief of this tribe will predict his future appearance in the form of a shark.

The base of the sculpture depicts the changing of a person into the shark form. The turtle is always present and is the peacekeeper of the ocean. The two fish held by the Shark God represent the balance of power in the ocean, and are also symbolic of the plentiful fish the ocean provides for the future generations.

My next exhibition will focus primarily on sculpture. Living in a place where the carving had disappeared and is now experiencing a revival has inspired me to take up my carving tools again to reinterpret some of our old traditional forms. The further I am away from it, the more I value our carving tradition. Seeing the work brings back memories from earlier days. I am the only member of my family who has carried on the tradition since my grandparents. Seeing the disappearance of carving skills, I feel a responsibility to keep it alive.

To carve a bowl now is an art form; once it was a part of the culture. Now, when a ceremonial offering is made, containers of western materials are used. In the past, master carvers were commissioned to create works for ceremony, but with the passing of the elders, many of the stories that inspired these events have been lost.

To honour my grandfather, I have chosen to create a bowl using garamut wood from home. He used to carve bowls that were used to mark the passing of land rights to the next generation. They also represented generosity and a sharing of knowledge. On visits home, I treasure every moment that I spend back in the culture, and I want to share my knowledge with the next generation [fig. 13.3].

Since coming to Canada, I have significantly advanced my career in ways that would not have been possible had I stayed in the Solomons. It is to the credit of my instructors and fellow students at North Island College, Alcheringa Gallery, and my wife Diane that I have been able to learn new creative techniques and applications as well as the technical business aspects for which I was not prepared.

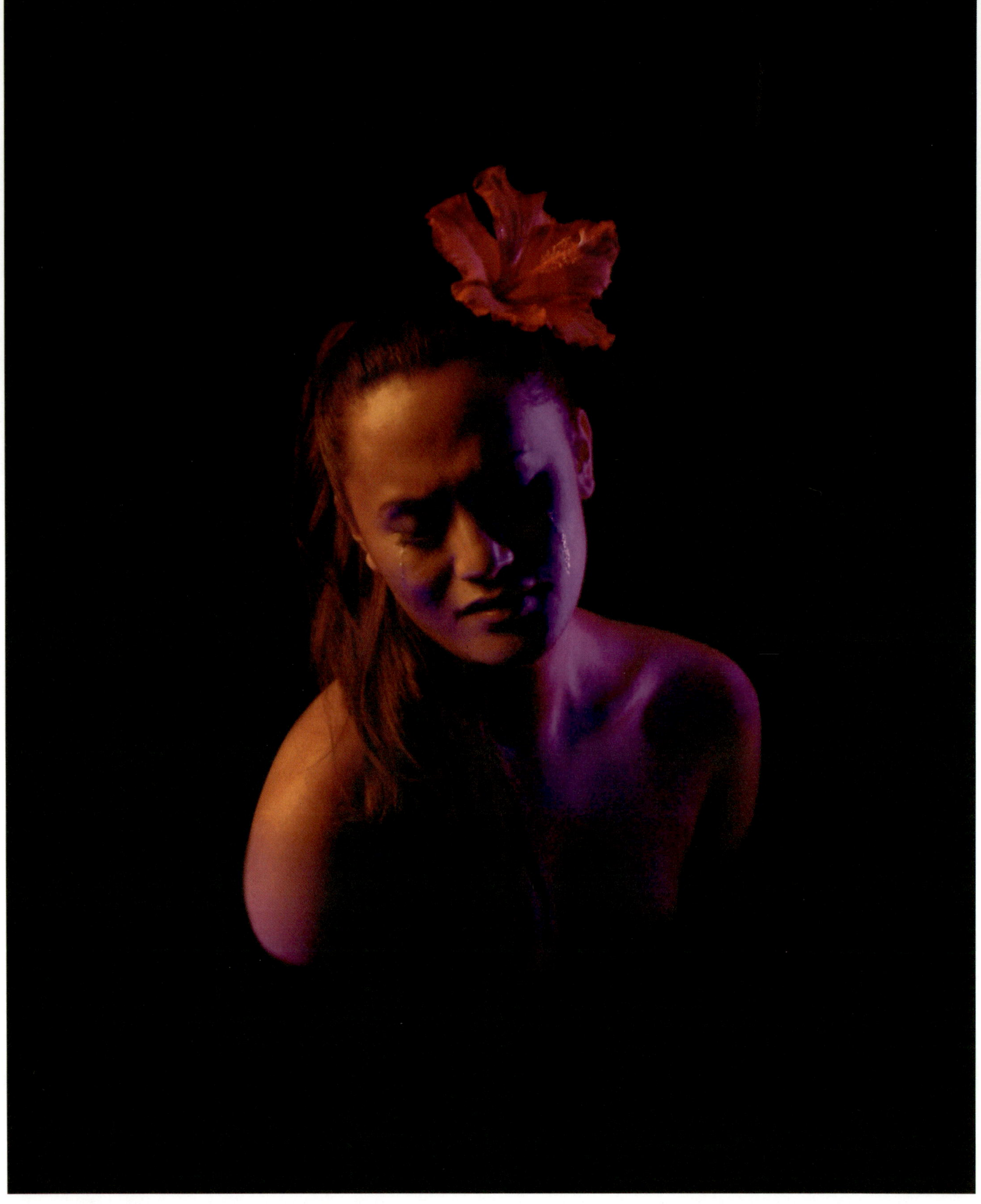

Figure. 14.1. *Le loimata o Apaula; Tears of Apaula* (Dip tyck), 80cm x 60cm, Mixed media and Photography. Courtesy of Photographer Sean Coyle and Artist Shigeyuki Kihara.

Shigeyuki Kihara, An Interview with Jim Vivieaere

It's mid morning, Wednesday 29th September 2004, and I have an appointment to interview Shigeyuki Kihara at my house. I've made an event of it, kind of dressed up, styled the kitchen table with a potted flowering antherium and lemons and bananas and unripe mangoes. The jug has boiled and I've placed teacups and saucers and made a plate of small glazed boysenberry and fresh strawberry flans.

My first encounter with Kihara's work was at a Wellington fashion show in the late 90's. As a student she presented a collection made remarkable by the models and the Asiatic details on her garments. Then years later she had an exhibition at Archill Gallery in Auckland, Adorn to Excess, twenty six monogrammed T-shirts, vacuum packed and sitting like frozen foodstuffs in a hired supermarket freezer.

Now we are neighbours, 5 minutes away, maybe longer from her place, as it's a steep up hill climb. Yuki arrives. She's been partying the night before and assures me that she's in the right space to undergo interrogation, slightly hung over and open for shop. In fact she suddenly excuses herself rushes off to the Dairy at the top of the street to buy a toothbrush and toothpaste and a couple of litres of orange juice. Settled and seated at the table we 'do' morning tea and alternately hum and hah into a dinky hand size recording system.

J. Good morning Yuki, you realize that my intention for interviewing you is to give Hawaii some insight into which you are as an artist. Maybe you could give a general outline of your involvement in the arts; tell me a story.

Y. I received an email from Rosanna Raymond telling me about this conference that was taking place in Hawaii, and then I was contacted by Pamela Rosi who invited me to attend and be part of the forum. I was really interested in some of the issues that were going to be presented and felt that they reflected a lot of my personal views and inquiries into my own practice.

I suppose I see myself as a multimedia artist. In 2000 I made a commitment to become a fulltime artist (which coincided with me shifting to Auckland). I've had to supplement this direction by working in various other disciplines, fashion, theatre and performance related work and usually in the background under the supervision of others. In fashion shoots, working as a fashion stylist, I work collaboratively with the creative team and the magazine editor who selects the fashion editorial.

When it comes to my own photographic artwork I have learnt the process and I'm the one in control. What I can't do in a fashion editorial is what I do in my own artwork.

J. What I find interesting about who you are as an artist is perhaps the ethnic and cultural ties that define you. Born in Samoa, a Samoan mother and Japanese Dad; bought up in Samoa, Indonesia, Japan and New Zealand. I think as an artist you've got lots to share, beyond those boundaries. What kind of work are you going to show in Hawaii?

Y. I'm going to show my recent work called *Vavau — Tales of Ancient Samoa* [figs. 14.1-14.5], which was my first solo exhibition at the Bartley Nees Gallery in Wellington (July 2004). Some works from this show were selected for *Prospect 2004*, the Biennial survey of contemporary art in New Zealand held at the City Gallery Wellington. I guess I am considered as one of 50 artists that are making waves in New Zealand.

What was interesting with the marketing of this work is that my art dealer deliberately selected the month to show my work to be aligned with the group exhibition at the City Gallery Wellington. This dual exhibition serves to impact the arts community and the buyers in raising the standard and credibility of my work as an artist and also creating hype around it. It's a logical strategy for any dealer to maximize the moment.

J. Are you empowered or influenced by the work of say artists like Cindy Sherman or Yasumasa Morimura who practice this genre of photographically imaging themselves, mimicking or morphing into other characters.

Y. Yes I know who they are, but I don't really identify with their work. As a child and even now I look at photos of myself and wonder how my life would have been if I wasn't a Fa'a fafine/transgender, or what my life would have been if I had lived in one country,

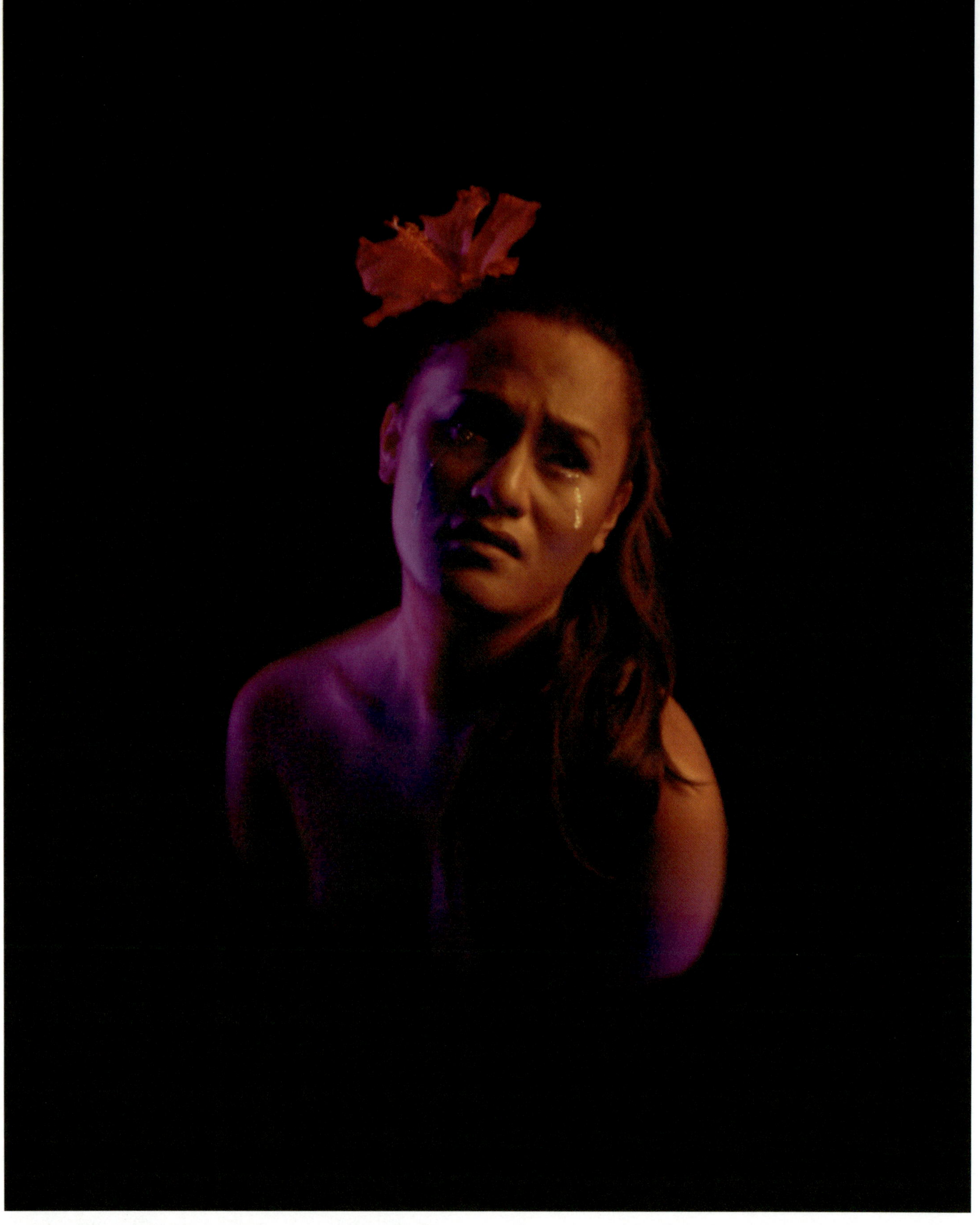

Figure. 14.2. *Le loimata o Apaula; Tears of Apaula* (Dip tyck), 80cm x 60cm, Mixed media and Photography. Courtesy of Photographer Sean Coyle and Artist Shigeyuki Kihara.

assumed one gender, experienced one culture, one religion and spoke one language.

My life has multiple facets and in principle I can be every thing all at once. What I like about my *Vavau* work is that I am basically telling a story, and of course, I end up taking on a variety of guises in order to realise the different narratives. By imaging myself as a Samoan, it was an opportunity for me to connect with my Samoan heritage and ancestry. There was a time when I didn't really acknowledge or understand that I was Samoan. My family shifted to Indonesia after I was born until I was 5 years old. We then went to live in Japan until I was 12, back to Samoa, then coming to New Zealand when I was 16.

J. Who are you talking to as an audience; your friends, the Samoan nation, I wonder who you are telling this story to?

Y. I'd like to think that I'm speaking to everybody even though my work extends from a Samoan cultural platform. I do believe that a lot of the issues that I speak of in the artwork are universal. If some people don't like it or don't get it then it's fine with me. The Samoan elders who have contributed by telling me the folklore have supported and appreciated my photographic work, so I think I've done my job.

J. I saw a great exhibition the other day, Martin Ball's super large canvasses, oil paintings of John Pule, Lisa Reihana, Ralph Hotere and Elizabeth Ellis. A palagi painting Polynesians. I ask the same rhetorical question, who'd buy them? Such incredible dexterity and draughtsmanship, I guess he probably gets commissions.

With regards to your portraits Yuki, being the creative mind and all, you don't actually press your finger on the shutter; you work collaboratively with a technician. Dumb question, is he recognized as partly responsible for your work?

Y. The photographic work that I've been doing is a collaborative process. I'm very much reliant on other people's capabilities when conceiving my work. I mastermind and fund the project and feel that I have the right to claim it as my own artwork. I have an agreement with my photographer that if the work gets published that he gets credited. I could say that the photographer is in part, one of my 'tools' for making my work

J. What sets you apart is that you're more than the sum of the parts. You started studying to be a dress/clothes designer that veered into making art; your T-shirt installation, screen-printed canvasses, photographs and then quite recently your performance work with the Pacific divas. Do you make a separation between your performances and your other work — your photos for example?

Y. I feel that there is a strong link between my visual art and my physical performance work, because a lot of my performances are informed by the critique of my visual art so they do reflect each other. When I'm doing a performance the music, gesture, emotion and movement is centred on an artwork that I have already made or am thinking about making.

J. It was good timing that Ann D'Alleva witnessed your performance at the Den Adult Store and I understand that she and Rosanna are delivering a paper in Hawaii referencing your work. In fact Rosanna is creating a performance piece; I wonder if she'll get a chance to see Markarita Urale's brilliant documentary beforehand. What do you think of Rosanna's intentions?

Y. It's quite an honour that the performance has affected some people, even now people are still talking about it. However, I have no control of people responding to what I do.

J. I remember being at a conference in Wellington "Under Capricorn, Is art a European idea?" (1994) and Yasumasa Morimura gave a paper, obviously he didn't look like any of his personae, very conservative he had a black suit on and…

Y. Sounds like my Dad (giggles).

J. When you go to Hawaii, in principle you'll be a total stranger. Will you make your entrance as one of your characters?

Y. I think I'll walk in with my jandals and lavalava and be myself really. But in terms of a persona or a character, I'm in 'drag' everyday anyway.

J. I'm sure Hawaii will be looking forward to your appearance and...

Y. I hope so. I hope they love me. I'm sure that I'll love them.

J. I understand that you have a show at Sherman Gallery in Sydney next year. Is that going to be an extension of the works that you'll be showing in Hawaii?

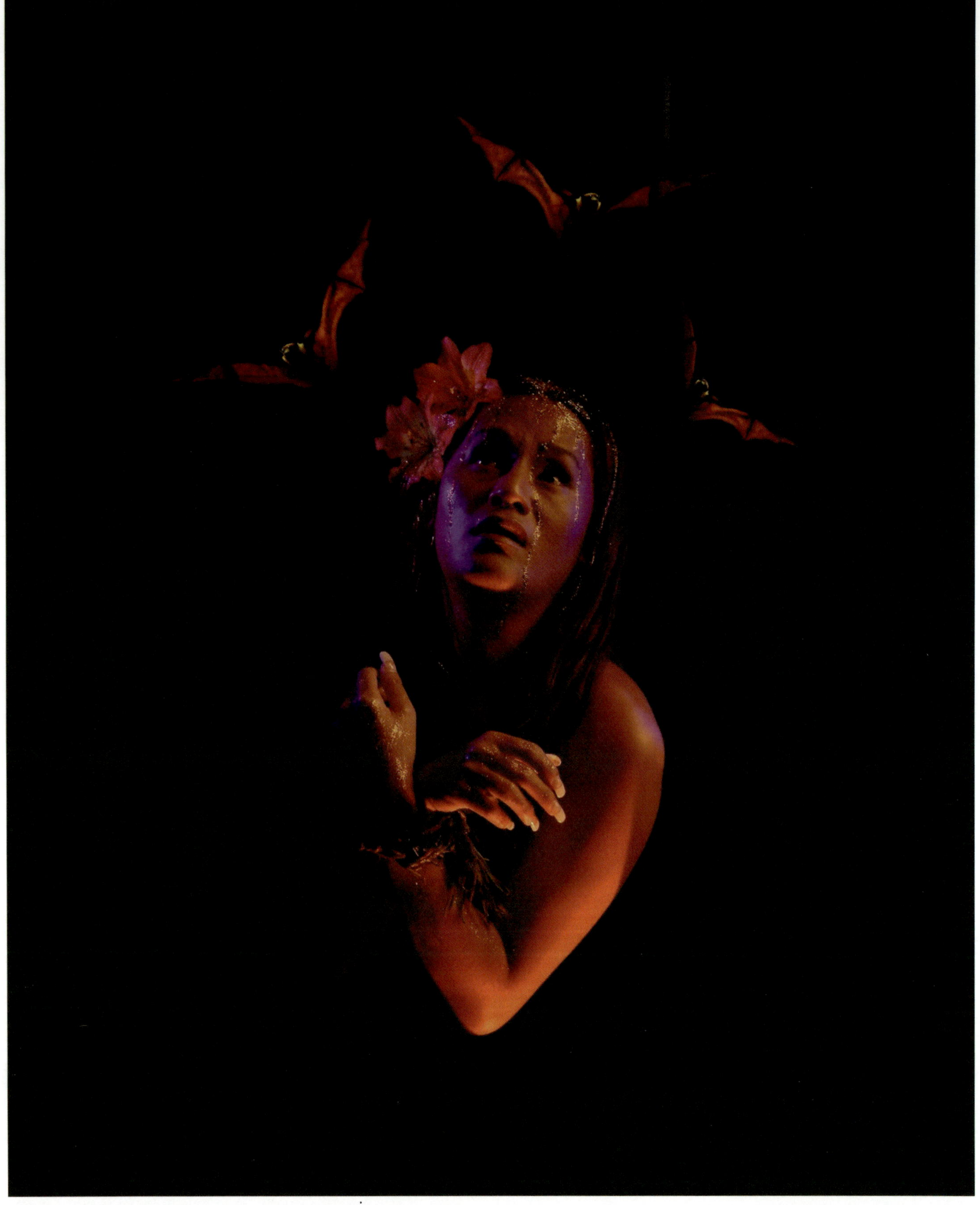

Figure. 14.3. *Tonumaipe'a; How she was saved by the bat*, 80cm x 60cm, Mixed media and Photography. Courtesy of Photographer Sean Coyle and Artist Shigeyuki Kihara.

Y. It is going to be photographs again, self-portraiture but different all together. This time I'm exploring ethnographic images of Samoans in the 19th century. In many ways I'm playing with issues of the European gaze.

J. Are you going to be using a lot of different characters — photoshopping? I recall Morimura's face being a piece of fruit in a French impressionist still life by Cezanne, Braque or Matisse.

Y. I'm going to mimic the poses that derive from these ethnographic postcards keeping in mind that a lot of the photographs were posed and structured around the orientalist art movement. I've been digging up a lot of information about this period. What, how and why this image making took place. Basically I want to come in and re-occupy the whole gaze issue and make it gutsier from what was formally romantic.

J. Maybe you'll do some research at the Bishop Museum.

Y. Oh yes it will be great.

J. Yuki as a young, emerging career driven Polynesian artist, have you any marketing strategies. Your movement in the art world is contingent on having a dealer. Do galleries sell your work, how many dealers have you got?

Y. I have three dealer galleries so far. Bartley Nees in Wellington, Whitespace in Auckland and most recently Sherman Galleries in Sydney. How I manage things is that I make a distinctive body of work for each gallery. For obvious reasons, dealers don't like leftovers that have been shown at other galleries. Because I'm bursting with ideas I see myself as an ideas machine; making new work is not a problem. I just need time and the money! Having dealers in three different cities I'm able to tap into a new audience and market as well and it allows me to have an excuse to travel to my openings and meet up with friends.

J. Because you're multi-dimensional multi-talented lots of multis...

Y. (Laughter)

J. Not only are you marginalized on ethnic levels but also gender levels. This kind of characteristic that you were born with or that you've engineered, is it something that you have to work with or against, in terms of your art practice. You've been in frivolous beauty contests and serious film documentaries. Do you make a separation?

Y. The only thing I don't do is to sensationalise and bull shit about it. What I am is what you get and I'm not going to change anything for anyone just because they feel insecure about what I am and what I do. I also wish that people would see the art for what it is rather than it being marginalized. When white artists have an exhibition people go along and see art for what it is, but when you're not White, not straight and not a man people immediately perceives your art as something political. I remember one time walking into a dealer gallery, seeking representation, showing them my artwork, and the director of the gallery said, "I'm not interested in your work as we are only interested in contemporary New Zealand art" and I replied by saying "then what is contemporary New Zealand art?" and he couldn't answer my question.

I do get these attitudes as though I'm bracketed as queer, and that my work could be construed as lowbrow. I do feel that there are things working against me. But I feel resolved about my work, and what I do and I can't change it and I've learnt to deal with other people's indifference and not take it so seriously.

Every year I'm invited to the various arts schools in Auckland to give lectures to the students, which I really enjoy, it gives me the opportunity to tell my story, my journey...

J. As you were talking I was thinking of the performance artist Luke Roberts. These personas "Pope Alice"... Will you make films? It's photography now... maybe acting...

Y. I went to Fashion Design School not Fine Art School. So I've been involved in a similar creative activity but a different industry I'm bringing all those experiences into my current practice. Where am I going now?...Video is something I would like to become involved in. When I imagine an artwork for the photos it's like imagining a still from a movie and I'm the lead actor of this film. I've done female impersonations on stage in clubs and would imagine myself as a character from a movie or from a music video. I watch a lot of movies and MTV and I'm constantly inspired to do something similar. Pope Alice? Fantastic. Oh there is the Cremaster series as well. Being aware of all these things makes me want to do my own versions.

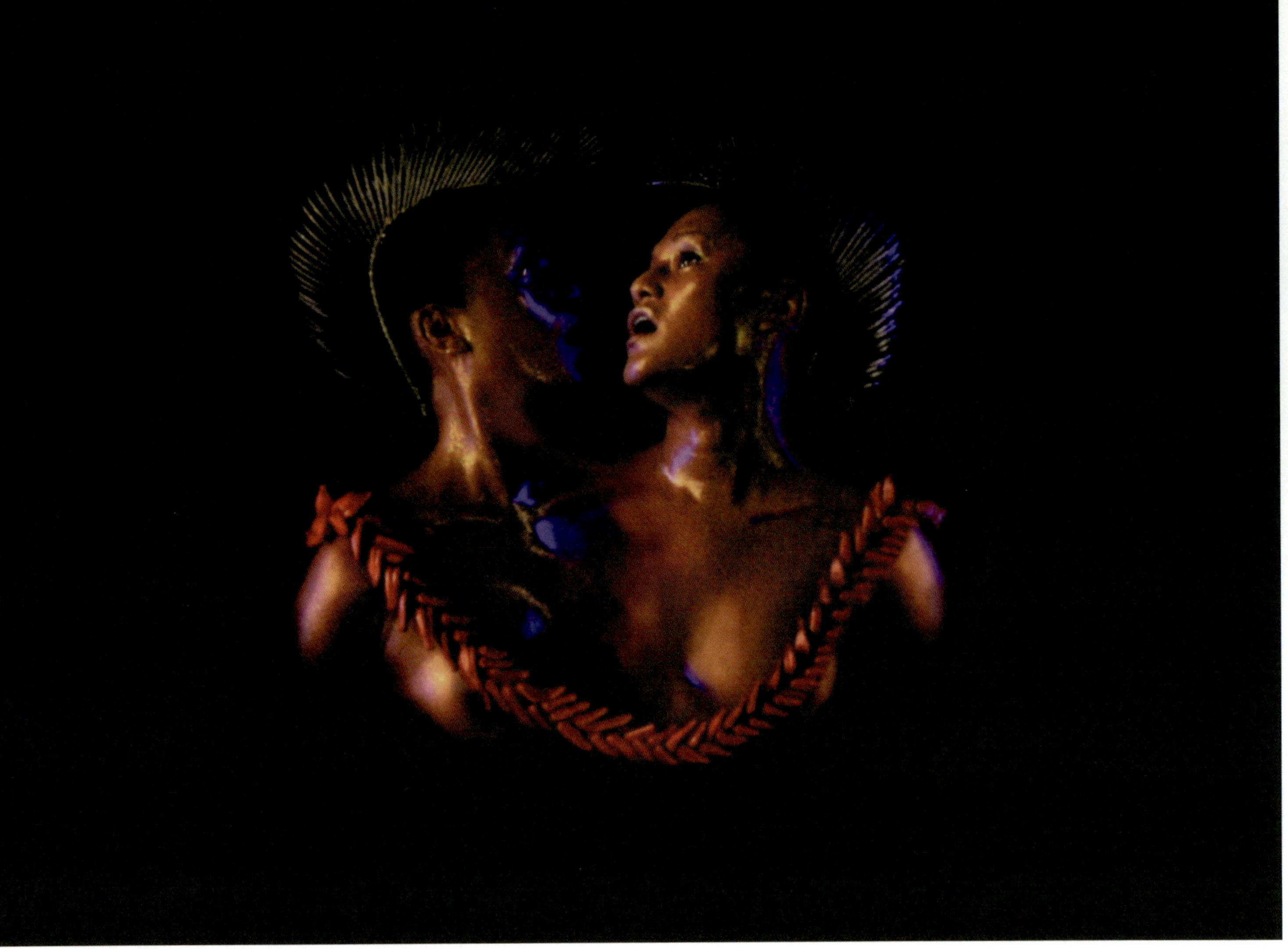

Figure. 14.4. *Taema ma Tilafaiga; Goddesses of Tatau*, 90cm x 70cm, Mixed media and Photography. Courtesy of Photographer Sean Coyle and Artist Shigeyuki Kihara

J. I'm thinking of Tracey Moffat's photographic work as well. Are you looking forward to going to Hawaii? Are there people that you need to connect with?

Y. I am looking forward to meeting other participating Pacific Island artists at the conference. I really think it is important to connect and share about what we are doing, and to encourage each other to keep on doing what we do.

J. I look forward to seeing you when you get back. I wish you all the best.

In 2008, The Metropolitan Museum of Art, New York, acquired two of Kihara's works for their permanent collection. Following that Shigeyuki Kihara had her first solo museum exhibition in North America at The Metropolitan Museum of Art entitled, *Shigeyuki Kihara; Living Photographs.* This was a survey of her early art practice. On exhibit from 7 October 2008-1 February 2009, this exhibition surveyed her early art practice from 2002 till 2006.

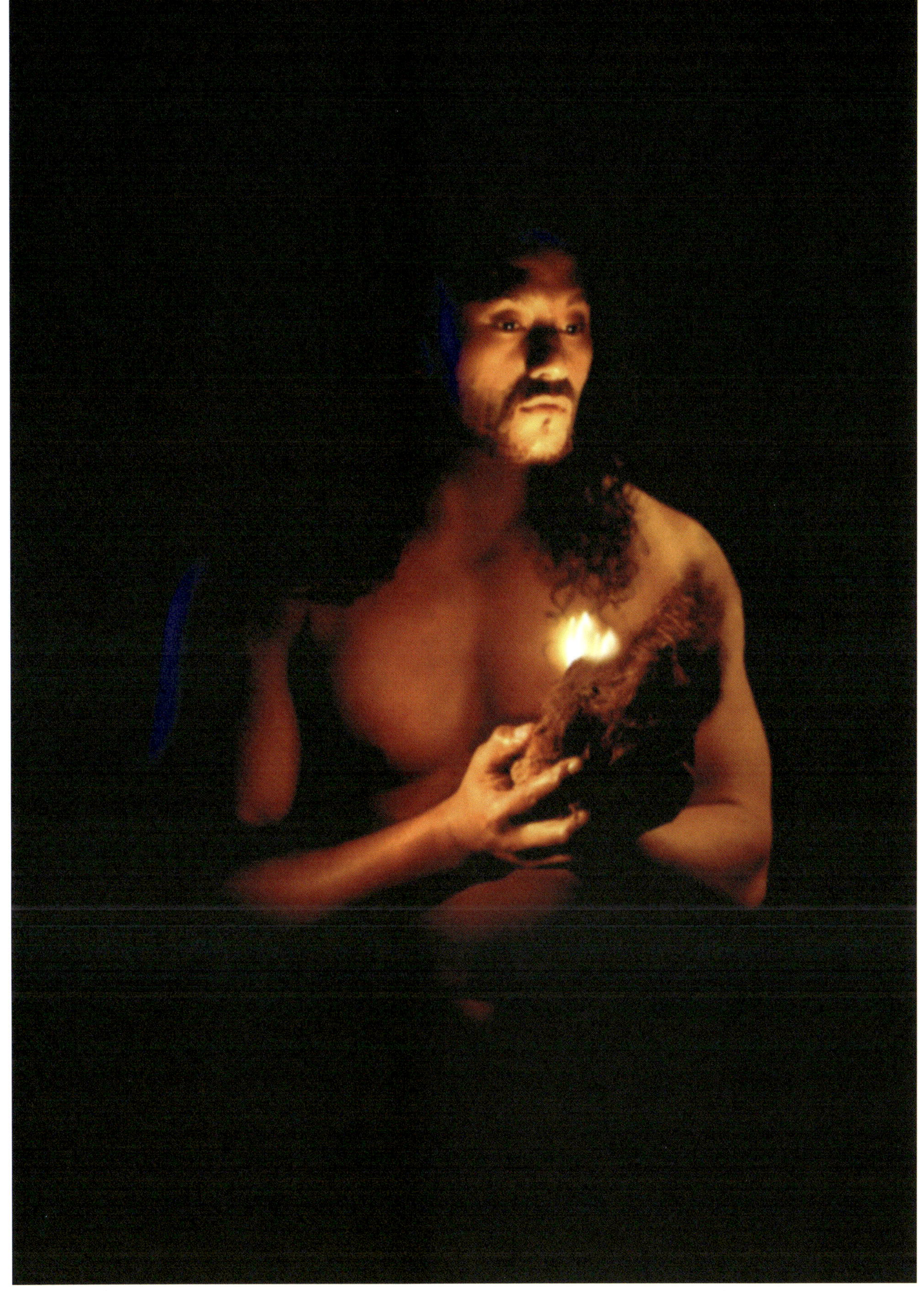

Figure. 14.5. ***Maui Ti'eti'e Talaga; Maui and the first fire of Samoa***, 80cm x 60cm, Mixed media and Photography. Courtesy of Photographer Sean Coyle and Artist Shigeyuki Kihara.

Konousi (Koni) Aisake, an Interview with Alan Howard

Konousi (Koni) was born on the isolated island of Rotuma in 1960. Konousi left Rotuma for Fiji at age 14 and attended D.A.V. Boy's College in Suva. He worked for the Blue Lagoon Cruise Company for ten years until 1987 and was one course short of attaining an inter-island master's certificate when the coup overthrowing the Fiji Government occurred. He met his future wife, Sandra, in 1985, and they married on 14 November 1987. After the second coup, they emigrated to Canada. For ten years, Konousi worked in a stained glass factory where he learned the art of making stained glass. In 1996, he set out on his own as a self-taught woodcarver and maker of art objects from stained glass.

A. You were born and raised on Rotuma and lived in the rather remote village of Fapufa. What was it like as a child growing up there?

K. As a child growing up in remote village, I had a great life. I enjoyed fishing, farming, and trapping. I most enjoyed going out on my own to see new places that I hadn't been to before. Somehow, my parents knew that I was different from my brothers and sisters, and I was.

A. Were you artistic as a child?

K. As a child I had no idea that I had artistic talent. It was just our way of life, being around Dad. In 1990, I started creating art and found it fulfilling to come up with something that I created. It took me back to my childhood days.

A. Was there anything in your childhood that influenced you to become the artist you are today? Was there anyone in your family, or any teachers, who particularly influenced your artistic development?

K. I looked up to my dad and know how blessed I am for the knowledge that he gave me. When you have little money, creativity is the key, like learning how to build a traditional house, or mixing coral to build a stronger house.

A. After leaving school, you spent 10 years working with the Blue Lagoon Cruise Company out of Lautoka. Did you have any opportunities during this period to express yourself artistically?

K. During my ten years with the Blue Lagoon Cruise, working with ropes was the only creative thing I got to do — making fenders, rope nets, and many different kinds of knots.

A. What would you say are the dominant artistic traditions on Rotuma?

K. The dominant artistic traditions in Rotuma are dance and mat weaving.

A. In what ways do you see your art as consistent with these traditions? In what ways do you see your work as different from them?

K. The difference is in the way I express my work; it is to show my people that we can bring back this type of skill [woodcarving], which has been lost for some time, so we can get in touch with our roots. The gift is always there, and the time has come to do something about it.

A. How did you happen to get a job in a stained glass factory in Canada? How did this influence your artistic development?

K. I found an ad in the local paper looking for someone who was willing to learn about decorative glass known as stained glass. All I knew then was I needed to restart my life. I first started working in the putty room; after glass doors and windows are built, putty is packed in to hold the glass pieces in place. As the company grew, I was chosen to start up the double-glazing section. Double-glazing involves using two pieces of clear glass to protect the stained glass unit. In 1989, the company grew again and bought a master glass machine that had numeric controls for making incisions. The software used a CAD program that was copied to a floppy disk for the machine to use. The program was made for particular designs on particular sizes and thicknesses of glass. To do this correctly you had to calculate the co-ordinates for the placement of the design on the glass. You also had to calculate the depth for the grooves of the diamond wheel(s) and the polishing wheel(s). These calculations had to be precise so glass wouldn't break, and so flaws and un-joined lines wouldn't happen because they are very visible on glass. I personally designed a test program that ran the master glass machine. This test allowed me to tell the machine how I wanted the etching to be done, and what groove size I wanted on that particular thickness of glass. I was also responsible for sand blasting. This included training, solving problems, and supervision. If the design is blasted incorrectly on the pieces of glass, it won't work out. I taught workers how to cut glass. From this work, I gained an understanding of glass and admiration for it. The color of stained glass and its beauty influenced me a lot in my artistic development.

A. After you left the stained glass factory in 1996 you started woodcarving in addition to making items out of stained glass. You have described yourself as a "self-taught" woodcarver. What inspired you to take up woodcarving?

K. I was deeply drawn to and inspired by how the American Indians have struggled to hold on to their culture, especially knowing that the art of woodcarving has been almost forgotten by my people. I knew I had to do something about it before it was too late.

A. How did you learn the art of woodcarving?

K. I learned woodcarving by using a few good ideas from books, which I made work. I knew that I was good with my hands, so I just worked at it. And listening to Rotuman music helped along in the process.

A. What equipment and materials do you use?

K. The only special tools I use are a box-cutter knife, very few carving chisels, a drill and a sander. Ninety-nine percent of my work is done manually. I believe that this way I can use my good energy to give my work life. Yellow cedar is the wood that I use mostly for carvings. It's not as cheap as other wood, but it is the best for carvings.

A. Can you tell me something about the technique you use?

K. My technique is to draw a picture on a piece of cardboard, then transfer it to a piece of wood. Then I cut out the shape before carving.

A. How long did it take before you felt like you had mastered the art?

K. It took me five years. When I compare my earlier carvings to those I do today, I can tell that I've improved. Designs that took me hours to complete no longer take that much time. I feel that I still have a lot to learn before I'll be a master in woodcarving.

A. How does your carving style reflect your life experiences as a Rotuman?

K. I started carving as a gift to my dad. The goal was to spread his name and to create a smile and joy in anyone with an interest in art. My style of carving reflects my family history and Rotuma. For example, my preferred designs are tropical fish. There are some bad fishing practices going on in Rotuma today. I am trying to bring fish artwork into Rotuman households in Rotuma, and hope that this will lead to people fishing in a different way and with a better understanding.

The designs I use are my own and the carvings tell a lot about my family, and about Rotuma.

Konousi uses a variety of symbols, many drawn from Rotuman culture, in his work. He provided the following set of signs that appear on his artwork and their meaning (see opposite page).

A. What objects that you create give you the most satisfaction? What are your inspirations for making these objects?

K. Working with coconut shells brings me the most satisfaction. It's an interesting material that I can bend and fold in any shape I want. But you must have respect for it because it can break. It teaches me about life — that there's a limit to every life form and one must know when and how to stop going further. It's also easy for my people to relate to, and it's something that is Rotuman. That brings me a lot of pride.

A. How often have you returned to Rotuma? Do your visits affect your art in any way?

K. So far my family has been to Rotuma four times in seventeen years. My plan is to visit Rotuma every five years with my wife and children, but because of the cost of flying, and arranging time off from school and work, it is getting harder. If we could, we would visit Rotuma every year. Being home inspires me and grounds me. Every time I visit Rotuma it makes me proud to see my artwork everywhere I look. That gives me determination to do more. I do hope that some day I'll have more time to express my art and points of view there. My plan is to open a studio in Rotuma someday.

A. When you are selling to Canadians or other non-Pacific buyers, do you have a sense of whether they

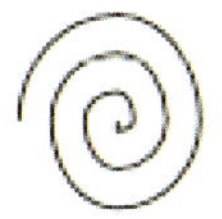
This is how I see life;
it starts small and continues

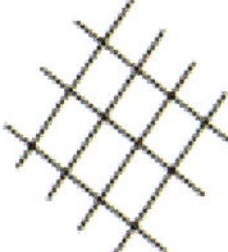
These lines come from
a human hand

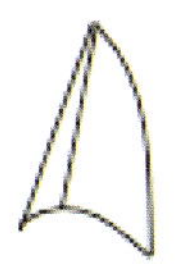
Main sail of a sailboat;
shows that I used to have a life
out at sea

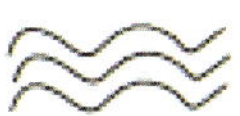
The sea

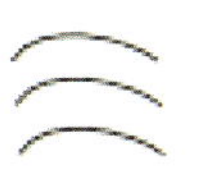
Hani
si = Hanisiof
of

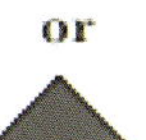
Means how many kids in my
Dad's family or my own

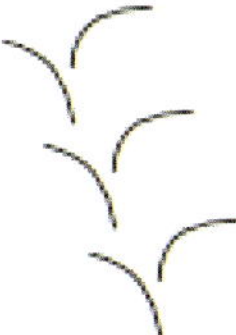
Birds

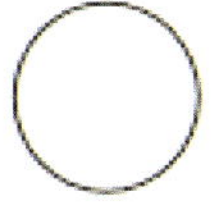
Circle of life: living creatures
need one another to create a life

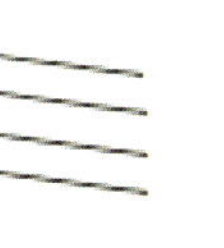
Sometimes I use these lines to
tell how many hours or days I
spent on a piece

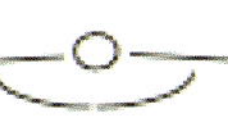
Sunrise (mostly seen as an eye)

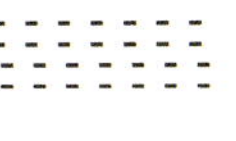
Reflections of light on a nice calm
day at sea, or at night

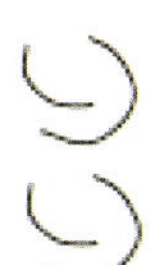
Waves breaking

buy your work for its artistic properties (they like how it looks) or because of what it represents? Do you specifically represent your work to customers as Rotuman art?

K. People buy my work because they like how different my work is compared to that of others. Usually a buyer wants to know who I am and where Rotuma Island is on the world map. I tell them to search the Internet for Rotuma Island. I specifically tell them my work is Rotuman art.

A. Do you have any idea of how many sales of your work have resulted from the display on the Rotuma website (http://www.rotuma.net/)?

K. Yes. The Rotuma website plays a major role in my sales, especially among Rotumans. All I know is that three thousand plus carved coconut shell hair holders have been sold in Rotuma.

Endnotes

Introduction

1 In literature, an idealized concept of uncivilized man, who symbolizes the innate goodness of one not exposed to the corrupting influences of civilization. The noble savage is a dominant theme in the 18th century writings of Jean-Jacques Rousseau, and many associated Pacific Islanders with this concept.

2 The Tahitian women offered sexual favours to the early explorers in exchange for gifts, primarily, iron. The British termed this 'the old trade', whereas the Tahitians were acquiring a desired commodity. These antics, described in the journals, quickly became integrated into Britain's popular culture (see Denning 1992).

3 Each officer was required to maintain a journal of his voyage. These were first published and edited by Hawkesworth in 1773. In the 1960s, J.C. Beaglehole edited and published the journals of Cook and Banks, which inspired new interest in these explorers.

4 Cannibal Tours (O'Rourke 1987), is a cringingly honest depiction of tourism and the preconceived notions the west holds about Papua New Guinea.

5 These discussions were highlighted by publications from Nelson Graburn (*Ethnic and Tourist Arts of the fourth World*, 1976), and Adrienne Kaeppler (Polynesian Dance as Airport Art, 1977). Conversations about these issues were frequently a part of the Pacific Arts Association conferences and their subsequent publications. See Mead, Mead and Kernot, Hanson and Hanson, Rose and Dark, Anderson and Craig, and Herle, et al.

6 Anthropologists began to address issues of authenticity and the reinvention of tradition (see Hobsbawm, Linnekin, and Keesing), which led to further discussion concerning issues of identity. This in turn led to a period of self-reflection (see Clifford), as well as a critique on how Pacific peoples were 'represented' in print as well as in museum exhibitions. These debates changed many of the perceptions/misconceptions about the pacific.

7 Artificial Curiosities was the title of an exhibition of Cook era objects at the Bishop Museum in 1979. Cook and his men made a distinction between the artificial (man made) as opposed to the natural curiosities they collected.

8 Collecting the world and the beginning of the curio cabinet, which turned into the 'ethnographic museum' is detailed in M. Ames Cannibal Tours and Glass Boxes (1992).

9 This group offers a different take on the typical conference paper/presentation. Here a session organizer proposes a topic and interested parties meet annually over a 3-year period. During this time, much discussion takes place and there is a large give and take as the participants realize what issues are prevalent and which ones are unique to their situation.

10 See Keesing and Tonkinson (1982), Hobsbawm and Ranger (1983), Keesing (1989), and Linnekin (1991).

11 See Linnekin and Poyer (1990), Nero (1992), and Hereniko 1994. Kaeppler (1992) offers a concise summary of the key issues associated with Pacific arts.

12 The importance of women's arts in the Pacific has not had the recognition it deserves. Textiles, which were under the control of women, were the backbone of Pacific economy. For further information see Weiner, Bolton, Kaeppler and Teilhet-Fisk.

13 This is not to say that some PNG women artists do not achieve recognition. Some sell their works alongside the men at the markets, others have immigrated to or have found dealers Australia.

14 See Herle (2001), Raymond and Henare (2008) *Pasifika Styles* and Reed and Stevenson (2009) *Conversations Across Time.*

15 Creative New Zealand has done much to support the integration of contemporary Pacific art into the global art market. This has been seen in *Paradise Now?, Pasifika Styles,* and *Dateline.* They have also supported New Zealand's participation in the Venice Biennale and the Asia-Pacific Triennial.

16 Exhibitions and residencies have also been held in London, New Caledonia, San Francisco, Taiwan, and Vancouver.

17 For a compilation of many of these sources, see Stevenson 2008.

18 The following is a short list of the exhibitions, publications and residencies that have included Pacific art and artists. Alcheringa and October Gallery websites provide listings of their exhibitions and publications. Other key exhibitions were: *Paradise Now?* (New York), *Pasifika Styles* (Cambridge), *Turning Tides: Gender in Oceania* (San Diego), *Island Affinities* (Los Angeles), *Dateline* (Berlin), the *Asia Pacific Triennials* (Brisbane), the Pacific Arts Festivals, and various biennales across the Pacific. Residencies have been offered by the deYoung Museum (San Francisco), the Sainsbury Institute (Norwich), Museum of Anthropology (Vancouver), Jean-Marie Tjibaou Cultural Center (Noumea) and the Kaohsiung Museum (Taiwan).

Chapter 1

1 Whilst the term "indigenous" is often used to refer to the aboriginal peoples of land later settled and colonised by others — fourth worlds - and less to define national or majority identities, it also makes sense to use in reference to post-colonial societies, who have negotiated independence often through recourse to similar discourses of sovereignty, priority and native nationhood. In addition, Pacific islanders connect across these different national contexts, forging links that unite islanders in a different category to later migrants to islands, frequently using the term indigenous (see Kalinoe 2004:passim). For instance in Vanuatu, whilst ni-Vanuatu citizenship may include people of French, British, Vietnamese and Chinese descent — there is a strong discourse of indigeneity that delineates exclusive fundamental connections between people and place, which often in turn give exclusive rights to identify with images and identities. The transition of these local identities into national ones remains instructive to fourth world claims to certain kinds of citizenship as do the slippery boundaries between indigenous and national identities, as Kuper (2002) notes.

2 See Helmreich (2005) for a fascinating discussion of indigeneity and being native in relation to plant species in Hawaii.

3 Sero Kuautonga, talking in Port Vila, 11 July, 2001, translated from Bislama.

4 Nelson Rockefeller 1979, speaking at the opening of the Rockefeller wing at the Metropolitan Museum of Art, New York.

5 Michael Busai, ni-Vanuatu artist, author interview Port Vila, 11 July 2001.

6 Translated by myself from Bislama, the national lingua franca of Vanuatu 16 August, 2000.

7 Despite the emphasis on indigeneity, the Coat of Arms itself was taken from a colonial etching, originally representing a ni-Vanuatu family: man, woman and child (see Jolly 1997).

8 Nawita presents itself like this primarily in the international arts arena. For instance, during the year 2000, Nawita was involved in several international and wide ranging projects ranging from participation in the 6th Festival of Pacific Arts, the 8th Pacific Arts Association meeting, a calendar of women artists from around the world, and an international Francophone exhibition to be held in Canada, as well as the development of several workshops and projects within Vanuatu.

9 Linda Bayer, personal communication, 2000.

10 Taken from the New Traditions web page: http://arts.anu.edu.au/arcworld/vks/exhib.htm accessed December 05, 2005.

11 This was funded by the New Zealand Government, organised in conjunction with the Pacific Development and Conservation Trust and the Australian Government.

12 These were: *Origins* (the creation of the people and the land of Vanuatu), *Darkness* time (the period prior to the arrival of traders and missionaries), *Missionisation* (from 1839 — to the early part of the twentieth century), Depopulation (following the arrival of traders and missionaries, the population of some Vanuatu islands was radically reduced through disease), *Blackbirding* (from 1863 to 1094, thousands of ni-Vanuatu were recruited to work on the sugar plantations of Queensland a practice known as blackbirding), *Condominium* (from 1906 to 1980 Vanuatu (then known as the New Hebrides) was jointly ruled by Britain and France, a period known as the Anglo-French Condominium., *World War II* (the New Hebrides was a major base for allied forces fighting in the battles of the Solomon Islands. Over 500,000 troops passed through Vanuatu during the war), *Independence and Nationhood* (Vanuatu became independent in 1980), *Development after Independence, The Future* (VCC 2000: 8).

13 Taken from the New Traditions web page: http://arts.anu.edu.au/arcworld/vks/exhib.htm, last accessed December 2, 2005.

14 Kake Buko, Port Vila, December 2000.

15 Author interview, in Port Vila, 11 July 2001.

Chapter 2

1 The Kriol noun kartiya refers to a person of European ancestry or, when used as an adjective, to any object, plant, animal, concept, or practice derived from Western as opposed to Aboriginal culture.

2 In writing this essay it must be noted that the majority of material presented here was not spontaneously volunteered but came in response to specific questions which I put to the artists such as: "Why do you think kartiya want Aboriginal paintings?", "What did you do at the exhibition?", or "How did you feel about seeing your paintings in the museum?" Hence, the particular topics chosen reflect my own research agenda and priorities more so than in much of my other East Kimberley research. The comments and perspectives in the responses, however, are entirely those of the artists.

3 This era of initial creation is frequently called the dreamtime in the literature and the term is occasionally used by Aboriginal Kriol speakers as well. However, most recent authors and Aboriginals prefer to use the word dreaming as this term reflects the Aboriginal belief that the supernatural power of the dreaming is an ongoing phenomenon that is not confined to a finite period in the distant past.

4 Jack Britten, interview July 2, 1996. This interview and all the other interviews with East Kimberley painters quoted in this essay were originally conducted in Aboriginal Kriol. For the sake of clarity, I have translated the artists' observations into standard English throughout.

5 The total population of the East Kimberley is approximately 6000 people of whom roughly 1800 are Aboriginal. Some East Kimberley Aboriginal painters describe Warmun (population ca. 400) as a "big city."

6 Freddie Timms, interview June 27, 1996 (emphasis original).

7 Rover Thomas, personal communication, 1996.

8 The Kriol term law denotes the sacred corpus of rules and customs established during the dreaming by which Aboriginal people are expected to live their lives and which governs their relations to other members of the group and the natural and supernatural worlds.

9 Peggy Patrick, interview August 1, 1998.

10 Hector Jandulu, interview July 28, 1998.

11 Queenie McKenzie, interview July 3, 1996.

12 Hector Jandulu, interview July 28, 1998.

13 Hector Jandulu, interview July 28, 1998.

14 Queenie McKenzie, interview July 22, 1998.

15 Shirley Purdie, interview June 26, 1996.

16 Shirley Purdie, interview June 26, 1996.

17 Shirley Purdie, interview June 26, 1996.

18 Shirley Purdie, interview July, 2000.

19 The annual rainy season, also called "The Wet Season" or simply "The Wet," which occurs between November and March.

20 Shirley Purdie, interview July, 2000.

21 Hector Jandulu, interview July 5, 1996.

22 Hector Jandulu, interview April 12, 1996.

23 Rover Thomas, personal communication, 1996.

24 Lorna Thomas, interview April 17, 1996.

25 Shirley Purdie, interview June 26, 1996.

26 Juju Wilson, interview April 17, 1996.

27 Two of Thomas' massacre paintings devoted to the killings at Ruby Plains, however, show the severed head of one of the massacre victims inside a hollow tree (see Thomas et al., 1994: 44-5, 60).

Chapter 3

1 However, this was not always and everywhere the case. As shown later in this article, early collectors of Humboldt Bay and Lake Sentani material culture were either not interested in, or unable to collect a substantial amount of barkcloth (Hermkens 2007a: 6-7). For example, in 1922 and 1926 the Swiss ethnographer Paul Wirz collected about 300 Sentani artefacts, which include only two pieces of painted barkcloth.

2 Fieldwork in Lake Sentani took place in 1996 and subsequently in 2009 when Dr. Muridan Widjojo travelled to Asei, assisting the author in conducting interviews with local artists on the topic of barkcloth paintings and gender. Fieldwork in Collingwood Bay took place from 2001 till 2002 and in 2004.

3 Agus Ongge, personal communication, Asei 1996.

4 Marta Ohee, interview with M. Widjojo, Asei 2009.

5 Marta Ohee, interview with M. Widjojo, Asei 2009.

6 Personal communication, Airara 2001.

7 Clifford Taniova, personal communication, Airara 2001.

8 Lina, personal communication, Airara 2001.

9 John Barker, personal communication, 2002.

10 Lina, personal communication, Airara 2001.

11 Personal communication. Airara 2001.

12 Monica Taniova, personal communication, Airara 2001.

Chapter 4

1 See Cecelia Perez, 1997: Introduction.

2 (Census 2000). Government of Guam Department of Commerce.

3 The spelling of "Chamorro" or "CHamoru" is contested. (The CH combination is a consonant in the Chamorro alphabet.) The latter spelling is preferred by activists. The author chooses to use the first spelling when writing in the English language and the latter spelling is used when writing in the CHamoru language; or to respect the preference of the interviewee or quoted writer.

4 Panel discussion, Guam Humanities Council Pacific Film Festival series, University of Guam. Mar 18, 2009.

5 See Pacific Daily News articles dated 24 Sept. 1967: 11; 18 Feb. 1973: 24; 21 Jan. 1977: 6; and 3 Aug. 1978: 4.

6 See Pacific Daily News 24 Apr. 1974: 13.

7 Interview with Alejandro Lizama, 1998.

8 Interview with Rob Limtiaco, 1996.

9 The South Pacific Arts Festival was held in Fiji in 1972 and New Zealand in 1976. The name was changed for the 1980 festival to the Festival of Pacific Arts. These festivals are held every four years in a different island nation.

10 Panel discussion, Guam Humanities Council Pacific Film Festival series, University of Guam. Mar 18, 2009.

11 Frank (Ko) San Nicolas interview, 1996.

12 Early missionary observations and archaeological records state that *Spondylis* beads were worn by high-caste women.

13 Interview with Frank (Ko) San Nicolas, 1996.

14 Interview with Frank (Ko) San Nicolas, 1996.

15 Interview with Frank (Ko) San Nicolas, 1996.

16 Both in formal interviews and in many casual conversations about the presence of taotaomo'na, people have referred to a feeling of intense chill when one is nearby. This chill raises the hairs on the skin, which has led to the use of the Chamorro term fugu' to describe the sensation. One interviewee playfully called this association with the taotaomo'na the "fugu' factor".

17 See also, Flores 2002.

18 See Firth 1973:18

19 Personal communication, Frank Rabon, 2004.

20 Benjie Santiago at the Intergenerational Conference on Chamoru Language and Culture, 1999.

21 Joe Peredo, at the Intergenerational Conference on Chamoru Language and Culture, 1999.

22 Bill Paulino at the Intergenerational Conference on Chamoru Language and Culture, 1999.

23 See Jolly, 1992:49.

Chapter 5

1 Bernard Narokobi, 1990: 20-21.

2 Although these questions are similar to the title of Gauguin's famous painting, Narokobi does not acknowledge he has drawn on this source.

3 The Creative Arts Center was funded by the Department of Education and the University of Papua New Guinea. In 1974, a large grant from Australia permitted the Center (renamed the National Arts School in 1976) to expand its facilities to include an exhibition hall, a theater, music and graphic design studios, and a production workshop. Funding for the National Arts School program held into the mid-1980s when, as the result of fiscal crises and devaluation of the kina, the government made severe cuts to its budget. By 1998, all public exhibitions were eliminated and, in 2000, the school was amalgamated into University of Papua New Guinea. See also Rosi 1994 and 2006.

4 The educational nationalism of Papua New Guinea's school system also encouraged Santana to include traditional designs and subjects linked to PNG customs and concepts of national identity in his work.

5. In 2005, Santana received a commission from the Vice-Chancellor of the University of Goroka for several large works. In 2006, 2007, and 2008 he sold several paintings (each priced at Kina 3,000 [$US 1,000]) at the annual Independence Day *Luk Save* exhibition at the Royal Yacht Club in Port Moresby.

6 Issue of copyright in Papua New Guinea has become increasingly political as owners of design motifs or dances have recognized that asking for compensation can be a profitable source of income. See J. Lewis-Harris 2006: 225-45.

7 Personal communication, Larry Santana, 1986.

8 Personal communication, Larry Santana, 1986.

9 January and February picture the mythic origins of the lake and how oil was used originally for body decoration. March and April depict the first white explorers taking oil samples, followed by boring of the first oil shafts. The images of the remaining months show the construction of the Chevron oil well and laying the main coastal pipeline after Independence. The message conveyed is that Chevron's oil production in Papua New Guinea must not destroy the natural environment or traditional PNG village life, but help preserve both through policies of environmental protection.

10 Personal communication, Larry Santana, 1998.

11 This painting is now lost. Santana told me (1986), it was executed in dark vibrant colors to symbolize grief and pain, and showed shadowy women magically inserting poisonous leaves into his father's body.

12 In 2009, there was only one-woman parliamentarian (Dame Carol Kidu) in the PNG national parliament.

13 Personal communication, Larry Santana, 1987.

14 Personal communication, Larry Santana, 2005.

15 As noted by Georgina Beier (1974), after Kauage built a settlement house his village wantoks moved in expecting him to support them. To stop this invasion of wantoks at the National Arts School, only wives and children could live with resident staff and artists.

16 This sentiment remains valid today. Several artists proposed that the government should re-established a Creative Arts Center because an open admission policy would enable artists from all levels of society to experiment with new techniques and media through educational workshops.

17 See Monds, this volume, on the importance of quality standards vis-à-vis the art market.

18 For further information see G. Beier (1974) and Rosi (1994, 1998a).

19 Bride price is a contentious issue in Papua New Guinea because modern demands now include goods and cash which puts a heavy burden on the husband's kin group to meet the costs collectively. When, as in Larry's situation, the husband is from an area where bride price is not traditionally

practiced, his relatives feel no obligation to meet the demands of strangers. Without his own relatives to protect him in Port Moresby, Santana was fearful of violent retribution in 1986.

20 Personal communication, Larry Santana, 2010.

21 Imagining Papua New Guinea as "paradise" is paradoxical since its traditional cultures are associated with headhunting and cannibalism. But the national symbol of Papua New Guinea is the Bird of Paradise; the in-flight magazine of Air Niugini is also named Paradise. Fantasies of a wild land of exotic flora and fauna with villagers living close to nature are promoted by the international tourist industry. Travel brochures and internet pictures depict beautiful island scenery and luxury tourist retreats whose architecture includes thatched roofs. These exotic stereotypes are contradicted by Pacific press reports of PNG urban violence, tribal fights, and growing threats of AIDS, poverty, and environmental destruction from mining and logging.

22 Personal conversation Pine Manor College, 1998.

23 The monthly Ela Beach Arts and Crafts Market became popular in the mid 1980's. Today, the variety of work displayed includes traditional and contemporary work from all regions of the country, facilitated by migration and island-mainland wantok connections. In addition to local nationals, expatriates, and tourists, art dealers from Australia buy for their shops and galleries. Embassy personnel and Government ministers also attend to buy work for their private collections and offices and to network with artists.

24 This exhibition was held at the Art Galleries, California State University, Northridge. See Rosi 2007b.

25 Teddy Balangu is a carver from the Iatmul people of the East Sepik River. He was featured in the 2007 Canadian documentary film Killer Whale and Crocodile. Michael Mel is a performance artist and Pro-Vice Chancellor of Goroka University, and the winner of the 2006 Prince Claus Award in Culture and Development. Cathy Kata is a textile artist from Goroka who creates bilums (looped string bags) and new bilum wear clothing. Martin Morububuna, from the Trobriand Islanders, is one of PNG's most celebrated painters.

26 Vol. 18, No. 2.

27 Larry Santana. Artist's Statement, Island Affinities: Contemporary Art of Oceania, 2007.

Chapter 6

1 Robert Davidson, Tony Hunt Jr., John and Luke Marston, Susan Point, Isabel Rorick, Ron Telek, Christian White, and others.

2 Among these are the University of British Columbia's Museum of Anthropology, the Museum of World Cultures in Germany, The Cultural Centre in Noumea, the Sculpture Garden at Stanford University, the Daetz-Centrum Museum in Germany, and the Musical Instrument Museum in Arizona.

3 Catalogues for most of these are in the archives at http://www.alcheringa-gallery.com/

Chapter 7

1 Salvage collecting was common at the end of the 19th century. Museums and anthropologists rushed to areas of colonization that were being disseminated by European contact in the belief that objects as cultural expressions were going to disappear. Such collecting was particularly prevalent in North America, Africa and the Pacific.

2 During a discussion about early collecting practices Emmanuel Kasarherou, Director of the Jean-Marie Tijbaou Cultural Centre in New Caledonia, identified what he called "a real paradox." Wryly, he note how interesting it was that Europeans will express so much pride in their own culture, yet when they display other cultures they don't want to show those things made after contact - only those things made before contact.

3 The organisation of storage in museums is usually based on a management retrieval system that delineates objects by geography, culture and usually type: all spears together, all masks together. The relationship between objects is sometimes reconstructed when they are included in an exhibition.

4 Objects that are considered culturally sensitive are stored separately as are textiles and other fibre based objects that are vulnerable to high level lighting.

5 The book chronicling the Burnett collection is due to be published in late 2012.

6 Mali Voi, personal communication, 2000.

7 Research was carried out in Kiribati, Fiji, Solomon Islands, Cook Islands and Papua New Guinea in 1998, New Caledonia, Fiji and Samoa in 2000, New Caledonia, Vanuatu and Australia in 2001, Vanuatu, Fiji, Australia and Torres Strait in 2002

8 In 2010 the open storage system was replaced by new Multiversity Galleries where the re-organisation of the collections was guided by diverse knowledge systems and multiple ways of seeing.

9 About 40% of the collection is Asian; the rest is African, Americas and European.

10 The Tseshaht people live on the west Coast of Vancouver Island, British Columbia, Canada, one of the 14 Nations that make up the Nuu chah nulth Tribal Council.

11 The curatorial expertise (6 curators) was concentrated on the British Columbian Collection. Two curators shared the responsibility for the rest of the world.

12 Prior to changes in policy Canada Council did not fund exhibitions or purchases of contemporary aboriginal art.

13 Governments attribute authenticity by adopting indigenous arts as symbols of the State, illustrations of national identity, and metaphors of homogeneity. In Canada images of totem poles, sculptures, masks and so on, appear as logos on embassy stationary, postage stamps, at world fairs and the 2010 Olympic Games, and in the Pacific images of canoe prows, tapa, clubs, shields are similarly used. This government-approved recontextualisation serves to afford authenticity to these images and ensure their appeal to the museum visitor and the buying public, both seeking the real thing.

14 Alcheringa in Victoria imports Papua New Guinea art and Spirit Wrestler in Vancouver brings in Maori art.

15 Teweiariki Taearo, personal communication, 2002.

16 Gloria Cranmer, personal communication, 2001.

17 Ralph Regenvanu, email correspondence, 2004.

18 http://laws.justice.gc.ca/en/C-42/39253.html.

19 Ralph Regenvanu, email correspondence, 2004.

20 At MOA the term culturally sensitive refers to those objects in the collection that for various reasons should not be on public display. An obvious example would be human remains; other examples include objects not meant to be viewed by outsiders.

2 http://www.news.vu/en/ae/Art/050420-Red-Wave-advocating-for-Vanuatu-artists-rights.shtml.

22 Moses Jobo is well known for reviving the painting on barkcloth — using both modern motifs and traditional techniques. See Browne Joy (ed) "New Traditions: Contemporary Art of Vanuatu" Vanuatu Cultural Centre, 2000, p. 11.

23 Moses Jobo, personal communication, 2002.

Chapter 8

1 Personal Communication, Frank Rabon — Master of Chamorro Dance, November 2001.

2 Ibid.

3 Ibid.

4 Personal Communication, Benjie Santiago — Founder/Owner, Natibu Dance Academy, November 2001.

5 Personal Communication, Leonard Iriarte — Group Leader, I Fanlalai'an, November 2001.

6 Personal Communication, Frank Rabon — Master of Chamorro Dance, November 2001.

7 Personal Communication, Eileen Meno — Group Leader, Irensian Taotao Tano Cultural Dance Group, November 2001.

8 Personal Communication, Benjie Santiago — Founder/Owner, Natibu Dance Academy, November 2001.

9 Personal Communication, Eileen Meno — Group Leader, Irensian Taotao Tano Cultural Dance Group, November 2001.

10 Personal Communication, Benjie Santiago — Founder/Owner, Natibu Dance Academy, November 2001.

11 Personal Communication, Eileen Meno — Group Leader, Irensian Taotao Tano Cultural Dance Group, November 2001.

12 Personal Communication, Benjie Santiago — Founder/Owner, Natibu Dance Academy, November 2001.

13 Personal Communication, Eileen Meno — Group Leader, Irensian Taotao Tano Cultural Dance Group, November 2001.

14 Personal Communication, Benjie Santiago — Founder/Owner, Natibu Dance Academy, November 2001.

15 I was a recipient of the Association of Social Anthropologist in Oceania Pacific Islands Scholarship Fund, which allowed me to attend this meeting.

16 Personal Communication, Eileen Meno — Group Leader, Irensian Taotao Tano Cultural Dance Group, November 2001.

17 Personal Communication, Frank Rabon — Master of Chamorro Dance, November 2001.

18 ibid.

19 Personal Communication, Leonard Iriarte — Group Leader, I Fanlalai'an, November 2001.

20 Personal Communication, Benjie Santiago — Founder/Owner, Natibu Dance Academy, November 2001.

21 Personal Communication, Eileen Meno — Group Leader, Irensian Taotao Tano Cultural Dance Group, November 2001.

Chapter 9

1 Gazellah Bruder, personal conversation at May 8, 2000.

2 Jane Wena, personal communication, October 11, 1998.

3 Winnie Weoa, personal conversation, June 1, 2000.

4 Gazellah Bruder, personal conversation, June 1, 2000.

5 Julie Mota, personal conversation, November 27, 1998.

6 Julie Mota, personal conversation, May 8, 2000.

7 Gazellah Bruder, personal conversation, October 10, 1998.

8 *Post-Courier*, October 29, 1998.

9 *The National*, November 5, 1998.

10 *The National*, December 18, 1998.

11 The artists participating in *Images of Germany* were: Julie Mota, Gazellah Bruder, Jane Wena, Winnie Weoa, Mathias Kauage, Gigs Wena, Alexander Mebri, John Siune, Oscar Towa, Apa Hugo, Laben Sakale John, Maik Yomba Kagle, Daniel Holland, Philip Yobale, Kenneth Rokure.

12 The artists participating in *Laip Bilong Meri (Everyday Life of Women)* were: Julie Mota, Gazellah Bruder, Jane Wena, Winnie Weoa, Mathias Kauage, Gigs Wena, Alexander Mebri, John Siune, Oscar Towa, John Bobby Charlie, Daniel Holland, Apa Hugo, Laben Sakale John, Barleyde J. Katit, Agatha Waramin Horambe, Morea Morea, Maik Yomba Kagle, Mealisy Ilamia, Chris Kauage, Gickmai Kundun, Larry Santana, Charlie Nebita, Maria Santana, Philemon Yalamu, Philip Yobale, Tom Yependohe, Milan Boie, Martin Lance, Leo Lapu, Kenneth Rokure, Martin Morububuna, and Joe Nalo.

13 See Totu in Herle, A. et al, 2002, p. 341.

14 *The National*, February 2, 1999.

15 *Laip bilong Meri (Everyday Life of Women)*, exhibition catalogue, 2000, p. 5.

16 1 PNG-Kina = 0.37407 US Dollar.

17 These artists are now working in a very abstract style.

18 Comments overheard during the exhibition *Zwischen den Welten (Between Worlds)* in Lübeck, September 27, 2005.

19 Comments overheard at various Papua New Guinea exhibition openings.

20 Personal communication with the owner of the Galerie am Schlump, Hamburg, October 23, 2001.

21 In 2004, *Paradise Now?* was shown at the Asia Society in New York and Date Line was shown at three locations in Germany (Neuer Berliner Kunstverein, Stadtgalerie Kiel and Galerie der Stadt Sindelfingen) in 2007 and in 2008.

22 Churches were often willing to open their doors for Papua New Guinean artists and allowed us to use their rooms for free; for instance in Saint Lorenz Church in Lübeck, Haus am Schüberg, and other locations of the Lutheran Church. To date, this work has not appeared in a major art museum or gallery venue in Germany.

23 Although Kauage was recognized with two retrospective exhibitions in Great Britain and was honored by the Queen with an OBE, this did not secure him a lasting position within the global art world.

Chapter 10

1 The Museum of World Cultures at Frankfurt (formerly the Museum of Ethnology) is an ethnographic museum that began collecting contemporary non-western art during the 1970s.

2 The kula is a ceremonial exchange system among the island groups of Southeast Papua New Guinea. Necklaces (soulava in Trobriand language) are traded clockwise from island to island. Armrings (mwali) circulate anti-clockwise in exchange of the necklaces.

3 In an interview at Port Moresby, 1999.

4 Interview with Julie Mota, Port Moresby, 1999.

5 Interview with Julie Mota, Port Moresby 1999. Peles is the pidgin word for place, the titles mean a 'Place in Papua' and a 'Place in the highlands'.

6 Interview with Julie Mota in April 1999, Port Moresby.

7 Interview with Julie Mota in April 1999, Port Moresby.

8 The sickle-shaped plates cut from the goldlip pearl shell (*Pinctata margaritifera*) are important indicators of wealth in many highland societies. They are also worn as breast plates.

9 Interpretation based on information given by Jane Wena in April 1999, Port Moresby.

10 Interview with the artist 1991, Port Moresby.

11 Interview with the artist 1999, Port Moresby.

Chapter 12

1 Dr. Carol Ivory is Professor of Art History at Washington State University in Pullman. "Dr. Ivory's research focuses on the art, history, and culture of the Marquesas Islands, French Polynesia.... A recent project was the exhibition, *Adorning the World, Art of the Marquesas Islands*, at the Metropolitan Museum of Art in New York May 2005-January 2006. She is currently working on an exhibition with the Art Centre Basel, Gauguin and Polynesia: South Pacific Encounters, which will open in Copenhagen, Denmark, in 2011." Washington State University website, Faculty Bios, http://finearts.wsu.edu/faculty/ivory.html.

2 Christina Hellmich is curator of the Jolika Collection of New Guinea Art and curator of Oceanic Art at the deYoung Museum in San Francisco.

3 The Mahina Movement is a multimedia, multi-cultural performance trio based in New York City. The members are Erica R. DeLaRosa, Gabriella Callender, and Vaimoana Litia Makakaufaki Niumeitolu. Information on their past and current projects can be found at http://www.mahinamovement.org/.

4 Filipe Tohi is an international sculptor and performance artist. Details about his art, current projects, and his perspectives on lalava as an enduring process and philosophy can be found at http://www.lalava.net/.

5 Dr. Richard S. Cooper is a painter/sculptor/public artist and teacher. Interesting to note that Cooper's paintings resemble many of his sculptures in his reduction of forms to simple abstract, organic shapes. As a sculptor, Cooper works in a variety of media, ranging from small to monumental in scale. "My work is based on the most important unit in society: the family…." http://www.cooperartworks.com/contact.php.

6 James Luna is a Luiseño Indian, international performance and installation artist whose work is collected by and exhibited internationally at museums and galleries including the Whitney Biennale, and The New Museum of Contemporary Art, New York, The National Museum of the American Indian in New York, and the National Gallery of Canada. Recently Luna's work was exhibited in Australia and New Zealand. From December 2007-January 2008 Luna's video installation, Spinning Woman, was featured in the Raw Space Galleries' exhibition titled, In the Meantime, organized by Jenny Fraser in South Brisbane, http://www.qcp.org.au/news/34. In May 2009, The Museum of New Zealand Te Papa Tongarewa commissioned his performance/installation, Urban (Almost) Rituals, which was presented at the Sounding Theatre in Te Papa, in Wellington. Luna lives on the La Jolla Reservation in San Diego, California. For more information on his work visit his website at http://www.jamesluna.com/.

7 Richard Lou is a Chicano performance artist, photographer, and curator, He is presently Chair of the Department of Art at Memphis University, and past Art Department Chair at both Georgia College and State University in Milledgeville and San Diego Mesa College in San Diego, CA. He was one of the founding members of the Border Art Workshop/Taller de Arte Fronterizo (BAW/TAF) in San Diego. "…Through his work, Lou constantly engages in the analysis and deconstruction of cultural, social and ethnic identity, a process that reveals how contemporary consciousness is profoundly shaped by negative stereotypes of people of color." DePaw University website, http://www.depauw.edu/news/index.asp?id=13628. Lou's work is exhibited internationally and is included in the Museum of Contemporary Art San Diego's permanent collection.

8 James Luna, interview, Palomar College, San Marcos, CA, December 2007.

9 Dr. Pamela Rosi teaches at Bridgewater State College, in Bridgewater, Massachusetts. She has published numerous articles on Oceanic art, particularly the work of contemporary Papua New Guinea artists. Her recent projects include the exhibition, Hailans to Ailans, Contemporary Papua New Guinea Art. For more details see http://www.hailanstoailans.com/.

10 Dan Taulapapa McMullin is a poet, painter, performance artist, playwright, and curator based in both Laguna Beach, CA, and Samoa. He is author of the book of poems titled, A Drag Queen Named Pipi. For more details on his art and current projects visit his website at http://www.taulapapa.com/.

11 Insurmountable obstacles having to do with visa issues for the main performance artist, ultimately forced us to cancel the performance event.

12. Fonofale McCarthy email, October 2005.

13 Jane Wena's artist statement for Turning Tides exhibition, University of California San Diego, CA, 2005.

14 Julie Mota's artist statement for Turning Tides exhibition, University of California San Diego, CA, 2005.

15 Larry Santana's artist statement for Turning Tides exhibition, University of California San Diego, CA, 2005.

16 Daniel Waswas' artist statement for Turning Tides exhibition, University of California San Diego, CA, 2005.

17 Filipe Tohi's artist statement for Turning Tides exhibition, University of California San Diego, CA, 2005.

18 Regina Meredith is Professor of Art at the Samoan Community College.

19 Regina Meredith's artist statement for Turning Tides exhibition, University of California San Diego, CA 2005.

20 Information on Rosanna Raymond and Pasifika Styles is available at http://www.pasifikastyles.org.uk/artists/rosanna-raymond.php.

21 Dr. Peri Klemm is a Professor of Art History at California State University Northridge (CSUN) where she teaches "a range of courses in African, Oceanic, and Native American art history and gallery design" (from http://www.csun.edu/art/faculty/fulltime/klemm/pklemm.html). Her research focus is African art with concentration in Ethiopia, (in 1999-2000 as Fulbright Scholar). Her current research includes masquerade and performance in Zambia and continued research on Oromo women's art in Ethiopia.

22 Current exhibition information for the McCarthy Art Gallery can be found at http://www.mccarthygallery.co.nz/.

23 James Luna, interview, Palomar College, San Marcos, CA, December 2007.

24 Sean Mallon is Senior Curator of Pacific Cultures at the Museum of New Zealand Te Papa Tongarewa and author of the book, titled, *Samoan Art & Artists: O Measina a Sāmoa.*

25 Sean Mallon, interview, email, December 2007.

26 Richard Lou, interview, email, November-December, 2007.

27 Shigeyuki Kihara, interview, email, November-December, 2007.

References

Agence de Développement de la Culture Kanak. 2000. *Biennale d'art contemporain de Noumea: Noumea-Pacifique.* Noumea: Agence de Développement de la Culture Kanak.

Ames, M. 1992. *Cannibal Tours and Glass Boxes: The Anthropology of Museums.* Vancouver: University of British Columbia Press.

Anderson, C. and B. Craig (eds.). 1999. *Art and Performance in Oceania.* Bathurst: Crawford House Press.

Anderson, B. 1983. *Imagined Communities: Reflections on the Origin and Spread of Nationalism.* London: Verso.

Anderson, C. and F. Dussart. 1988. Dreamings in Acrylic: Western Desert Art. In: Sutton, P. (ed.), *Dreamings: The Art of Aboriginal Australia.* New York: The Asia Society in Association with George Brazillier Publishers. pp. 89-142.

Anderson, R. L. 1990. *Calliope's Sisters: A Comparative Study of Philosophies of Art.* Englewood Cliffs, New Jersey: Prentice Hall.

Anonymous. 1992. Designs for Living, in M. Barr (ed.), *Headlands: Thinking through New Zealand Art.* Sydney: Museum of Contemporary Art. p. 13.

Barker, J. 1985. *Maisin Christianity: An Ethnography of the Contemporary Religion of a Seaboard Melanesian People.* Unpublished doctoral thesis, University of British Columbia.

_____. 2008. *Ancestral Lines. The Maisin of Papua New Guinea and the Fate of the Rainforest.* Canada: Broadview Press.

Baxandall, M. 1985. *Patterns of Intention. On the Historical Explanation of Pictures.* New Haven and London: Yale University Press.

Beaglehole, J. C. (ed.). 1961.*The Journals of Captain James Cook on his Voyages of Discovery. The Voyage of the Resolution and Adventure, 1772-1775.* Cambridge: Cambridge University Press for the Hakluyt Society.

_____. 1962. *The Endeavour Journal of Joseph Banks 1768-1771.* 2 vols. Sydney: Angus and Robertson.

_____. 1967.*The Journals of Captain James Cook on his Voyages of Discovery. The Voyage of the Resolution and the Discovery, 1776-1780,* 2 vols. Cambridge: Cambridge University Press for the Hakluyt Society.

_____. 1968 [1955]. *The Journals of Captain James Cook on his Voyages of Discovery. The Voyage of the Endeavour 1768-1771.* Cambridge: Cambridge University Press for the Hakluyt Society.

Becker, H.S. 1982. *Art Worlds.* London: University of California Press

Beier, G. 1974. *Modern Images from Niugini.* Special Kovave Publication, pp. 1-60. Queensland: Jacaranda Press.

Beier, U. 1976. The Artist in Society, Lecture given in the Foundation Course of the University of Papua New Guinea.

_____. 2005. *Decolonizing the Mind: The Impact of the University on Culture and Identity.* Canberra: Pandanus Books.

_____. n.d. The Artist's Struggle for Integration in a Changing Society. Lecture given in the Foundation Course of the University of Papua New Guinea. Typescript in the possession of the author.

Berman, M. 1990. Samting Tru, or Samting Nating? What is Contemporary Melanesian Art? In S. C. Simmons and H. Stevenson, eds., *Luk Luk Gen: Contemporary Art from Papua New Guinea,* pp. 59-64. Townsville: Perc Tucker Gallery.

Bink, G.L. 1896. *Drie maanden aan de Humboldtsbaai.* Overdruk uit: Tijdschrift voor Indische Taal-, Land-, en Volkenkunde deel 39. Batavia: Albrecht & Rusche.

Bijkerk, J. 1924. *Naar Sentani.* Oegstgeest: Zendingsbureau.

Boissevain, J. (ed.). *Revitalizing European Rituals.* London and New York: Routledge.

Bolton, L. 1993. *Dancing with Mats: Extending Kastom to Women in Vanuatu.* PhD thesis, Manchester University.

_____. 1996. Tahigogona's Sisters: Women, Mats and Landscape on Ambae, in J. Bonnemaison, K. Huffman, C. Kaufmann and D. Tryon (eds.), *Arts of Vanuatu.* Sydney: Crawford House. pp. 112-119.

_____. 2001. What Makes Singo Different? North Vanuatu Textiles and the Theory of Captivation, in C. Pinney and N. Thomas (eds.), *Beyond Aesthetics. Art and the Technologies of Enchantment.* Oxford: Berg. pp. 97-115.

_____. 2003. *Unfolding the Moon: Enacting Women's Kastom in Vanuatu.* Honolulu: University of Hawaii Press.

Bonnemaison, J., K. Huffman, C. Kaufmann and D. Tryon (eds.). 1996. *Arts of Vanuatu.* Australia: Crawford House Publishing

Burnett, F. 1910. *Through Tropic Seas.* London: Francis Griffiths.

Campbell, S. F. 2002. *The Art of Kula.* Oxford: Berg.

Carrier, J. 1998. Property and Social Relations in Melanesia, in C. M. Hann, (ed.), *Property Relations: Renewing the Anthropological Tradition.* Cambridge: Cambridge University Press. pp. 85-103.

Celes, R. 1995. *Latte Magazine.* Hagåtña, Guam: May 1995:38-45.

Census 2000, Government of Guam Department of Commerce.

Chiu, M. (ed.). 2004. *Paradise Now?: Contemporary Art from the Pacific.* Auckland: David Bateman in association with Asia Society.

Clerq, F. S. A. de. 1893. De West- en Noordkust van Nederlandsch Nieuw-Guinea. *Tijdschrift van het Koninklijk Nederlandsch Aardrijkskundig Genootschap* 10:151-219, 438-465, 587-649, 841-844, 981-1021.

Clerq, F. S. A. de and J. D. E. Schmeltz. 1893. *Ethnographische Beschrijving van de West- en Noordkust van Nederlandsch Nieuw Guinea.* Leiden: P. W. M. Trapp.

Clifford, J. 1986. Introduction: Partial Truths, in J. Clifford & G. Marcus (eds.), *Writing Culture: The Poetics and Politics of Ethnography.* Berkeley: University Of California Press.

_____. 1988. *The Predicament of Culture.* Cambridge: Harvard University Press.

Cochrane, S. 1997. *Contemporary Art in Papua New Guinea.* Sydney: Craftsman House.

_____. 2001. *Bérétara, Contemporary Pacific Art.* Noumea: Agence de Développement de la Culture Kanak.

_____. 2007. *Art in Life in Melanesia.* Newcastle: Cambridge Scholars Publishing.

Cochrane, S. and H. Stevenson (eds.). 1990. *Luk Luk Gen (Look Again): Contemporary Art from Papua New Guinea.* Townsville: Perc Tucker Regional Gallery.

Colchester, C. 2003. Introduction, in C. Colchester (ed.), *Clothing the Pacific.* Oxford: Berg. pp. 1-22.

Cruces, F. and A. de Rada. 1992. Public Celebrations in a Spanish Valley, in: J. Boissevain (ed.), *Revitalizing European Rituals.* London: Routledge. pp. 62-79.

Dark, P. J. C. (ed.). *Development of the Arts in the Pacific.* Occasional Papers of the Pacific Arts Association, No. 1. Wellington: National Museum.

Dark, P. J. C. and R. G. Rose (eds.). 1993. *Artistic Heritage in a Changing Pacific.* Honolulu: University of Hawaii Press.

Davis, J. 1992. History and the People without Europe., in K. Hastrup (ed.). *Other Histories.* London & New York: Routledge. pp. 17-27.

Dening, G. 1992. *Mr. Bligh's Bad Language: Passion, Power, and Theatre on the Bounty.* Cambridge: Cambridge University Press.

Eves, R. 1996. *Colonialism, Corporeality and Character: Methodist Missions and the Refashioning of Bodies in the Pacific.* History and Anthropology 10(1): 85-138.

Fajans, J. 1997. *They Make Themselves: Work and Play among the Baining of Papua New Guinea.* Chicago: University of Chicago Press.

Firth, R. 1973. *Symbols Public and Private.* London: George Allen & Unwin.

Flores, J. S. 1996. *Reinventing Artistic Traditions: The Chamorro Search for Identity.* Master's thesis. Mangilao, Guam: University of Guam.

_____. 2002. Art and Identity in the Mariana Islands: The reconstruction of "ancient" Chamorro dance. In A. Herle, N. Stanley, K. Stevenson, R. L. Welsch, (eds.). *Pacific Art: Persistence, Change and Meaning,* Adelaide: Crawford House Publishing.

Forsyth M. 2003. Intellectual Property Laws in the South Pacific: Friend or Foe? *Journal of Pacific Law* (7)1. http://www.paclii.org/journals/fJSPL/vol07no1/8.shtml (accessed January 6, 2006).

Foster, R. J. 2002. *Materializing the Nation: Commodities, Consumption, and Media in Papua New Guinea.* Bloomington: Indiana University Press.

_____. (ed.). 1995 . *Nation Making: Emergent Identities in Postcolonial Melanesia.* Michigan: University of Michigan Press.

Foucault, M. 1986. Of Other Spaces. *Diacritics*, Spring (16): 22-27.

Friede, J. A. and R. A. Peltason. 2005. *New Guinea Art: Masterpieces from the Jolika Collection of Marcia and John Friede.* San Francisco: de Young Museum.

Galis, K. W. 1955. *Papua's van de Humboldt-baai.* Proefschrift, Rijksuniversiteit te Leiden. Den Haag: J. N. Voorhoeve.

_____. 1968. Nogmaals Sentani. *Kultuurpatronen: Bulletin Ethnografisch Museum Delft* 10-11:59-95.

Gathercole, P. 1970. *From the Islands of the South Seas, 1773-74: An Exhibition of a Collection made on Captain Cook's Second Voyage of Discovery by J.R. Forster.* Oxford: Pitt Rivers Museum.

Geismar, H. 2001. What's in a Price? An Ethnography of Tribal Art at Auction. Journal of Material Culture, 6(1), March 2001, pp. 25-49.

_____. 2004. The Materiality of Contemporary Art in Vanuatu. *Journal of Material Culture,* 9(1). 43-58.

_____. 2005. Copyright in Context: Carvings, Carvers and Commodities in Vanuatu. *American Ethnologist* 33(3): 437-459.

Geismar, H. and R. Empson. 2004. Fieldwork: A Review. *Cambridge Anthropology* 24(1): 39-50.

Geismar, H. and H. Horst. 2004. Introduction: Materializing Ethnography. *Journal of Material Culture* 9(1): 5-10.

Gegeo, D.W. 2001. Cultural Rupture and Indigeneity: The Challenge of (Re)visioning "Place" in the Pacific. *The Contemporary Pacific* 13 (2): 491-507.

Gell, A. 1992. The Technology of Enchantment and the Enchantment of Technology, in J. Coote and A. Shelton (eds.), Anthropology, *Art and Aesthetics.* Oxford: University Press.

Gell, A. 1998. *Art and Agency.* Oxford: University Press.

Ginsburg, F. and F. Myers. 2006. A History of Aboriginal Futures. *Critique of Anthropology* 26(1): 27-45.

Goes, H.D.A. van der, et al. 1862. Aantekeningen nopens de Humboldts-baai en hare bewoners. In H.D.A. van der Goes, et al. Nieuw Guinea, ethnographisch en natuurkundig onderzocht en beschreven in 1858 door een Nederlandsch Indische commisie. *Bijdragen tot de Taal-, Land- en Volkenkunde van Nederlandsch Indië* 5:168-184.

Graburn, N. 1976. *Ethnic and Tourist Arts: Cultural Expressions of the Fourth World.* Berkeley: University of California Press.

Hanson, A. 1989. The Making of the Maori: Cultural Invention and its Logic. *American Anthropologist* 91(4): 890-902.

Hanson, F. A. and L. Hanson (eds.). 1990. *Art and Identity in Oceania.* Honolulu: University of Hawaii Press.

Hassan, J. 2001. Boomerang Effect. *Fuse Magazine*, June (http://www.ccca.ca accessed August 9, 2009).

Hau'ofa, E. 2000. Opening address at James Harvey Gallery, Sydney, 27 September.

Hawkesworth, J. 1773. *An account of the voyages undertaken by the order of his present Majesty, for making discoveries in the southern hemisphere, and successfully performed by Commodore Byron, Captain Wallis, Captain Carteret, and Captain Cook, in the Dolphin, the Swallow, and the Endeavour drawn up from the journals kept by several commanders and from papers of Joseph Banks, Esq.* London: Printed for W. Strahan and T. Cadell.

Hawthorn, A. 1993. *A Labour of Love: The Making of the Museum of Anthropology, UBC. The First Three Decades 1947-1976.* Museum Note No.33. Vancouver: UBC Museum of Anthropology.

Heermann, I. 1979. *Tingting blong mi. Zeitgenössische Kunst aus Papua Neuguinea.* Ausstellungskatalog des Linden Museums: Stuttgart.

Helmreich, S. 2005. How Scientists Think about 'Natives', for Example. A Problem of Taxonomy among Biologists of Alien Species in Hawaii. *The Journal of the Royal Anthropological Institute.* 11(1): 107-129.

Hereniko, V. 1994. Representations of Cultural Identity, in B. Lal and R. Kiste (eds.),*Tides of History: The Pacific Islands in the 20th Century.* Honolulu: University of Hawaii Press. pp. 406-434.

Herle, A. 2001. *Exhibition and Representation: Stories from the Torres Strait Islanders Exhibition*, Museum International. UNESCO, 8-18.

Herle, A., N. Stanley, K. Stevenson, R. L. Welsch (eds). 2002. *Pacific Art. Persistence, Change and Meaning.* Honolulu: University of Hawai'i Press.

Hermkens, A. 2005. *Engendering Objects. Barkcloth and the Dynamics of identity in Papua New Guinea.* Unpublished Ph.D. Thesis, Radboud University Nijmegen.

_____. 2005a. *Painting the Past and the Future. Barkcloth of the Maisin People in Papua New Guinea* (39 pages). Leiden: National Museum of Ethnology:E-publication, http://www.rmv.nl/publicaties/23Maisin/e/fr_pub.html

_____. 2007. Gendered Objects. Embodiments of Colonial Collecting in Dutch New Guinea. *Journal of Pacific History* 42(1): 1-20.

_____. 2007a. Stretching the Cloth. Hybrid Meanings, Styles, and Gender Structures in Maisin Barkcloth. *Journal of Pacific Arts* 3-5: 104-114.

_____. 2007b. Church Festivals and the Visualization of Identity in Collingwood Bay, Papua New Guinea. *Visual Anthropology* 20(5): 347-364.

Hermkens, A. and M. Widjojo 2011. Sentani Art and Artists Today, in: V.-L. Webb (ed.), *Ancestors of the Lake.* Yale University Press.

Hobsbawm, E. and T. Ranger (eds.). 1983. *The Invention of Tradition.* Cambridge: Cambridge University Press.

Hollander, H. 2007. E*en man met een speurdersneus. Carel Groenevelt (1899-1973), beroepsverzamelaar voor Tropenmuseum en Wereldmuseum in Nieuw Guinea.* Amsterdam: KIT Publishers.

Hoogerbrugge, J. 1995. Notes on the Art of Barkcloth Painting in the Jayapura Area, Irian Jaya, Indonesia. In D. A. M. Smidt, P. ter Keurs, and A. Trouwborst, eds., *Pacific Material Culture: Essays in honour of Dr. Simon Kooijman on the Occasion of his 80th Birthday*, pp. 167-179. Leiden: Rijksmuseum voor Volkenkunde.

Howard, A. 1990. Cultural Paradigms, History, and the Search for Identity in Oceania. In J. Linnekin and L. Poyer (eds.) *Cultural Identity and Ethnicity in the Pacific.* Honolulu: University of Hawaii Press. pp. 259-280.

Howard, M. C. 1996. Irian Jaya's Barkcloth Revival. *Arts of Asia* 26(5):114-124.

_____. 1998. Maro Paintings of Irian Jaya. *ART Asia Pacific* 18: 54-61.

Iamo, W. and J. Simet 1998. Cultural Diversity and Identity in Papua New Guinea: A Second Look, in V.R Dominguez and D.Y.U Wu (eds.), *From Beijing to Port Moresby: The Politics of National Identity in Cultural Policies.* Amsterdam: Gordon and Breach Publishers.

Ian Potter Museum of Art, 2002. *Blood on the Spinifex.* Melbourne: Ian Potter Museum of Art, University of Melbourne.

Jolly, M. 1992. Specters of Inauthenticity. *The Contemporary Pacific*, 4(1): 49-72.

_____. 1997. Women-Nation-State in Vanuatu: Women as Signs and Subjects in the Discourses of Kastom, Modernity and Christianity, in T. Otto and N. Thomas (eds.), *Narratives of Nation in the South Pacific.* Amsterdam: Harwood Academic Publishers.

Jones, P. 1988. Perceptions of Aboriginal Art: A History. In P. Sutton (ed.), *Dreamings: The Art of Aboriginal Australia.* New York: The Asia Society in Association with George Brazillier Publishers. pp. 143-79.

Jules-Rosette, B. 1984. *The Messages of Tourist Art: An African Semiotic System in Comparative Perspective.* New York: Plenum Press.

Kaeppler, A. L. 1975. *The Fabrics of Hawaii.* Leigh-on-Sea: F. Lewis.

_____. 1978. *"Artificial Curiosities": Being an Exposition of Native Manufactures Collected on the Three Pacific Voyages of Captain James Cook.* R. N. Bernice P. Bishop Museum special publication 65. Honolulu: Bishop Museum Press.

_____. 1977. Polynesian Dance as Airport Art, in A. Kaeppler, J. Van Zile and C. Wolz (eds.), *Asian and Pacific Dance:*

Selected Papers from the 1974 CORD-SEM Conference. New York: Committee on Research in Dance.

_____. 1992. Epilogue: States of the Arts. The Arts and Politics, Special Issue, *Pacific Studies* 15(4): 311-318.

Keesing, R. M. 1989. Creating the Past: Custom and identity in the Contemporary Pacific. *The Contemporary Pacific,* 1(1 & 2):19-39.

Kalinoe, L. 2004. Legal Options for The Regulation Of Intellectual and Cultural Property in Papua New Guinea, in M. Strathern and E. Hirsch (eds)., *Transactions and Creations: Property Debates and the Stimulus of Melanesia.* Oxford: Berghahn Books.

Keesing, R. 1989. Creating the Past: Custom and Identity in the Contemporary Pacific. *The Contemporary Pacific* 1(1-2): 19-42.

Keesing, R. and R. Tonkinson (eds.). 1982 Reinventing Traditional Culture: The Politics of Kastom in Island Melanesia, Special Issue of *Mankind* 13(4).

Kenrick, J. and Lewis, J. 2004. Indigenous People's Rights and the Politics of the Term 'Indigenous'. *Anthropology Today* 20(2): 4-9.

Killer Whale and Crocodile, DVD, directed by P. Campbell and A. Holbrook (Vancouver: Moving Images Distribution, 2007).

Kjellgren, E. 2000. They Make Us Go Artist Now: East Kimberley Painters on the Art World, in S. Kleinert and M. Neale (eds.), *The Oxford Companion to Aboriginal Art and Culture.* Oxford: Oxford University Press. pp. 490-2.

_____. 2001 Mingmarriya: Art as Autobiography in the Paintings of Queenie McKenzie. *Pacific Arts,* 23 & 24: 11-20.

Kofod, F. 2002. Introduction, in Ian Potter Museum of Art 2002, *Blood on the Spinifex.* Melbourne: Ian Potter Museum of Art, University of Melbourne. pp. 16-17.

Konau B. and M. W. Smith. 2006. *Dreaming Their Way: Australian Aboriginal Women Painters.* Washington, DC: National Museum of Women in the Arts.

Kooijman, Simon. 1959. *The Art of Lake Sentani.* New York: Museum of Primitive Art.

Küchler, S. 2002. *Malanggan: Art, Memory and Sacrifice.* Oxford: Berg Publisher.

Kuper, A. 2003. The Return of the Native. *Current Anthropology* 44(3): 389–395.

Layton, R. 1991. *The Anthropology of Art.* Cambridge: Cambridge University Press.

Lepsoe, D. 2008. Introduction to Voices and Visions: Contemporary Sepik Art. Retrieved July 1, 2009 from http://www.alcheringa-gallery.com/exhibit.html/v5/75/.

Lewis-Harris, J. 2006. Gender, Location, and Tradition: A Comparison of Two Papua New Guinea Societies, in E. Venbrux, P.S. Rosi, R.L. Welsch (eds.), *Exploring World Art.* Long Grove, Illinois: Waveland Press.

Lincoln, L and E. Monds. 1993. Malagans: *The Ceremonial Art of New Ireland.* Victoria, BC: Alcheringa Gallery.

Lindstrom, M. 1998. Pasin Tambuna: Culture and Nationalism in Papua New Guinea, in V. R. Dominguez and V.R. Dominquez (eds.), *From Beijing to Port Moresby: The Politics of National Identity in Cultural Policies.* The Netherlands: Gordon and Breach Publishers. pp.141-167.

Lindstrom, L. and G. White (eds.). 1994. *Culture, Kastom, Tradition: Developing Culture Policy in Melanesia.* Suva: Institute of Pacific Studies.

Linnekin, J. 1990. The Politics of Culture in the Pacific, in J. Linnekin and L. Poyer (eds.), *Cultural Identity in the Pacific.* Honolulu: University of Hawai'i Press.

Linnekin, J. 1991. Cultural Invention and the Dilemma of Authenticity. *American Anthropologist* 93: 446-449.

Linnekin, J. and L. Poyer (eds.). 1990. *Cultural Identity and Ethnicity in the Pacific.* Honolulu: University of Hawaii Press.

Lorentz, H.A. 1905. *Eenige maanden onder de Papua's.* Leiden: E. J. Brill.

MacCannell, D. 1992. *Empty Meeting Grounds: The Tourist Papers.* New York: Routledge.

MacClancy, J. (ed.) 1997. *Contesting Art: Art, Politics and Identity in the Modern World.* London: Berg.

MacKenzie, M.A. 1991. *Androgynous Objects: Stringbags and Gender in Central New Guinea.* Amsterdam: Harwood Academic Publishers.

Macnair, P. L. 1994. *Northwest Coast Indian Art for Sale: A Long Tradition, in Life of the Copper: A Commonwealth of Tribal Nations.* Victoria, BC: Alcheringa Gallery.

Macnair, P., R. Joseph, and B. Grenville. 1998. *Down from the Shimmering Sky: Masks of the Northwest Coast.* Seattle: University of Washington Press.

MacNayr, L. and E. Monds. 1994. *Epama Epam: Everything Has Meaning.* Art Gallery of Greater Victoria, BC Canada.

McFadden, D. R. and E. N. Taubman. 2005. *Changing Hands: Art without Reservation 2.* New York: Museum of Arts & Design.

Malinowski, B. 1922. *Argonauts of the Western Pacific: An Account of Native Enterprise and Adventure in the Archipelagoes of Melanesian New Guinea.* London: G. Routledge & Sons.

Mallon, S. .2002. *Samoan Art and Artists: O Mesina a Samoa.* Nelson: Craig Potton Publishing.

Mallon, S. and F. Pereira 1997. *Speaking in Colour.* Wellington: Te Papa Tongarewa.

_____. 2002. *Pacific Art Niu Sila: The Pacific Dimension Of Contemporary New Zealand Arts.* Wellington: Te Papa Press.

Maquet, J. 1986. *The Aesthetic Experience.* New Haven: Yale University Press.

Marcus, G. E. and F. R. Myers (eds.). 1995. *The Traffic in Culture: Refiguring Art and Anthropology.* Berkeley: University of California Press.

Mason, N. 2000. New Horizons: Future Directions. *Biennale d'Art Contemporain de Noumea. Noumea: Agence de Développement de la Culture Kanak.*

Mathews, G. 2000. *Global Culture/Individual Identity: Searching for Home in the Cultural Supermarket.* London: Routledge.

McGonagle, D. 2004. The Temple and the Form Together: Re-configuring community arts. *Fusion* 28(2): 25.

Mead, S. 1979. Exploring the Visual Arts of Oceania. Honolulu: University Press of Hawaii.

_____. 1984. *Te Maori: Maori Art from New Zealand* collections. New York: Abrams in association with the American Federation of Arts.

_____. 1993. The Maintenance of Heritage in a Fourth World Context: The Maori Case. In P. Dark & R. Rose, (eds.), *Artistic Heritage in a Changing Pacific*, Honolulu: University of Hawaii Press.

Mead, S. and B. Kernot (eds.). 1983. *Art and Artists of Oceania.* Palmerston North: Dunmore Press.

Megaw, M. R. and J. V. Megaw. 1993. Black Art and White Society: Some Bicentennial Observations on Contemporary Australian Aboriginal Art, In Dark, P. and R. Rose (eds.), *Artistic Heritage in a Changing Pacific*, Honolulu: University of Hawaii Press. pp. 162-172.

Mel. M. 1997 Pasin Bilong Bilas, in S. Cochrane (ed.), *Contemporary Art in Papua New Guinea.* Sydney: Craftsman House.

_____. 2002. Ples Bilong Mi: Interfacing Global and Indigenous Knowledge in Mapping a Pacific Vision at Home and Abroad. *Pacific Arts* 25:41-47.

Mel, M. and P. Rosi. 2009. *Hailans to Ailans: Contemporary Art from Papua New Guinea.* Vancouver: Hemlock Printing. Exhibition at Alcheringa Gallery and Rebecca Hossack Art Gallery.

Mellow, J. R. 1968. The Stein Salon was the First Museum of Modern Art. New York Times, December 1. (http://nytimes.com/books/98/05/03/specials/stein-salon.html accessed January 6, 2006).

Miller, D. 1987. *Material Culture and Mass Consumption.* Oxford: Blackwell Publishing.

Miller, D. (ed.) 1995. *Worlds Apart. Modernity through the Prism of the Local* (ASA Decennial Conference Series. The Uses of Knowledge: Global and Local Relations). London, New York.

Milroy, S. 2001. Nothing Sacred in the Peyote Tent. Globe Review, *Globe & Mail*, Toronto, May 16.

Mithlo, N. 2006. Native American Art in a Global Context: Politicization as a Form of Aesthetic Response, in E. Venbrux, P. S. Rosi, and R. Welsch (eds.), *Exploring World Art.* Long Grove, Il: Waveland Press.

Monds, E. and H. Tutton. 1996. *Ceremony and Passage: Mastercarvers of the Sepik River and Maprik Area.* Victoria, BC: Alcheringa Gallery.

Morphy, H. 1991. *Ancestral Connections: Art and an Aboriginal System of Knowledge.* Chicago: University of Chicago Press.

_____. 1998. *Aboriginal Art.* London: Phaidon.

Morphy, H. and M. S. Boles. 1999. *Art from the Land: Dialogues with the Kluge-Ruhe Collection of Australian Aboriginal Art.* Charlottesville: University of Virginia.

Morphy, H and Perkins, M (eds). 2006. *The Anthropology of Art: A Reader.* Oxford: Blackwell Publishing.

Mulitalo, T. 2001. *My Own Shade of Brown.* Christchurch: University of Canterbury, School of Fine Arts and Shoal Bay Press.

Myers, F. 2002. *Painting Culture: The Making of an Aboriginal High Art.* Duke University Press.

_____. 2004. Ontologies of the Image and Economies of Exchange. *American Ethnologist.* 31(1):5-21.

_____. 2004a. Unsettled Business: Painting, Tradition, and Indigenous Being. *Visual Anthropology* 17:247–271.

_____. 2005. Review of "Paradise Now! Contemporary Art from the Pacific. The Contemporary Pacific 17:1:273-277.

Narokobi, B. 1983. *The Melanesian Way.* Boroko: Institute of Papua New Guinea Studies.

_____. 1990. Transformations in Art and Society, in S. Cochrane Simons and H. Stevenson (eds.), *Luk Luk Gen: Contemporary Art from Papua New Guinea.* Townsville: Perc Tucker Regional Gallery. pp. 17-21.

Nero, K. (ed.). 1992. The Arts and Politics, Special Issue, *Pacific Studies* 15(4).

Neuer Berliner Kunstverein. 2008. *Dateline. Zeitgenossische Kunst des Pazifik/Contemporary Art from the Pacific.* Berlin: Hatje Cantz.

Oliver, T. 2002. Blood on the Spinfex, In *Blood on the Spinifex.* Melbourne: Ian Potter Museum of Art, University of Melbourne. pp. 6-11.

O'Rourke, D. 1987. *Cannibal Tours* (a film). Port Moresby: Institute of Papua New Guinea.

_____. 1997. *Yumi Yet: Papua New Guinea Gets Independence.* A film by Film Australia. Mt. Vernon, NY: Macmillan Films. [VHS, 1989, Direct Cinema, Los Angeles.]

Otto, T. 1993. Empty Tins for Lost Traditions, in T. Otto (ed.), *Pacific Islands Trajectories: Five PersonalViews.* Canberra: Australian National University Press.

Otto, T and N. Thomas (eds.). 1997. *Narratives of Nation in the South Pacific.* Australia: Harwood Academic Publishers.

Pacific Daily News. A daily Gannett Publication for Guam. Selected articles as cited.

Panoho, R. 1990. *Te Moemoea no Iotefa, The Dream of Joseph: A Celebration of Pacific Art and Taonga.* Wanganui: Sarjeant Gallery.

Pearce, S. 1995. *On Collecting: An Investigation in Collecting in the European Tradition.* London: Routledge.

Peltier, P. 1992. Jacques Viot, the Maro of Tobati, and Modern Painting: Paris-New Guinea: 1925-1935. In S. Greub (ed.), *Art of Northwest New Guinea*, pp. 155-175. New York: Rizzoli.

Perez, C.T. 1997. *Signs of Being — A Chamoru Spiritual Being.* Unpublished manuscript quoted with permission from the author.

Perez, M. 1997. *The Dialectic of Indigenous Identity in the Wake of Colonialism: The case of Chamorros of Guam.* Doctoral dissertation, Riverside: University of California, Riverside.

Petersen, G. 1992. Off-the-Shelf Tradition: Variation Versus Invention. In D. Rubinstein (ed). Mangilao, *Pacific history: Papers from the 8th Pacific History Association Conference*, Guam: University of Guam Press and Micronesian Area Research Center. pp. 201-212.

Petersen, G. 2007. Pacific New Wave: Hot Spot/Cambridge. *Art AsiaPacific* 52:66-67.

Phillips, R. B. 1995. Why Not Tourist Art? In G. Prakesh (ed). *After Colonialism.* Princeton: Princeton University Press.

Port Vila Press, November 23, 2004.

Powell, G. 1987. *Through Melanesian Eyes: An Anthology of Papua New Guinea Writing.* Melbourne: The Macmillan Co.

Price, S. 1989. *Primitive Art in Civilized Places.* Chicago: University of Chicago Press.

Puri, K. 1999. Protection of Expressions of Indigenous Cultures in the Pacific. XXXIII UNESCO's Copyright Bulletin 6-34.

Queensland Art Gallery. 1993. *The Asia-Pacific Triennial of Contemporary Art.* Brisbane: Queensland Art Gallery.

_____. 1996. *The Second Asia-Pacific Triennial of Contemporary Art.* Brisbane: Queensland Art Gallery.

_____. 1999. *Beyond the Future: the Third Asia-Pacific Triennial of Contemporary Art.* Brisbane: Queensland Art Gallery.

Raabe, E. Ch. 1992. Collecting Contemporary Art at the Museum für Völkerkunde, Frankfurt a. M., Germany, *Pacific Arts* (The Journal of the Pacific Arts Association) 5:14-18.

_____.1995. Modernism or Folk Art? The Reception of Pacific Art in Europe, *Art and Asia Pacific* 2(4):96-104.

_____. 1997a. Sinnwelten. (Galerie 37 — Kunst im Museum für Völkerkunde 1). Ed. with Mona Suhrbier. Frankfurt: Museum für Völkerkunde.

_____. 1997b. A Modern Pacific Painter and his Tradition. Joseph Nalo's "Universal Man", *Pacific Arts* (The Journal of the Pacific Arts Association) 15/16:61-67.

_____. 1998. *Im Auge des Betrachters. Kunst und Sehen in Papua Neuguinea.* Gallery 37 — Kunst im Museum für Völkerkunde 3. Frankfurt: Museum für Völkerkunde.

_____. 1999. Understanding Pacific Identity and Individual Creativity: Two Paintings from Papua New Guinea, *Australia Art Monthly* 21: 21-23. Canberra: Canberra School of Arts, Australian National University.

Rabon, F.B. 2001. *Pa'a Taotao Tano': A way of Life, People of the Land.* Hagatna, Guam: Irensia Publishing.

Raymond, R. and A. Henare. 2008. *Pasifika Styles: Artists Inside the Museum.* Cambridge: University of Cambridge Museum of Archaeology and Anthropology.

Reed, M. and K. Stevenson 2009. *Conversations Across Time.* Christchurch: Christchurch Institute of Technology.

Regenvanu, R. 1996. Transforming Representations: A sketch of the Contemporary-Art Scene in Vanuatu, in J. Bonnemaison, K. Huffman, C. Kaufmann and D. Tryon (eds.), *Arts of Vanuatu.* Australia: Crawford House Publishing.

Rice, R. 1998. *Tradition in Transition: Bridging Past and Present with the Most Beautiful Cloth in New Guinea.* http://www.citypaper.net/articles/o51498/art.tapa.shtml

Roper, R. 1999. *Traditional Arts, Contemporary Artists: A study of Influence and Change in Irian Jaya, Indonesia.* MA thesis, University of Victoria, Canada.

_____. 2001. The Bronze Asmat Warrior: Contemporary Art in Papua is about New and Contested Identities. *Inside Indonesia,* Jul.-Sept. http://www.insideindonesia.org/edit67/roper.htm, last visited 6/02/07.

Rose, D. 1991. *Hidden Histories: Black Stories from Victoria River Downs, Humbert River and Wave Hill Stations.* Canberra: Australian Institute of Aboriginal and Torres Strait Islander Studies.

Rose, R. and P. J. C. Dark (eds.). 1993. *Artistic Heritage in a Changing Pacific.* Honolulu: University of Hawaii Press.

Rosi, P. C. 1989. *Contemporary Art from Papua New Guinea.* Exhibition Catalogue. Bridgewater, MA: Anderson Gallery, Bridgewater State College.

_____. 1991. Papua New Guinea's New Parliament House: A Contested National Symbol. *The Contemporary Pacific* 3:2:289-323.

_____. 1992. Larry Santana, in G. McLaughlin (ed.), *Discover Paradise: A Selection of stories from Air Niugini's In-Flight Magazine — Paradise.* Lae: La Galamo Books.

_____. 1994. *Bung Wantaim: The Role of the National Arts School in Creating National Culture and Identity in Papua New Guinea.* Ph.D. dissertation, Bryn Mawr College.

_____. 1997. O Meri Wantok (My Countrywoman): Images of Indigenous Women in the Contemporary Arts of Papua New Guinea. Paper delivered at the Association of Anthropologists in Oceania Meetings. San Diego, CA, 1997.

_____. 1998a. Cultural Creator or New Bisnis Man?: Conflicts of being a Contemporary Artist in Papua New Guinea, in L. Zimmer-Tamakoshi (ed.), *Modern Papua New Guinea.* Kirksville: Thomas Jefferson University Press. pp. 31-54.

_____. 1998b. *Nation-Making and Cultural Tensions: Contemporary Art from Papua New Guinea.* Exhibition Catalogue. Boston: Pine Manor College.

_____. 2002. "National Treasures" or "Rubbish Men": The Disputed Value of Contemporary Papua New Guinea (PNG) Artists and Their Work. *Zeitschrift für Ethnologie* 127:241-267.

_____. 2006a. About the Artist: Larry Santana. *The Contemporary Pacific* 18(2):ix.

_____. 2006b. The Disputed Value of Contemporary Papua New Guinea Artists and their Work, in E. Venbrux, P.S. Rosi, R.L. Welsch, (eds.), *Exploring World Art*. Long Grove, Il. Waveland Press, Inc. pp. 245-71.

_____. 2007a Profile: Shigeyuki Kihara: Subverting Dusky Maidens and Exotic Tropes of Pacific Paradise. *Art Asia/Pacific* 51:72.

_____. 2007b. Review of: "Island Affinities: Contemporary Art of Oceania." *Art Asia/Pacific* 53:125-126.

Ryan, J. 1989. *Aboriginal Art of the Desert*. Melbourne: National Gallery of Victoria.

Said, E. 1978. *Orientalism*. Pantheon Books.

Sande, G. A. J. van der. 1907. Ethnography and Anthropology. *Nova Guinea* 3. Leiden: E. J. Brill.

Santana,M.2007.PaintingsforSchoolFees.http://www.pngbd.com/forum/showthread.php?p=67369#post67369. Posted Sunday 12 August

Schneider, A. and C. Wright. 2005. Introduction: The Challenge of Practice, in *Contemporary Art and Anthropology*. Oxford: Berg.

Seear, L. (ed.). 2002. APT 2002: *Asia-Pacific Triennial of Contemporary Art*. Brisbane: Queensland Art Gallery.

Seear, L. and S. Raffel (eds.). 2006. *The 5th Asia-Pacific Triennial of Contemporary Art*. Brisbane: Queensland Art Gallery.

Shaw, B. 1983. Heroism Against White Rule: The 'Rebel' Major, in Fry, E. (ed.). *Rebels and Radicals*, Sydney, London, and Boston: George Allen and Unwin.

Simmons, S. C. and Stevenson, H. (eds.). 1990. *Luk Luk Gen!: Contemporary Art from Papua New Guinea*. Exhibition Catalogue. Townsville: Perc Tucker Gallery.

Sisii, Y. 2004. Creating Art Out of Pain and Hardship, in *Inspirational People: Role Models for a Developing Nation*. Madang: Divine Word University Press. pp, 34-35.

Smidt, D. 1995 (ed.). *Asmat Art. Woodcarvings of Southwest New Guinea*. Leiden: Periplus Editions.

Smith, B. 1985 [1960]. *European Vision and the South Pacific*. New Haven: Yale University Press.

_____. 1992. *Imaging the Pacific: In the wake of Cook's Voyages*. New Haven: Yale University Press.

Smith, L. 1999. *Decolonizing Methodologies: Research and Indigenous Peoples*. London: Zed books.

Spyer, P. 1998. Introduction, in P. Spyer (ed.), *Border Fetishisms: Material Objects in Unstable Spaces*. London: Routledge.

Somare, M.T. 1979. Our Pride and Strength, in The Arts of the People. Special Issue of *The Post Courier* (Port Moresby), 2 September 1979.

_____. 1979a. Foreword, in S. Mead, *Exploring the Visual Arts of Oceania*. Honolulu: University Press of Hawaii. pp. xiii-xv.

Stanley, N. 1998. *Being Ourselves for You: The Global Display of Cultures*. Middlesex: University Press.

Stanton, J. 2004. *On Track: Contemporary Australian Aboriginal Art*. University of Western Australia. Berndt Museum of Anthropology, Occasional Paper No.6.

Steiner, C. 1994. *African Art in Transit*. Cambridge: University Press.

Stevenson, K. 2004. Refashioning the Label, Reconstructing the Cliché: A Decade of Contemporary Pacific Art, 1990-2000, in M. Chiu (ed.) *Paradise Now: Contemporary Art From the Pacific*. New York: Asia society.

_____. 2008. The Frangipani is Dead, *Contemporary Pacific Art in New Zealand, 1985-2000*. Wellington: Huia.

_____. 1990. Structuring a New Art Environment. In S.C. Simons and H. Stevenson, eds. *Luk Luk Gen!: Contemporary Art from Papua New Guinea*. Townsville: Perc Tucker Regional Gallery. pp. 23-30.

Stevenson, K. and V-L. Webb (eds.). 2007. *Representing Pacific Art*. Crawford House Press.

Struck-Garbe, M. 2009. Contemporary Art from Oceania, In *The Pacific Islands — At the Beginning of the 21st Century — Society, Culture, Religion*. Suva: The Pacific Theological College. pp. 267-277.

_____. 1998. *PNG Meri Artists Soim Piksa*. Exhibition catalogue. Port Moresby 1998.

_____. 2000. *Laip Bilong Meri: An Exhibition of Paintings and Textiles*. Papua New Guinea National Museum and Art Gallery, 16.6.-14.7.2000. Port Moresby: National Museum and Art Gallery.

Sutton, P. 1988. Dreamings: *The Art of Aboriginal Australia*. New York: The Asia Society Galleries.

Suzman, J. 2003. Response to Adam Kuper. *Current Anthropology* 44(3):399-400.

Taylor, M. 2004. Prologue. In *Inspirational People: Role Models for a Developing Nation*. Madang: Divine Word University Press. p.5.

Teilhet, J. 1983. The Role of Women Artists in Polynesia and Melanesia. In Sidney Mead and Bernie Kernot, (eds.), *Art and Artists of Oceania*, Palmerston North. pp. 45-56.

Teilhet-Fisk, J. 1991. To Beat or Not to Beat, That is the Question: A Study on Acculturation and Change in an Art-Making Process and its Relation to Gender Structures. *Pacific Studies* 14(3):41-68.

Thomas, N. 1991. *Entangled Objects: Exchange, Material Culture, and Colonialism in the Pacific*. Cambridge: Harvard University Press.

_____. 1995. *Oceanic Art*. London: Thames and Hudson.

_____. 1996. Contemporary Art and The Limits of Globalisation, in C. Turner and R. Devenport (eds.), *The Second Asia Pacific Triennial of Contemporary Art*. Brisbane: Queensland Art Gallery. pp. 17-18.

_____. 1999. *Possessions: Indigenous Art/Colonial Culture*. London: Thames and Hudson.

Thomas, R., Akerman, K., Macha, M., Christensen, W. and W. Caruana. 1994. *Roads Cross: The Paintings of Rover Thomas.* Canberra: National Gallery of Australia.

Tilley, C. 1997. Performing Culture in the Global Village, *Critique of Anthropology* 17(1):67-89.

Trask, H.-K. 1991. Natives and Anthropologists: The Colonial Struggle. *Contemporary Pacific* 3:159-67.

Torgovnick, M. 1990. *Gone Primitive: Savage Intellects, Modern Lives.* Chicago: University of Chicago Press.

Totu, V. 2002. The Impact of Commercial Development of Art on Traditional Culture in the Solomon Islands, in Herle, A., N. Stanley, K. Stevenson, R. L. Welsch (eds.), *Pacific Art. Persistence, Change and Meaning.* Honolulu: University of Hawai'i Press. pp 338-341.

Vanuatu, 1990. *Vanuatu: 10 Yia blong Independens.* Australia: Other People Publications.

Venbrux, H.J.M. 2006. The Postcolonial Virtue of Aboriginal Art from Bathurst and Melville Islands. In H.J.M. Venbrux, P.S. Rosi & R.L. Welsch (eds.), *Exploring World Art*, pp. 201-218. Long Grove, IL: Waveland Press.

Venbrux, E., P.S. Rosi and R.L. Welsch, eds. 2006. *Exploring World Art.* Long Grove: Waveland Press.

Wassmann, J. 1988. Introduction. In J. Wassmann (ed.) *Pacific Answers to Western Hegemony: Cultural Practices of Identity Construction*, Oxford: Berg. pp. 1-36.

Webb, J. (ed). 1999. *Objects and Expressions.* University of British Columbia Museum of Anthropology. Museum Note #35.

Weiner, A. B. 1980. Stability in Banana Leaves: Colonisation and Women in Kiriwina, Trobriand Islands, in M. Etienne and E. Leacock (eds.), *Women and Colonisation, Anthropological Perspectives.* New York: Praeger, pp. 270-293.

_____. 1989. Why Cloth? Wealth, Gender, and Power in Oceania, in A. B. Weiner and J. Schneider (eds.), *Cloth and Human Experience.* Washington: Smithsonian Institution Press. pp.37-72.

_____. 1992. *Inalienable Possessions: The Paradox of Keeping While Giving.* Berkeley: University of California Press.

Weiner, A. B. and J. Schneider (eds.). 1989. *Cloth and Human Experience.* Washington: Smithsonian Institution Press.

Welsch, R. L. 2002. Introduction: Changing Themes in the Study of Pacific art, in A. Herle, N. Stanley, K. Stevenson and R. L. Welsch (eds.), *Pacific Art: Persistence, Change and Meaning.* Adelaide: Crawford House Press. pp. 1-12.

Wendt, A. 1983. Contemporary Arts in Oceania, in S. Mead and B. Kernot, eds., *Art and Artists of Oceania.* Palmerston North: Dunmore Press.

Whiteley, P. and L. Dubin. 2004. *Totems to Turquoise: Native North American Jewelry Arts of the Northwest and Southwest.* New York: American Museum of Natural History.

Wingert, P. 1953. *Art of the South Pacific Islands.* London: Thames and Hudson.

Wirz, P. 1928. Beitrag zur Ethnologie der Sentanier (Holländisch Neuguinea). *Nova Guinea* 16:251-370, pl.16-32. Leiden: E. J. Brill.

Zimmer-Tamakoshi, L. 1993. Nationalism and Sexuality in Papua New Guinea. *Pacific Studies* 16(4):61-98.

_____. ed. 1998. *Modern Papua New Guinea.* Kirksville: Thomas Jefferson University Press.

Author Biographies

Karen Stevenson, of Tahitian heritage, was born and raised in Los Angeles. She received her PhD in Oceanic Art History from the University of California, Los Angeles in 1988. The following year was spent as a Rockefeller Fellow at the Center for Pacific Studies at the University of Hawaii. Her writings and research have focused on the politics and institutionalisation of culture, art and identity, the Pacific Arts Festival, and most recently on Contemporary Pacific Art. She has published widely including *Art AsiaPacific*, the *Art Journal, Art New Zealand, Pacific Studies, Pacific Arts*, and *The Contemporary Pacific*. She recently published *The Frangipani is Dead, Contemporary Pacific Art in New Zealand* (2008), was a co-editor for *Re-Presenting Pacific Art* (2009) and *Pacific Arts: Persistence, Change and Meaning in Pacific Art* (2002), and guest editor for *Pacific Arts* — the Festival of Pacific Arts (2002). Karen is currently an Independent Researcher based in Christchurch, New Zealand.

Konousi (Koni) Aisake was born in the isolated village of Fapufa on the island of Rotuma in 1960, the 13th of 16 children. He left Rotuma for Fiji at age 14 and attended Dayanand Anglo-Vedic Boys College in Suva. He worked for the Blue Lagoon Cruise company for ten years until 1987, when the coup overthrowing the Fiji Government occurred, leading him to emigrate to Canada, where he worked in a stained glass factory for ten years learning the art of making stained glass. In 1996 he set out on his own as a self-taught wood carver and maker of art objects from stained glass. He uses a variety of symbols, many drawn from Rotuman culture, in his work.

Jewel Castro (MFA, Visual Arts, University of California at San Diego) is a multi-media artist who looks for ways to celebrate her Samoan ancestors, living elders, and to honor the integrity of her family's indigenous history. In addition to making art, Jewel is a curator, writer, public speaker, and part-time teacher of studio art at both Mesa College in San Diego and MiraCosta College in Oceanside. Her own art and writing are published in books and academic journals including the *Pacific Studies Journal, The Contemporary Pacific Journal, Pacific Arts: The Journal of the Pacific Art Association*, Sean Mallon's book, *Samoan Art and Artists O Measina a Samoa*, and Kay Flavell's book, *Moon Over the Pacific*. She is a member of the Pacific Art Association, the College Art Association, and The National Pacific Islander Educators' Network. For more information visit her website at www.jewelcastro.com.

Judith Selk Flores is a folklorist, historian, teacher, and visual artist who has lived and worked in the island of Guam since 1957. She earned a BA from the University of Guam and an MA from the University of Washington. She taught secondary school art for 10 years, then served as folklorist for the Guam arts council for another 10 years. She helped found Gef Pa'go, Guam's only living museum of Chamorro culture; serving successively as advisor, director and president. She earned a second MA in Micronesian Studies from the University of Guam; and PhD in Arts of Oceania from the University of East Anglia in Norwich, England. She returned to teach at the University of Guam, retiring in 2005. She is widely recognized as a professional visual artist of batik paintings that depict Guam's culture and history that can be seen in many of Guam's public buildings.

Haidy Geismar is Assistant Professor of Anthropology and Museum Studies at New York University. Her research focuses on issues surrounding value and materiality, using museums as a filter. Her research interests are intellectual and cultural property, indigenous contemporary art in the Pacific and the ways in which museums and markets influence and engender relations between persons and things. Since 2000 she has worked as a researcher and curator in Vanuatu and Aotearoa New Zealand, England and the US. She has curated two exhibitions about Vanuatu, Vanuatu Stael at the Cambridge Museum of Archaeology and Anthropology (2003) and Port Vila Mi Lavem Yu at the East West Center, Honolulu (2011).

Anna-Karina Hermkens is a cultural anthropologist working as a postdoctoral researcher at the Institute for Religious Studies, Radboud University Nijmegen, Netherlands. Her main fields of interest are: material culture; gender; religion; conflict and peace studies. In 2005, she received her PhD, which dealt with the interplay between gender and material culture among the Maisin people (*Engendering Objects: Dynamics of gender and identity in Papua New Guinea*). Between 2005 and 2008 she worked as a postdoctoral researcher in the programme 'The Power of Pilgrimage' at the Institute for Gender Studies at Radboud University Nijmegen. As part of this research she co-edited a volume entitled '*Moved by Mary. The Power of Pilgrimage in the Modern World*,' published by Ashgate in 2009. Her current research focuses on the role of religion and ritual in process of warfare and peacemaking on Bougainville, Solomon Islands and Ternate, Indonesia.

Alan Howard is professor emeritus of anthropology at the University of Hawai'i-Manoa. He has been doing research on the island of Rotuma and among Rotumans in diaspora since 1959. Since retirement in 1999 he has managed the Rotuma Website, which he created in 1996. Among his publications are "Symbols of Power and the Politics of Impotence: The Mölmahao Rebellion on Rotuma" (1992); "Speak of the Devils: Discourse and Belief in Spirits on Rotuma" (1996); and (coauthored with his wife, Jan Rensel) "Where Has Rotuman Culture Gone? And What Is It Doing There?" (2001); and *Island Legacy: A History of the Rotuman People* (2007).

Shigeyuki Kihara is a leading Inter-disciplinary Artist and Independent Curator who explores the intersection between Visual arts, Performance and Theatre. A native of Samoa, Kihara has represented New Zealand in 4th Asia Pacific Triennial (AUS) and 4th Auckland Triennial (NZ). Kihara's first solo museum exhibition in North America entitled *Shigeyuki Kihara; Living Photographs* (2008-09) was held at the Metropolitan Museum of Art, New York following the acquisition of her works by the museum for their permanent collection. Kihara has participated in selected group exhibitions including Te Papa Tongarewa Museum of New Zealand; Museum of Contemporary Art (AUS); Gallery of Modern Art (AUS); University of Cambridge Museum of Archeology and Anthropology (UK); Shanghai Zendai Museum of Modern Art; Kaohsiung Museum of Fine Arts, Taiwan; National Museum of Poznan, Warsaw; Centro Ricerca Arte Attuale, Italy and de Young Fine Arts Museum of San Francisco. www.shigeyukikihara.com

Eric Kjellgren is the Evelyn A. J. Hall and John A. Friede Associate Curator for Oceanic Art at The Metropolitan Museum of Art in New York. A former Fulbright scholar and Fellow of the Royal Geographical Society, he has worked extensively with contemporary Aboriginal painters in the East Kimberley region of Western Australia. He has also done research in Vanuatu, Indonesia, French Polynesia, and Rekohu (the Chatham Islands). Dr. Kjellgren has written extensively on Australian Aboriginal art is also the author of *Oceania: Art of the Pacific Islands in the Metropolitan Museum of Art* as well as exhibition catalogues and articles on a diversity of Oceanic artistic traditions. He has curated numerous exhibitions on the arts of the Pacific and recently completed the redesign and reinstallation of the Metropolitan's permanent galleries for Oceanic Art.

Ake Lianga is a painter, sculptor, and muralist from the island of Guadalcanal, Solomon Islands. His works, which often depict traditional stories and cultural practices, are in public collections in North America and the South Pacific. Lianga was born in 1975 into a large family of carvers and weavers. He learned how to carve as a small child, and taught himself to paint. He has been the recipient of numerous awards including; the South Pacific Contemporary Art Competition (1995) and the Commonwealth Arts and Crafts (1996). This brought him to Canada where he graduated in Fine Arts from North Island College in Courtenay, British Columbia, in 1999. He has exhibited in Australia, New Caledonia, the United States and Canada. During regular trips to the Solomon Islands, he provides training and advice for emerging artists. His dream is to help revive traditional wood-carving in the Solomon Islands.

Carol E. Mayer is head of the curatorial department and curator of Oceania at the UBC Museum of Anthropology. She is also an associateto the Department of Anthropology. She has taught museum-related courses in Canada, and has lead workshops in Fiji, Australia, New Caledonia and Vanuatu. She has been awarded Fellowships at the Smithsonian Institute and the Sainsbury Research Centre. She currently serves on the boards of the Pacific Peoples' Partnership and the Pacific Arts Association. She is an expert examiner for the Cultural Property Review Board, and a reviewer and editor for several publications. She has delivered papers at numerous conferences and has published widely on topics relating to museum practice. In 2009 she received the ICOM (Canada) International Award of Excellence for her work in the Pacific. In 2010 she received the Thirtieth Anniversary of Independence Medal for her cultural contributions to the Republic of Vanuatu.

Elaine Monds' interest in world cultures began early, during a childhood in Kenya and Australia. She arrived in Canada in the 1970s and opened a business that developed into Alcheringa Gallery. In 1984, she fell in love with the arts and peoples of Papua New Guinea during the first of many trips to that region. Alcheringa Gallery began introducing Papua New Guinean art to North American audiences, then expanded to represent eminent and emerging Indigenous artists from Australia, Canada's Northwest Coast, and other Pacific traditions. Over more than 25 years of exhibitions, publications, artist exchanges, and collaborations with major cultural institutions worldwide, Alcheringa

Gallery has become recognized as a leading promoter of contemporary Indigenous fine arts and cultural exchange. Elaine continues to make regular trips to visit artists in the South Pacific. Alcheringa Gallery's extensive website, featuring complete exhibition catalogues, artist interviews, biographies, stories, and more, is at www.alcheringa-gallery.com.

Eva Raabe is curator of the Oceania Department at the Museum of World Cultures Frankfurt, Germany. She specialized on contemporary art forms in Pacific cultures and their representation at European museums. She collected contemporary art in Papua New Guinea and curated several exhibitions for the museum.

She was co-founder of the Gallery 37, which was the Museum's special exhibition space for contemporary art from non-European countries (1997-2010). This gallery was acknowledged as a project of the World Decade of Cultural Development by the UNESCO. 1998/99 Eva Raabe was an International Research Fellow at the Centre of Cross-Cultural Research at the Australian National University and did research on contemporary art in Papua New Guinea.

Rosanna Raymond was born in Auckland New Zealand of Samoan decent and currently lives and works in London. A 'Tusitala' (a teller of tales) at heart her art practice takes a variety of forms ranging from installation works, spoken words and body adornment, fusing traditional pacific practises with modern innovations and techniques.

Raymond has forged a role for herself over the past 15 years as an artist, writer, producer and commentator on contemporary PI culture. She has worked within museums and higher education institutions in Aotearoa NZ, the UK and the USA.

Raymond has undertaken art residencies at the de Young Museum San Francisco, University of Hawaii and the Cambridge University Museum of Archaeology and Anthropology UK, where she curated the internationally acclaimed *Pasifika Styles* exhibition with Dr Amiria Salmond. Raymond remains an active member of the London based Polynesian cultural groups *Beats of Polynesia* and *Ngati Ranana.*

Vince Reyes is the Program Director and Fafa'nague (Traditional Teacher) for the Inetnon Gef Pa'go Cultural Arts Program. Mr. Reyes has successfully pioneered and implemented one of the first cultural arts programs in the Guam Department of Education, which has achieved a notable reputation in Chamorro dance, winning numerous dance competitions and awards both on island and abroad. He is the recipient of the 2003 Traditional Teacher of the Year Award by the Guam Humanities Council and has presented at many international conferences and festivals, speaking on behalf of the Chamorro people and culture. Today he services over 120 students in the middle school 60 students in the community-based after school program and provides Guam's only Full-Chamorro Dinner show at the Sheraton Laguna Guam Resort. His group has traveled extensively throughout Asia, U.S. Mainland, Australia, Philippines, the Pacific, and Europe, promoting Guam's rich culture and heritage through dance.

Pamela Rosi is Adjunct Associate Professor of Anthropology at Bridgewater State University, Massachusetts. She received her Ph.D. from Bryn Mawr College, Pennsylvania. Following research at Papua New Guinea's National Arts School in 1986, her publications and curatorial work have focused on the contemporary arts of Papua New Guinea (PNG) and their contested value to an emerging PNG national culture. She also studies the problems which PNG artists encounter promoting their work in PNG and on the global art market. In addition to articles and book chapters on these topics, she is co-editor with Eric Venbrux and Robert L. Welsch of *Exploring World Art*, Waveland Press, 2006. In 2009, she co-curated with Michael Mel the international multimedia art project *Hailans to Ailans*, and edited the exhibition catalogue (http://hailanstoailans.com).

Marion Struck-Garbe is a graduate in Ethnology and Socio-Economics. She has worked on diverse subjects such as violence, international relations, ecology and contemporary art and literature in Oceania. As a student she lived and researched in Tonga and Fiji. In the 1990s she lived in Papua New Guinea for several years and during this period worked with woman artists in Port Moresby. Today she lives in Hamburg, where she works at the Greenpeace office and teaches in the Asia-Africa Institute of the University of Hamburg. Since 2002, she has been Chairperson for the Network of Pacific Groups in Germany. Marion has organized numerous exhibitions of contemporary Papua New Guinea art both in PNG and Europe

Jim Vivieaere's visibility can be attributed to his bi-cultural politicization as a New Zealand-born Polynesian. This positioning over the last three decades has offered him roles of writing, mentoring and curating. It has enabled him to travel extensively and work collaboratively with a diverse range of practitioners in the local and international art community. He is a multi-media artist with a strong interest in geomancy and the ephemeral, drawing small distinction between daily living and making art.

CPSIA information can be obtained
at www.ICGtesting.com
233426LV00001B
* 9 7 8 0 9 7 1 4 1 2 7 7 4 *